# THE POLITICS OF COALITION

*The Politics of Coalition* is the tale of two parties embarking on the first coalition government at Westminster for over 60 years. What challenges did they face in the first couple of years, and how did they deal with them?

With the authorisation of Prime Minister David Cameron, Deputy Prime Minister Nick Clegg and the then Cabinet Secretary, Sir Gus O'Donnell, the Constitution Unit has interviewed over 140 ministers, MPs, Lords, civil servants, party officials and interest groups about the Coalition and the impact coalition government has had upon Westminster and Whitehall.

*The Politics of Coalition* tells how the Coalition has operated in the different arenas of the British political system: at the Centre; within the Departments; in Parliament; in the parties outside Parliament; and in the media. It will be of interest to politicians, policy makers, academics, students and anyone interested in how the UK Coalition works in practice and not just in theory.

# The Politics of Coalition

## How the Conservative–Liberal Democrat Government Works

Robert Hazell and Ben Yong

·HART·
PUBLISHING

OXFORD AND PORTLAND, OREGON
2012

Published in the United Kingdom by Hart Publishing Ltd
16C Worcester Place, Oxford, OX1 2JW
Telephone: +44 (0)1865 517530
Fax: +44 (0)1865 510710
E-mail: mail@hartpub.co.uk
Website: http://www.hartpub.co.uk

Published in North America (US and Canada) by
Hart Publishing
c/o International Specialized Book Services
920 NE 58th Avenue, Suite 300
Portland, OR 97213-3786
USA
Tel: +1 503 287 3093 or toll-free: (1) 800 944 6190
Fax: +1 503 280 8832
E-mail: orders@isbs.com
Website: http://www.isbs.com

© Robert Hazell and Ben Yong 2012

British Library Cataloguing in Publication Data
Data Available

ISBN: 978-1-84946-310-2

Typeset by Hope Services, Abingdon
Printed and bound in Great Britain by
TJ International Ltd, Padstow, Cornwall

# Contents

# Preface

The origins of this book lie in two previous pieces of work by the Constitution Unit. The first was Ben Seyd's 2002 report, *Coalition Government in Britain: Lessons from Overseas*. The second was a project we embarked upon in 2009, preparing for the possibility of a hung parliament after the 2010 general election. That led us to work closely with the then Cabinet Secretary Sir Gus O'Donnell and his officials. So it was understandable when a coalition government was formed in 2010 that we should want to revisit Ben Seyd's earlier study, and to ask the Cabinet Office for their help and cooperation.

Sir Gus O'Donnell responded positively, and we wish to thank the Prime Minister David Cameron, the Deputy Prime Minister Nick Clegg and the Cabinet Secretary for generously agreeing to allow us access. It was an extraordinary privilege to be permitted to observe the inner workings of the Coalition, and we are very grateful to all the ministers, senior officials, parliamentarians and special advisers who kindly agreed to be interviewed. We hope that they recognise the picture that we have gradually built up of how the Coalition operates, seen from the inside; and that they feel the time they kindly gave us was justified. We are also grateful to the members of the political parties, interest groups and media commentators who gave us interviews.

This was a daunting project in several respects. There is almost no literature on coalition government in Britain, apart from the honourable exceptions mentioned in chapter one. In academic literature generally, there are few studies of how coalition government works in practice. That is in part because of difficulties of access, which Sir Gus and his colleagues so generously overcame; and in part because of the academic predilection for theoretical modelling, for studying the formation and termination of coalitions, but not their actual operation.

This book attempts to be both an academic study and a practical study aimed at policy makers, with the risk of falling between the two. And it is a study of the Coalition only in its first 18 months. We fully recognise that some of our conclusions may be overtaken by subsequent events; but it seemed too important to wait until the end of the Coalition before attempting to learn any lessons about its operation.

The Nuffield Foundation were willing to back the risk, with their long record of supporting academic research with a strong policy focus. We are grateful to them and to their Deputy Director, Sharon Witherspoon, for agreeing to fund our research; and for hosting a seminar of UK coalition experts to discuss some of our draft chapters in November 2011.

We originally planned to interview 60 people for the study, but in the end interviewed almost 150. That we managed to do so was largely thanks to Peter Waller and Brian Walker, both honorary Senior Research Fellows of the Constitution Unit. Peter Waller was formerly a senior civil servant, and Brian Walker in the BBC, and they brought to the project their deep knowledge of how government works, and how it interacts with the media. They conducted many of the interviews, and kindly wrote the chapters on Whitehall departments, and the Coalition and the media. Chapter 2 was written by Eimear O'Casey, who joined the Constitution Unit part-way through the project, and was tasked with pulling together the data we had collected on how coalitions work in other countries. She quickly did that and more, proof reading and copy editing all the chapters – for which we are very grateful. The final member of the project team was David Laughrin, also a former senior civil servant, and now Fellow of the Ashridge Public Leadership Centre; he generously helped with some of the Whitehall interviews, attended our monthly project meetings, and offered wise comments on our progress and our draft chapters.

All the chapters were sent in draft to several reviewers. We are grateful to all those who kindly commented on our work in progress. Several of our reviewers were also interviewees, and to protect their anonymity we do not name them all here. But those we can thank publicly include Sir Christopher Foster, who nobly read a copy of the entire manuscript; Nick Anstead, Tim Bale, Sir John Elvidge, Oonagh Gay, Chris Hanretty, Andrew Ladley, Meg Russell, Jean Seaton, Ben Seyd and Nick Timmins.

We also wish to thank Vicki Spence, the Constitution Unit administrator, for helping to organise interviews and seminars. Finally, thanks must go to all the interns who worked on the coalition government project: Chris Appleby, Katherine Benson, Jessica Carter, Patrick Graham, Rachel Heydecker, Ian Jordan, Andreas Kutz, Ashley Palmer and Robbie Fergusson; as well as David Busfield-Birch, former intern with the Unit. They did a lot of the background research, and also helped to produce the weekly 'coalition updates', which we will leave on the Unit's website as part of the record of the Coalition and how it was reported in 2011.

We have attempted to describe the Coalition as it stood from its formation on 11 May 2010 until 31 December 2011.

Robert Hazell and Ben Yong
January 2012

# List of Figures and Tables

# List of Abbreviations

ACP      Association of Conservative Peers
AV       Alternative Vote
BIS      Department for Business, Innovation and Skills
BNP      British National Party
BSG      Backbench Support Group
CCHQ     Conservative Campaign Headquarters
CO       Cabinet Office
COI      Central Office of Information
COSPG    Coalition Operation and Strategic Planning Group
CPF      Conservative Policy Forum
DCLG     Department for Communities and Local Government
DCMS     Department for Culture, Media, and Sport
DECC     Department of Energy and Climate Change
Defra    Department for Environment, Food and Rural Affairs
DfE      Department for Education
DfID     Department for International Development
DfT      Department for Trade
DH       Department of Health
DPM      Deputy Prime Minister
DPMO     Deputy Prime Minister's Office
DUP      Democratic Unionist Party
DWP      Department for Work and Pensions
ECA      European Communities Act 1972
ECHR     European Convention on Human Rights
EDS      Economic and Domestic Affairs Secretariat, Cabinet Office
FCO      Foreign and Commonwealth Office
FEC      Federal Executive Committee
FPC      Federal Policy Committee
HMT      Her Majesty's Treasury
HO       Home Office
MoD      Ministry of Defence
MoJ      Ministry of Justice
NGO      non-governmental organisation
NHS      National Health Service
NIO      Northern Ireland Office
NSC      National Security Council
NUS      National Union of Students
PM       Prime Minister

PPC     Parliamentary Party Committee
PPS     Parliamentary Private Secretary
PVSC    Parliamentary Voting System and Constituencies (Bill)
SDLP    Social Democratic and Labour Party
SNP     Scottish National Party
SO      Scotland Office
SoS     Secretary of State
spad    special adviser
UKIP    UK Independence Party
WO      Wales Office

# 1

# Introduction: Why Study the Conservative-Liberal Democrat Coalition?

## BEN YONG

'SINGLE PARTY GOVERNMENT is the British norm', said David Butler, doyen of British political scientists, and most observers of Westminster would agree with him.[1] That is why the formation of the Conservative-Liberal Democrat Coalition (the Coalition) after the 2010 general election came as such a surprise. While many academics and commentators had predicted a hung parliament, very few predicted a coalition, let alone a coalition of two apparently ideologically opposed political parties.

It is not clear that this opinion has changed. With the exception of the Liberal Democrats, most in the 'Westminster Village' continue to regard the current Coalition as an aberration – something which will be remedied come the 2015 election (or perhaps even earlier). This caution has some merit. In 2010, there had been no coalition formed at the national level for 65 years; prior to that there had only been four coalitions formed between 1900 and 1945 – most formed

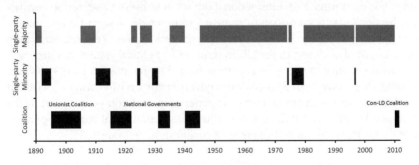

**Figure 1.1 Timeline: Types of Government at Westminster, 1890–2010**

Source: Adapted from R Hazell and A Paun (eds), *Making Minority Government Work: Hung Parliaments and the Challenges for Westminster and Whitehall* (London, Constitution Unit, 2009) 18

[1] D Butler, *Coalitions in British Politics* (London, Macmillan, 1978) 112.

in national emergencies such as war.[2] Minority government has been a more frequent occurrence than coalition.

Various hypotheses are advanced to explain the British predilection for single-party government, many sliding subtly from the descriptive to the normative. Single-party government provides a much clearer line of accountability: electors know whom they voted for and what they voted for. By contrast, multiparty government leads to confusion over responsibility ('decisions made in smoke filled rooms'), or to smaller parties having excessive influence over government ('the tail wagging the dog'). The British value stable government, and single-party government is more stable. Multiparty governments are unstable because there is constant pressure exerted on the parties within government to differentiate themselves – the centrifugal pressures within coalition governments eventually tear them apart. There is a sense that coalition government is not just unusual; it is something to be avoided.[3]

Table 1.1   Differences between Single-Party Majority Government and Coalition Government

| Single party majority government | Coalition government |
| --- | --- |
| Stable | Unstable |
| Fast | Slow |
| Firm decision making | Consensual / weak decision making |
| Autocratic | Deliberative |
| Clear lines of accountability | Blurred lines of accountability |
| Clear and coherent policy | Compromise / incoherent policy |
| Ineffective, weak legislature | Stronger legislature |
| Adversarial | Consensual |

And yet, Westminster is an international outlier in terms of being run so consistently by single-party majority governments. In much of Western Europe, multiparty government is the norm and not the exception. New Zealand, for a long time thought of as closest to the UK in terms of its political system, has had various coalitions since the adoption of proportional representation in 1996. Closer to home, there have been four coalition governments over ten years in Scotland and Wales. There is an abundance of experience in coalition government in the developed Western world. If so many other jurisdictions treat coalition government as 'normal', should British views of coalitions be re-evaluated?

---

[2] These were: the brief Asquith Coalition of 1915–16; the Lloyd George Conservative-Liberal-Labour Coalition of 1916–22; the National Government of 1931–40; and the wartime Coalition of 1940–5. See the 'Historical Coda' at the end of ch 2 for a summary of the British coalition experience.

[3] See, for instance, the Conservative Party briefing *A Hung Parliament will be Bad for Britain*, available at www.conservativehome.blogs.com/files/a-hung-parliament-will-be-bad-for-britain.pdf. This briefing conflates hung parliaments with minority and coalition governments, but is representative of some of the fears set out above.

Of course, many of those countries where coalition government is prevalent have proportional representation electoral systems. But a number of psephologists have argued in recent years that the first past the post electoral system has come under increasing pressure: it has looked less likely to produce single-party governments and more likely to produce hung parliaments, and thus potentially more coalitions.[4] That is because of the emergence of third parties like the Liberal Democrats and the various nationalist parties (the SNP, Plaid Cymru), and the decline of marginal seats (ie, 'swing' seats held by one party with a small majority). This can be illustrated by the decline of the proportion of votes cast for Conservative and Labour combined (the 'two-party vote') (see Figure 1.2). In the early 1950s, the two-party vote hovered around 96 per cent. By the mid-1970s that had dropped to three-quarters of all votes cast, with 'third parties' receiving the other quarter. In the 2010 election, the two-party vote had dropped to two-thirds, with third parties (including the Lib Dems) receiving one-third of the vote.[5] So there is a real need for a clear discussion of the peculiar problems and opportunities coalitions may face, and a need to show how the Coalition has worked in practice, as opposed to theory and speculation. We elaborate on this below.

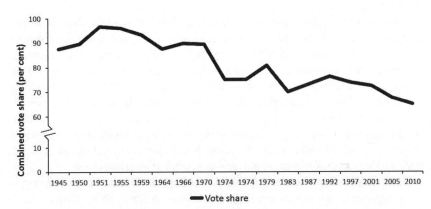

Figure 1.2 Decline of Two-Party Vote Share 1945–2010

Source: Adapted from D Butler and G Butler, *British Political Facts*, 10th edn (Basingstoke, Palgrave Macmillan, 2010) 267–71

The Constitution Unit's initial impetus for undertaking a study on the Coalition came from the Unit's previous work on how to manage hung parliaments. In 2009, the Constitution Unit in conjunction with the Institute for Government carried out a yearlong comparative study looking at hung parliaments in other Westminster countries. *Making Minority Government Work: Hung Parliaments*

---

[4] J Curtice, 'So What Went Wrong with the Electoral System? The 2010 Election Result and the Debate about Electoral Reform' (2010) 63(4) *Parliamentary Affairs* 623; P Dunleavy, 'Facing Up to Multi-Party Politics: How Partisan Dealignment and PR Voting have Fundamentally Changed Britain's Party Systems' (2005) 58(3) *Parliamentary Affairs* 503.

[5] Curtice, 'So What Went Wrong', ibid.

*and the Challenges for Westminster and Whitehall* made a number of predictions and recommendations about how Westminster and Whitehall might change under a hung parliament, and how actors in key arenas of the British political system might best respond.[6]

The Constitution Unit had also done work on coalition government ten years ago, in a Nuffield Foundation-funded project to learn the lessons of coalition government from overseas. Ben Seyd's report *Coalition Government in Britain: Lessons from Overseas* was published in 2002, followed by a later supplementary report.[7] Then, our main audience was the new Coalition Governments in Scotland and Wales; but we always had an eye to the possibility of coalition government at Westminster.

Given this, and the Constitution Unit's remit of doing work which has a sharply practical focus which is timely and relevant to policy makers and practitioners, it seemed natural that the Unit would want to see how the Coalition would play out. How difficult was it for a coalition at Westminster to govern? What lessons could be learned from how the Coalition operated in its first 18 months? And what could be learned from the experience of countries overseas and from academic writing on coalitions?

Until recently, coalition government was considered an esoteric subject in British political science, due to the perceived unlikelihood of multiparty government. Where British political scientists have covered minority or coalition government, this has usually taken the form of historical case studies.[8] Perhaps because of the limited and distant nature of British experience, these studies have tended to focus mostly on the formation, duration and termination of coalitions, but slide over the 'pedestrian' business of making coalition government work. There were a small number of works examining the practical issues specific to multiparty government, but these remained exceptional.[9] In short, British literature still lacked in-depth studies of how to make coalition governments work at a national level.

The literature on Western Europe (and elsewhere) is far more extensive: proportional representation is widespread and coalition government is relatively common.[10] But, even in those cases, earlier work on coalition government was mostly about 'the wedding, not the marriage', addressing three main questions: who gets in? (which parties form the coalition); who gets what? (how they allocate portfolios between them); and how long does it last? In recent years, however, there have been

---

[6] See Part Three in R Hazell and A Paun (eds), *Making Minority Government Work: Hung Parliaments and the Challenges for Westminster and Whitehall* (London, Constitution Unit, 2009).

[7] B Seyd, *Coalition Government in Britain: Lessons from Overseas* (London, Constitution Unit, 2002).

[8] Butler, *Coalitions in British Politics* (n 1); D Butler, *Governing without a Majority: Dilemmas for Hung Parliaments in Britain* (Basingstoke, Macmillan, 1986); V Bogdanor, *Multi-Party Politics and the Constitution* (Cambridge University Press, 1983); Seyd, *Coalition Government in Britain* (n 7).

[9] Seyd, *Coalition Government in Britain* (n 7); M Oaten, *Coalition: The Politics and Personalities of Coalition Government from 1850* (Petersfield, Harriman House, 2007); Hazell and Paun (eds), *Making Minority Government Work* (n 6).

[10] K Strøm and WC Müller (eds), *Coalition Governments in Western Europe* (New York, Oxford University Press, 2000).

more systematic attempts at analysis. Strøm and Müller's work provides a comprehensive and up-to-date synthesis of the literature on coalition governance.[11]

But even later works are not a guide to action. The studies on which they draw are mainly large comparative studies, developing and testing theoretical models with regression analysis to achieve the best statistical fit. Many of the variables studied (the party system; 'critical events') lie beyond the control of political actors. The studies leave a large unexplained residue of variation between countries, suggesting that each country develops its own habits and traditions of coalition government.[12] And there remains a serious gap in terms of how coalition government works on a day-to-day basis.[13] As Strøm and Müller themselves acknowledge, 'the territory remains largely uncharted'.[14]

There are a number of reasons for this, but the major reason is the difficulty of securing access. Governments are generally unwilling to grant access to researchers, especially access in real time: there are very real issues about political sensitivity, which are perhaps even more pressing in multiparty government. This colours much of the literature: what is studied is that which is publicly accessible or observable. And so the day-to-day details of conflict management, consultation and coordination of coalition activity and policy remain mostly unexamined.

There is an additional problem, which has already been hinted at: the preponderance in political science of quantitative over qualitative work.[15] One scholar, in his conclusion to an authoritative overview of the literature on coalitions, opined:

> [A]fter forty years of intense scholarly work we have only come to lift a tip of the veil. . . . given the current state of the art, research resources would be more efficiently invested in thick descriptions rather than in testing ever more complex formal theories with ever more sophisticated statistical techniques, a line of research that has not significantly enhanced our understanding of real world formations. In other words, coalition researchers should abandon their computer screens and get their hands dirty again.[16]

So we chose to 'get our hands dirty', or in more scholarly terms, engage in thick description. Constitution Unit Director Robert Hazell approached Sir Gus O'Donnell, the (then) UK Cabinet Secretary, shortly after the formation of the Coalition with the idea of a project in real time on the working of the Coalition. We were granted access by Prime Minister David Cameron, Deputy Prime Minister Nick Clegg, and Sir Gus O'Donnell to interview ministers, officials from 'the Centre' – Cabinet Office and No 10 – and in three case study departments,

---

[11] ibid; K Strøm, WC Müller and T Bergman (eds), *Cabinets and Coalition Bargaining: The Democratic Life Cycle in Western Europe* (Oxford University Press, 2008).

[12] Strøm, Müller and Bergman (eds), *Cabinets and Coalition Bargaining*, ibid.

[13] For an exception see J Boston and A Ladley, 'The Efficient Secret: The Craft of Coalition Management' (2006) 4 *New Zealand Journal of Public and International Law* 55.

[14] Strøm, Müller and Bergman (eds), *Cabinets and Coalition Bargaining* (n 11) 35.

[15] We exaggerate, but only slightly. This is more noticeable in the literature on coalitions than in, say, the literature on the core executive.

[16] L de Winter, 'Parties and Government Formation, Portfolio Allocation, and Policy Definition' in KR Luther and F Müller-Rommel (eds), *Political Parties in the New Europe: Political and Analytical Challenges* (Oxford University Press, 2002) 206.

and special advisers. The Nuffield Foundation generously agreed to fund the project in late 2010.

We decided on a qualitative, action research approach: that is, our research would be based mostly on interviews and done in real time. This had both advantages and disadvantages. The key advantage of an action research project done in real time over one year (2011) was that the contemporaneous views of key participants were captured, without the subtle reshaping of experience by hindsight. Too often 'lessons' or insights become matter of fact and common sense – they are no longer insights but are taken for granted. We wished to capture that sense of discovery. The key disadvantage, of course, was that historical depth and perspective is lost: events which seem significant at the time may be shown in retrospect to be quite trivial in the life of the Coalition.

But there was another reason for studying the Coalition in real time. Scholars of coalition governments have noted that coalition governance is characterised by path dependence.[17] That is, later coalitions draw on and are shaped by experience of previous coalitions. Initial decisions made may become the set way of doing things because of inertia and because it is difficult to begin afresh (economists and political scientists call these factors 'transaction costs'). But this simply brings home that now is the time to study the current Coalition: these formative years may determine how future coalitions are governed. If there are coalitions in the future, they may simply adopt the procedures of the current coalition, unaware of why the procedures were adopted in the first place or their pitfalls.

In short, we decided to study the Conservative-Liberal Democrat Coalition because of the various concerns expressed about coalitions as a viable form of government in Britain; because of the dearth of practical advice on how to govern under a coalition; because of the extraordinary opportunity of access to a coalition government; and because we hoped to capture that sense of discovery before it all became matter of fact.

## SCOPE OF THE BOOK

Our focus is strongly on *coalition governance*. 'Governance' here means 'the practice of governing, and the stage in the life cycle of governments that is devoted to policy execution and implementation'.[18] This includes political coordination of the Cabinet, but also the political executive's relationships with the civil service, Parliament and the political parties. So we were most interested in how the Coalition operated day to day rather than in its formation (although as we acknowledge in chapter three, the method of formation has had an impact upon its operation) or its termination.

All coalition governments face two sets of difficulties. One is *instability*, and the challenges associated with that. Coalition governments in Europe are more short

---

[17] Strøm, Müller and Bergman (eds), *Cabinets and Coalition Bargaining* (n 11) 54.
[18] ibid, 9.

lived than single-party majority governments. Half of coalition governments end because of conflict between the governing parties or within them.[19] So procedures to manage conflict and resolve disputes between the coalition partners, as well as those to facilitate communication and coordination, are particularly important.

The second difficulty is the *unity/distinctiveness dilemma*. A coalition must devise means of ensuring that its constituent parts remain coordinated and coherent if it is to govern effectively – this is the problem of unity. But coalitions are also composed of political parties, which have separate histories and values, and which compete for votes separately. These political parties must therefore devise means by which they can ensure that at least some of the coalition's policies are identified as specific to their party, thus satisfying internal factions and party supporters – and more importantly, the electorate. In short, parties to the coalition must also preserve their identity – this is the problem of distinctiveness.[20] These competing considerations are fundamental to understanding how a coalition government acts in relation to administration and policy making.

We wished to see how these tensions played out in real time, and in a number of arenas within the political system: at the centre; in departments; in Parliament; outside Parliament; and in the media. We formulated a number of research questions, set out below:

*The Political Executive*

What mechanisms has the Coalition Government used to reinforce internal stability?

Have the coordination, consultation and dispute resolution mechanisms devised by the Coalition provided a workable balance between unity and flexibility?

How has coalition government affected policy making, as it requires agreement between two or more parties?

*The Civil Service*

What changes have been made in Whitehall's working practices to accommodate the Coalition?

Does coalition government strengthen the role of the civil service, as the custodians of the collective and consultative procedures?

*Parliament*

How effectively does the Government present a united front to Parliament?

How do the coalition parties use Parliament as a forum to present their distinctive policies to the country?

How do the coalition parties in Parliament seek to influence government policy?

Has coalition government made Parliament stronger or weaker?

[19] E Damgaard, 'Cabinet Termination' in Strøm, Müller and Bergman (eds), *Cabinets and Coalition Bargaining* (n 11).

[20] Boston and Ladley, 'The Efficient Secret' (n 13); see also K Strøm, WC Müller and T Bergman, *Delegation and Accountability in Parliamentary Democracies* (Oxford University Press, 2003).

### Political Parties

How have the coalition parties managed the tension between needing unity in government and the preservation of ideological and policy distinctiveness in the eyes of the electorate?

Have there been changes in the relationships between the leaders and the party in government, the party in central office and the party 'on the ground'?

### The Media

How does the Coalition present itself to the media: as a united government, or as two distinct parties?

How do the media report on the Coalition: as united or divided?

And underlying these was a question about how we should evaluate the performance of the Coalition. What are the measures of success? That depends on the observer and their point of view. For officials, success may be measured by the extent to which the coalition partners use the proper channels in Whitehall; by the degree of cooperation between the parties; and by the absence of leaks, projecting a unified and effective government. For the media, that is going to be boring: politics is about the clash of arms, with winners and losers, and preferably blood. And for the parties, unified and effective government is only one measure of success. Getting re-elected is the other: for that, they will need to project their distinct identity and contribution. Finally, for the citizen, success is measured not by processes but by outcomes: does coalition government lead to better policies? That final question we cannot answer. This book is about how coalition government works, not what it does.

## RESEARCH METHODS

Robert Hazell and Ben Yong (Constitution Unit Research Associate) gathered a wider coalition government team, including Peter Waller (Honorary Research Fellow at the Constitution Unit and former senior civil servant at the Department of Trade and Industry), Brian Walker (the Unit's press officer and former BBC journalist) and Eimear O'Casey (Unit Research Assistant as of July 2011).

The four key members of the coalition government team, Robert Hazell, Ben Yong, Peter Waller and Brian Walker, carried out almost 150 one-to-one interviews to test the issues identified by Hazell and Yong. The team also conducted a small number of group interviews with special advisers from both the Conservatives and the Liberal Democrats. Each member was responsible for one or more key 'arenas' of government. Robert Hazell interviewed those at the centre; Peter Waller in departments; Ben Yong in Parliament, the political parties and interest groups (as well as some at the centre and in departments); and Brian Walker the media. They were ably assisted in interviews at the centre by David

Laughrin, a Fellow of the Ashridge Public Leadership Centre and a former senior civil servant. These interviews were done on the basis of anonymity: where we name a source, that is because they either granted us an on-the-record interview, or because we went back to them for permission.

In all we conducted 147 interviews. The selection of interviewees depended on the arena. In the case of the centre, we identified key interviewees through news articles and organograms published by the Coalition Government in late 2010. For parliamentarians we opted for a broad range of interviewees, from the chairs of both parties' backbench groups to party whips; those who were pro-coalition and those who were coalition-sceptics. There was also significant 'snowballing': interviewees would often suggest or refer us to someone else who had more in-depth knowledge on a particular matter.

The three case study departments – the Department for Communities and Local Government (DCLG); the Department of Energy and Climate Change (DECC); and the Department for Environment, Food and Rural Affairs (Defra) – were chosen for two reasons. First, all three departments had a different ministerial configuration. One was led by a Conservative Secretary of State with one junior Lib Dem minister (DCLG); one by a Lib Dem Secretary of State with a number of Conservative junior ministers (DECC); and one was led by a Conservative Secretary of State with no Lib Dems in the department (Defra). Second, the three departments' subject matter or 'jurisdictions' overlapped to some extent. Our aim was to see how the differently configured departments might have an impact on policy.

Earlier in the project we carried out a small number of interviews with interest groups, partly to identify key actors in the Coalition, but also to get a sense of how the Coalition was seen to be working. We chose organisations which had regular dealings with our case study departments (DCLG, DECC and Defra), and that were also well resourced enough to have a team devoted to government relations.

Each team member had a set of questions derived from the research questions set out above. We pressed interviewees, where possible, for concrete examples. We then cross-checked our findings by asking similar questions of interviewees from other arenas. For example, we hypothesised that Liberal Democrat junior ministers would act as 'watchdogs', having a broader remit than the 'ordinary' junior minister to watch over his or her department. So we asked about this when interviewing junior ministers and special advisers from both coalition parties, backbench parliamentarians, and also those from the party outside Parliament.

Table 1.2 below categorises interviewees by arena and by party affiliation.[21] We recognise that those falling under 'No 10' and 'Deputy Prime Minister's Office' could all technically fall under 'Cabinet Office', but we separate them here so that readers have some idea of whom and how many we interviewed at the centre. The category 'official' refers to civil servants; 'other' to those not in the Coalition: Labour, or in the case of the House of Lords, Crossbenchers; or those outside government, either in interest groups or in the media. Interviewees were not

---

[21] Table 1.2 counts the number of interviewees rather than the number of interviews: so someone we interviewed twice was only counted once.

broken down by specific role: so, for instance, special advisers (spads) were counted as interviewees with a party affiliation in the centre, in departments and in Parliament. We interviewed significantly more special advisers than ministers, but that was a product of ministerial workload rather than bias on our part.

Overall we had more Lib Dem interviewees than Conservative, possibly reflecting the fact that the smaller party in the Coalition were keen to talk about the novel experience of being in power, at least in comparison with the party that was more used to government. We also interviewed very few people from Labour, mostly because of limited resources. As a result, we do not discuss in any detail the impact upon the official opposition of having a coalition at Westminster.

Table 1.2 Interviewees

| Arena | Organisation | Affiliation | | | | |
|---|---|---|---|---|---|---|
| | | LD | Con | Official | Other | Total |
| Whitehall | No 10 | 5 | 4 | 3 | | 12 |
| | Cabinet Office | 2 | | 8 | | 10 |
| | Deputy Prime Minister's Office | 1 | | 2 | | 3 |
| | Departments | 9 | 7 | 17 | | 33 |
| Parliament | House of Commons | 10 | 10 | | | 20 |
| | House of Lords | 15 | 15 | | 4 | 34 |
| Extra-parliamentary | Political party | 10 | 5 | | | 15 |
| | Media | | | | 10 | 10 |
| | Interest groups | | | | 10 | 10 |
| Total | | 52 | 41 | 30 | 24 | 147 |

In June 2011, we released a report online with our interim findings, titled *Inside Story: How Coalition Government Works.*[22] At that point we had done two-thirds of our interviews. Where possible we then tested the findings of the interim report by asking the remaining interviewees whether they thought the report reflected the truth as they saw it, and where it did not, to explain why and where possible to give concrete examples. We finished our final interview in late October 2011.

OUTLINE OF THE BOOK

*The Politics of Coalition: How the Conservative-Liberal Democrat Government Works* consists of 11 chapters. Following the Introduction, chapter two, written by Eimear O'Casey, looks to the experience of coalitions in Germany, Ireland,

---

[22] Available at www.ucl.ac.uk/constitution-unit/research/coalition-government/interim-report2.pdf

New Zealand, Scotland and Wales. Taking the international and subnational experience of coalitions, O'Casey examines the common problems that coalitions face and the range of responses, and asks to what extent the UK Coalition is typical or atypical in comparison to the experience of other countries.

Chapter three by Ben Yong examines the formation of the Conservative-Liberal Democrat Coalition, looking at the factors that led to the formation of a coalition, and a Conservative-Liberal Democrat coalition rather than one led by Labour; and the nature of the substantive and procedural Coalition Agreements.

Chapters four and five look at how the Coalition works in Whitehall. Chapter four by Robert Hazell examines the centre – No 10, the Office of the Deputy Prime Minister and Cabinet Office, and in particular the formal and informal machinery that has emerged to deal with the tensions of being in a coalition.

Chapter five, written by Peter Waller, examines the impact of the Coalition on departments and the civil service, with a particular focus on our three case study departments: the Department of Energy and Climate Change, Environment, Farming and Rural Affairs, and the Department for Communities and Local Government. It also looks at the roles of ministers – and in particular the role of Liberal Democrat ministers – in the Coalition.

Chapter six looks at how the Coalition works in Westminster. Ben Yong examines the problems that the Coalition faces in Parliament: in particular, the problems of ensuring sufficient and efficient interparty cooperation; maintaining good frontbench/backbench relations; monitoring the Coalition Agreement; and the difficulty of expressing party distinctiveness where there is pressure to speak with one voice.

Chapters seven and eight look at how the Coalition works outside Westminster and Whitehall. In chapter seven Yong looks at how the two coalition parties have responded to their parliamentary party and leadership having agreed to form a coalition, and takes a brief look at the Labour Party.

Chapter eight, written by Brian Walker, examines the Coalition and the media: how the Coalition and coalition partners handle the media, and how the media have portrayed the Coalition. Walker asks if the Coalition is able to speak with a single voice, particularly given a mostly hostile Tory media looking for evidence of 'splits'. As befits a contribution from a former political journalist, this chapter is written in a more narrative and journalistic style than the other chapters in the book.

Chapters nine and ten look at a number of case studies. In chapter nine Hazell examines the Coalition's constitutional reforms. Chapter ten, written jointly by Peter Waller and Ben Yong, examines tuition fees, NHS reforms and nuclear policy. These case studies aim to illustrate how the internal and external structures of the Coalition have worked in practice.

Chapter eleven sets out our conclusions. The first part considers the future of the Conservative-Liberal Democrat Coalition: will it survive until 2015? What are the key obstacles it faces in the near future, and what are the exit strategies for the two coalition parties? The second part sets out the 'lessons learnt' from the first year and a half of the Coalition for future coalition governments.

# 2

# *The Experience of Coalition: Domestic and Abroad*

EIMEAR O'CASEY

## INTRODUCTION

WHILST IT WAS a rare and daunting prospect for Westminster, coalition government is both expected and institutionalised in democracies in much of the rest of the world. Indeed, coalition is a far more common form of government in most parliamentary systems than the single-party governments which have dominated in the UK. Consequently, it is worth surveying some of the most important aspects of coalition government elsewhere before we launch into findings about our own.

In this chapter we take the three key phases of coalition governance in turn – formation, management, and termination – and pose four broad questions for each: what are the most common features of coalitions elsewhere? What are the most common problems that arise? What mechanisms have countries adopted to deal with these problems, and how successful have they been? And finally, how did the UK Coalition in its first 18 months match up to the comparative experience?

In this short survey we draw on the general comparative literature, but focus on the experiences of five countries in particular: Germany, Ireland, New Zealand, Scotland and Wales. NZ, Scotland, Ireland and Wales have been chosen because they are Westminster systems with several features comparable to the UK; Germany has been chosen for its rich coalition history and successful approach to coalition management. In sum, this chapter should provide a comparative context against which to view the UK experience and the themes and problems running through the book.

## OVERVIEW

The normalisation of coalition government in Western parliamentary democracies is longstanding and comprehensive. In the European Union in December 2011, 20 of 27 governments were coalitions. Of the seven that were not, five were single-party governments (Bulgaria, Cyprus, Hungary, Malta and Spain) and the remaining two were the recently created technocratic governments of Greece and Italy. The dominance of coalition governments is not a recent development. Since the Second World War, coalitions have accounted for about 70 per cent of European governments.[1]

Traditionally there has been a clear link between a country's voting system and the kind of government formed. Majoritarian systems like the UK's have long tended to produce a two-party system and single-party government, while proportional systems tend to make it very difficult for one party to pass the 50 per cent threshold needed to govern alone. The dramatic shift from single-party governments to a string of five successive multiparty governments in New Zealand following their switch from a majoritarian to a more proportional voting system embodies this trend. However, a general erosion in the traditional class and left-right cleavages and a process of 'dealignment' has been observed across the Western world, in both proportional and majoritarian systems.[2] The UK has been no exception: since 1975, the Liberals/Liberal Democrats have won sufficient support to markedly reduce the two main parties' vote share at each election, and there has been a gradual increase in the number of parties present in Parliament, with 10 parties represented in the 2010 House of Commons. This has increased the likelihood of parties having to share power to form a government.[3] It remains to be seen how the recent coalition experience will affect this trend, and the probability of future coalition governments being formed in the UK.

## FORMATION

Formation of a single-party majority government is a relatively straightforward affair. As Westminster practice demonstrates, a majority government can be in place within a matter of hours after election results are confirmed. Where no one party has a clear majority, however, formation can take a lot longer, as different parties negotiate to find a viable government and agree on a programme. One of the standard criticisms of coalition is that the formation process gives rise to uncertainty and delay while negotiations take place.

A combination of factors informs the coalition formation process: the arithmetic of the election – if there are many viable government configurations or only a few; the ideological fit between the negotiating parties; and finally, contextual factors – if there are national emergencies or public pressure to form a government. The Belgians, for example, managed to break their 18-month negotiation deadlock in November 2011 only when the Eurozone crisis necessitated urgent reforms which required a government agreement.

The timeframe for coalition formation varies considerably both within and across different countries. We can see from Figure 2.1 that the UK was unusual in

---

[1] M Gallagher and P Mitchell (eds), *The Politics of Electoral Systems* (Oxford University Press, 2005) 401.

[2] See primarily RJ Dalton, 'The Decline of Party Identifications' in RJ Dalton and M Wattenberg (eds), *Parties without Partisans* (Oxford University Press, 2000).

[3] Gallagher and Mitchell (eds), *The Politics of Electoral Systems* (n 1) 164–7.

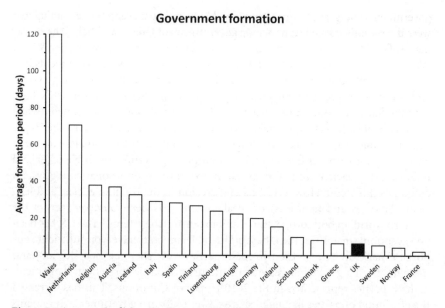

Figure 2.1 Average Coalition Government Formation Time

Source: Adapted from K Strøm, WC Müller and T Bergman (eds), *Cabinets and Coalition Bargaining: The Democratic Life Cycle in Western Europe* (Oxford University Press, 2008) 130

Note: The unusually high figure for Wales is an average of the 2002 Labour-Lib Dem negotiations, which took six months (conducted while a temporary government had been put in place), and the 2007 Labour-Plaid Cymru negotiations, which took two months.

the European context in terms of the speed with which it negotiated the coalition deal in 2010 (five days).

We discuss the causes of this haste in chapter three. To discourage the long delays experienced elsewhere, the devolution legislation in Scotland and Wales introduced a statutory 28-day deadline for formation. However, some, including the negotiators, believe that this caused the process to be rushed and made policy plans inconsistent.[4] The Belgian experience is certainly not the inevitable result where there is no such deadline. In Germany, for example, the average formation time is only 20 days.

In countries where coalition is the norm, a range of other constitutional rules and conventions exist to regulate the formation process. These include pre-election pacts between parties (used on occasion in Ireland and Germany); the appointment of a designated *formateur* to lead the negotiation process (common across continental Europe); and the requirement of an investiture vote whereby a new government must formally test its support in Parliament (which exists in

---

[4] R Blackburn, R Fox, O Gay and L Maer, *Who Governs? Forming a Coalition or Minority Government in the Event of a Hung Parliament* (London, Hansard Society & Study of Parliament Group, 2010) 5.

Germany, Ireland, Scotland and Wales).[5] The shape of the formation process in a given country, and whether it relies more on institutionalised rules (like Scotland and Wales, Finland and Belgium) or informal conventions (like Ireland or Germany) is very much a product of history and habit, as countries re-create methods that have worked in the past.

The negotiations typically result in a coalition agreement. This exists as a means of recording joint objectives, facilitating communication and providing avenues for dispute resolution.[6] By setting down policies on paper, the coalition agreement becomes a means by which the parties relinquish veto power over coalition policies and outline common discipline.[7] It is also a means by which the public and parties can have a clear idea of the government's objectives so that they can hold it to account.[8] Agreements vary enormously in length and degree of detail. Table 2.1 below demonstrates this variation across 15 Western European countries.

Junior partners have shown a particular fondness for longer, more detailed agreements. But in several cases longer documents have been criticised for causing inflexibility. The agreement negotiated in NZ in 1996 between National and New Zealand First ran to 74 pages, at the behest of the smaller party. But it proved to be a straitjacket, and may have been one of the causes of the Coalition's collapse in 1998.[9] There is also an issue about the balance between policy and process. The Welsh Agreement between Labour and the Lib Dems in 2000, which ran to 6,000 words, was subsequently criticised by some ministers for focusing too heavily on coalition management mechanisms and not enough on policy.[10]

At 16,000 words, the principal UK agreement (the 'Programme for Government') was of about average length by comparative standards. What was unusual was that there were in fact three documents: the Interim Coalition Agreement, the more detailed Programme for Government proper, both of which laid out coalition policy, and the Coalition Agreement for Stability and Reform, which laid out the procedural framework for coalition management. Chapter three provides a full discussion of these documents.

## MANAGEMENT

Managing a coalition presents distinct challenges compared with managing one-party government. Drawing on experiences elsewhere, we can distil most of these

---

[5] For a comprehensive discussion of these various factors see B Seyd, *Coalition Government in Britain: Lessons from Overseas* (London, Constitution Unit, 2002).

[6] For a comprehensive survey of coalition agreements across Western Europe see WC Müller and K Strøm, 'Coalition Agreements and Cabinet Governance' in K Strøm, WC Müller and T Bergman (eds), *Cabinets and Coalition Bargaining: The Democratic Life Cycle in Western Europe* (Oxford University Press, 2010).

[7] ibid.

[8] A Paun, *United We Stand?* (London, Institute for Government, 2010) 23.

[9] B Yong, 'New Zealand's Experience of Multiparty Governance' in R Hazell and A Paun (eds), *Making Minority Government Work* (London, Institute for Government and Constitution Unit, 2009) 41.

[10] Seyd, *Coalition Government in Britain* (n 5) 16.

Table 2.1 Size and Content of Coalition Agreements in 15 European Countries, 1945–99

| Country | Size (number of words) | | Policy content (mean in %) | General procedural content (mean in %) |
|---|---|---|---|---|
| | Range | Mean | | |
| Austria | 700–23,300 | 6,593 | 48 | 18.5 |
| Belgium | 3,150–43,550 | 14,166 | 93 | 1.5 |
| Denmark | 910–5,613 | 3,619 | 88 | 0 |
| Finland | 204–4,541 | 1,163 | 100 | 0 |
| France | 870–3,390 | 1,976 | 99 | 1 |
| Germany | 513–16,536 | 5,934 | 91.5 | 7.5 |
| Ireland | 1,248–23,500 | 10,161 | 100 | 0 |
| Italy | unknown | 3,680 | 31 | 38 |
| Netherlands | 3,100–36,000 | 14,223 | 90.5 | 3 |
| Norway | 2,919–31,138 | 12,435 | 99.5 | 0 |
| Portugal | 2,461–34,300 | 13,746 | 77 | 16.5 |
| Scotland (1999–2011) | 4,623–14,730 | 9,677 | unknown | unknown |
| Sweden | 1,100–5,200 | 2,443 | 97.5 | 0 |
| Wales (1999–2011) | 6,900–11,597 | 9,249 | unknown | unknown |

Source: Adapted from 'Coalition Agreements and Cabinet Governance' in K Strøm, WC Müller and T Bergman (eds), *Cabinets and Coalition Bargaining: The Democratic Life Cycle in Western Europe* (Oxford University Press, 2008) 173

challenges into the following two categories: the difficulty of reconciling the unity of the government with the need for each party to retain, and sell, its distinctiveness; and the need to maintain communication and coordination channels to limit disagreements, resolve disputes and above all ensure stability. Below we discuss these challenges as they have presented themselves internationally, first in terms of general aspects of coalition management, and then more specifically at the executive level.

## The Unity/Distinctiveness Dilemma

The unity/distinctiveness dilemma is an enduring theme running through this book. Coalition parties must work hard to construct cohesive policies and present a united front to the public. However, they must also protect their electoral support by maintaining a distinct party identity from their governing partner, who will be a competitor once more when the parties return to the polls.[11]

This dilemma has historically been a particular concern for junior partners, who are inevitably less influential and less visible than their senior partners. The inherent disadvantage of being the junior partner has often translated into poor performance at the polls.[12] In Ireland the Progressive Democrats lost all but two seats in 2007 and subsequently disbanded, while the Greens suffered a total wipe-out in the 2011 election.[13] NZ's Alliance Party lost all its seats in similar fashion in 1999 after splintering into two (although its 'other half', the Progressives, did secure two seats at the next election).

The German Free Democratic Party (FDP) is an example of a junior partner that has been unusually good at securing influence – in terms of high profile ministries – and at performing well at elections. The party has participated in government for a longer aggregate period than either of the two main parties, or indeed any other party.[14] However, this record seems to be critically dependent on an internal party structure in which vital decisions are taken at the top and then presented as a fait accompli to the party afterwards.[15] This stands in sharp contrast to the UK Lib Dems' strong tradition of internal party democracy – for instance, the 'triple lock' procedure required for securing approval of any agreement (see chapter three).

## Policy Coordination, Conflict Resolution and Collective Cabinet Responsibility

For both partners in a coalition, keeping tabs on the behaviour of the other party, and their compliance with the agreement, is the second core challenge. In the worst cases, failure to consult properly has prompted government breakdown. In the dramatic break-up of the Fianna Fáil-Irish Labour Coalition in 1994, for example, the main stimulus for the government's collapse was the junior partner Labour being angered and humiliated by the 'culture of secrecy' surrounding Fianna Fáil, with Labour being repeatedly misled on key decisions.[16]

Parliamentary government and modern party discipline require collective cabinet responsibility, in which ministers publicly defend all the policies of the

---

[11] J Boston, 'Multi-Party Governance: Managing the Unity-Distinctiveness Dilemma in Executive Coalitions' (2010) *Party Politics* 1.

[12] See for instance K Deschouwer, *New Parties in Government: In Power for the First Time* (Oxford, Routledge, 2008); and R Miller and J Curtin, 'Counting the Costs of Coalition: The Case of New Zealand's Small Parties' (2011) 63(1) *Political Science* 106.

[13] However, the Irish Greens' dismal showing in 2011 is only a sideshow to the historic defeat of senior coalition partner Fianna Fáil, who lost 57 of 77 seats, all in the context of the 2010–11 financial crisis.

[14] However, the FDP's long-standing pivotal role in government formation and their ability to influence coalition agreements is declining. See C Lees, 'Coalition Dynamics and the Changing German Party System' (2010) 28(3) *German Party Politics and Society* 130.

[15] EJ Kirchner and D Broughton, 'The FDP in the Federal Republic of Germany: The Requirements of Survival and Success' in EJ Kirchner (ed), *Liberal Parties in Western Europe* (Cambridge University Press, 1988) 68.

[16] J Garry, 'The Demise of the Fianna Fáil/Labour "Partnership" Government and the Rise of the "Rainbow" Coalition' (1995) 10(1) *Irish Political Studies* 192.

government, even if they have argued against them in private. In Ireland, collective responsibility is in fact a constitutional requirement, and coalition government has made no change to the doctrine. Voting against the government is not an option for a cabinet minister.[17]

In contrast, NZ has been experimental with the relaxation of collective cabinet responsibility. Since the 1999 Labour-Alliance coalition, a measure known as the 'party distinction provision', or the 'agreement to disagree', has become standard. This provision stipulates that where either party leader considers a policy to have implications for party identity, they are to raise it with the Coalition Management Committee. The Committee can then deem the matter suitable for public differentiation. The general assessment of the 'agreement to disagree' is a positive one, and it is credited with providing junior partners in particular with a 'useful and necessary' safety valve.[18] The UK's Programme for Government contains four specific 'agree to disagree' provisions, but a generic safety valve such as exists in NZ has not so far been deemed necessary.

## Coalition Committees

The most important formal mechanism unique to a coalition is a coalition committee, usually consisting of cabinet ministers, and sometimes senior party figures from outside the government.[19] The most recent 2007–11 Welsh Coalition established two formal committees, one for monitoring implementation of the Coalition Agreement and presentation of policy, the other for the budget. The First Minister and Deputy First Minister (leaders from each coalition party) sat on both.[20] In Germany, coalition committees have also been used, but only on an irregular basis. Instead, the Germans have typically relied on an array of informal mechanisms for dealing with these challenges, outlined below. We will see in chapter four that the UK Government's Coalition Committee was similarly underused in the first 18 months, despite being envisaged in the Coalition Agreement as one of the core dispute resolution mechanisms. In Ireland, there is no tradition of establishing official conflict management arenas. Instead, disputes are resolved outside official institutions, and Cabinet can even be suspended until an agreement is reached.[21]

---

[17] P Mitchell, 'Ireland: From Single-Party to Coalition Rule' in K Strøm and WC Müller (eds), *Coalition Governments in Western Europe* (New York, Oxford University Press, 2000) 141.

[18] J Boston and D Bullock, 'Experiments in Executive Government under MMP in New Zealand: Contrasting Approaches to Multiparty Governance' (2009) 7(1) *New Zealand Journal of Public and International Law* 39.

[19] RB Andeweg and A Timmermans, 'Conflict Management in Coalition Government' in Strøm, Müller and Bergman (eds), *Cabinets and Coalition Bargaining* (n 6) 272.

[20] J Osmond, *Crossing the Rubicon: Coalition Politics Welsh Style* (Institute of Welsh Affairs, 2007) 38.

[21] Mitchell, 'Ireland' (n 17) 140.

## Ministerial Allocation

A very common mechanism for coordination is the use of watchdog ministers, also known as ministerial 'twinning'. Twinning is the practice of assigning a junior minister from one party to a department headed by a minister from the other party. It helps communication, policy coordination and the build-up of trust. The twinning process has been used frequently in Germany, Ireland and Belgium, but never in Denmark or Finland.[22] The UK has also adopted the twinning mechanism: in 2010 Lib Dem ministers were appointed alongside Conservatives in all but five government departments (see chapter five).

Alternatively, a junior partner can go for depth rather than breadth and concentrate their ministers in just a few departments. Full control of a ministry allows the junior partner to surround itself with trustworthy colleagues, and to take full responsibility for successful policies in that subject area. The junior coalition partner in NZ, the Alliance, re-evaluated their decision to take a series of junior posts, and decided to hold only one high profile ministry in 2002. In interviews they cited the difficulty that the twinning approach had created in terms of presenting their achievements to voters.[23]

A further strategy is 'cross-cutting', whereby a junior partner minister holds a portfolio across several departments. This approach was used for women's affairs or equalities ministers in NZ in 1999–2002, and in Ireland in 1982–7. Its effectiveness is debatable. In Ireland, ministers and civil servants were not very cooperative, and felt hostile to interference from an outsider.[24] Cross-cutting portfolios are likely to be even more demanding for junior ministers, who find it hard enough to make an impact in just one department.

Finally, ministers may also be supported in monitoring implementation of the coalition agreement by staff dedicated to that role. The Partnership Programme Managers introduced by Irish Labour in 1993 are an example. These were quasi-political appointees – combined advisers and managers who were instructed to monitor the implementation of the Policy Agreement. They met once a week following Cabinet to review progress, and to provide a forum for difficulties to be ironed out.[25] However, some MPs within the Labour Party complained that Programme Managers were mere spin doctors. Programme Managers continued to be used under the following Coalition, where they also drew criticism for politicising the administration.[26] Whatever impact they may have had, they certainly did not prevent the dramatic break-up of the Coalition in 1994, mentioned above, following a total breakdown in trust between the party leaderships.

[22] L Verzichelli, 'Portfolio Allocation' in Strøm, Müller and Bergman (eds), *Cabinets and Coalition Bargaining* (n 6) 260–1.

[23] Seyd, *Coalition Government in Britain* (n 5) 90–91.

[24] Mitchell, 'Ireland' (n 17) 144.

[25] E O'Halpin, 'Partnership Programme Managers in the Reynolds/Spring Coalition 1993–1994: An Assessment', DCU Business School Research Papers Series (Paper No 6), Dublin University Business School, Ireland (1996), 8.

[26] B Connaughton, 'Politico-Administrative Relations under Coalition Government: The Case of Ireland' (Cracow, 10th Annual NISPAcee Conference, 2002) 13–14.

## Informal Mechanisms

Informal forums for coordinating policy and resolving disputes are important tools of coalition management. In several instances, these forums have come to be used more regularly than their formal counterparts. In Germany, informal mechanisms have included regular bilateral meetings between the Chancellor and Deputy Chancellor; smaller groups of government members holding monthly meetings (*Kreßbronner Kreis*); 'coalition talks' attended by cabinet members and leaders of parties, the decisions of which were usually ratified by Cabinet; the *Elefantenrund*, a group comprising party chairpersons, coalition party leaders, and secondary experts; as well as other similar configurations at different times over the last 50 years.[27] A comparable network of informal, regular meetings developed in the 1999–2002 New Zealand Labour-Alliance Coalition. These included meetings between each party's special advisers on particular problems, meetings between ministers' press secretaries, and various other ad hoc interactions between ministerial advisers as issues arose.[28]

International experience also suggests that a functional coalition depends crucially upon the relationship between the Prime Minister and Deputy Prime Minister. In both Wales and Scotland, the relationship between the First Minister and Deputy First Minister was considered the driving force behind coalition management.[29] In the Scottish Labour-Lib Dem coalitions of 1999–2003 and 2003–7 close cooperation between the two party leaders was favoured by the junior Lib Dem partner over a more formal collective coalition structure, and was even provided for in the two coalition agreements.[30] In practice this involved joint decision-making with regard to portfolio allocation, and consultation on items for inclusion on the cabinet agenda. Similarly, both the First Minister and Deputy First Minister were copied in to all papers regarding significant policy issues; this has also been the case in Wales.[31]

Closely linked to this is the 'good faith and no surprises' principle. It has become crucial in New Zealand, where it is cited in various agreements and in Cabinet Office Circulars. The Labour-Alliance Government required joint signatures to indicate joint approval before a paper was accepted for a committee or Cabinet. Departments were also told not to implement policies which were still subject to consultation between the parties. Crucially, the good faith element of this approach rests upon trust, and all those interviewed for a study conducted in 2009 cited the importance of strong personal relationships in multiparty government.[32]

---

[27] M Schmidt, *Political Institutions in the Federal Republic of Germany* (Oxford University Press, 2003) 33.

[28] J Boston and A Ladley, 'The Efficient Secret: The Craft of Coalition Management' (2006) 4(1) *New Zealand Journal of Public and International Law* 76.

[29] B Seyd, *Coalition Governance in Scotland and Wales* (London, Constitution Unit, 2004) 96.

[30] Seyd, *Coalition Government in Britain* (n 5) 95.

[31] ibid, 94.

[32] Yong, 'New Zealand's Experience of Multiparty Governance' (n 9) 48.

In its first 18 months the UK Coalition emulated many of these informal management tools for avoiding disputes and for coordinating policy. It espoused in earnest the 'good faith and no surprises' principle, and the interviews conducted for this book reveal the importance of the relationship between David Cameron and Nick Clegg in setting the tone for relations further down the chain (see chapter four). And while Cabinet and Cabinet Committees provided the formal machinery for joint signing off regarding policy, they were preceded by the informal group dynamics that are so common in Germany.

## TERMINATION

What are the main factors to precipitate the termination of coalitions? A study by Damgaard finds the most common reason for coalition government termination among 17 Western European countries to be controversies between cabinet parties, ie interparty tension. In the majority of cases, these tensions are policy rather than personality based. The study also finds that coalitions are no more likely than single-party governments to end because of intraparty conflict. Table 2.2 below shows the full range of coalition government termination types and their prevalence in these 17 Western European countries.

Table 2.2 Reasons for Government Termination across 17 Countries, 1945–99

| Termination type | Prevalence (%) |
|---|---|
| 'Technical' | 37 (total cases: 92 of 248) |
| of which regular election | 75 |
| of which other constitutional | 19.5 |
| of which death of PM | 5.5 |
| 'Discretionary' | 63 (total cases: 156 of 248) |
| of which early election | 35 |
| of which voluntary enlargement | 4 |
| of which cabinet defeat | 12 |
| of which intra-party conflict | 25 |
| of which inter-party policy conflict | 56 |
| of which inter-party personal conflict | 15.5 |

Source: Adapted from data in E Damgaard, 'Cabinet Termination' in K Strøm, WC Müller and T Bergman (eds), *Cabinets and Coalition Bargaining: The Democratic Life Cycle in Western Europe* (Oxford University Press, 2008) 308. Note that these categories are not mutually exclusive and thus add up to over 100 per cent.

Preventing interparty tensions from reaching the point at which they can precipitate a breakdown in government is a priority for all coalition partners. Many of the mechanisms and approaches discussed above are employed with a view to doing just that.

Not covered in the data above are the exogenous factors that can bring down a coalition government – or indeed a single-party government. These might include scandal, economic recession or international events.[33] The spectacular collapse of the 2007–11 Fianna Fáil-Irish Green Coalition was directly precipitated by the withdrawal of the junior partner, the Greens, from government. However, their withdrawal was, in turn, prompted by the Greens' lack of faith in the senior party's conduct in the context of the 2010–11 economic crisis in Ireland. Consequently, any fair appraisal of that government's termination would have to factor in an external cause.[34] It remains to be seen whether the exceptional economic circumstances in which the UK Coalition operated and the subsequent Eurozone crisis will play a part in the nature of its termination.

### Coalition Campaigning

The unity/distinctiveness dilemma is particularly acute for coalition parties towards the end of a government. While it is often presumed that coalition partners must distance themselves from one another, experience in Scotland suggests that this is not necessarily so. The two Labour-Liberal Democrat coalitions in Scotland stayed together for the full four years, and successfully campaigned as distinct parties in the 2003 and 2007 elections.

Mechanisms were put in place to avoid a clash between electoral and government interests. In line with Westminster practice, the Government reduced activity to a minimum in the election run-up.[35] In their election campaigns the parties did not engage in a process of detachment from the Coalition. One Scottish Liberal Democrat interviewee for this book insisted that this was critical to their success at the polls.

Several factors helped to reinforce the cohesion of these two coalition governments. Both enjoyed healthy majorities in Parliament, and benefited from generous budget increases. Labour and the Lib Dems avoided negative campaigning against each other because they knew that they might need each other again after the election: any chance of forming a government to rival the Scottish National Party would almost certainly involve the other party.[36]

---

[33] For a thorough discussion see T Saalfeld, 'Institutions, Chance and Choices' in Strøm, Müller and Bergman (eds), *Cabinets and Coalition Bargaining* (n 6) 327–68.

[34] Although, of course, it was the government's *actions* in the context of that financial crisis that provoked Fianna Fáil's historic losses at the polls as much as the crisis itself; evidence of the very integrated nature of all termination factors.

[35] Seyd, *Coalition Governance in Scotland and Wales* (n 29) 13.

[36] A Trench (ed), *The State of the Nations 2008* (London, Imprint Academic, 2008) 39.

CONCLUSION

Coalition government is an established norm throughout the Western world, and a multitude of conventions and mechanisms have developed to accommodate it. In formation, the core challenge is to secure a coalition agreement which is at once specific and flexible. In management, while in many respects the challenges of single-party and coalition government are parallel, we have identified two recurring themes that coalitions encounter: the unity/distinctiveness dilemma, and the need to coordinate policy and resolve conflict. A range of formal and informal mechanisms exist to meet these challenges, including the standard Cabinet and Committee arenas, as well as ad hoc meetings and reliance upon good personal relationships. Governance challenges are amplified for the junior partner, which tends to suffer more at the polls than its senior counterpart. And finally, regarding termination of coalition governments, interparty tensions have proved to be the most common cause of break-up – testament to the importance of putting in place effective mechanisms for managing such inevitable tensions.

How does the UK Coalition fit into this picture? As we will see, practices in the first 18 months matched several elements of the international experience. The Coalition Agreements were negotiated very quickly, but the main agreements, the Programme for Government and the Agreement for Stability and Reform, together were of average length and specificity, with plenty of procedural safeguards embedded in them. The distribution of ministers followed the practice of twinning, with a watchdog minister in almost every department. At the centre the Coalition put in place a combination of formal and informal mechanisms to ensure adequate consultation and policy coordination. In terms of the unity/distinctiveness dilemma, the Government has been stronger on unity than distinctiveness. At the end of the first 18 months, the Liberal Democrats were doing badly in terms of their poll ratings; it remains to be seen whether they suffer disproportionately at the next election.

**Historical Coda: Previous Coalitions in the UK**

Finally, this chapter offers some brief reflections on what can be learned from the experience of previous coalitions in the UK.[37] Four coalitions were formed in the twentieth century, led by Asquith (1915–16), Lloyd George (1916–22), Macdonald (1931–5) and Churchill (1940–5). There are not many direct lessons to be drawn, because of the unique circumstances of those coalitions and the different way in which politics was conducted. All arose in response to a national crisis: three in a world war, the fourth in the 1930s Great Depression.

[37] See generally D Butler, *Coalitions in British Politics* (London, Macmillan, 1978); V Bogdanor, *Coalition Government in Western Europe* (London, Heinemann Educational Books, 1983); and, most recently, V Bogdanor, *The Coalition and the Constitution* (Oxford, Hart Publishing, 2010).

Three out of the four coalitions continued even after the Conservatives had an outright majority, because of the need for national unity.

Following the rest of the chapter, the analysis will focus on their formation, management and termination. Formation was very different, resulting from informal talks rather than formal negotiations. The parliamentary parties were not consulted before their leaders entered coalition, with just one exception – the Labour Party Conference formally endorsed Labour's entry into Churchill's wartime coalition in 1940. There were no formal coalition agreements. In the wartime coalitions the agreed objective was simply victory. In 1918 the Conservatives and Lloyd George's 'coupon' Liberals fought under a joint manifesto: that coupon election is the leading example in British history of an electoral pact, which delivered short-term gains for the Liberals but proved disastrous in the longer term. The National Government in 1931 had a short seven-point statement of priorities, but it was nothing like the detailed coalition agreements of modern times.

Management of these coalitions was also much less formal. There were no Cabinet Coalition Committees. The War Cabinets were to give political direction to the conduct of the war, not to resolve coalition disputes. Management was directed primarily through individuals rather than parties or institutional mechanisms. This was especially the case for the WWI and 1930s coalitions, which were based on fractions of parties organised around key individuals. The lack of formal mechanisms has led some to call Macdonald's Government a quasi-coalition. Only under Churchill's government did coalition management become a little more formalised, with the War Cabinet also functioning as an assembly of party leaders, with watchdog ministers from the junior party in most departments, and with joint whipping of the coalition parties.

Termination of Britain's twentieth century coalitions does have a closer fit with the comparative analysis earlier in the chapter. They resulted from interparty and intraparty dissent. Although Conservative ministers were willing to continue under Lloyd George, their backbenchers and the Conservative grassroots were not. Conservative MPs rebelled in 1922 at the famous meeting in the Carlton Club, but the rebellion had begun in constituency associations, which had adopted large numbers of candidates opposed to the Coalition. In the 1931 Coalition there was an attempt to manage the divisive interparty issue of free trade by an 'agreement to disagree', but this was condemned by the Liberal Party Conference, and Liberal ministers resigned in protest at the imposition of the imperial tariff. In 1945 Churchill wanted to continue the Coalition, but the Labour Party voted to leave and to fight the election on their very different vision of post-war social policy.

Labour's success in the 1945 election showed dramatically that the junior coalition partner need not always suffer at the next election. But the Liberals definitely suffered as a result of their involvement in the 1918 and 1931

Coalitions. Although coalition was not the cause of the splits in the Liberal Party, it exacerbated them, with the Liberal Party split three ways under the 1930s Coalition. The history of all the coalitions also shows that, even before the advent of more formal internal party democracy, party leaders could not ignore their backbenchers or party members for ever. When a coalition dissolves, it is often from the bottom up.[38]

[38] Bogdanor, *The Coalition and the Constitution*, ibid, 76.

# 3

# Formation of the Coalition

## BEN YONG

Forming a coalition is an exercise of political leadership basically, and the longer you take over it, the more process you build around it, the more the ability of leadership to exercise itself is dissipated. (Liberal Democrat minister)

I think we got a completely duff deal. (Lib Dem minister)

It's like being stuck at the airport, isn't it? You know you can't do anything about the snow, but what people can do is tell you what's going on. (Conservative peer)

## INTRODUCTION

COALITIONS HAVE A life cycle, consisting of a set of stages: from formation, to governance, to termination. These stages are often treated as separate, but what happens at an earlier stage may have an influence on later stages.[1] Most of this book is about the second stage: coalition governance. In this chapter, however, we consider its formation. How that is handled can have a profound influence on how well it works thereafter.

The formation of a Conservative-Liberal Democrat coalition at Westminster came as a surprise to many observers of Westminster politics. We first ask how well the parties prepared for that as a possible outcome. We explain why it was that a coalition was formed following the 2010 general election, and why a Conservative-Liberal Democrat coalition. Following this, we examine the three key documents which collectively constitute the 'Coalition Agreement', to see what contributions the two coalition parties made, and offer thoughts on who won what. We then look at the division of ministerial office and resources and ask what factors were salient for the Liberal Democrats as the smaller party when they determined what portfolios to take and who would take them. Finally, we foreshadow findings in later chapters: that some of the decisions made in the formation process would have a negative impact on coalition management.

---

[1] K Strøm, WC Müller and T Bergman (eds), *Cabinets and Coalition Bargaining: The Democratic Life Cycle in Western Europe* (Oxford University Press, 2008); J Curtice, 'So What Went Wrong with the Electoral System? The 2010 Election Result and the Debate about Electoral Reform' (2010) 63(4) *Parliamentary Affairs* 623.

FORMATION OF THE CONSERVATIVE-LIBERAL DEMOCRAT COALITION

We noted in chapter one that various long-term trends (the decline of the two-party vote, the rise of third parties and the shrinking number of marginal seats) made it difficult for any one party to achieve an overall majority in the House of Commons, which was what happened in the 2010 general election. The results are set out in Table 3.1 below.

Table 3.1  UK 2010 General Election: Share of Votes and Number of Seats Won, and Changes from 2005

|  | Share of votes (%) | Change 2005–10 | Number of seats | Change 2005–10 |
|---|---|---|---|---|
| Conservative | 36.0 | 3.6 | 305* | 95 |
| Labour | 29.0 | -6.2 | 258 | -90 |
| Lib Dem | 23.0 | 1.0 | 57 | -5 |
| UKIP | 3.1 | 0.9 | 0 | 0 |
| BNP | 1.9 | 1.2 | 0 | 0 |
| SNP | 1.7 | 0.2 | 6 | 0 |
| Green | 1.0 | 0 | 1 | 1 |
| Independents | 0.8 | 0.4 | 1 | 0 |
| Sinn Féin | 0.6 | 0 | 5 | 0 |
| DUP | 0.6 | -0.3 | 8 | -1 |
| Plaid Cymru | 0.6 | 0 | 3 | 1 |
| SDLP | 0.4 | -0.1 | 3 | 0 |
| UCU-NF | 0.3 | -0.2 | 0 | -1 |
| Alliance | 0.1 | 0 | 1 | 1 |
| Speaker | 0.1 | 0 | 1 | 0 |

Source: House of Commons Library, *General Election 2010: Preliminary Analysis,* Research Paper 10/36 (18 May 2010) 12-3, www.parliament.uk/documents/commons/lib/research/rp2010/RP10-036.pdf

Note that the change in seats is calculated on the basis of 'notional' 2005 results in England and Wales due to boundary changes.

* The data here and throughout the paper exclude the delayed election in the constituency of Thirsk and Malton, which was later won by the Conservative Party, raising their overall number of seats to 306.

The civil service began to prepare for a hung parliament in 2009, with the Cabinet Office gaming the possible scenarios that might follow at the end of that year.[2] In early 2010 it issued a set of draft guidelines on government formation, recognising that there was a lack of clarity regarding the process of government formation in the event of an inconclusive election. Amongst other matters, the draft guidelines stated that the incumbent Prime Minister would remain in office until it was apparent who could form a government, and that it was the responsibility of those involved in the political process to determine and communicate clearly who that person should be.

Senior civil servants had pre-election contact with members of the Conservative Party, as was common practice: this was done to prepare for a possible government transition, and allowed officials to discuss with opposition parties the broad outlines of what they might do should they become the Government. Unsurprisingly, the Liberal Democrats had fewer opportunities to discuss their plans.[3] The civil service was also prepared to support the parties involved in the formation of a government, following the Scottish civil service's close involvement in brokering coalitions in Edinburgh. At the beginning of negotiations, however, both the Conservative and Liberal Democrat negotiating teams refused civil service support, perhaps because the teams thought this was a political matter, to be settled politically.[4]

All three parties differed in their levels of preparation. The Liberal Democrats are often presumed to have undertaken the most comprehensive preparation for the 2010 general election, but that is not quite correct: they prepared well for a hung parliament; they did not prepare well for government. A negotiating team had been secretly established at the end of 2009. They met several times in late 2009 and early 2010, and carefully laid out plans for both a coalition with one of the major parties, and for Lib Dem support on 'confidence and supply' issues (ie, agreeing to support a minority government on issues involving either the supply of public money or confidence matters). These discussions were carried out in secret.[5] This, according to Lib Dem negotiator David Laws, was done in order to ensure that the party concentrated on getting their message across to the public. But there was also concern that preparations for government might be perceived by the electorate as presumptuous. And because it was done in secret, less thought was given to what might happen following government formation:

> We didn't want to think about it. That's strange for my party, because if we were ever going to progress into government, we were going to be in coalition. [It] was the elephant in the room. (Liberal Democrat peer)

> I think we were good at working out what we wanted from the coalition negotiations. I don't think we were very good at working out what we wanted out of government.

---

[2] P Riddell and C Haddon, *Transitions: Lessons Learned* (London, Institute for Government, 2010) 31–35.

[3] ibid, 35.

[4] D Laws, *22 Days in May* (London, Biteback Publishing, 2010) 96.

[5] ibid, 13–23.

I don't think we had thought any of that through. [But] we would never be in that position again. (Liberal Democrat minister)

Some Liberal Democrats simply presumed that they would not enter government. Said another Lib Dem minister:

I go back to the views of [some] that there was no need to prepare for government as we were not going to be in it . . . My view that we needed to prepare very seriously for government was a minority one.

The Conservatives, on the other hand, appeared to have prepared for government rather well. That was partly because of their greater resources and partly because of the party's previous experiences of government. Preparation for negotiations was mostly done under the direction of senior Tory Oliver Letwin during the election campaign.[6]

The least preparatory work was put in by Labour – perhaps understandably, because they were still running the country. Most preparatory work was done during the election campaign – even though it might have been thought that a coalition was their only realistic hope of remaining in government at all.[7] Their feeble preparation, or lack thereof, would manifest itself in the period following 6 May 2010.

**Table 3.2  Chronology of 2010 Government Formation**

| Days from polling day | Date | Event |
|---|---|---|
| 0 | Thurs 6 May | Polling day. Buckingham Palace indicates to senior civil servants that in the event of a close result, the Queen will only consider seeing the politician who is likely to form the next government after 1pm, rather than the traditional morning meeting when there is an outright winner, thus imposing a 'cooling off period'. |
| 1 | Fri 7 May | BBC News declares a hung parliament. Brown signals he will remain as Prime Minister and extends civil service support to all parties in negotiations. Nick Clegg asserts that the Conservatives have the first right to try to form a government. Cameron makes his 'big, open offer' to the Liberal Democrats to work together in government. |

---

[6] Riddell and Haddon, *Transitions* (n 2) 42; R Wilson, *5 Days to Power* (London, Biteback Publishing, 2010) 52.

[7] D Kavanagh and P Cowley, *The British General Election of 2010* (Basingstoke, Palgrave Macmillan, 2010) 206.

Table 3.2  (*cont.*)

| Days from polling day | Date | Event |
|---|---|---|
| 2 | Sat 8 May | Conservative and Liberal Democrat negotiating teams meet in the Cabinet Office, with civil servants in attendance. Labour and Liberal Democrat negotiating teams meet unofficially in Portcullis House. Nick Clegg meets with David Cameron at Admiralty House. |
| 3 | Sun 9 May | Conservative-Liberal Democrat talks continue. Labour-Liberal Democrat talks continue between Clegg and Brown. |
| 4 | Mon 10 May | Brown resigns as Labour leader, but remains as acting Prime Minister. Labour and Liberal Democrat negotiating teams meet. Conservative Party agrees to hold a referendum on the Alternative Vote system. |
| 5 | Tues 11 May | Brown resigns as Prime Minister in the evening. The Queen appoints David Cameron as Prime Minister. Cameron announces that he intends to create a full coalition with the Liberal Democrats. Liberal Democrat parliamentary party and Federal Executive meet and approve coalition participation by the requisite majority as required by the triple lock procedure. |
| 6 | Wed 12 May | Interim Coalition Agreement published, setting out broad policy direction of Coalition. Clegg is appointed Deputy Prime Minister; four other Liberal Democrats are granted Cabinet seats. Allocation of ministerial office continues. Negotiation on the full Coalition Agreement continues. |
| 10 | Sun 16 May | Liberal Democrats hold special conference to ratify Interim Coalition Agreement as part of triple lock procedure. |
| 12 | Tues 18 May | First meeting of the new Parliament. |
| 14 | Thur 20 May | The Programme for Government is published, outlining substantive coalition policies. |
| 15 | Fri 21 May | Coalition Agreement for Stability and Reform is published, setting out the Coalition's inner organisation. The Ministerial Code is published. |
| 19 | Tue 25 May | The State Opening of Parliament and the Queen's speech take place. |

All three key parties faced choices following Thursday 6 May. The dilemma for the Conservatives was whether to attempt to form a minority government or a coalition.[8] Although the Conservatives had been successful in gaining 95 new seats, they had failed to achieve an overall majority. Even combined with the Democratic Unionist Party they would only have 314 seats in the Commons. Many Tories favoured a minority government, perhaps supported by agreements of confidence and supply, and, following a suitable period of time, a second election to gain an overall majority. But this was high risk: there was no guarantee that the outcome of a second election would be any different from the first – particularly given that all the factors that had led to a hung parliament in the first place were still present. Moreover, the public might blame the Conservatives for an unnecessary second election.

By the morning of Friday 7 May the minority government option was dismissed by Cameron, who argued that the problems at the time were so serious that Britain needed strong government. In contrast, a Conservative-Liberal Democrat coalition offered a de facto majority of 80. Moreover, a coalition with the Lib Dems would be strategically beneficial to Cameron and the 'modernising' wing within his party.[9] In the short term, Cameron's offer of a coalition would deflect criticism from factions within the Conservative Party about their 'poor' performance at the election. In the long term, a coalition would have the benefit of giving Cameron greater leverage with the right wing of his party. Following Nick Clegg's announcement that the Lib Dems would indeed talk first with the party who had won the most seats and votes (that is, the Conservatives), Cameron made his bold, game-changing move on Friday afternoon: his 'big, open and comprehensive offer' to the Liberal Democrats – without specifying the nature of the government to be formed.[10]

For the Liberal Democrats, the election results were a disappointment. The televised leaders' debates had caused a spike in support, but 'Cleggmania' failed to lead to an electoral breakthrough for the party. However, the outcome of the election was such that the Liberal Democrats were still in a pivotal position: should any party wish to form a coalition, the Lib Dems would need to be involved. For Clegg's party, a coalition was always the preferred choice rather than supporting a minority government on issues of confidence and supply.[11] The latter would be 'all pain and no gain': either they would be forced into day-to-day voting on issues over which they had no influence, or they would be blamed for a failing government and an early election. So they welcomed Cameron's bold statement.

Moreover, the Liberal Democrats had a vested interest in showing the public that coalitions could work in practice: they were the party who talked of a different, consensus-based politics; and they were only ever likely to enter government

[8]  R Fox, 'Five Days in May: A New Political Order Emerges' (2010) 63(4) *Parliamentary Affairs* 608.
[9]  See ch 7 for a discussion of this.
[10]  BBC News, 'Election: Cameron makes offer to Lib Dems on government' (7 May 2010), www.news.bbc.co.uk/1/hi/8667938.stm
[11]  Laws, *22 Days in May* (n 4) 17.

as part of a coalition. This may explain why the Liberal Democrats never considered staying outside government altogether.[12] And finally, the Lib Dems could not afford another election campaign. So their dilemma following the election was not whether but with whom they should form a coalition.

For Labour, the dilemma was whether they should enter coalition negotiations at all. While they had not done as badly as some had feared, they had clearly lost the election. Ideologically Labour and the Liberal Democrats were seemingly close, but the continuing presence of Gordon Brown posed a problem to any proposed coalition. However, the arithmetic was poor: Labour and the Liberal Democrats together had 315 seats; a 'rainbow' or 'traffic light' coalition with the Liberal Democrats, the SNP, Plaid Cymru, the SDLP and the sole Green MP would give 328 seats – a very thin majority with which to survive in Parliament, and difficult to work in practice over any length of time. In the end they demonstrated a desire to retain the levers of power and, however ill prepared, sought to begin discussions with the Lib Dems. It was, however, a Labour Party that was itself publicly divided over the benefits of entering into a coalition; and a Labour negotiating team that was ill prepared for negotiations. The Liberal Democrats continued to negotiate with Labour until the last minute to maximise their bargaining power in their negotiations with the Conservatives.

Over the 'five days in May', negotiations took place between the Conservatives and Liberal Democrats; and between the Liberal Democrats and Labour. Ultimately, however, the matter was determined by parliamentary arithmetic and political contingency.[13] Numbers pointed to a Conservative-Liberal Democrat coalition as the most simple majority outcome. But it was more than this: the Liberal Democrats were no longer as personally or ideologically aligned with Labour as many voters and commentators presumed. The Liberal Democrats had 'progressively fallen out of love with the Labour Party'.[14] Many Lib Dems still preferred a coalition with Labour, but they were not averse to doing a deal with the Conservatives either. Over 13 years of New Labour, the Liberal Democrat parliamentary party in particular had moved from being anti-Conservative to a position of political equidistance between the two main parties. This could be seen in their voting record: between 1997 and 2008, Liberal Democrat MPs had gone from voting 80 per cent in favour of Labour to 80 per cent against Labour. Moreover, over the long period in which Labour was in government, the two main opposition parties had begun to converge on a number of policy issues.[15] A younger generation of Liberal Democrats – the so-called Orange Bookers – now had positions of influence, and were to be located on the economically liberal

---

[12]  M Stuart, 'The Formation of the Coalition' in M Beech and S Lee (eds), *The Cameron-Clegg Government: Coalition Politics in an Age of Austerity* (Basingstoke, Palgrave Macmillan, 2011) 52.

[13]  V Bogdanor, *The Coalition and the Constitution* (Oxford, Hart Publishing, 2011) 31; Kavanagh and Cowley, *The British General Election of 2010* (n 7).

[14]  Stuart, 'The Formation of the Coalition' (n 12) 41.

[15]  M Debus, 'Portfolio Allocation and Policy Compromises: How and Why the Conservatives and the Liberal Democrats Formed a Coalition Government' (2011) 82(2) *Political Quarterly* 293.

wing of the party.[16] At the same time, Cameron and his modernisers had pushed the Conservatives towards the centre by adopting voter-friendly policies, such as the green agenda, and by downplaying totemic Tory issues like immigration and Europe.

Finally, there was the immediate concern about the economic state of the UK and of Europe in general. Prior to the general election there was great apprehension about the response of the markets to an 'unstable' hung parliament. This, coupled with the enfolding deficit crisis in Greece and the fear of 'contagion', gave a sense of urgency to the negotiations. The negotiating teams of the Conservatives and Liberal Democrats shared similar views on the need to respond to the UK's fiscal situation with a firm and explicit signal to the markets: a stable majority coalition of two parties rather than a potentially unstable multiparty coalition seemed the best way to do this.

The key problem for the Conservatives and Liberal Democrats was how they might come to an agreement. Cameron had laid out on Friday 7 May where the negotiating lines would lie: setting out common ground like the green agenda, political and education reform, but also the red lines beyond which the Conservatives would not go – more power to the EU, and the weakening of immigration and defence policy. The Conservatives had also offered the Liberal Democrats 20 ministerial posts, five of which would be in Cabinet, and an all-party committee of inquiry on political and electoral reform.[17] More generally, the thorough pre-election preparations by the Conservatives – particularly Oliver Letwin – on policy meant that the two teams were able to begin negotiations quickly.

As negotiations continued over the weekend of 8–9 May, progress between the Conservatives and Liberal Democrats was made on policies, but electoral reform remained an obstacle: this was a deal-breaker for the Liberal Democrats, who had long campaigned for electoral reform. While both parties' negotiating teams saw a coalition as being the optimal outcome, it was still possible at this point for the Liberal Democrats to opt to support a Conservative minority government on confidence and supply if no progress was made on electoral reform. Debate continues over how it came to be understood that the Labour negotiating team had offered the Liberal Democrats a referendum on the Alternative Vote (AV) system without legislation.[18] What was important was that the Conservatives, unnerved by the possibility of a Labour-Liberal Democrat arrangement, agreed with the Liberal Democrats to a referendum on adopting AV on Monday 10 May.

By midday on Tuesday 11 May, events were clearly moving away from the prospect of a Labour-led coalition, and towards the prospect of the Liberal Democrats and the Conservatives coming to an agreement. Gordon Brown, sensing that the moment had slipped away from him, went to the Palace that night. It had been five days since the general election. The Conservatives and Liberal

---

[16] For more on this see ch 7.

[17] Fox, 'Five Days in May' (n 8) 607–22.

[18] See for instance Wilson, *5 Days to Power* (n 6) 152–5; and Kavanagh and Cowley, *The British General Election of 2010* (n 7).

Democrats had not yet finalised a formal deal, and Cameron himself later stated to the Queen that he was not yet certain of the kind of government he would form.[19] That same evening, Nick Clegg received the requisite 75 per cent consent from both the Liberal Democrat parliamentary party and Federal Executive, meeting the first part of the 'triple lock' procedure required in circumstances where there was a substantial proposal to affect the party's independence.[20] On Wednesday 12 May the Conservatives and Liberal Democrats announced the formation of the Coalition and published the Interim Coalition Agreement.

The Conservative-Liberal Democrat Coalition came as a surprise to many, but its birth was consistent with the academic literature on coalition formation. This literature sees parties as primarily office seeking: parties want government office, and with as few partners as possible to reduce the potential for conflict. This suggests that where there is a hung parliament, a 'minimum winning coalition' – a coalition with the smallest number of parties necessary to form a majority in the legislature – would be the most obvious solution. In European Union countries at the end of 2009, 12 per cent of governments were single-party majorities, 42 per cent minimum-winning coalitions, 31 per cent minority governments and 15 per cent oversized coalitions.[21] But the Conservative-Liberal Democrat Coalition was not just a minimum winning coalition; it was a minimum *connected* winning coalition.[22] Parties are also policy seekers: they want to implement policy. So parties do not simply form coalitions on the basis of numbers alone: they will want to form a coalition with partners who share policy affinities to minimise conflicts while in government.[23] And as already noted, the Conservatives and Liberal Democrats had a surprising number of policies and values in common.

However, one Liberal Democrat minister expressed it differently, suggesting why a coalition with the Conservatives made more sense than one with Labour:

> If it had been a coalition with the Labour Party, I think we might have had more difficulty differentiating ourselves, in a funny sort of way. . . . We might have had difficulty distinguishing ourselves from a Labour Party who we'd worked with for five years on a joint progressive agenda. . . . that won't be a problem with the Tories.

[19] BBC News, 'Cameron "unsure of government's form" as he met Queen' (29 July 2010), www.bbc. co.uk/news/uk-politics-10794180

[20] The 'triple lock' procedure was initially developed in lieu of the possibility of a Labour-Lib Dem coalition at the Liberal Democrat 1998 Spring Conference. Where there was any substantial proposal affecting the party's 'independence of political action', consent from three-quarters of the Federal Executive and the parliamentary party in the Commons was required; failing this, a two-thirds majority at a Special Conference; and failing this, a simple majority of all Liberal Democrat members voting in a postal ballot.

[21] Bale also explains the incidence of oversized coalitions and minority governments. Oversized coalitions are often formed in states with deep ethnic and linguistic divisions: parties which are technically 'surplus' to achieving a majority are brought in for representational purposes. Minority governments are more often formed in countries with a history of minority government (such as Sweden), and/or where the pivotal party – one which all feasible coalitions would need to include – can rely on the fact that the other parties will not cooperate to defeat it. See T Bale, 'I Don't Agree with Nick: Retrodicting the Conservative-Liberal Democrat Coalition' (2011) 82(2) *Political Quarterly* 245.

[22] ibid; Debus, 'Portfolio Allocation and Policy Compromises' (n 15).

[23] Bale, 'I Don't Agree with Nick' (n 21) 245.

This argues against the idea of a 'minimum connected winning coalition': policy difference rather than affinity could be a factor in forming a coalition. But all this was said in retrospect – over a year after the Coalition's formation with its stability fairly well established, and by a Lib Dem minister confident enough to be thinking about a general election still four years away.

## THE 'BIBLE': THE COALITION AGREEMENTS

The formation of a coalition is usually marked by the publication of a coalition agreement. This provides a point of reference so that both sides know on what basis they are entering a power-sharing arrangement. By setting down policies on paper, the coalition agreement becomes a means by which the parties relinquish their veto over policies to which the coalition commits itself.[24] It is also a means by which the public and parties can have a clear idea of the objectives to which they can hold the Government to account.[25]

There were in fact three key coalition agreements, each with their own distinctive function. An interim coalition agreement (Interim Agreement) outlining the key policies agreed by the Coalition was published on 12 May.[26] This was followed by the Programme for Government (PfG) on 20 May, which dealt in more detail with the policy objectives of the Coalition.[27] Finally, the Coalition Agreement for Stability and Reform (the Procedural Agreement), published on 21 May, set out the principles and procedures on which the Coalition would operate.

In Appendix one, we provide a more comprehensive analysis of the Interim Agreement and PfG, but here we set out some key features.

### The Interim Coalition Agreement

The Interim Agreement was a 3,000-word document, setting out key issues that needed to be resolved in seven sections: deficit reduction and the Spending Review; tax measures; banking reform; immigration; political reform; pensions and welfare; education; relationship with the EU; civil liberties; and the environment. It stated that a much broader document would follow in due course, 'covering the full range of policy and including foreign, defence and domestic policy

---

[24] W Müller and K Strøm, 'Coalition Agreements and Cabinet Governance' in Strøm, Müller and Bergman (eds), *Cabinets and Coalition Bargaining* (n 1) 163.

[25] A Paun, 'United We Stand? Governance Challenges for the United Kingdom Coalition' (2011) 82(2) *Political Quarterly* 252.

[26] Curiously, the Interim Agreement is not to be found on the Cabinet Office website. It can be found here: BBC News, 'Full text: Conservative-Lib Dem deal' (12 May 2010), www.news.bbc.co.uk/1/hi/8677933.stm

[27] The PfG and the Coalition Agreement for Stability and Reform can be found on the Cabinet Office website: 'The Coalition: Our Programme for Government' (19 May 2010), www.cabinetoffice.gov.uk/news/coalition-documents

issues'. In addition to being agreed to by Liberal Democrat parliamentarians and the Federal Executive on the night of Tuesday 11 May, it was also ratified at a special party conference of the Liberal Democrats on the following Sunday, 16 May.

The Interim Agreement could be read in a number of ways. It could have been seen as a document signalling party gains, but the coalition partners at the time emphasised the high level of agreement between the parties, and a Constitution Unit analysis confirms this. Analysing the pledges by origin (ie, tracing pledges in the Interim Agreement back to one or other of the parties' manifestos or policy documents), 70 per cent of the Interim Agreement was Conservative (totalling up manifesto and non-manifesto pledges, plus those pledges classified as coming from both parties) and roughly 60 per cent was from the Lib Dems. These proportions were to change with the publication of the PfG.

## The Programme for Government

The PfG followed 10 days later. It was a 36-page document of almost 16,000 words – of average length by international standards. Coalition agreements in Western Europe have ranged from 200 words (Finland) to 43,000 words (Belgium) or more, with Scandinavian countries averaging over 10,000 words; their content is on average 90 per cent policy.[28] As with the collective set of agreements for the Coalition, the majority of coalition agreements in Western Europe are made public.

Drafting of the PfG was determined by a much smaller group of people than the government formation process. It was negotiated in detail by Lib Dem Danny Alexander and Conservative Oliver Letwin, who were best qualified to undertake the task, having been in charge of compiling their respective parties' election manifestos. They were supported by Polly Mackenzie (Liberal Democrat) and James O'Shaughnessy (Conservative), key party political staff members who later became special advisers (spads) in No 10; and by a small team of civil servants in the Cabinet Office who helped with drafting and policy advice. The policy experts in Whitehall departments were not involved, and departments were only shown 'their' chapters at the end of the process; in many cases they were given only 12 hours to comment.

Conservative Campaign Headquarters had constructed a very detailed analysis before the election of every item in both parties' manifestos. They had also drawn up draft business plans for each department, which also informed the PfG. Individual chapters of the PfG had been shown to the relevant Secretary of State, but they were not shown the whole document. One difficulty was that the Secretaries of State had by then been appointed, and some were already starting to get on with departmental business, which occasionally made the drafting of the PfG awkward. The final draft of the PfG was then submitted for approval to the PM and DPM.

---

[28] Müller and Strøm, 'Coalition Agreements and Cabinet Governance' (n 24) 172. See also ch 2.

The PfG differed in significant ways from the Interim Agreement. Most obviously, it was far longer. Some of the more controversial pledges in the PfG had not even appeared in the Interim Agreement – most notably, the proposed reforms of the NHS. In the Interim Agreement, there was a single pledge devoted to the NHS; in the PfG this had expanded to 30 pledges.[29] The proportions of pledges identified by party changed between the Interim Agreement and the PfG: in the Interim Agreement, the largest proportion of pledges came from both parties' manifestos; in the PfG, the largest proportion of pledges came from the Conservatives.

To some extent these differences were understandable: the Interim Agreement was, after all, only interim – it was understood as an initial set of understandings on which the two parties could build a relationship and quickly form a coalition. The detail was understood to come later: it was deferred so that the two parties could begin the business of being in government. And if later the balance of Conservative or Lib Dem 'coalition' pledges changed, this was also understandable: the Conservative manifesto was larger and more detailed; the Lib Dems' manifesto smaller and less fleshed out. But it is worth noting that what the Lib Dems had agreed to as part of their triple lock procedure was based on the text of the Interim Agreement, not the PfG.

The PfG consisted of approximately 400 pledges in 31 sections, each devoted to a particular policy area – from banking to defence, government transparency to universities. An initial analysis by the Constitution Unit, looking at how much of the respective parties' manifestos made it into the PfG, suggested that approximately 75 per cent of the Liberal Democrats' manifesto commitments made it into the PfG, compared with 60 per cent of the much larger Conservative manifesto. However, that analysis was subject to issues over coding consistency (see Appendix one). In any case, it is worth noting that, of the pledges that did not make it into the PfG, not all were dropped reluctantly: those which Letwin and Alexander regarded as liabilities would have been more easily traded away. As one Lib Dem peer put it, 'There's a lot of laying off issues which the other partner didn't want to do but which were commitments from the party'.

However, an analysis looking at the contribution of the manifestos to the PfG could be subject to misinterpretation. The Liberal Democrat manifesto on one count contained well over 300 pledges, while the much larger Conservative manifesto consisted of over 550. So even though a higher proportion of the Liberal Democrats' manifesto commitments made it into the PfG, in absolute terms the PfG included more Conservative pledges.

This can be seen in a later Constitution Unit analysis categorising PfG pledges by whether they were Conservative; Liberal Democrat; both; neither; or a compromise between Conservatives and Liberal Democrats. In this analysis, if the total contribution of the Conservatives was taken into account, this made the PfG roughly 75 per cent Conservative (counting those items classified solely as

---

[29] See ch 10 for a more detailed discussion of the NHS reforms.

'Conservative' pledges and those classified as 'both') and 40 per cent Lib Dem (counting items classified as 'Lib Dem' and those classified as 'both').[30]

On an aggregate analysis of the PfG, then, the Conservatives could be said to have done 'better', which might be expected of the larger party with the larger manifesto. However, we should make a caveat here: this presumes that the Conservatives 'won' on the basis of the net number of pledges classed as 'Conservative' in the PfG. That is not necessarily so: the Lib Dems may have been happy to accept Conservative policies that they had been considering themselves, or which also fit with their party's values. Put differently, identifying a pledge by its origin as 'Conservative' or 'Lib Dem' did not necessarily mean that that pledge represented a 'win' only for that party: the inclusion of one party's pledge may have been a 'win' for both parties.

Bearing in mind this caveat, a closer look at the PfG showed that sections tended to be dominated by one or the other of the coalition parties' commitments. Liberal Democrats had 'wins' on their key policies – for instance, the section on civil liberties was primarily Liberal Democrat. The Conservatives had similar – but far more – success in areas of their key party values: defence, foreign affairs, national security; family and children, jobs and welfare. Some sections were genuinely informed by both parties' manifesto commitments: for instance, culture, media and sport, energy and climate change, and government transparency.

There were also some unusual results. On the Constitution Unit's analysis, the Lib Dems led on taxation (with 44 per cent of the PfG's pledges coming from the Lib Dems), while the Conservatives led on political reform (70 per cent of the PfG's pledges came from the Conservatives).

At a more detailed level, both parties achieved significant policy goals. For instance, the Liberal Democrat pledges on House of Lords reform, fixed term parliaments, increasing the personal allowance income tax threshold for low earners, and the pupil premium were all included in the PfG. For the Conservatives, there was the renewal of Trident, free schools, and the ringfencing of the NHS budget.[31]

It was unclear that the public would be able to keep a tally of which pledges in the PfG were Liberal Democrat and which were Conservative, since most lacked a detailed knowledge of the parties' policies generally. It was more likely that they would focus on the flagship commitments that defined each party.[32] For the Liberal Democrats, there were the four key pledges: fair taxes (eg by taking poorer people out of tax); a fair future (eg through green policies); a fair chance for every child (eg through the pupil premium); and a fair deal by cleaning up politics. Some of these would be implemented in the period studied – for instance, raising the income tax threshold and the pupil premium. Arguably, however, the Lib Dems were defined in the first 18 months by their policy failures: tuition fees and the AV referendum.

---

[30] This analysis also took into account pledges which had their origins not in party manifestos but rather in party policy documents. See Appendix one.

[31] Fox, 'Five Days in May' (n 8) 616.

[32] ibid, 617.

The Conservatives, on the other hand, dominated on the economy, which was the raison d'être of the Coalition. It is worth noting that the Liberal Democrats conceded to the Conservative line to cut further and faster on the deficit – agreeing to cut £6 billion in the 2010–11 fiscal year and to eliminate the deficit within one parliamentary term. The Liberal Democrats had campaigned against the Conservative approach prior to the election, but readily agreed to it during the negotiations – perhaps because the negotiating team included senior Lib Dems David Laws and Chris Huhne, both of whom had economic backgrounds and worked in the City of London; and because Vince Cable, Deputy Lib Dem leader and vociferous critic of deep and fast cuts during the campaign, was not part of the negotiating team.[33]

There were also various issues on which the two parties did not agree, and which were reflected in the PfG. Disagreement could be seen in the vague language over the renewal of Trident, or in the three areas where the Liberal Democrats explicitly 'agreed to disagree': student loans, the building of new nuclear stations, and transferable tax allowances for married couples. However, agreeing to disagree did not mean that the Liberal Democrats could vote against such proposals in Parliament: the PfG provided that Liberal Democrat MPs could only abstain. But abstention on the part of all Liberal Democrat MPs would simply reduce the majority necessary for the Conservatives to win a vote in the Commons. More importantly, it was not clear that voters would understand the difference between voting for and abstaining on such policies.

'Disagreement' could also be seen in the 25 policy reviews and five commissions laid out in the PfG. Establishing reviews or commissions did not necessarily indicate irreconcilable conflict: it would have been unrealistic for the negotiators to have resolved these issues in such a short time. For some of these issues, however, it was anticipated that there would be serious differences between the parties, best resolved in an 'external arena' (ie, an arena from which ministers were excluded). This is not uncommon in countries with coalitions.[34] The PfG proposed commissions dealing with various issues on which the parties disagreed – for instance, banking, a bill of rights, and the West Lothian Question.[35]

Contentious issues were sometimes papered over in ambiguous language. As one Liberal Democrat peer noted:

> The difficulty for the Liberal Democrats was that the [Coalition Agreement] used the usual phrases in coalition agreements which . . . have a stretch of some ambiguity to them. For example, with Lords reform where it says we will bring forward proposals, it doesn't say 'we will implement', which is a typical frontend language . . . the first few

[33] BBC News, 'Lib Dems will not back early cuts, says Nick Clegg' (13 March 2010), www.news.bbc.co.uk/1/hi/uk_politics/8565722.stm

[34] R Andeweg and A Timmermans, 'Conflict Management in Coalition Government' in Strøm, Müller and Bergman (eds), *Cabinets and Coalition Bargaining* (n 1) 273.

[35] These commissions were often composed of a mixture of former civil servants and representatives chosen by the two coalition parties: see, for instance, the Independent Commission on Banking, www.bankingcommission.independent.gov.uk; or the Commission on Human Rights, www.justice.gov.uk/about/cbr/index.htm

words of any statement are crucial to whether or not you're intending to execute the changes.[36]

In short, while the Liberal Democrats probably achieved some significant gains, it was not clear how aware the public would be of them. Following formation, at least two flagship policies – the AV referendum and tuition fees – were disastrous for the Liberal Democrats. The PfG was strongly Conservative flavoured, but perhaps that should not be surprising – the Conservatives, after all, were the larger party in the Coalition. And the Liberal Democrats' focus on 'minor' policies blinded them to the far more important issue of how to manage the economy, a matter on which they agreed with – or conceded to – the Conservatives.[37]

### The Coalition Agreement for Stability and Reform

The third coalition document was the three-page, 1,300-word Procedural Agreement, which set out how the two parties were to operate as a coalition (see Appendix four). Although the two parties were keen to stress their initial agreement on policy, the Procedural Agreement implicitly recognised that there would be differences, and provided various mechanisms by which both coalition partners could monitor and manage coalition issues. In short, the PfG dealt with coalition policy; the Procedural Agreement with coalition procedure.

The preamble to the Procedural Agreement stated that the parties would work together 'on the basis of goodwill, mutual trust and agreed procedures which foster collective decision-making and responsibility while respecting each party's identity'. It re-emphasised that legislation to ensure a fixed parliamentary term of five years would be put forward: in effect, a vital source of leverage was to be removed from the larger party – the power to request early dissolution.[38]

The Procedural Agreement provided that the Deputy Prime Minister was entitled to be consulted about all government policies, and on some matters he had an effective veto. He had to agree to all ministerial appointments, including whips and special advisers; he was to nominate Liberal Democrat ministers, and no Liberal Democrat minister or whip could be removed without his full consultation; and his agreement was also required for the establishment of Cabinet Committees, their membership and terms of reference.

In terms of the functioning of the Coalition, both the Prime Minister and Deputy Prime Minister were to 'have a full and contemporaneous overview of the business of government', and each had the power to commission papers from the Cabinet Secretariat. This arrangement only applied to the PM and DPM; it did not apply between a Secretary of State and a junior minister. Implicitly, that

---

[36] The exact language is: 'We will establish a committee to bring forward proposals for a wholly or mainly elected upper chamber on the basis of proportional representation'. See PfG, 27.

[37] Stuart, 'The Formation of the Coalition' (n 12) 53.

[38] This was later implemented with the Fixed Term Parliaments Act 2011.

meant that no junior minister could have the clout equivalent to a Secretary of State (on this, see chapters four and five).

It was originally envisaged that the cabinet system would also be central to the operation of the Coalition. Two committees were created specifically to manage coalition issues. The first was the Coalition Committee; the second was the Coalition Operation and Strategic Planning Group (COSPG).[39] The Coalition Committee was to be co-chaired by the Prime Minister and the Deputy Prime Minister, with equal representation from both parties: five Liberal Democrat ministers, and five Conservatives. COSPG was technically a working group and not a Cabinet Committee, with just four members: Oliver Letwin and Danny Alexander as co-chairs, and Francis Maude and Lord (Jim) Wallace as the other members.

In theory, then, coalition disputes would be referred upwards from department to Cabinet Committee, and/or then from COSPG to the Coalition Committee. COSPG was an intermediate arena where most coalition matters would be dealt with and cleared; the Coalition Committee was envisioned to be the final arbiter of coalition issues. As shall be seen in chapter four, these two committees were later supplanted by other, more informal mechanisms.

Finally, the Procedural Agreement provided for discipline. Collective cabinet responsibility was to apply unless explicitly set aside – ie where there was an agreement to disagree. The two parties were expected to support government policy and legislation, except where the PfG provided otherwise. Future exceptions had to be agreed by the Coalition Committee and Cabinet. Neither parliamentary party was to support proposals brought before Parliament other than by the Government, unless considered and agreed to by both parties.

## DISTRIBUTION OF PORTFOLIOS AND MINISTERIAL OFFICE

The allocation of ministerial office (or 'portfolio allocation') was determined mostly on Wednesday 12 May.[40] During the earlier negotiations, the Liberal Democrat team deliberately chose not to discuss the allocation of ministerial offices until there was a coalition agreement, so that one did not drive the other. Clegg nominated Liberal Democrat ministers, but the portfolios to which they were allocated were determined between himself and Cameron. The wider group involved in the division of office included Edward Llewellyn, William Hague and George Osborne for the Conservatives; and for the Liberal Democrats, Danny Alexander.

---

[39] COSPG was not in fact mentioned in the Procedural Agreement: its existence was first disclosed in another 'coalition document' listing all coalition ministers and Cabinet Committees. This can be found at www.cabinetoffice.gov.uk/sites/default/files/resources/cabinet-committees-system.pdf

[40] The list of government ministers as of July 2010 can be found at www.cabinetoffice.gov.uk/resource-library/government-ministers-and-responsibilities

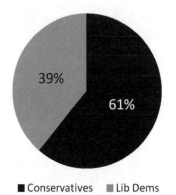

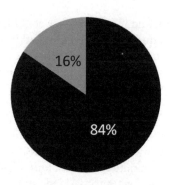

■ Conservatives   ■ Lib Dems

■ Conservatives   ■ Lib Dems

**Figure 3.1 Proportion of Vote Share between Conservatives and Lib Dems after the 2010 General Election**

**Figure 3.2 Proportion of MPs Share between Conservatives and Lib Dems**

Source: Institute for Government, *United We Stand*, 31

Source: IFG, ibid

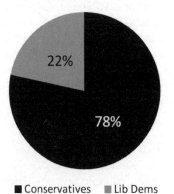

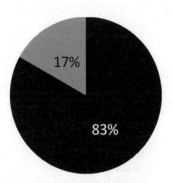

■ Conservatives   ■ Lib Dems

■ Conservatives   ■ Lib Dems

**Figure 3.3 Proportion of Cabinet Ministers Share between Conservative and Lib Dems in the 2010 Coalition Government**

**Figure 3.4 Proportion of Junior Ministers Share between Conservatives and Lib Dems in the 2010 Coalition Government**

Source: IFG, ibid

Source: IFG, ibid

The first step was for Cameron and Clegg to decide upon the division of ministerial posts: this was broadly determined by the number of *seats*, rather than votes, won. The difference was substantial: if by seats, the ratio of Liberal Democrats to Conservatives would have been one to five – or roughly 20 Liberal Democrat ministers to 100 Conservative ministers; but by votes the ratio would have been two to three – or almost 50 ministers to 70-odd Conservatives. The Liberal Democrats ended up with five cabinet ministers and 18 ministers outside Cabinet.[41] This gave

[41]   Whips (paid or unpaid) are counted here as ministers.

them 22 per cent of all frontbench positions, while their share of coalition MPs was 16 per cent.

These proportions accorded with international experience: generally speaking, in coalitions ministerial portfolios are allocated in proportion to seats won in the legislature, but the smaller party will often receive a slightly disproportionate share of ministerial offices.[42] Of course, in most Western European states proportional representation is the norm, and so there is no disparity between votes won and seats won – they are one and the same.

In terms of distribution, senior Liberal Democrats had a brief discussion about whether to go for depth over breadth – that is, packing certain departments with Liberal Democrat ministers as opposed to spreading them throughout government. Depth was quickly dismissed. Almost all Liberal Democrat parliamentarians interviewed, frontbench and backbench alike, rejected the idea of going for depth over breadth. One Lib Dem minister commented,

> I don't think you can be a party which is only interested in a limited number of issues and a restricted number of departments. To be a credible coalition partner . . . you have to be engaged and involved across the whole patch.

Another minister thought that selecting signature departments risked 'ghettoisation':

> There's a danger then that you have ghetto departments in the views of the Conservative backbenches. . . . 'Oh, we can have a pop at them'. We see this to a certain extent with [the Deputy Prime Minister's] department.

Almost all Conservative interviewees thought that the Lib Dems' decision to go for coverage across government was correct, and expressed distaste for the alternative (depth). There needed to be 'joint ownership' of government decisions – although a cynic might say they needed a fall guy. A single Conservative interviewee thought differently:

> From a governing point of view, [breadth] may be right. But from a political strategy point of view, I think if they said, 'Okay. We're going to have some slightly Lib-Demy stuff: we're going to have International Development, we're going to have Energy and Environment Change, and we're going to have Education or Health. Then we'll go back to the British people and say, 'Look at the things we did. Give us more'. I think that's an easier way to carve out a distinctive legacy . . . than it is to say, 'Oh, well. The Pupil Premium was us, and we stopped them doing this and we got them to do more of that'.

That is often the logic informing the action of parties going into coalition as the smaller partner (see chapter two). But the negotiating team – now just Clegg and Alexander – wanted to 'coalitionise' as many departments as possible. Thus, three front-line departments were headed by Liberal Democrat Secretaries of State and ten line departments had Liberal Democrat junior ministers. The Department

---

[42] L Verzichelli, 'Portfolio Allocation' in Strøm, Müller and Bergman (eds), *Cabinets and Coalition Bargaining* (n 1) 238.

for Business, Innovation and Skills (BIS), curiously, had two Liberal Democrat ministers – Vince Cable and Ed Davey.

For the Liberal Democrats, portfolio allocation and the question of who would take ministerial office was determined by a mixture of personality, policy, experience and the insistence on broad involvement across government. So it was perhaps obvious that the negotiating team and Vince Cable would be cabinet ministers.[43] And while the 'depth over breadth' argument was quickly dismissed, Clegg and Alexander did attempt to secure departments whose policies the party wished to be identified with.[44]

To some extent, the choices were obvious. Indeed, during his discussions with Nick Clegg, Gordon Brown offered almost exactly the same cabinet positions that the senior Lib Dems ended up taking.[45] Clegg was made Deputy Prime Minister, but chose not to take a line department, wanting a greater reach across departments. Instead, he took control of political and constitutional reform – a key policy area identified with the Liberal Democrats – and was situated in the Cabinet Office. Vince Cable with his high economic profile was given BIS, as George Osborne was made Chancellor. Chris Huhne, with his background in environmental and economic issues, took the office of Energy Secretary: environmental issues had become a policy priority identified with the Liberal Democrats.[46] Danny Alexander took the Scotland Office (SO), being the only high ranking member of government who was a Scot. The light workload of the SO would free Alexander to deal with coalition issues. He would in effect be the Liberal Democrat 'coalition minister', and he was given a second office in the Cabinet Office where he was expected to support Nick Clegg in his cross-departmental role.

The Liberal Democrats also had to choose between taking the office of Transport Secretary or a 'lesser' cabinet role, the Chief Secretary to the Treasury. It was thought absolutely necessary to have at least one Liberal Democrat in the Treasury, given the pressing need to deal with the economic crisis and because of the role of the Treasury in government generally.[47] David Laws, with his economics background and experience in the City, took this post.[48] Thus, three of the five cabinet-level posts chosen by the Liberal Democrats gave broad coverage across government (the Cabinet Office, Treasury, and the Scotland Office).

---

[43]   Andrew Stunell, one of the Liberal Democrat negotiators, was made 'only' a Parliamentary Under-Secretary of State in the Department of Communities and Local Government, with responsibilities for community cohesion, race equality, building regulations and the implementation of the Big Society.

[44]   Laws, *22 Days in May* (n 4) 207.

[45]   A Seldon and G Lodge, *Brown at Ten* (London, Biteback Publishing, 2010) 450–1. Chris Huhne was to be offered the office of Environment or Local Government Secretary; and although Nick Clegg was offered a 'constitutional position', it was not clear whether he was also to be Deputy Prime Minister in a Labour-Liberal Democrat coalition.

[46]   Laws, *22 Days in May* (n 4) 203.

[47]   ibid, 205.

[48]   But only briefly. Laws resigned as Chief Secretary on 29 May 2011 after it was reported that he had claimed expenses for second house costs contrary to parliamentary regulations which prohibit MPs from renting and claiming accommodation costs from a partner.

The same factors were present in the allocation of junior ministerial posts, but perhaps the overriding factor here was the potential for policy conflict. The number of ministerial posts allocated to the Liberal Democrats meant that some departments – ultimately, the Department for Environment, Food and Rural Affairs (Defra), the Department for Culture, Media and Sport (DCMS), the Department for International Development (DfID), the Northern Ireland Office and the Wales Office – could have no Liberal Democrat representation at all. One senior Liberal Democrat interviewee involved in portfolio allocation stated: 'The selection of departments with no ministers was broadly on the basis [that] these were areas where [the two parties'] policies were more aligned.' Thus, DfID, where both political parties shared similar policies, was thought not to need Liberal Democrat ministerial representation. DCMS was a similar case: the pledges in the PfG section on culture, media and sport were evenly divided between Conservatives and Liberal Democrats (see Appendix one). The converse of this was that departments in which the Liberal Democrats saw the potential for conflict between the parties did require Liberal Democrat representation.[49] Thus, departments such as the Foreign and Commonwealth Office, Home Office, and the Ministry of Justice, where controversies would arise naturally as a result of their subject matter, all had Liberal Democrat ministers.

For the Conservatives, the allocation of office remained primarily about balancing considerations of competence, ensuring cohesion and balancing interests within the party. The Coalition need to ensure adequate representation, and monitoring government business was not a pressing issue for the Conservatives: the large number of ministerial posts available would ensure cross-departmental coverage. Most line departments were headed by a Conservative Secretary of State, and in particular those closely connected with key Tory concerns: the Treasury, Home Office, the Ministry of Justice, the Foreign Office and the Ministry of Defence – the one exception being BIS. The Conservatives also had key ministers exercising a cross-government remit: the Prime Minister, the Chancellor, and Oliver Letwin in the Cabinet Office.

The key complication for the Conservatives arising from being in a coalition government was that there was a smaller set of ministerial offices available to be used as patronage. Numerous interviewees talked about the anger of those Conservative parliamentarians who had expected to take ministerial office upon entering government, but were unable to because these went to Liberal Democrats instead.

## The Lords

The Coalition was a Commons-based government, which would have implications for business management in the Lords. Little thought was given by Cameron,

---

[49] This is consistent with the literature on coalitions, which sees junior ministers placed in departments where there are potential policy conflicts between the parties in government. See Verzichelli, 'Portfolio Allocation' (n 42) 259–60.

Clegg or their advisers to the appointment of peers as ministers. Under the Brown Government there had been an unusually high number of ministers in the Lords, including two Secretaries of State. But under the Coalition, the number of ministers (and whips) in the Lords shrank to the bare minimum. This was pragmatic politics on the part of both the Conservatives and the Liberal Democrats: priority for ministerial office had to be given to MPs, not peers. But the result was that 'only' 24 peers were given government posts.

This had a disproportionate impact on the Liberal Democrats in the Lords. Of 14 peer ministers, only two were Liberal Democrats (Lords McNally and Wallace of Tankerness) – or one in seven. This left Liberal Democrat party whips to pick up the slack: in the Lords, whips will often deputise for ministers. Of 10 Lords whips, four were Liberal Democrat – but only one was paid.[50] Of course, it would have been hypocritical of the Liberal Democrats to appoint more ministers from the House of Lords when the party advocated its eventual abolition. But the result was that the Liberal Democrats denied themselves an important pool of ministerial talent, and remained overstretched in the upper house.

### Special Advisers

One other early decision reached by Cameron and Clegg was to have a deep impact on how the Coalition worked in the first 18 months. Both leaders agreed to limit the number of special advisers, having criticised Blair and Brown for their growing numbers under New Labour. As a rule, only cabinet ministers and those regularly attending Cabinet could appoint spads. Initially there were 68 special advisers in the Coalition, and their distribution disproportionately favoured the Liberal Democrats. One in four was a Liberal Democrat, and of them half were responsible to Nick Clegg.[51]

However, the initial limit on spads to ministers attending Cabinet meant that Liberal Democrat junior ministers were given no political support, despite expectations by the party that they act as the Liberal Democrat voice in a department. This weakened the ability of frontbench Liberal Democrats to exercise influence across government, and to reconnect with the backbench. As we shall see in chapter five, the lack of ministerial support was a common complaint amongst Liberal Democrats. This weakness was finally redressed in October 2011, with six additional special advisers being appointed to assist Liberal Democrat junior ministers.[52] The number of special advisers had reached almost 80 – more than under Brown, and closing in on the later Blair years.

[50] Lord Shutt, Chief Whip of the Liberal Democrat peers; Deputy Chief Whip for the Government in the Lords.

[51] By June 2010 there were 16 Lib Dems spads out of a total of 68; eight reported to Nick Clegg.

[52] Written Ministerial Statement on Numbers and Costs of Special Advisers (9 December 2011), www.cabinetoffice.gov.uk/sites/default/files/resources/LIST_AND_COSTS_9_DECEMBER_0.pdf. The statement records 21 Lib Dem spads, but lists only four of the additional six Lib Dem spads agreed in late 2011.

## THE NEGOTIATION PROCESS: AN EVALUATION

By international standards, the Conservative-Liberal Democrat Coalition was formed in an extraordinarily short time.[53] As was noted in chapter two, it is usual for prospective coalition partners to take at least two to three weeks to negotiate the terms of a coalition. By British standards, however, five days was unusually long, with most governments being formed the day the election results are announced.

There was a difference of opinion amongst Liberal Democrat interviewees regarding the impact of the speed with which the Coalition was formed. The overwhelming majority of Lib Dem backbenchers interviewed thought that the negotiations had been rushed, resulting in problems emerging further down the line, particularly in terms of support for the Party, both in and outside Parliament (see chapter six). One Lib Dem minister complained:

> If we're going to be in coalition for five years, then you do want to spend a bit of time and avoid having tired people make a decision over four days . . . what I would do differently is to at least have a fortnight doing these things and getting things like support and . . . protocols. . . . and not having to backfill the whole time. And we're still backfilling.

Another Liberal Democrat minister expressed disappointment at the negotiating team's performance in the latter stages:

> I think at the end of that [the negotiating team] had completely exhausted themselves. Precious little thought really went into the machinery of the Coalition which was part two of it. And by part three of it, which was bums on seats, Nick did this completely on his own with Cameron . . . I think we got a completely duff deal.

But one senior Liberal Democrat involved in the negotiations was unrepentant:

> [In] the British system there is a premium on getting government sorted relatively quickly. . . . the key issues about that are not the time you take . . . it is the goodwill on all sides and the ability to find the areas of agreement . . . that can be done as easily in an intensive process as it can in a dragged out one. The problem with a dragged out process is that the centrifugal forces get stronger because the longer the process goes on the more you will find pressures within parties, you will find every word pored over. . . . Forming a coalition is an exercise of political leadership basically, and the longer you take over it, the more process you build around it, the more the ability of leadership to exercise itself is dissipated.

On the Conservative side, very few interviewees expressed unhappiness about the speed of government formation – they were much more concerned about whether or not the Coalition had been formed on the basis of misinformation about an AV referendum. Some Conservative peers were upset, however. One described how

---

[53] See Political and Constitutional Reform Committee, 'Lessons from the Process of Government Formation after the 2010 General Election' HC (2010–11), as well as Figure 2.1, Average Government Formation Times, in ch 2.

Conservative peers here were extremely peeved that they were not consulted in any way whatsoever, unlike Liberal peers. . . . eventually somebody invited us to a meeting which was going to take place at 10 o'clock at night . . . bearing in mind Parliament wasn't sitting at that particular time, and most of us don't live in the centre of London – it was really sort of inviting us to a non-meeting. . . . It's like being stuck at the airport, isn't it? You know you can't do anything about the snow, but what people can do is tell you what's going on.

There was a sense from some of the Conservatives and the small number of Labour parliamentarians interviewed that the formation process had exposed their internal party mechanisms, which had been found wanting. For instance, the Labour parliamentary party never met; and the Conservative parliamentary party was never given copies of the Interim Agreement prior to formation.[54] After the first 18 months, however, neither of the two larger parties had sought to amend their party procedures in preparation for another hung parliament.

## CONCLUSION

The hung parliament following the 2010 general election was widely predicted. But what came as a surprise to many was the formation of a Conservative-Liberal Democrat coalition, determined above all by parliamentary arithmetic and political contingency. In terms of numbers, a Labour-Liberal Democrat coalition, or a 'rainbow coalition', would have been too unstable to function – particularly given the perceived need to deal firmly with fiscal issues; a Conservative-Liberal Democrat coalition provided a comfortable majority. The only obstacle to such a coalition was thought to be ideological distance, but 13 years of New Labour had led to a Liberal Democrat position of equidistance, and changes in the Liberal Democrat leadership meant a party more favourably predisposed towards the Conservatives.

The resulting arrangements broadly mirrored the outcome of the 2010 election. The Conservatives dominated on both policy and the division of office, but that reflected their larger numbers and superior bargaining position. The Liberal Democrats, on the other hand, won a number of policies key to their party, but many of these were likely to be overshadowed by the handling of the economy. They did less well on the allocation of ministerial office and resources. While receiving more than their proportionate share of ministers, the Liberal Democrats chose to spread their ministers across government in the hope of having broad influence, but were unable to secure adequate support at the legislative or executive level to ensure that they could achieve that goal.

---

[54] Kavanagh and Cowley, *The British General Election of 2010* (n 7) 221.

# 4

# *How the Coalition Works at the Centre*

ROBERT HAZELL

Inevitably coalition has placed a greater reliance on using the Cabinet Committees and machinery. (Cabinet Office official)

A S WE SAW in chapter one, coalition government has the reputation in Britain of being unstable, quarrelsome, slow and indecisive. One would expect the epicentre of quarrels, delays and indecisiveness to be at 'the Centre' of government – that is, No 10, the Deputy Prime Minister's Office and the Cabinet Office – where disputes between coalition partners and between Whitehall departments get referred for resolution. So we made a special study of these arenas. We wanted to explore what changes the new Government had introduced to facilitate the operation of the Coalition, and how effective those changes were deemed to be. In particular, we wanted to understand the machinery for coordination at the Centre, and for dispute resolution. What is the balance between formal and informal machinery; between No 10 and the Cabinet Office; and between the Centre and departments? How do the coalition partners ensure unity in government, and the maintenance of collective cabinet responsibility? How do they project the parties' distinct identities, especially for the junior partner? And finally, what is the impact of coalition on the role of the civil service: does it make the civil service weaker or stronger?

Underlying our answers is the same set of questions running through the book about how we should evaluate the performance of the Coalition. What are the measures of success? That will depend on the observer and their point of view. For officials, success may be measured by the extent to which the coalition partners use the proper channels; and by the absence of leaks and negative briefing, projecting a unified and effective government. For the media, that is going to be boring: politics is about splits, and who is up and who is down. And for the parties, unified and effective government is only one measure of success. Getting re-elected is the other: for that, they will need to project their distinct identity and contribution.

This chapter describes how the Coalition worked in 10 Downing Street and the Cabinet Office, but does not cover the Treasury. So far as we know, the Treasury operated effectively in coalition terms, thanks to Danny Alexander's combined roles as the Liberal Democrats' chief negotiator and as Chief Secretary responsible for expenditure cuts. The Treasury was unusual in Whitehall in being a department where issues could be 'coalitionised' within the department. Unlike junior Lib Dem ministers in other departments, Danny Alexander had the seniority to negotiate with the Chancellor on sufficiently equal terms, both within the Treasury and in the Quad (the 'inner Cabinet' for spending decisions, discussed further below).

The chapter is based upon 25 interviews in No 10 and the Cabinet Office, conducted in the spring and summer of 2011. The Cabinet Secretariat supports the Cabinet as a whole, but the Prime Minister sets the agenda and broad priorities of the government. He decides the establishment, membership and terms of reference of Cabinet Committees. They provide the central decision-making machinery of the government, coordinating departments' competing objectives and priorities. Under the Coalition the classic roles of No 10 and the Cabinet Office, to provide leadership and coordination at the Centre, have not changed; but the ways in which they operate have changed considerably.

## A RETURN TO CABINET GOVERNMENT

The Coalition Government moved into a Downing Street which had lapsed into a sorry state. Historically No 10 has been the epitome of the highest traditions of Whitehall, attracting top-flight civil servants who work closely together alongside the Prime Minister's political staff. The house itself creates a unique working atmosphere, and the long hours and intense tempo forge a fierce loyalty and powerful esprit de corps.

Some of that ethos continued under New Labour, but with a fatal flaw. A chasm opened between No 10 and No 11, with the bitter rivalries and infighting of the Blair/Brown years. Blair favoured informal discussions with his ministers, 'sofa government' over cabinet government, which reached a very low ebb in Blair's first two terms. And Brown when Chancellor systematically denied information to Blair and his colleagues, running the Treasury as a secretive and tightly controlling operation. When Brown became Prime Minister his working habits transferred next door. No 10 became a bunker, issuing commands interspersed with long periods of silence. Collegiality was non-existent. Cabinet government revived a little under Brown; but for much of the period 1997–2010 Cabinet and its committees remained hollow shells.[1]

The civil service must have been anxious that coalition government would open up similar fault lines, this time between the coalition partners. But the

[1] T Blair, *A Journey* (London, Hutchinson, 2010); A Rawnsley, *Servants of the People: The Inside Story of New Labour* (London, Hamish Hamilton, 2001); A Rawnsley, *The End of the Party* (London, Viking, 2010); P Mandelson, *The Third Man: Life at the Heart of New Labour* (London, HarperPress, 2010); A Seldon and G Lodge, *Brown at 10* (London, Biteback Publishing, 2010).

Coalition spawned a determination to revive cabinet government, and to use Cabinet and its Committees as the prime machinery for negotiation between the coalition partners, and for resolving coalition disputes. As we shall see, cabinet government was indeed revived; but negotiation between the coalition partners took place in a series of more informal groupings, with the deals negotiated then being brought to Cabinet Committees for formal ratification.

It was originally envisaged that Cabinet and its committees would be the main forum for negotiation between the coalition partners because they were strangers to each other. But working together in government they quickly developed a rapport, and at the Centre high levels of trust. This was partly good luck: David Cameron and Nick Clegg came from similar backgrounds, found that they got on well together, and set the tone for those around them. But the relationship also had to be worked for: the constant pressures of government provide plenty of scope for slights and misunderstandings. However, in the interviews we conducted it was hard not to be impressed by the emotional intelligence of the key participants, and the consideration they showed for each other. This was in sharp contrast not just with the Blair/Brown years, but also with the last Conservative government under John Major, where the Prime Minister had to endure a disloyal and leaking cabinet.[2]

Trust and the importance of good personal relations were stressed by many of our interviewees. Those around Cameron and Clegg worked very hard to maintain good relations, at every level, and displayed a lot of sensitivity in doing so. One No 10 special adviser (spad) commented:

> Particularly at the Centre, the relationships are so important. Not doing anything that surprises the coalition partner. We don't always get this right: there are occasions when we do slip up. But going the extra mile, making sure you inform each other about things, make a big effort to sort problems out before they become festering sores: all of that is incredibly important.

THE FORMAL MACHINERY (1): THE COALITION PROCEDURAL AGREEMENT

The Interim Coalition Agreement of 11 May and the more detailed Programme for Government (PfG) of 20 May were silent on the processes by which the coalition parties would reach agreement with each other. These were set out in a third document, the Coalition Agreement for Stability and Reform (the Procedural Agreement), published on 21 May 2011 and reproduced in Appendix four.

The procedural agreement was just three pages long, and is analysed in chapter two. It emphasised the need for mutual trust and close consultation to underpin all the coalition partners' working arrangements.

At the Centre this meant the Deputy Prime Minister being consulted about everything. Both the Prime Minister and Deputy Prime Minister were to have 'a

---

[2] P Routledge, 'Major hits out at Cabinet' *Observer* (25 July 1993); J Major, *John Major: The Autobiography* (London, HarperCollins, 2010).

full and contemporaneous overview of the business of government', and the power to commission papers from the Cabinet Secretariat. When the Prime Minister was consulted on the Budget, the Deputy Prime Minister was also to be consulted. The Prime Minister also had to consult the Deputy Prime Minister on all public appointments.[3]

## THE FORMAL MACHINERY (2): LITTLE USE OF COALITION COMMITTEES

The Procedural Agreement stipulated that the Deputy Prime Minister had also to agree the establishment of Cabinet Committees, their membership and terms of reference. It was originally envisaged that the cabinet system would be central to the operation of the Coalition. Two committees were created specifically to manage coalition issues. The first was the Coalition Committee; the second was the Coalition Operation and Strategic Planning Group (COSPG).

Table 4.1 List of Cabinet Committees and their Size in May 2010

| Committee/sub-committee | Con | LD | Chair |
|---|---|---|---|
| Coalition Committee | 5 | 5 | Con |
| National Security Council | 8 | 3 | Con |
| NSC: Threats, Hazards, Resilience, Contingencies | 15 | 3 | Con |
| NSC: Nuclear Deterrence & Security | 5 | 2 | Con |
| European Affairs Committee | 10 | 4 | Con |
| Social Justice Committee | 7 | 3 | Con |
| Home Affairs Committee | 16 | 4 | LD |
| Public Health Sub-committee | 14 | 5 | Con |
| Olympics Sub-committee | 7 | 1 | Con |
| Economic Affairs Committee | 9 | 3 | Con |
| Reducing Regulation Sub-committee | 7 | 2 | LD |
| Banking Reform Committee | 4 | 2 | Con |
| Parliamentary Business & Legislation Committee | 6 | 7 | Con |
| Public Expenditure Committee | 4 | 1 | Con |
| *Note: by November 2011 the following Sub-committees had been added:* | | | |
| *NSC: Emerging Powers* | *8* | *3* | *Con* |
| *NSC: Libya** | *Unknown (7 attend)* | | |
| *Social Justice: Child Poverty*** | *5* | *2* | *LD* |

Sources: Cabinet Office, *Cabinet Committee System* (23 September 2010), www. cabinetoffice.gov.uk/sites/default/files/resources/cabinet-committees-system.pdf; Intelligence and Security Committee, *Annual Report 2010–2011* (11 July 2011) 36, isc. independent.gov.uk/files/2010-2011_ISC_AR.pdf

\*   www.isc.independent.gov.uk/files/2010-2011_ISC_AR.pdf?attredirects=0, 36.

\*\*   http://webarchive.nationalarchives.gov.uk/+/http://www.cabinetoffice.gov.uk/ media/425203/cabinet-committees-system.pdf

[3] Coalition Agreement for Stability and Reform, 21 May 2010, sections 1–3, 5–6, reproduced in Appendix four.

The Coalition Committee was listed first in the published list of Cabinet Committees. It was co-chaired by the PM and the DPM, with equal representation from both parties: five Liberal Democrat ministers, and five Conservative ministers. In terms of the formal machinery of the Coalition, it was the topmost body. Other Cabinet Committees all have a chair from one party and a deputy chair from the other, and unresolved issues may be referred up to the Coalition Committee by the chair or deputy chair of any other Cabinet Committee.[4] In practice this right was not exercised in the Coalition's first 18 months.

The Cabinet Office had expected the Coalition Committee to meet frequently: its terms of reference said weekly. But in 2010 and 2011 the Coalition Committee met only twice, in summer 2010, in the first three months of the new government. It met to test the machinery and establish ground rules for coalition management, rather than to resolve any dispute. It also had an early discussion about the planned reforms to the health service, because the decision to drop directly elected health boards represented a departure from the PfG (see chapter ten).

In its first 18 months, the Coalition experienced no formal disputes. The most common disputes in Whitehall were interdepartmental, and they were generally between ministers of the same party. If they pitted ministers from different parties against each other, they would also raise a coalition issue. 'Coalition issue' is used in this chapter to mean a dispute or difference between the coalition partners. This may arise within one department, between departments, or at the Centre between the PM and DPM. Coalition issues were resolved in informal meetings, not in Cabinet or its committees. The issue might subsequently have come before a Cabinet Committee for signing off, but resolution of coalition differences was negotiated earlier and informally. As our interviewees explained, 'The Coalition Committee was designed as the ultimate arbiter. It quickly became clear that anything elevated to that level would be pretty bad news'. 'It is important that it exists, but better that it never meets: like a hotline' (senior adviser, No 10).

If the Coalition Committee was intended to be the quarterdeck of the Coalition, the Coalition Operation and Strategic Planning Group was to be the engine room. Technically it was a working group and not a Cabinet Committee, with just four members: Oliver Letwin and Danny Alexander as co-chairs, and Francis Maude and Lord (Jim) Wallace as the other members. Its terms of reference envisaged that it would meet at least weekly. In fact it did not meet at all. Instead Oliver Letwin and Danny Alexander met very frequently. Their informal bilateral meetings (discussed below) have supplanted the need for formal meetings of COSPG.

THE FORMAL MACHINERY (3): REVIVAL OF CABINET GOVERNMENT

Although the cabinet system was not used much for explicit coalition management, everyone agreed that Cabinet and its committees had been greatly revived under the

---

[4] ibid, para 3.5.

new government. As one cabinet official said, 'Inevitably coalition has placed a greater reliance on using the Cabinet Committees and machinery'. Cabinet Committees which had never met under the last government began to do so. They were used as a forum for strategic and general policy discussions, as well as for resolving the frequent differences that arose between Whitehall departments when addressing difficult policy problems. Most of the differences resolved in Cabinet Committees were inter-departmental issues, not differences between the coalition parties.

Cabinet Committees were particularly important for those departments with no Lib Dem minister, such as Defra. As described in chapter five, Defra did not think a policy had been properly approved until it had been signed off by a committee in which the Lib Dem view could potentially be expressed. So the committees served a coalition purpose, even though the disputes they resolved were mainly interdepartmental, not coalition disputes. This also underlines the importance of the Centre in relation to departments. It was at the Centre that disputes got resolved, and not in departments.

**Figure 4.1  Two Cabinet Committees**

The European Affairs Committee and the Home Affairs Committee illustrate how Cabinet government works under the Coalition. Under the Brown government the European Affairs Committee did not meet; it was used simply as a network to clear EU business by means of inter-ministerial correspondence. Chaired by William Hague, in 2010 and 2011 it met monthly, and Chris Huhne as the Lib Dem deputy chair was closely involved in agreeing the agenda. Hague liked to use the Committee for wider discussions than just forthcoming EU business, such as the EC's annual work programme, its budget, and how to forge stronger alliances with the bigger European powers.

The Home Affairs Committee, chaired by Nick Clegg, also met regularly, every couple of weeks. It gave Clegg an overview of the whole of domestic policy.

> For the Deputy Prime Minister, his role as chair of the Home Affairs Committee is crucially important . . . it's a very hard gateway on policy. Policy announcements cannot happen until he has signed the clearance letter . . . it's quite an important part of the coalition machinery. (Cabinet Office official)

Like Hague, Clegg used the Home Affairs Committee in the early days for big strategic discussions on issues such as immigration, welfare reform, NHS reforms, localism, planning, and housing.

> These issues wouldn't always be bottomed out through a wide ranging discussion in committee; but it's helpful for clearing the ground. Cabinet Committee provides a good forum for setting a framework for the policy then to be developed. (Cabinet Office official)

The more controversial issues were resolved not in Cabinet Committee, but in a series of informal forums described in the next section.

Overall the new Cabinet system was a great deal more collegiate. Some offi-cials said it had slowed things down; but they added that taking time to reach collective agreement was not necessarily a bad thing. Cabinet Office insisted on papers being circulated in good time for Cabinet Committees, and on 10 days to clear anything by correspondence. That is part of the general 'no surprises' rule: there is much less scope under coalition government for bounces, because of the need always to consult the coalition partner. The Liberal Democrats gradually strengthened their responses, looking out not just for issues affecting their own department, but also (for example) for EU issues where they might take a different line from the more eurosceptic Conservatives; in this they were assisted by their European Affairs adviser based in the Whips' Office. All papers for Cabinet Committees had to state what had been done to ensure collective approval: that the policy had been checked against the Coalition Agreement, and cleared with the Treasury and parliamentary business managers. The chair and deputy chair (one from each party) had to sign everything off. So although Cabinet Committees were not the forum in which coalition deals were bro-kered, they were the forum in which those deals were formally signed off. Reinstatement of the 10-day rule was welcomed by the civil service, and it strengthened their role as the guardians of due process.

Two other points about the Cabinet system are worth noting. First is the strain felt by Liberal Democrat Cabinet ministers due to the number of Cabinet Committees they had to attend. Danny Alexander sat on 12 Cabinet Committees, Chris Huhne on nine, and Vince Cable on seven. They served on disproportion-ately more committees than their Conservative counterparts, and the pressure told. Their departmental private secretaries noted how much more of the Secretary of State's time was devoted to Cabinet business. In recognition of the extra demands placed on the smaller party, the second point to note is the inno-vation that entitled ministers to send a substitute from their department or their party. The Liberal Democrats did sometimes exercise this right; for example, Nick Clegg as deputy chair of the National Security Council occasionally nomi-nated his Lib Dem colleagues Nick Harvey (MoD), Jeremy Browne (FCO) and Lord Wallace of Saltaire (Lords whip, FCO) to attend in his stead.

## THE INFORMAL MACHINERY: CIRCLES OF POWER IN NO 10

Although Cabinet Committees were revived, no one claimed that they were the place where coalition deals got done. All governments have their circles of power at the Centre,[5] and the Coalition was no exception. The difference was that the Deputy Prime Minister or his advisers were included in all the key circles of

---

[5] P Hennessy, *The Prime Minister: The Office and its Holders since 1945* (London, Allen Lane, 2001); D Kavanagh and A Seldon, *The Powers Behind the Prime Minister: The Hidden Influence of Number Ten* (London, HarperCollins, 1999); Rawnsley, *Servants of the People* (n 1); Rawnsley, *The End of the Party* (n 1).

power. The Centre is where all the key coalition brokerage took place, before going through the formal machinery. Cabinet Committees remained the place where interdepartmental issues got resolved; and where policies were submitted for final policy clearance through 'write rounds' to cabinet colleagues, and signing off by the chair. Any coalition issues should have been spotted well before that stage. They were resolved in half a dozen different forums, which are illustrated on the right-hand side of the diagram in Figure 4.2.

**Figure 4.2  The Formal and Informal Machinery for Resolving Coalition Issues**

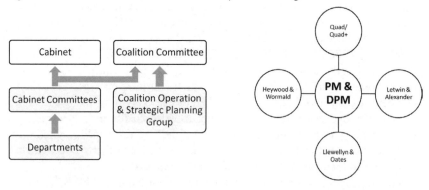

Formal Mechanisms                    Informal Mechanisms

A coalition issue would generally be raised first in one of the informal forums. It might have surfaced in any of the informal groups, and then be referred up to the PM and DPM; or occasionally be raised first by the PM and DPM and referred on to the Quad, or to Letwin and Alexander to resolve. If it was a policy issue which then required collective approval, it would be put through the formal machinery for signing off by the relevant Cabinet Committee. The process was not always neat and sequential; it could be iterative, with the issue being bounced around more than one of the informal forums, or from departments to the Centre and back. But the final stage was always formal sign-off by a Cabinet Committee.

The same names recurred again and again in the informal forums. To introduce the main players, Table 4.2 sets out the key advisers and officials working for Cameron and Clegg in the first year. The top half sets out the special advisers – political staff appointed directly by the PM and DPM, often from amongst the staff who worked for them in opposition. They leave government when their minister does. The bottom part of the table shows the senior officials – permanent civil servants who stay in office from one government to the next. Four of the Liberal Democrat special advisers – Lena Pietsch, Sean Kemp, Polly Mackenzie and Tim Colbourne – were outposted to No 10, where they worked alongside their Conservative colleagues. This was a key part of the integrating mechanism at the Centre, especially in terms of media handling: two of the four Liberal Democrat advisers in No 10 worked in the Press Office.

Table 4.2  The Top Advisers to the Prime Minister and Deputy Prime Minister in 2010–11

|  | Prime Minister's staff | Deputy PM's staff |
|---|---|---|
| **Special Advisers** | | |
| Chief of Staff | Ed Llewellyn | Jonny Oates |
| Deputy Chief of Staff | Kate Fall | Alison Suttie, replaced by Jo Foster in Sep 2011 |
| Head of Political Strategy | Andrew Cooper | Richard Reeves |
| Director of Strategy, Head of Policy | Steve Hilton | Polly Mackenzie (Head of Policy for DPM, based in No 10). Replaced by Julian Astle in Dec 2011 |
| Director of Communications | Andy Coulson, replaced by Craig Oliver in Feb 2011 | Lena Pietsch (in No 10); replaced by Olly Grender in autumn 2011 |
| Deputy Director of Communications | Gabby Bertin | Sean Kemp (in No 10) |
| **Officials** | | |
| Top Official | Jeremy Heywood, Permanent Secretary, No 10 | Chris Wormald (Director General, and until Aug 2011 Head of Economic and Domestic Affairs Secretariat, Cabinet Office) |
| Principal Private Secretary | James Bowler | Calum Miller |
| Official spokesman | Steve Field | James Sorene (from Feb 2011) |

Note: these advisers are presented in a single table to show their opposite numbers. But not all posts have a precise analogue in the other office. No 10 is much larger than the DPM's Office, with a wider range of staff.

## Prime Minister/Deputy Prime Minister Bilaterals

Everyone agreed that these were the summit meetings for the Coalition, where all the big coalition issues got decided. A senior No 10 official noted that 'At those PM-DPM bilaterals, which are regular and frequent, an awful lot gets done'. The meetings generally took place once a week, on Monday mornings; and occasionally twice. Those attending were Ed Llewellyn and Kate Fall (Cameron's chief of staff and deputy), Jonny Oates (Clegg's chief of staff), Jeremy Heywood (Permanent Secretary in No 10) and Chris Wormald (Clegg's senior official). Cabinet colleagues and senior officials could ask for items to go on the agenda to get resolved at this level. Most issues involved the question of how to handle their respective parties; but that would sometimes take them into discussions of substantive policy. For example, issues about the AV (Alternative Vote) referendum, reducing the size of the House of Commons and reform of the House of Lords were resolved at this level (see chapter eight).

Cameron and Clegg often talked by phone on Sunday evenings. They were not just reactive, responding to an agenda set by their officials and advisers. They set the agenda as well:

> The PM and DPM do think ahead, and they go faster than quite a lot of people around them. They are the sort of minds who do range ahead: which is one reason why I think they get on very well. (Senior official, Cabinet Office)

### The Quad: PM/DPM plus the Chancellor and Chief Secretary to the Treasury

The next level down in the informal machinery was the Quad, consisting of David Cameron and Nick Clegg, plus George Osborne and Danny Alexander. It was the main forum for resolving any coalition issues which had spending implications. It first came into being for the comprehensive spending review, in the summer and autumn of 2010.

> The Quad didn't really become properly institutionalised for a few weeks, and I think no one anticipated that it would be such an important forum. It's rather supplanted the role of the Coalition Committee. The Coalition Committee was Oliver [Letwin]'s original thought as to how we might resolve disputes, but we've not really used that particularly. (Senior adviser, No 10)

The Quad came to acquire semi-formal status, meeting on average once a month, but more frequently in the run-up to the budget or autumn statement.

It was sometimes expanded to include other cabinet ministers, so the 'Quad plus' might include Iain Duncan Smith to discuss welfare reform, or Vince Cable to discuss banking. The Quad did not cover all policy areas; it was used primarily for resolving tax and spending issues. As with the other informal mechanisms, it was not formally a decision-making body.

> It is used to get a common position for the Centre, and help bind together the parties for that. And that of course carries weight in Whitehall, but it's not Cabinet clearance in itself. The outcome is generally that there needs to be another process, a committee, Cabinet itself or correspondence that actually makes the final decision. (Cabinet Office official)

### Ministerial Bilaterals or Trilaterals

Certain issues were resolved by the PM with the relevant Secretary of State, or the PM/DPM and the Secretary of State. A senior Cabinet Office official noted: 'The

DPM has frequent meetings with the Home Secretary which are robust conversations'. But in the first year and a half there were no complaints about 'sofa government' of the kind which became commonplace under Blair. This was because the Coalition precluded purely bilateral deals; and any informal deals had subsequently to be ratified through the formal machinery. Sofa government under the Coalition was effectively in the antechamber to the Cabinet room, because those deals were then put to the relevant Cabinet Committee. By contrast, under Blair, sofa government tended to be where the decision was made; it was then decreed by No 10, with no further collective discussion.

## Oliver Letwin/Danny Alexander

The next level consisted of Oliver Letwin, Minister of State in the Cabinet Office, and Danny Alexander, Chief Secretary to the Treasury. Letwin was the Conservatives' director of policy and in charge of writing the Conservative manifesto. Alexander was his opposite number: the man in charge of writing the Liberal Democrat manifesto, and Nick Clegg's chief of staff. Both had been key members of their respective parties' negotiating teams, since they knew the party policy inside out. Alexander was initially appointed as Scottish Secretary, an undemanding job which enabled him to continue as Clegg's right hand man, with an office next to Clegg in the Cabinet Office. But when David Laws was forced to resign as Chief Secretary to the Treasury on 29 May 2010, after only three weeks in government, he was replaced by Danny Alexander.

It seemed like a double blow at the time, not just to lose David Laws, but to remove Alexander from his crucial role as coalition broker. But the evidence from most of our interviews was that Alexander managed to combine both roles. As one No 10 adviser put it:

> Danny Alexander has done everything that was expected of his coalition role . . . Even after Danny became Chief Secretary, that made very little difference: because the majority of issues were budget and spending decisions, which involved Treasury anyway. So it still works in the way originally envisaged.

Alexander certainly held frequent meetings with Oliver Letwin, and the Letwin/Alexander axis was a crucial part of the Coalition's negotiating machinery. Both men commanded a high degree of trust from their respective masters, and they had a high degree of trust in each other. A special adviser to Clegg said:

> Oliver often acts as a broker on all sorts of things. He might act on our side if he agrees with us, but he's an honest broker . . . He likes the Coalition and wants it to work. Oliver works better as a broker, and Danny is our champion.

Danny Alexander and Oliver Letwin spoke on the phone every Sunday night, and both of them put things on the agenda. According to Alexander:

> It will often depend on a Liberal Democrat minister coming to me or a Conservative minister going to Oliver or it being clear from our quarterly updates on the [departmental]

business plans which we do together as well that there is an issue brewing. Or just the political antennae that perhaps the PM or the DPM may mention to one of us, what is happening with X or Y? . . . You don't want the Prime Minister and Deputy Prime Minister to have to solve these sorts of problems. You want to go to them and say 'This is our proposed solution'.

In terms of the issues that got discussed, these included:

Anything and everything. It is really areas where either there is a lower level dispute brewing which we think we can sort out, or areas that we can foresee have a political salience . . . Sometimes very small things. Sometimes it can be things that have a financial dimension; we are working together on a white paper on defence industrial strategy . . . We had a session about badgers . . . Quite a lot of the environmental issues . . . often there are issues between DECC and the Treasury which we can sometimes help to try and resolve. I think we see ourselves as problem solvers.

### Oliver's 'Policy Catch-ups'

Oliver Letwin also held a weekly policy catch-up meeting, jointly chaired by him and Danny Alexander. It lasted for about an hour, with a mix of a dozen ministers, officials and special advisers. The meeting ran through progress on the Government's policy agenda, and flagged up potential problems. Any coalition issues might be referred to Letwin and Alexander to sort out.

### Ed Llewellyn/Jonny Oates

The next levels also consisted of pairs of people working for the Prime Minister and Deputy Prime Minister: their top advisers, and top officials. The top advisers were their respective Chiefs of Staff, Ed Llewellyn in No 10, and Jonny Oates who was Nick Clegg's chief of staff in the Cabinet Office. They talked to each other several times a day and, unlike other special advisers, they had sufficient authority that they could themselves resolve some coalition issues. A No 10 senior official noted: 'They have been given a sufficiently clear mandate by their respective bosses that on occasion they have reached the final agreement of an issue'.

In addition to policy issues, they resolved a lot of party political matters.

Ed Llewellyn and Jonny Oates will tend to deal with party political things, or things like special adviser numbers, or if the DPM has a particular concern about a political speech that the PM might have been making. (No 10 official)

Clearance of speeches by members of the other party covered not only ministerial speeches, but also party political speeches, and even extended to speeches given at their respective party conferences.

## Jeremy Heywood/Chris Wormald

Working very closely with Ed Llewellyn and Jonny Oates were the two senior officials supporting Cameron and Clegg, Jeremy Heywood and Chris Wormald. Heywood had been the top official in No 10 for three different governments. He was brought back by Brown in 2008, and helped manage the transition to the new Coalition Government in 2010. Chris Wormald was head of the Economic and Domestic Affairs Secretariat in the Cabinet Office, and in addition became Clegg's top official in October 2010 when it became clear that Clegg's team needed some bigger guns to fight their Whitehall battles.

As they gained the confidence of their respective masters, more coalition business was delegated to them:

> I suppose in the very early days probably somewhat more was brokered on the pure PM/DPM, Ed/Jonny net, and one trend has been . . . as the PM's got more comfortable with Jeremy Heywood and the DPM's got more comfortable with Chris Wormald, more's been delegated down that channel. (Senior official, No 10)

## Integrated Staffing

For simplicity, these informal forums have been presented as matching pairs. But there was also a lot of cross-working between special advisers and civil servants, with Ed Llewellyn talking to Chris Wormald, or Jonny Oates to Jeremy Heywood, etc. In addition, a key integrating mechanism at the Centre was the inclusion of both coalition parties' staff in No 10. There were Conservative and Liberal Democrat special advisers working alongside each other on both policy and communications. Nick Clegg had four advisers outposted to No 10: Lena Pietsch and Sean Kemp, working on communications and the media; and Polly Mackenzie and Tim Colbourne, working on policy and strategy. They shared offices with their Conservative colleagues. Another potentially integrating mechanism could be the new Policy and Implementation Unit in No 10, which reports to both the PM and the DPM; but that depends on what use the DPM makes of it (see below).

## INITIAL PROBLEM AREAS

There were a number of formal and informal mechanisms which did not work so well in terms of coalition governance in the first year. These were the Deputy Prime Minister's Office; the No 10 Policy Unit; and special advisers.

## The Deputy Prime Minister's Office

Just as no one had forecast a coalition after the 2010 election, so the Cabinet Office was unprepared for a Deputy Prime Minister, let alone one who might require substantial support. It was not easy for them: with Oliver Letwin and Baroness Warsi being parachuted in, they had more than the usual number of Cabinet Office ministers, even before trying to accommodate Nick Clegg. And with the Cabinet Office being required to set an example to the rest of Whitehall in trimming staff and budgets, there was little scope for finding additional staff.

Initially Nick Clegg's Private Office was the same size as that of other Secretaries of State. It quickly became apparent that this was seriously inadequate for a Deputy Prime Minister who wanted to cover every aspect of government policy. Following a review in autumn 2010, he was assigned a Cabinet Office Director General, Chris Wormald, to be his senior official; until September 2011, however, Wormald continued also to be the head of the Economic and Domestic Affairs Secretariat (EDS), in itself a demanding role. The 2010 review also concluded that Clegg needed a separate resource for his cross-departmental role, with a Research and Analysis Unit of six people; and that his Press Office needed strengthening. A Cabinet Office senior official noted how:

> There was not enough time and resource for the DPM to develop his own proactive agenda. We do now have a much clearer grip on his three main priorities: political and constitutional reform; social mobility, where we lead; and rebalancing the economy, which is Treasury-led but where we seek to exert influence.

Mindful of the debilitating rivalries of the Blair/Brown years, the Cabinet Office was understandably reluctant to create twin centres of power in Whitehall.

> The DPM would really have liked to have had a [Permanent Secretary]. But he was made to realise he could not establish a rival power base to No 10: it would have led to endless conflict . . . So the decision was made to enmesh the Lib Dems in a more inter-dependent way. That was a seminal decision: it affected the dynamics of the Coalition in an integrating way. (Cabinet Office official)

The inadequate initial staffing and subsequent patchwork solutions took their toll. Nick Clegg's ministerial colleagues appreciated the immense burden placed on their leader. One Lib Dem minister noted:

> For the DPM for quite a while the machine wasn't working. Things were not responded to; there was a backlog of mail; meetings were not well organised. People underestimate the strain on Nick of having no proper support.

But they continued to be critical of his office, even after its numbers had been strengthened. One Liberal Democrat minister said in August 2011:

> They need to communicate more effectively what Nick wants from individual Lib Dem ministers, or ministers collectively: in the way that No 10 does very well. It is all a bit fuzzy. The Office needs clearer direction, with clear deployment of specific tasks within it.

It was particularly difficult for Nick Clegg's special advisers. They had not expected to be in government and they had no experience of working in Whitehall. In the first year they suffered the added burden of starting an office from scratch.

They were primarily ideas people – policy creators, not fixers, negotiators or power brokers. The civil servants had hoped they would do a lot of the unblocking, like New Labour's spads; but at least initially, this was not how they conceived their role.

Behind these criticisms lay the underlying difficulty that Nick Clegg was trying to keep abreast of all government policy, and retained the right to intervene in any aspect of policy, foreign as well as domestic. Just as the Liberal Democrats might find it hard to demonstrate their influence by spreading themselves thinly across the whole of government, so the DPM might find it hard to point to his own tangible achievements:

> The matrix arrangement for the DPM (whereby he retains the right to intervene in all policy issues) is high maintenance. What does he want to achieve? What are his hard deliverables at the end of this? (Cabinet Office official)

Clegg's main priorities in 2011 were constitutional reform, social mobility, and rebalancing the economy. These priorities were not well known in Whitehall. They made little impact amongst the media, and none with the wider public. The public were notoriously indifferent to constitutional reform, as the AV referendum result showed. Social mobility was deeply intractable, and the launch of Clegg's social mobility strategy was a damp squib.[6] And if the economy was successfully revived and rebalanced, the credit will be given to the Chancellor, and not to Clegg. So the question remained: what did Clegg want to achieve? And what did he want to demonstrate as his achievements? Without a sense of clear priorities and achievable targets, it was that much harder for his staff and his advisers to give a lead to his ministerial colleagues, the rest of Whitehall and the wider world.


## Special Adviser Networks

The special advisers were another under-utilised resource in terms of coalition management. They provided information networks, but initially at least, and unlike in some other countries, they did not prove to be coalition brokers. At the Centre these networks were closely integrated, thanks to the four Liberal Democrat advisers outposted to No 10. But in departments special advisers came from just one party, with only the Treasury and the Department for Business having a mix of Conservative and Lib Dem spads. It was not until late 2011, when the Lib Dems gained six extra spads, that they became a little more mixed.

The entire special adviser network came together each Friday for a meeting chaired by Ed Llewellyn. From summer 2011 these meetings became fortnightly, or sometimes less.

> They are coalition meetings. They are only one of the mechanisms of keeping the political teams within departments in touch with each other. They are useful, but I cannot

[6] M Savage, S Coates and R Bennett, 'Clegg's big moment backfires over interns' *Times* (6 April 2011), www.thetimes.co.uk/tto/news/politics/article2974671.ece; J Glover, 'Nick Clegg's social mobility plans should not be lost amid mockery' *Guardian* (6 April 2011), www.guardian.co.uk/commentisfree/2011/apr/06/nick-clegg-social-mobility

> pretend that they are massively useful . . . frankly there is a limit to how much you can say in a gathering of potentially 60–70 people. (No 10 special adviser)

Later on Fridays there was a meeting of Liberal Democrat special advisers chaired by Jonny Oates.

> In this latter meeting we might look at the grid for the week; conference planning; policy; big things that are upcoming – keeping the information flowing. Holding the party together is harder because you are all in different places. (Lib Dem special adviser)

Once a month these meetings were supplemented by a separate meeting with a wider group of people: staff from the Lib Dem party headquarters, and ministers' parliamentary staff.

The Conservative special advisers also held separate meetings. They did not do so initially, for a reason which displays their sensitivity towards the junior partner:

> In the early months of the Government, the first six to nine months, it was very important to get the thing off on the right footing, to get relationships established, and trust and collegiality; and so not to have lots of separate meetings. That applies particularly to Conservatives, because we are the bigger partner. (No 10 special adviser)

The special advisers were not coalition brokers. In countries such as New Zealand, Scotland and Wales, spads to the coalition party leaders have been key go-betweens, doing deals on behalf of their political masters (see chapter two). The main reason why this did not happen so much in the UK was that for Cameron and Clegg this role was largely being performed by Letwin and Alexander. Another reason was that the Conservative and Liberal Democrat special advisers were still getting to know each other. A third was that they lacked experience of government, and did not yet have the confidence or authority to negotiate on behalf of their ministers. Several civil servants commented on their lack of clout compared with their Labour predecessors, and the absence of any 'super spads'; but that may change over time, as they grow in experience and stature.

A final reason might simply be that there were not enough of them. Many of our interviewees commented on this, and said that a coalition needed more special advisers because there was so much more negotiation required: between ministers, with the parliamentary party, and with the party outside Parliament. This view was expressed by civil servants, as well as by ministers and their advisers. It was expressed particularly strongly by Liberal Democrats. One Lib Dem spad said:

> I would get rid of the cap on spads. I know they aren't well regarded, but in a coalition there is so much more politics to be done that you need special advisers. Ideally, one for every minister.

This began to be remedied with the arrival of six additional Lib Dem spads from October 2011, allowing one spad for every two junior Lib Dem ministers.[7]

---

[7] Written Ministerial Statement on Numbers and Costs of Special Advisers (9 December 2011), www.cabinetoffice.gov.uk/sites/default/files/resources/LIST_AND_COSTS_9_DECEMBER_0.pdf. The statement records 21 Lib Dem spads, but lists only four of the additional six Lib Dem spads agreed in late 2011.

**No 10 Policy Unit**

Nor did the Policy Unit prove to be a forum for management of coalition issues At the start its numbers were drastically reduced. The number of special advisers in Downing Street had famously trebled under New Labour, going from eight working for John Major to 25 under Blair. Cameron was determined to reverse that, and the No 10 Policy Unit was greatly slimmed down in May 2010. It did not comprise any of the senior people listed in Table 4.2.

The initial decision to slim down the Policy Unit was soon regretted. No 10 realised its lack of capacity during the autumn 2010 spending review, and took stock afterwards. As one No 10 official said:

> We eventually came to the conclusion that to bind together the Coalition whilst giving us the right firepower relative to departments, it made sense to have one policy unit serving both [the PM and DPM]. Therefore it had to be civil servants, because the DPM wasn't going to take advice from a Conservative spad on immigration policy for example.

So the new Policy and Implementation Unit created in spring 2011 consisted of a dozen more senior and experienced people, working jointly to the Prime Minister and Deputy Prime Minister. In practice only half of the new Policy Unit were civil servants from Whitehall departments. The other half were outsiders from the private sector, and the membership looked more favourable to Cameron than to Clegg (for the full list see Appendix seven). Two of the outsiders had worked on secondment for the Conservative Party before the 2010 election, and one led on the Big Society. It was seen by the rest of Whitehall as No 10's Policy Unit, and not Nick Clegg's.

Papers from the Policy and Implementation Unit were copied to both the Prime Minister and the Deputy Prime Minister, but they could commission something for their eyes only.

> Clearly the PM and the DPM will have slightly different focuses and different priorities but I think it's perfectly possible for the Policy Unit to provide advice and support to both of them. Particularly given the fact that these appointments are civil servants or apolitical specialist advisers. (Cabinet Office official)

It promised to be an interesting experiment in terms of how the two leaders of the Coalition were supported. One Downing Street official noted that 'It was felt that it was important to bind the Coalition together rather than allow it to bifurcate. It was important to have one integrated unit'. Potentially it could represent a big expansion in the policy capacity available to Nick Clegg, who retained his own smaller Research and Analytics Unit. But it could also be seen as a small precedent for the more radical idea floated by some of our interviewees, that a future Deputy Prime Minister should ask to be based in Downing Street, and have the support of the entire Downing Street machine.

IMPACT OF THE COALITION ON THE CIVIL SERVICE

The Cabinet Secretary was Head of the Civil Service, and the Cabinet Office offered central guidance to Whitehall on the conduct of the civil service.[8] We asked our interviewees how the Coalition had affected the work of the civil service, and the role of the Centre in Whitehall. Formally there was very little change.

> There has been no need to change any of the civil service guidance. We made one change to the Ministerial Code, about setting aside collective responsibility on those issues where the parties agree to disagree. There have been no ethics or propriety issues specific to the Coalition. (Cabinet Office official)

The civil service was very keen to demonstrate that it could work for a coalition government just as effectively as for single-party government. A month after the election Sir Gus O'Donnell issued a letter to Permanent Secretaries which included advice on handling coalition issues. The full text is set out in Appendix five, with key extracts below:

> The role of the Civil Service is to serve the Government of the day. This is of course no different for a coalition government, with majority and minority partners . . . collective agreement through the Cabinet Committee clearance process is therefore of additional importance, as one means of making the Coalition work.

> The Coalition Programme for Government was agreed collectively through the Coalition Committee, and departments should consider this an agreed position . . . it would be helpful for departments to adopt a requirement for submissions to ministers to include a section on 'coalition considerations' under which officials should set out how the Coalition has been taken into account in framing the advice.

> In thinking about coalition issues, officials should consider the importance both sides of the Coalition attach to a 'no surprises' culture . . . civil service advice can flag the need to engage on a point of party political difference relevant to the functioning of the Coalition. Permanent Secretaries may also advise ministers that an issue should be taken to the Coalition Committee.

This guidance did not prevent civil servants from providing advice to just one side of the Coalition, as this Cabinet Office official explained:

> Sometimes we are commissioned by a minister, or No 10, or others to do work solely for them, and we do. So they may want something that explains something entirely from their point of view, or to do some research on something which they know the other side of the Coalition – and both sides have done this – would not like. Sometimes both sides want some thinking space to themselves.

---

[8] Sir Gus O'Donnell held both posts. But when he retired in December 2011, his successor Jeremy Heywood became Cabinet Secretary but not Head of the Civil Service. The new Head of the Civil Service was Sir Bob Kerslake, Permanent Secretary at the Department for Communities and Local Government.

Nor did it prevent the civil service from proffering advice to just one side on particular issues. For example, on the Fixed Term Parliaments Bill, the Cabinet Office decided to advise the Prime Minister separately about the prerogative powers he was about to relinquish. The policy lead lay with the Deputy Prime Minister, in conjunction with the Prime Minister; but because the PM was about to lose significant political power, officials felt they owed him a separate note about the potential consequences (see chapter nine).

Such private briefings are nothing new. It has long been the case that a Secretary of State might ask for a note which will not be shared with his junior ministers; or the Treasury or No 10 might do some blue sky thinking without telling the relevant department. It may be more common in No 10 and the Cabinet Office; we found no evidence of separate briefing in our interviews in departments. But it probably happens, and it is not necessarily wrong.

The civil service were less flexible in offering additional support to Liberal Democrat ministers. In a couple of departments (Education and Health) Lib Dem junior ministers were supplied with an additional civil servant as a policy adviser to support them in their cross-departmental role. But these were the exception, with the initiative coming from the Secretary of State: in most departments they got the standard Private Office appropriate to their status (see chapter five). This was politically a sensitive issue, and not one in which the Centre sought to intervene.

In two respects the civil service were empowered by the Coalition. The first was a return to more evidence-based policy making. As David Willetts put it to the *Guardian*, 'Because it's a coalition, it's evidence-based. You can't get anywhere with an appeal to tribal loyalty'.[9] The civil service were encouraged to intervene in Whitehall policy debates, and to offer more evidence and advice. In the words of Jeremy Heywood:

> Our experience so far has been that the Coalition has made it easier if anything to have open debates . . . about what the evidence suggests . . . If there is not a very clear presumption one way or the other, often the starting point is 'what does the civil service think the right evidence is'?[10]

The second was a return to due process in terms of collective policy clearance. The Cabinet Secretariat had been sidelined under a series of Prime Ministers who tended to bypass Cabinet and its Committees.[11] That tendency was reversed by the Coalition, because of the central role of Cabinet Committees in formally signing off on all government policy on behalf of both coalition partners.

---

[9]  D Aitkenhead, 'David Willetts: "Many more will go to university than in my generation – we must not reverse that"' *Guardian G2* (20 November 2011), www.guardian.co.uk/politics/2011/nov/20/david-willetts-university-student-loans-debt

[10]  P Wintour, 'Cabinet Secretary calls for social policy "kitemark" to highlight quality initiatives' *Guardian* (10 January 2012), www.guardian.co.uk/politics/2012/jan/10/cabinet-secretary-social-policy-kitemark

[11]  See n 1 above.

We have made steps to more strictly enforce the proper processes and timetables for securing cabinet clearance, and with the support of the PM and the DPM, have been more active in pushing back departments. There was a time when this was honoured more in the breach than in adherence to the rules. We have got considerably better at making sure that departments do give appropriate time so that things can be 'coalition-ised' if necessary. (Cabinet Office official)

The Cabinet Secretariat also helped to support the crucial Oliver Letwin/Danny Alexander nexus, which underpins so much coalition management.

It is Oliver Letwin in the Cabinet Office rather than No 10 who is the one we're working to. Although we also work to the Chief Secretary in his coalition management capacity . . . For our advice on every substantive bit of correspondence, we send a small pro forma, as we call it, to Oliver Letwin and to the Chief Secretary . . . this is in their coali-tion roles just so that they're aware of what the issue is and aware of coalition issues, between the special advisers and others here, just to try and help smooth the process more effectively. (Cabinet Office official)

## CONCLUSION

In its operation at the Centre the Coalition proved to be the antithesis of the neg-ative stereotype with which we opened this chapter. Far from being quarrelsome, slow and indecisive, it proved remarkably harmonious, smooth and effective in its decision-making. That was achieved through a combination of formal and infor-mal machinery. The ultimate formal machinery for dispute resolution, Cabinet's Coalition Committee, was not deployed for that purpose because no disputes escalated to that level. There were of course disputes – that is the stuff of govern-ment – but they were anticipated and brokered in a series of informal forums before going through the formal hoops of Cabinet Committees for final signing off. No 10 was central, but so was the Cabinet Office, which was less marginalised than under previous Prime Ministers for two reasons. It supported the DPM, who was directly involved in all the coalition brokering; and the Cabinet Office sup-ported the revived system of Cabinet Committees.

Of course, the revival of cabinet government might have happened anyway under a new Prime Minister with a commitment to collegiality. It is important to try to distinguish what is a necessary consequence of coalition government and what is merely contingent. But as our interviews show, the Coalition required a revival of cabinet government: enforcing the proper clearance procedure became the final stage in ensuring that both coalition partners signed off on every aspect of government policy.

The informal forums in which government business got brokered between the coalition parties before going through the formal hoops of Cabinet Committees might also have been replicated to some extent. All governments develop infor-mal machinery for coordination between No 10, the Treasury and departments. But the extent of the informal machinery, and the central role of the Prime

Minister and Deputy PM's weekly meetings, the Quad, and Oliver Letwin and Danny Alexander, were distinctive products of the Coalition. The Quad became a semi-formal institution, and the Treasury became much more open to No 10 and the Cabinet Office in the process.

So No 10, the Cabinet Office and Treasury were better integrated than in previous governments. In its first 18 months the Centre showed that coalition government could be unified and effective. Both partners observed collective cabinet responsibility; there were almost no leaks, and there was little negative briefing. Seen from the inside, the Coalition seemed remarkably harmonious and successful.

But as we noted at the beginning of the chapter, this is not the only measure of success. Seen from the outside, it was a rather different story. It was a different story in the media, which persisted with reports of coalition splits (see chapter eight). This was despite the point made by many Whitehall interviewees that differences between ministers of the same party were more frequent, and more serious, than differences between the coalition partners. Perhaps because of the media reporting, the public's perception of coalition government one year on still conformed to the negative stereotype. Coalition government was seen as 'weaker' than single-party government by 68 per cent of people surveyed in April 2011, 'more indecisive' by 73 per cent, and a 'bad thing' by 58 per cent (see also Appendix two).[12]

The other different measure of success was for the Liberal Democrats. Their strong support for the smooth and harmonious working of the Centre reflected their determination to show that coalition government could be unified and effective, and that the Lib Dems could be relied upon to be loyal and disciplined coalition partners. But in terms of poll ratings only the Conservatives seemed to reap the benefit. The Lib Dems' polling figures slumped in 2010 to half the support they had received at the election. Because of the difficulties involved in getting Nick Clegg's office established in the first year, it was not easy for the Lib Dems to demonstrate greater distinctiveness. As the pressures mount on them to differentiate, greater strains may build within the Coalition. But it may still prove futile, because their attempts at differentiation in the first 18 months were too subtle and too varied to be noticed by the public. Whether the junior partner is doomed to be eclipsed in this way is a theme to which we return in chapter eleven.

A third feature, stressed by many interviewees, was the importance of good personal relationships. Cameron and Clegg, who hardly knew each other before the election, got on famously well. But those around them worked very hard to maintain good relations, at every level, and displayed much emotional intelligence in doing so.

It was striking how harmonious the Centre seemed to be, seen from the inside: particularly by comparison with the Blair/Brown years. It seemed almost too good to be true; and it may be too good to last. As the pressures mount on the Liberal

---

[12] Rick Nye, 'What is the State of Public Opinion after 12 Months of the Coalition Government?' in *One Year On: The First Year of Coalition Government* (London, Institute for Government, 2011) 71–74.

Democrats in subsequent years to demonstrate more distinctiveness, tensions may begin to grow. But it will be hard for the Lib Dems, having started in government as civilised partners, to turn themselves into more brutal ones: it does not come naturally to them.

# 5

# Departments: Ministers and the Civil Service

## PETER WALLER

I was not at all sure how the Coalition would work and even whether it would work. But it's been far better than anyone could have expected. (Senior government official)

## INTRODUCTION

T HE PREVIOUS CHAPTER discussed how 'the Centre' of Whitehall – No 10, the Deputy Prime Minister's Office and Cabinet Office – developed to support the Coalition. This chapter looks more closely at how the Coalition has impacted on mainstream Whitehall departments. It considers the following: how departments prepared for the possibility of a coalition; what arrangements were put in place to ensure that both partners in the Coalition were fully engaged in the development of policy; how those arrangements worked in practice; and what conclusions can be drawn, both positive and negative.

We interviewed ministers and special advisers from a wide range of departments. But a feature of the current Coalition was that departments had different ministerial configurations. We therefore paid particular attention to the impact of the Coalition in three departments with different models:

- the Department for Communities and Local Government (DCLG), a department headed by a Tory Secretary of State, but with a Lib Dem junior minister – one of the nine major[1] departments;[2]

---

[1] We loosely defined 'major' departments as those departments with substantial budgets responsible for a major sector of government administration. On that basis the territorial 'departments' (the Scottish Office, Wales and Northern Ireland Offices) would not be considered major departments, for instance.

[2] The major departments with a Conservative Secretary of State and a Lib Dem junior minister in 2010–11 were: Department for Communities and Local Government, Home Office, Foreign and Commonwealth Office, Department for Education, Department of Health, Department for Work and Pensions, Ministry of Justice, Ministry of Defence, Ministry of Transport. We do not include the Treasury here.

- the Department of Energy and Climate Change (DECC), one of only two Whitehall major departments headed by a Lib Dem cabinet minister;[3]
- the Department for Environment, Food and Rural Affairs (Defra), the largest of three major departments which had no Lib Dem ministers.[4]

**Figure 5.1  Ministers in Departments by Party Affiliation, 2010–11**

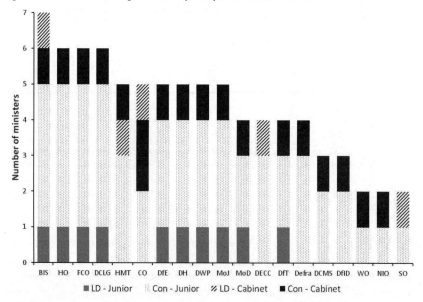

Source: adapted from Institute for Government, *United We Stand*, 34

In each of those departments we were given access to a number of senior officials in order to discuss how the civil service had adapted to the Coalition. Each faced different challenges. But the chapter also draws in experience from other departments where relevant.

ANTICIPATING THE NEW GOVERNMENT

Whitehall is used to preparing for new governments. It is a convention that as the date of the general election gets closer, the Prime Minister of the day will authorise civil servants to hold initial discussions with shadow ministers in the opposi-

---

[3] Of the five Lib Dem Cabinet ministers, only Chris Huhne (DECC) and Vince Cable (BIS) were appointed to lead major departments. The DPM role in the Cabinet Office was *sui generis*, Danny Alexander was second in command at the Treasury, and the Scotland Office, headed by Michael Moore, was a tiny department with few functional responsibilities.

[4] The three major departments were: Defra, the Department for Culture, Media and Sport (DCMS) and the Department for International Development (DfID). Two other territorial departments – the Northern Ireland Office and the Wales Office – were headed by Conservative Secretaries of State with no Lib Dem junior ministers.

tion parties to discuss their immediate priorities should they win the election. Those discussions took place in the early months of 2010, with Tory shadow ministers having talks with the Permanent Secretary in their shadow department. There was similar – but considerably less – contact with Lib Dem frontbench spokesmen.

Once an election is called, each department produces three sets of initial briefings for the incoming government in 'blue, red and yellow' versions for the three main parties. These briefs – comprehensive to the point of overkill – serve a dual purpose: first, they brief incoming ministers on their new responsibilities; second, they set out the department's thoughts on how it might implement the manifesto policies. Inevitably, more effort is put into the briefing for the likely winning party, whether that be the current Government or the official Opposition; and the Lib Dem briefing would always come third in order of priority.

The 2010 preparations in departments differed in only limited ways from the conventional approach, even though it was clear that the likelihood of a hung parliament was considerable. Most attention was paid to preparations for a Tory government. One official involved commented:

> The first thing we did was a textual analysis of the various manifestos. We started before the first leaders' debate when we had no idea what would happen, though we were essentially expecting a Conservative government, though perhaps one without a majority. We included the Liberal Democrat manifesto not in the expectation of a coalition but because we thought there might be some horse trading on individual policies.

In contrast to the Centre, where the Cabinet Secretary had engaged in a significant degree of pre-planning for the possibility of a hung parliament, none of the three departments had given much thought to how a coalition would impact on departmental routines. An official commented:

> I remember before the election discussing whether if we had a coalition we would copy submissions to ministers from both parties; or should we give them separate briefs, reflecting there were two parties? In hindsight it's obvious that they must have the same submission, but it's interesting that it wasn't so obvious then. The reality is we didn't give serious thought to a coalition before it happened.

However, in each of the three departments examined, the review by officials of the party manifestos showed that the policy differences between the Tory and Lib Dem parties – which inevitably get exaggerated during an election campaign – were in practice less significant than might have been expected. And to some extent this broad similarity in approach applied even when compared to the Labour Party manifesto. In DECC, for example, officials emphasised that the department's objectives had barely changed under the Coalition – though the practical policies to achieve those objectives had changed. The only major issue between the Lib Dem and Tory policies for the department was on nuclear energy, and as the case study of nuclear energy (chapter ten) demonstrates, even there the differences proved fewer upon detailed examination than they had appeared at headline level.

An official at DCLG made the same point:

> A technique we used [in preparing our briefing] was to overlay the Lib Dem proposals for our departmental responsibilities on to the Conservative and Labour proposals which we had already plotted. Where they were similar we used green; and where they were different we used red. And, contrary to our expectations, there was a heck of a lot of green on the Lib Dem/Tory analysis and a heck of a lot of red on the Labour side.
>
> When we looked at it in detail it became clear that the Labour focus was on regions; but the Lib Dem and Tory emphasis was on localism, even if that specific word was more Tory than Lib Dem. It came through in such policies as abolishing the RDAs [Regional Development Agencies] and Government Offices, and transferring power to communities and local government. So we realised that the Lib Dems and the Tories were not that far apart on our patch. And we were thus really quite prepared for the Coalition when it happened.

And there was a similar story at Defra:

> There was consternation immediately after the election when we realised we were facing a coalition. But when we revisited the Tory and Lib Dem briefing packs for an incoming Government, there were virtually no distinctions between the two coalition parties in their stated aims for the department's agenda. There was the odd iconic issue such as foxhunting, which is not on the Coalition agenda so has not in practice proved problematic. But on the core aspects of Defra activities, there were really no Lib Dem/Tory disagreements.

Clearly there were departments such as the Department of Health, the Home Office and the Ministry of Defence where there were significant differences between the coalition partners. But beyond the headline issues that decide an election, there was usually a significant degree of consensus between the parties as to how to manage the numerous executive functions for which every government is responsible. So although Whitehall civil servants inevitably and excitedly speculated about what a change of Government would mean for their policy area, for a significant number of them it turned out to be business as usual. A Lib Dem junior minister endorsed this conclusion:

> When you strip away the rhetoric there's just this huge bit that's shared. Shared values, shared approach, shared reasonable behaviour – and I think that's a strength, I don't think it's a weakness at all; I think it's very important in a mature, law-based democracy.

## THE NEW GOVERNMENT ARRIVES

Clearly, no department had any forewarning of what the Coalition would mean in practice for them, or what combination of ministers they would get. Each department did, however, quickly experience two things. First, their immediate policy priorities were set out for them in the Programme for Government (PfG). The emphasis on 'implementing the Agreement' was made clear by ministers from day one, quickly followed by the mantra 'if it's in the Programme we are doing it; if it's not, we aren't'. This gave departments clear direction from the outset, to a degree which was unusual: the general Whitehall reaction to an incoming Government election manifesto could usually best be described as closer to 'guidance' than a detailed programme for action.

Second, incoming ministers immediately embraced the Coalition as something which they were determined to realise. Presumably Tory ministers would privately have preferred a majority Government – but there was a clear initial message to departmental officials that both parties had signed up to a deal and they were going to make it work. By taking such a strong position from the outset, incoming ministers effectively removed from the civil service the need for officials to work out how it was going to function at departmental level. Officials were told to behave as if the Coalition were a single Government, and the thinking they had done about the need to 'coalitionise' their activity was effectively redundant.

An example of this was the letter sent by Sir Gus O'Donnell, then Cabinet Secretary, to all his Permanent Secretary colleagues in June 2010. Alongside explaining the arrangements the Centre was putting in place for coalition management (discussed in chapter four), the letter discussed how officials should react to the Coalition within departments, and included the following recommendation:

> It would be helpful for departments to adopt a requirement for submissions to ministers to include a section on 'coalition considerations' under which officials should set out how the Coalition had been taken into account in framing the advice . . .
>
> . . . in thinking about coalition issues, officials should consider the importance both sides of the Coalition attach to a 'no surprises' culture . . .
>
> . . . civil service advice can flag the need to engage on a point of party political difference relevant to the functioning of the Coalition.

A year later, however, the officials we spoke to could only recall this advice vaguely; and none of the departments we studied in detail were including 'coalition considerations' as a heading in their submissions.[5] The reality was that officials observed ministers working together as a team and had limited need to think independently about how the Coalition might impact on their advice. It was 'business as usual' with one Government and one set of ministers in each department, regardless of their political party of origin. So what changed?

The consensus was that the Coalition had had less impact on normal business than officials had expected at the outset. Incremental changes were identified in a number of areas – although the Whitehall 'veterans' interviewed tended to see the 2010 changes as rather less radical than those brought about by the previous new Government, namely the arrival of New Labour in 1997.

---

[5] BIS, however, used the suggested heading in submissions. That may reflect the fact that BIS was the only department with at least two ministers from each coalition party, and had a minister from each party (Vince Cable and David Willetts) attending Cabinet.

The key areas where changes in approach were discernible under the Coalition are discussed below.

### 1. Greater Ministerial Emphasis on Discussion and Teamwork

A core tenet of the civil service is that any Secretary of State is entitled to run their department in the style they wish – and the department will adjust its working practices to accommodate that. Secretaries of State vary considerably in their working styles, from those who welcome open discussion with officials, junior ministers and special advisers to those who tend to restrict discussion about new policies and ideas, often preferring to keep a 'tight circle' of colleagues whom the Secretary of State trusts. Several senior members of the outgoing Labour Government were known in particular to employ the 'tight circle' approach. Individual junior ministers were often outside that inner circle.

However, across Whitehall Secretaries of State were overtly making an effort to widen discussion with regular, usually weekly, meetings of all ministers, accompanied by spads, Parliamentary Private Secretaries and sometimes the relevant whips, regardless of party affiliations. Even Defra, though lacking a Lib Dem minister, included a Lib Dem spokesman (Andrew George) in many such meetings, as did the Department for Culture, Media and Sport (DCMS), which sent along Don Foster. In each case, discussion at such meetings was wide-ranging, with debate and challenge welcomed. Interviews carried out in other departments left a similar impression.

It was possible that this generation of cabinet ministers happened to be unusually consensual in their approach. But it is in practice much more likely that the fact of there being a coalition obliged ministers to be more open and collegiate in the way they ran discussion within their departments. There was a clear sense within Defra, for example, that any significant policy proposal ought to be run past Andrew George before it was taken to Cabinet Committee – and no policy could be considered to be authorised until the Lib Dems had had a chance to comment at Cabinet Committee. In DCLG, the Secretary of State was known to take pains to check whether Andrew Stunell had been consulted on issues – and to want Stunell to attend meetings even when the subject matter was not relevant to his direct responsibilities. And while the dynamic was different in DECC – with a Lib Dem Secretary of State (SoS) – the same regular ministerial meetings and discussions took place. As one senior official put it:

> The Coalition obliges all the ministers to look slightly wider in their perspectives. When a single-party government is taking legislation through, for example, they might have to take account of a few rebels on their backbenches but that is about it. But here there is much more of a conscious effort to recognise that there are two parties and two perspectives.

A Tory junior minister in a department with a Lib Dem Secretary of State took a similar line:

> I think the team work is stronger because of the Coalition. If we had come in with a clear majority, we would have handed our policy over to the civil service and told them to get on with it. The fact that we had to discuss what we wanted to do, what the other party wished to do – or indeed whether there were other options – made it much better.

This was echoed by a Lib Dem junior minster in a Tory-led department:

> The team of ministers in our department works together well on a day-to-day basis in a constructive spirit. The civil service support that positively; and the good relationship is at the heart of how it is all working. When there are issues which require ironing out there will inevitably be a discussion either with ministers as a whole or with the SoS bilaterally.

It did not follow that a greater degree of discussion and debate necessarily led to better outcomes in terms of policy making. But almost all interviewees believed the day-to-day atmosphere within each department was more positive that it had been under the previous Government; and officials contrasted the current regime very positively with what they had encountered in 'the days of Brown and Blair'. This was particularly so in the case of DCLG, where under Labour two ministers regularly attended Cabinet (the Secretary of State and the Housing Minister) with relations between the two of them being described, with typical Whitehall understatement, as 'quite difficult'.

## 2. Greater Emphasis on Formal Government Structures

As described in chapter four, the Coalition began life with a set of formal processes for resolving disputes between the parties. Arrangements were also set in place for a revised list of Cabinet Committees, with membership carefully designed to provide a balance of Tory and Lib Dem ministers (see chapter four).

In the departments examined here, the formal dispute resolution procedures had zero impact (though they were used by the Department of Health on the NHS reforms). None of them appeared to have come near a level of impasse which necessitated even thinking about invoking the Coalition dispute procedures, on any policy. Indeed, there was no issue in any of the three departments where there had been an internal split along overtly party lines.

But the renewed focus on formal resolution of policy through Cabinet Committees was very noticeable. Most officials we interviewed were supportive of this, in that it provided greater clarity, with proposals needing to be fully thought through and written down, with less risk of unrecorded 'backroom deals' outside formal structures. Having to take everything through committee slowed down the process of policy development, though this was often seen as something of a benefit in that it avoided rushed decision-making.

That said, it would be wrong to over-emphasise the importance of the change. Incoming governments tend to arrive with a commitment to 'good habits', such as the use of formal processes; but over time more informal ways of conducting business become increasingly common. Departments have a natural tendency to want to agree the outcome before they put any paper forward for formal clearance. One department, for example, quickly moved to ensuring that the Deputy Prime Minister was sent all papers for the committee he chaired in draft well before the formal paper was circulated, in effect seeking to pre-empt any risk of dissent on the day.

A critique of reliance on formal Cabinet Committee structures, however, was that it can lead to departments focusing on their own policy position without worrying about other perspectives. One senior official observed:

> In moving back to a more Cabinet Committee style of government, we are also moving back to a position where departments take up entrenched positions. And with something of a hollowed-out Centre, there is less emphasis on joined-up government and collective management of cross-cutting issues. Each department runs its own show and sets out its own business plan. We have lost the heavy handed centralist model which drove the Labour Government but have replaced it with a rather federal model. What would be better would be a more corporate model of government. I am certainly not hankering back to the Labour days. What we have now is a reaction to the Labour approach, but something of an overreaction.

There were echoes of this in a comment from an official in another department:

> The Centre would argue that the widespread use of Cabinet Committees means that departments come out of their silos and work more constructively together. But I haven't seen much sign of that and that is disappointing. There is still the sense of departments working on the basis of 'we win, you lose' or vice versa. I would have liked to think the Coalition would have made a difference to that, but I haven't seen much sign of that.

Throughout our interviews, there were also numerous references to the relative lack of resource at the Centre – notably No 10 and the DPM's office – compared to Labour. Views were decidedly ambivalent on this subject. In some respects there was a considerable sense of relief that No 10 was no longer scrutinising every aspect of any given policy and was no longer constantly announcing new initiatives regardless of whether the department concerned agreed with them (a regular feature of the Treasury under Gordon Brown and then in his time at No 10). But against this there was a concern that departments felt that they could not always get the engagement of the Centre even where they thought they needed it. One official commented:

> There is an unusual degree of crawling over our business plan to check whether we are meeting the targets in it. But it's all about timetables and milestones, not substance. And no one is really concerned about the underlying outcomes of policies . . . we never get challenged on whether the policies themselves are the right ones. There is a noticeable lack of an 'intelligent customer' focus.
>
> The much bigger problem we have had is that there has been no real way to get the Prime Minister played into our issues. Our interaction has been negligible. Under Labour, when we needed to get a sense of the PM's views, we would go to [the No 10 spad operating in their area] who would put a note into the PM and we would get the necessary steer coming back.

But a senior press and communications officer from the same department saw less sign of change:

> It took the Centre a while to get organised, especially needing to think about Lib Dems as well as Tories – so things were slow at first. But in terms of intrusiveness it's actually not much different. The new Government wants roughly the same degree of interaction with departments on major policy issues as its predecessor did, no more no less.

### 3. A Limited Role for Special Advisers – but a Stronger Role for Elected Politicians

Under the Labour Government, special advisers had immensely important roles to play in the functioning of departments. There were in effect two parallel lines of policy making: one through officials and the formal machinery, and one through the special advisers and their networks. In the most important areas, the spad network tended to dominate, being more flexible and quicker – and obviously more overtly political. The downside, of course, was that there was at times a disconnect between the two networks, with the spad network being focused more on the next announcement and far less concerned with the detailed nitty-gritty of decision making. Another feature of the Labour administration was that several 'super spads' emerged, most obviously those with a career in No 10 or the Treasury, and became very powerful figures in their own right, often with much more influence than junior ministers and occasionally even cabinet members.

On entering government, the Prime Minister made it one of his messages that the number of spads should be curtailed; he set a strict limit of two for each cabinet minister and none for junior ministers – an approach which changed at the end of 2011 when the number of Lib Dem spads was increased as the Government recognised the need for greater resources. Until that decision, the spads were directly linked to the party of the Secretary of State: so in our study departments, DECC had Lib Dem spads, while Defra and DCLG had Tory spads.

Interviews showed clearly that spads retreated a certain amount compared with the breadth of influence they enjoyed under Labour. The consensus was that spads were collectively less influential and were focusing more on advising their Secretaries of State on the political and presentational implications of policies emerging from officials, rather than being very hands-on with the policy making process. One official in DCLG said:

> The spads here have stepped back a bit in their role and relationships with officials compared to what I've seen previously . . . Their attitude is to be a little more careful in differentiating their role. They are still important and I don't want to exaggerate this but they operate more directly with the Minister and less overtly with officials.

By and large, interviewees welcomed this. A corollary of a reduced role for spads was that officials felt more empowered and there was less scope for confusion. At the same time, several officials thought something was missing, most obviously the ability that spads previously had to broker deals with other departments. One official in Defra commented:

> The spads here are obviously Tories and they find it difficult to ring up Nick Clegg's spads for example and sort something out. It's easier for ministers to sort things out, so a single-party set of ministers is probably less of a handicap than a set of single-party spads. This matters because without the informal brokering of spads, departments too often develop their policies in isolation and produce papers for committees which are their pure position, without being tempered by other perspectives. We miss the spad brokering role.

The Coalition introduced a new dynamic: spads found it harder to broker deals because any points of disagreement were resolved by elected ministers rather than unelected advisers. A Lib Dem spad said:

> One impact of the Coalition is that more issues have to go to ministers than would be the case under single-party government, where spads have a common understanding and set of values which can be used to resolve issues. We don't have that shared understanding with Tory spads.

Another Lib Dem demonstrated that the difference was partly cultural:

> There is a difficulty in being in coalition with people who are not natural allies. I was brought into politics by my opposition to the Tories and all they stood for. So it's difficult for me to go to spads meetings at No 10 which are full of Tories.

In contrast to the rather more restricted role of spads, however, there was evidence of an enhanced role for elected politicians in deal-making between departments, notably Oliver Letwin but also Danny Alexander (fully discussed in chapter four). The same phenomenon was echoed in departments, first from a Defra official:

> Letwin is a difference from the previous regime. He does up to a point try to initiate policy in some areas. But he is a benign influence – he is quite green, he is good at joining up. Though I have to say that there is still a lot more joining up to do.

A DECC official who had been involved in the DECC negotiations with the Treasury on DECC spending said:

> Letwin had a key role. He didn't take sides as such between departments and the Treasury but was instrumental in drawing out issues and seeking alternative solutions. It was a broker role which fitted very well with the way that a coalition might be expected to resolve complex issues. It was different from the autocratic discussions under Labour. But whether the same approach might have been taken under a Tory-only government with the current personnel is hard to say.

### RELATIONSHIPS WITH OTHER DEPARTMENTS

Our interviews probed whether the Coalition had made any difference to the way departments worked together. The aim was to see whether 'Tory-led' departments were more likely to have strong relationships with each other – perhaps with friction more obvious where departments were led by ministers of different parties.

No examples of this were uncovered. That did not mean that departments under the Coalition were in total agreement with each other. As we have indicated, departments arguably behaved rather more in silos than under Labour, with 'joined-up government' being less of a battle cry than it had been previously. But we could not detect any suggestion that such disputes were exacerbated by party differences.

Tory-led DCLG, for example, had rows with Lib Dem-led BIS over regulatory issues and the 'localism or regionalism' debate; but Lib Dem-led DECC had just as many debates with BIS on the green agenda (and higher energy costs in particular), with no suggestion that two departments with Lib Dem Secretaries of State were any more likely to be in agreement. Moreover, Defra seemed to have more disputes with DCLG, though both were Tory-led departments, than with DECC. Junior ministers were asked whether they naturally went to junior ministers of the same party in other departments – but again the response was no.

The position with respect to relationships between the Treasury and other departments was more nuanced. There was a tendency for Lib Dem ministers to engage most naturally with Danny Alexander and for Tories to speak more often to the Chancellor. But this was driven by the fact that politicians were more likely to speak initially to someone they already knew well, rather than by any expectation that the Chancellor or the Chief Secretary would favour 'their' party in the spending settlements.

## RELATIONSHIPS WITH THE CIVIL SERVICE

Ministers and officials were asked whether they thought the relationship between them was working well. Officials often commented in detail both positively and negatively (though on the whole more positively) about how the new ministers affected the way they operated. At the same time, they were unanimous that such impacts were all about personalities and policies rather than anything to do with the Coalition.

Ministers similarly had a range of views on the civil service (again mostly positive). But there were only occasional suggestions that they felt the civil service had any difficulty in supporting the Coalition. The most commonly stated issue was that ministers felt it took too long to get things done – but that was nothing new.

## RELATIONSHIPS WITH WESTMINSTER

Whitehall and Westminster are obviously strongly linked, but only a modest proportion of departmental activity has a parliamentary component. Clearly legislation is of major importance, but most departments will have a bill before Parliament only every couple of years; and such bills are likely to impact on only one or two of the ministers and a handful of officials. Each department has a monthly 'departmental questions' session, which can be nerve-wracking for ministers, but is not a major time commitment. The work of Select Committees is increasingly important – and higher profile – but Select Committee appearances are rare for both ministers and officials. Having said that, all ministers are members of the Commons or Lords, so Parliament is crucial to their overall role as politicians.

There was no evidence of a change in the relationship between Whitehall and Westminster. The odd anecdote from interviewees in Westminster suggested that the Government was less flexible in taking legislation through Parliament because it was more difficult to change detailed policy once a policy line had been brokered between the two coalition partners. That may have been a result of the particular departments we studied.

Ministers were, however, a little more forthcoming in this area, no doubt reflecting their greater day-to-day engagement with Parliament. The main theme, applying more to Lib Dem ministers than Tory ministers (and reflecting the different nature of the two parties), was the need for regular liaison with the backbench policy committees discussed in chapter six. This was particularly the case where there were no Lib Dem ministers in a department, as discussed in the Defra case study below. But a Lib Dem junior minister in another department thought that party liaison was becoming more important:

> For the first nine months or so I felt it was my role to explain and justify the Government's position to the party and to stakeholders – but it wasn't to broker agreement between the parties and the Government. But as a result of our experiences, the role has changed to a degree and has become more one of brokering agreement with the party.

Several ministers commented that it was easier – at least emotionally – to be enthusiastic about the Coalition from the comfort of ministerial office. One Tory junior minister noted the disappointment felt by a number of his colleagues who had hoped to have a ministerial post but had been squeezed out by Lib Dem ministers. Another observed:

> It's great for us in ministerial roles. We have got some power after all these years; and it's even better for the Lib Dems in that they were not expecting that. But it's not the same when you are on the backbenches – and where there are obviously hard-liners who are not reconciled to the Coalition.

## RELATIONS WITH THE MEDIA

The media response to the Coalition is discussed in chapter eight. But during the course of our interviews, we interviewed some departmental heads of communications to gauge their perspective. It was difficult, however, to detect any Coalition-specific developments, though all our interviewees noted that budgets for paid publicity had been severely cut, whereas press office functions had been less affected.

Generally the mood was quite positive. One head of communications mentioned the same drive within the Coalition to demonstrate togetherness that has been recorded elsewhere:

> I think there is less briefing of disputes – much more care is taken collectively and at the Centre to ensure that there is a single voice. There is a real attempt to avoid factionalism; there is less scope for it than under Labour with its large majorities. They are determined not to fall out.

Another noted that there were modest changes in terminology according to which party the minister came from:

> There is some difference of tone between them in that Tory ministers are more inclined to talk about market solutions, whereas Lib Dems are more likely to talk about the role of the state. But they don't really disagree on the substance so that is OK.

Another noted that incoming ministers in his department had a clear preference for getting messages across in 'the language of the tabloids' rather than in the more moderate tone of the broadsheets, and this had proved slightly problematic. But he doubted it was anything to do with the Coalition.

The communications professionals were slightly more concerned about the future than other officials. They observed that the No 10 communications team had generally been hands-off compared to their Labour counterparts, but that this was already changing, which had both positives and negatives. Another saw issues arising between the coalition partners in future:

> Before the election, I went to a public discussion with the communications directors in Wales and Scotland and I remember one of them remarking that as time goes on, there is a tendency for suspicion to grow among the coalition partners that the officials are subconsciously beginning to favour the majority partner. So we have had to be very careful to show that we are even-handed. But as it goes on – as everyone gets more tired and fractious and elections come along – I fear that the risk will grow, especially where the majority party is in charge of the department.

## DIFFERENT DEPARTMENTAL MODELS

In this section we flesh out how our three study departments managed their specific structure, and draw on interviews conducted with other departments with the same structure.

### The Tory-led Model: DCLG

In the period we studied, the Department of Communities and Local Government was headed by a Conservative Secretary of State (Eric Pickles) but had a Lib Dem junior minister (Andrew Stunell). This structure was the most dominant within the Coalition, with nine mainstream departments following such a model.

In principle, having a junior minister in a department seemed self-evidently better for the junior partner in the Coalition than having no minister. But the reality was characterised by three things: first, in terms of numbers, the odds were stacked against any junior Lib Dem minister in a Tory-led department. DCLG had six ministers in all, five Tories and one Lib Dem – and both spads were from the Tory Party. This effectively meant that there were eight full-time politicians in the department, only one of whom was a Liberal Democrat. Second, ministers are appointed in a three-tier hierarchy, with the Secretary of State alone in the top tier. No junior minister could have clout equivalent to a Secretary of State. Third, the resources associated with being a minister diminish with seniority – so a junior minister does not have the level of support staff that a Secretary of State enjoys.

There was nothing in our interviews with DCLG officials to suggest that ministers were not putting a focus on the Coalition team. Indeed the 'team' concept amongst the ministers was regularly commented on with strong endorsement. One DCLG official said:

> The SoS came in and said from day one that this was a coalition department and he simply was not going to have a separate Tory caucus within it. He lived up to that rhetoric. He used the weekly ministerial meetings to have a sort of second reading debate on policy questions that the team were tackling. So everyone could have their say. And he went out of his way to encourage that with good humour – saying for example 'and what does our Lib Dem colleague say on that point'?

It was also clear that the Secretary of State was content for Andrew Stunell – and indeed all his ministers – to raise comments across the whole of the department's activities and not just in relation to his ministerial portfolio. In respect of local government finance in particular – a key issue for any politician in the department – the SoS was regularly concerned to check that Andrew Stunell had been fully engaged.

It was recognised that Stunell had a difficult role, as he had very limited support in keeping on top of the volume of work. As a senior official said:

> If resources were not a constraint, the obvious solution would be for Andrew Stunell to have his own spad (or at least dedicated policy support, though he really needs political support) . . . it would even things up a bit and allow more of a Lib Dem voice to be heard, which is rather crowded out at present with the SoS having two people dedicated to that function while Andrew has to do it all on his own.

The Lib Dem influence on DCLG was, however, by no means limited to the influence of the one Lib Dem minister in the department. The department was expected to clear all its key policies through the relevant Cabinet Committees, notably the Home Affairs Committee chaired by the DPM. An official engaged in preparing for that committee said:

If we are having a difficulty about the reform of local government finance and the DPM has reservations about the direction, then Stunell is a very important channel in getting the DPM on side. And the only way he can be effective on that is if he can say that he has been in all the meetings, has been engaged fully in the policy making and that the way forward proposed is a sensible way forward.

Underlying this was recognition that the Tory voice in DCLG was much stronger than the Lib Dem voice. An official suggested that:

You could ask whether the Lib Dem perspective has been submerged in the department – and I would have to say it has been in that the ministerial team overall is pursuing a very clear and rather traditional Tory agenda.

This theme – of the odds being against a single Lib Dem junior minister being able to operate effectively within a department which is otherwise Tory – was a recurring one in other departments operating on the same ministerial model as DCLG. In that context there were various examples of informal support being provided to Lib Dem junior ministers, including a department allocating an additional member of staff to the Private Office of the minister concerned and allowing parliamentary researchers to have some access to ministerial meetings though not departmental papers. It also seemed – though it was difficult to demonstrate conclusively – that the more assertive a junior Lib Dem minister had been, the more likely it was that he had been granted additional logistical support. One junior minister who had been given extra resources told us:

During the summer break I made a point of writing down my key strategic priorities and concerns and getting both the DPM and the SoS here to sign them off. So that provided a framework not only for my direct responsibilities but also for the issues I was concerned about across the department as a whole.

But a Lib Dem minister in another department was clear that it could be an uphill struggle:

There's an issue with the civil service in that they are not used to a junior minister wanting to take a wider role. They feel nervous when I say 'I'm not just a Parliamentary Under-secretary, I am also the coalition partner in this department'. That's been a bit of a hurdle in terms of access to information, inclusion. I often find stuff going on that I don't know about.

In the longer term, therefore, a junior minister from the minority coalition partner needed additional political support if they were to have a realistic chance of ensuring the minority party voice was considered across the department as a whole. In autumn 2011 it was decided that a number of new Lib Dem spads would be recruited primarily as a shared resource between Lib Dem ministers in Tory-led departments. Some Tories might argue that these resources give the Lib Dems disproportionate political support compared to the number of Lib Dem ministers – and there were no plans to allow Tory junior ministers to have spads. But if all contentious policy issues were to be considered by both coalition partners, that could not happen if adequate resources were not available to the minority partner.

### The Lib Dem-led Model: DECC

The Department of Energy and Climate Change was one of only two mainstream departments headed by a Lib Dem Secretary of State. Chris Huhne was also unique in having only Tory ministers working for him.[6] Although this structure is relatively unusual in any coalition, it produced in DECC a balance that was not apparent in the other departments we studied. In particular, there was no struggle against the odds for the minority partner to make its voice heard. As a senior official said:

> In most departments, the challenge has been to consider on each issue which arises whether there might be a Lib Dem perspective and how to take account of that. For us, with a Lib Dem SoS, the Lib Dem perspective is much clearer from the outset. We don't have to research it in the same way.

In theory the corollary would be that the Tories feel their entitlement to a leading role in policy making on DECC issues might be compromised. But in practice no SoS from the minority party is likely to wish – or be able – to override the Coalition majority partner and must reach agreement.

It was very clear that the Coalition was working well within DECC and that tensions were few. A factor in this was that the DECC agenda received a considerable amount of attention in the PfG, reflecting, first, the potential of civil nuclear power to become a dividing line between the coalition partners and, second, the fact that both Oliver Letwin and Chris Huhne were persuaded of the fundamental importance of the department's agenda. The result was that DECC officials felt that the agenda was clear from day one and the debates were more technocratic in nature, with discussion focusing on the best means to achieve the objectives, rather than debate as to what the objectives should be. One official summarised it as follows:

> DECC has more words devoted to its agenda in the Programme for Government than any other department. And that is really helpful because it gives us a very detailed guide to determine our activities. And ministers are focused very much on the practicalities, not the politics.

One minister in the department also noted that all three parties were in broad agreement on the objectives: 'There is quite a difference between what Labour were doing and what we are doing. But it's not necessarily an ideological point about ends so much as differences of approach on means'. There was consensus that the ministers worked seamlessly as a team, with practical economic analysis and 'what works' dominating discussion. But one official did suggest that the fact of a coalition led to changes in the way the ministerial team operated:

---

[6] BIS, in addition to having a Lib Dem Secretary of State, also had a junior Lib Dem minister. Technically, the Scotland Office was in the same position as DECC in having a Lib Dem Secretary of State and a Tory junior minister – but in reality it was not really comparable because of its size and scope.

In my own Whitehall experience, it has been the norm to have a dominant SoS who takes the decisions, no doubt having listened to the views of the other minister, but still being very clearly the one in charge. But in DECC it's harder for the SoS to say to the other ministers, 'this is my decision, just shut up'. Things have to be brokered more.

Being on numerous Cabinet Committees placed particular demands on the Secretary of State, and this was a significant factor in the way the department was run. One official noted that, 'the SoS is much busier than his predecessor was because of the number of committees he sits on. In some weeks, the amount of time he has left for the department can be very limited'. So it was perhaps not surprising that the Secretary of State was obliged to delegate a great deal:

The SoS works well with junior ministers. Compared to many Secretaries of State, he does give them a fair amount of rein. But that's as much about personalities as the Coalition. It's very much his style to work in that way.

### The Tory-only Model: Defra

Defra was the largest of three main government departments without a Lib Dem minister. The challenge for Defra's ministers and officials was, therefore, how best to ensure that Defra 'coalitionised' its policies.

The Secretary of State, Caroline Spelman, set the tone from the top. An official noted:

The SoS takes the Coalition seriously and works hard to make it work. She is the most collegiate cabinet minister I have ever worked with. She is devoted to working constructively with her colleagues and she works hard at ensuring all our policies are discussed with Lib Dem ministers across the Cabinet.

But it was also recognised that Defra was not a hotbed of political disagreement between the coalition partners:

Ministers don't sit around the table wearing their party hat when tackling the issues they are responsible for. It's portfolio first and party second, not the other way around. That said, once they have reached a view, they then pause and say to themselves, 'How would this look from the perspective of the Coalition?'

In practical terms, Defra sought to respond to the lack of a Lib Dem minister in two ways: First, a weekly 'Coalition business meeting' was established. This was chaired by the Secretary of State and attended by all the Defra ministers, the spads, the Parliamentary Private Secretaries and, crucially in this context, Andrew George, co-chair of the Lib Dem Defra backbench committee, or Parliamentary Party Committee (see generally chapter six). This essentially political meeting – which officials did not attend – gave Defra ministers the opportunity to discuss emerging policies and allowed George the opportunity to influence policy making – if not at its inception, then at least before it was announced. Second, emerging policies were to be cleared through the Cabinet Committee system, which ensured that the Lib Dems had the opportunity to scrutinise Defra policies. As a result, 'committee clearance' came to have a much greater importance for Defra under the Coalition than it had previously – and more than for departments with different models.

The role of Andrew George was consistent with the growing importance of backbench co-chairs in the Lib Dem Party and was paralleled by Don Foster who led for the Lib Dems in DCMS, also a Tory-only department. However, Andrew George had no office support and no right of access to papers or formal briefings from civil servants. One senior official noted that because George attended 'political meetings' he had met him only once and he was not aware of policy changing as a result. But another official, closer to the Secretary of State's office, observed:

> It is important to recognise that Andrew George has no formal power, he has no veto; the formal agreement is given through the Cabinet Committee system, usually after we have spoken to Andrew but sometimes in parallel. George is there to ensure ministers understand the Lib Dem perspective before they seek formal approval. But there are issues where his views have led to a change in approach. His role is advisory but ministers will reflect on what he has said and may well decide to change their approach accordingly.

Andrew George himself was broadly supportive of the way the role was developing. He felt he got on well with the Defra ministers and that there was respect on both sides. He was clear that there had been several issues in relation to which he had influenced the outcome, mainly in terms of presentation and handling, but also with regard to policy. He noted that he was not bound to support the government position in a way that a Parliamentary Private Secretary (PPS) would be – so he was free to speak against the government position in the House. But he often found himself defending Defra ministers against criticism from Lib Dem backbenchers, as he had been satisfied through his discussion with ministers of the logic of their proposals. He also often provided background briefings on Defra issues for the Lib Dem ministerial members of the various Cabinet Committees, in that special advisers would often contact him to see if he had been consulted on the issue concerned. A frustration with the role, however, was the lack of support he received from Defra officials: for example, the limits on his ability to receive papers or background briefings for public meetings. But overall, he thought that Defra ministers were genuinely seeking to make the Coalition work as it should.

The increased importance of Cabinet Committees was broadly welcomed by Defra officials and ensured that Defra policies had formal 'sign-off' from the Lib Dems. It did, however, involve more work for officials in briefing the committee chairs than they thought would have been the case if there had been a Lib Dem minister in the department. An unexpected 'perverse outcome' for the department was that in order to ensure that all committees had substantial representation from both coalition partners, those departments with no Lib Dem ministers had fewer committee places than they had previously, and Defra were irritated that they no longer had a place by right on the European Affairs Committee where much Defra business had previously been done.

It is important to stress, however, the considerable degree of overlap between the coalition parties on Defra-related issues. It was not clear that there had been any issues in the first 18 months of the Coalition where the two parties would have been expected to split along party lines. There was agreement that the most controversial Defra policy in the first 12 months – the Forestry Commission – would not have worked out differently with a Lib Dem minister in the department. Nor was it expected that the most sensitive future issue – the possible culling of badgers – would lead to coalition tensions as that was seen as causing a potential rift between rural farming and urban animal protection lobbies, with many Lib Dems supporting the farming perspective.

Overall, therefore, Defra officials reported that they approved of the way that the Coalition was working in the department, but also that relatively little had changed. One official noted that for the first six or nine months, 'the most note-worthy aspect was how "undifferent" it felt from single-party government. There was so little disagreement between the coalition partners on our agenda'. That said, there was a certain disappointment amongst some officials that the Coalition might be passing them by. Another official said:

> Not having a Lib Dem minister has meant that the Coalition has been very low impact on us. We did not really need to think about 'coalitionising' our policies and no one thought very much about the Coalition . . . Our only real check comes at the level of the Cabinet committee stage at which point we get the DPM and other senior Lib Dem input. But officials aren't really thinking about the Coalition in the development of policies before that stage . . . The central strategy team might be aware of the specific issues of difference but officials at working level are not. The decision to make us a Tory only department may well have been the right one, given the policies overlap so much. But it does make us rather disengaged from the Coalition and the dynamic of making it work.

It is arguable that the existence of departments with no Lib Dem ministers, such as Defra, DCMS and DfID, created a 'coalition deficit' in that the junior partner had to take a great deal on trust. Even when a backbench Lib Dem MP such as Don Foster or Andrew George had a defined role, their impact was limited to seeking to modify policy with no real opportunity to initiate it. But the overall arithmetic in any given coalition is unlikely to permit the minority partner to have a ministerial appointment in every department. So choices are going to have to be made – and the degree of consensus over policy in Defra, DfID and DCMS suggests that they were correctly identified as being the most appropriate Tory-only teams.

CONCLUSION

The impact of the Coalition on how departments conduct the business of government can be broadly summarised as follows:

1. change has been less dramatic than the civil service expected; and
2. to the extent that there have been changes, those changes have been broadly regarded by departments as positive or, at worst, neutral.

There should perhaps be no surprise at either of these conclusions. First, the way a government operates is largely handed down from one government to the next and changes in conduct are incremental and measured. Moreover, the new Government had much political capital tied up in not only working together constructively as a coalition but also in being seen to be working together. So radical change in internal processes was perhaps never likely. Indeed, the pre-election approach of both coalition partners had been to accuse the Labour Government of riding roughshod over the usual checks and balances of government.

Moreover, the tone of the new Government had been set so clearly by the incoming Prime Minister and Deputy Prime Minister that all ministers felt a duty to make the Coalition work. Earlier Governments might have had more detailed policy plans for office – and the incoming Labour administration in 1997 was in many respects better prepared for government – but there is no recent precedent of an incoming government being so committed to working in unison. And each of the Secretaries of State at DCLG, DECC and Defra put in place the necessary arrangements to ensure that both coalition parties were signed up to their policies.

Similarly, it should come as no surprise that departments regarded those changes positively. A focus on more internal discussion, the use of formal processes through the Cabinet Committee machinery and a more modest role for special advisers were all issues which were likely to be supported by a civil service which felt it had been significantly marginalised in recent years.

None of this means that the initial enthusiasm for the Coalition will last – nor indeed does it mean that the civil service could be said to have any natural bias in favour of coalition. Just as political parties get tired and jaded by too many years of government, so the civil service can become jaded by serving the same set of ministers through successive elections. So any incoming government is usually treated with some enthusiasm, and the positive reaction to the Coalition in 2010 was not substantively different from the support that Tony Blair's government received in 1997.

The issue was just how long the initial Whitehall optimism and enthusiasm for the style of the Coalition would last. There were undoubtedly some straws in the wind which suggested that it might not last all that long.

First, government is always tougher in practice than incoming administrations anticipate. Policies that look attractive in opposition prove in government to be more problematic and the benefits prove harder and slower to realise than expected. For the first year of government, there is a massive agenda and a broad assumption that new policy approaches will produce results. When they prove disappointing, a sense of frustration follows.

Second, as noted, some of the changes in process following the election had negative aspects which might not have been entirely apparent after only 18 months. Perhaps the most worrying was the concern that departments were more focused on their own agenda and priorities and paid less attention to the interaction between their policy priorities and those of other departments. The last

Labour Government was regularly accused of being over-centralised in the way it ran Whitehall – but there are dangers in both directions.

Third, over time, all governments develop internal tensions which arise from the fact that politics is about personal ambition and rivalries as well as the battle of ideas. At the time of writing, the Coalition Government seemed remarkably free of such rivalries – but it would be foolish to assume from this that they will not develop in due course.

Fourth, the most striking distinction between a coalition and single-party government is that a coalition marches to a different timetable. Single-party governments may have internal arguments but the closer they get to the next general election, the more they tend to unite and demonstrate a united purpose. But in coalition government, while the initial priority is unity, the more the general election comes into focus, the more the parties will seek to demonstrate their differences, not their similarities. In our interviews, we asked how people saw the 'disengagement' process between the coalition partners being managed. We were given no answers; the common response was 'we will deal with it when we get there'.

Finally, one potential advantage of a coalition – at least in the eyes of Whitehall officials – is that there should be less frenetic activity towards the end of the current Parliament than usual. A feature of single-party governments in the run-up to a general election is an obsession with new announcements which are often short-term 'headline grabbers', rather than fully developed policies. Given that both coalition partners will want to be emphasising differences not similarities at that point, it seems likely that the final year of the Government may turn out to be somewhat calmer than usual in Whitehall – though no doubt the political debate outside Whitehall will be intense.

# 6

# *The Coalition in Parliament*

## BEN YONG

What we have is a coalition government, not a coalition Parliament. (Lib Dem peer)

### INTRODUCTION

COALITIONS GOVERN JOINTLY, but at election time the partners must compete for votes separately. We have called this the unity/distinctiveness dilemma. These competing incentives create problems in the management of the Coalition in the legislature.

In the case of the Conservative-Lib Dem Coalition, for the frontbench what mattered was getting legislation through Parliament. To achieve this, they needed to coordinate their two sets of backbenchers. For the backbenchers, cooperation was important, but equally important was re-election and asserting their distinctive party identity. To this end, each set of backbenchers sought to influence their frontbench to implement party – rather than government – policy.

This chapter looks at the impact of being in a coalition on the Conservative and Liberal Democrat parliamentary parties, and to a lesser extent at the impact of the Coalition on Parliament as an institution. The next chapter will look at the parties more generally: in particular the relationship between the leadership and the party, and the longer term considerations for the two coalition parties.

### THE WESTMINSTER PARLIAMENT

The Westminster Parliament has long been thought of as a 'weak' legislature, with the Executive generally dominating the legislature and the legislative agenda. Parliamentary sovereignty is, in practice, executive sovereignty, because of the fusion of executive and legislature, and single-party majority rule. So coalition government seemed to promise something new – possibly, a loosening of the Executive's stranglehold over the legislature – because there were now two parties in government with different values and ideologies. For those who believed in 'strong government', then, coalition government suggested weakness, delay and indecision; for those who believed in a stronger role for Parliament, coalition government suggested greater influence for the backbench and greater autonomy from the Executive.

In truth that image of a weak, impotent Parliament is a caricature, and in recent years it has come under criticism from academics, who have pointed to increasingly rebellious backbench MPs, a more independent House of Lords and other indicators of backbench influence.[1] That did not mean that the Executive was weak: rather, the picture was more nuanced. Government will normally get its way. But this is more often a matter of cajoling and persuasion than command and fiat.

As a result of forming a coalition, the Government had a majority in the House of Commons and a larger working majority in the House of Lords. In the Commons the Government had a total of 363 MPs (Conservatives 306, Liberal Democrats 57) and a working government majority of around 80 MPs. In the Lords, there was now a larger number of government peers than under the previous New Labour Government. Combined, government peers numbered 309 (Conservatives 217, Liberal Democrats 92), while Labour peers numbered 242. This was a *relative* government majority, as discipline, attendance and voting patterns in the Lords have always differed from the Commons; and because the Lords also consisted of other groups, such as the Crossbenchers, who made up almost one-third (238) of the chamber's membership as a whole.

So at least in terms of arithmetic, the management of Parliament looked favourable for the Coalition. But the new Parliament had an unknown quality about it. Over one-third of all MPs (225) were new to the House of Commons: this was slightly fewer than in 1997, when 260 MPs entered the Commons for the first time, but it still signalled a change to how Parliament might work. New entrants made up almost half (148 MPs) of the Conservative Party in the Commons, almost one-fifth (10 MPs) of the Liberal Democrats, and a quarter (67 MPs) of Labour.

The House of Lords also saw many new arrivals. One hundred and seventeen life peerages were created between May 2010 and April 2011, in part to redress the perceived imbalance in numbers between government and Labour peers. This brought the formal total number of Lords close to 800. The added pressure on scarce resources, peers competing to contribute to debates in the chamber, and the sudden influx of new peers not acculturated to the courteous, non-partisan ethos of the House led to a more fractious atmosphere in the Lords.[2]

---

[1] P Cowley, *The Rebels: How Blair Mislaid his Majority* (London, Politico's, 2005); M Russell and M Sciara, 'The Policy Impact of Defeats in the House of Lords' (2008) 10 *British Journal of Politics and International Relations* 571; M Russell and M Benton, *Selective Influence: The Policy Impact of House of Commons Select Committees* (London, Constitution Unit, 2011).

[2] M Russell, *House Full: Time to Get a Grip on Lords Appointments* (London, Constitution Unit, 2011).

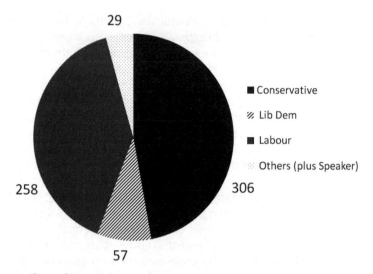

Figure 6.1 Share of Seats in House of Commons 2010–11

Source: Parliament website: www.parliament.uk/mps-lords-and-offices/mps/state-of-the-parties

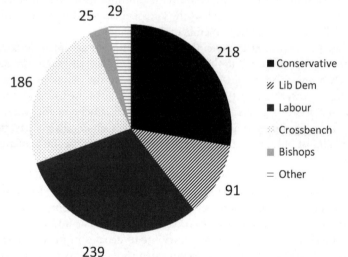

Figure 6.2 Share of Seats in House of Lords 2010–11

Source: Parliament website: www.parliament.uk/mps-lords-and-offices/lords/lords-by-type-and-party

There were also institutional changes, which had carried over from the last Parliament – in particular, the Wright reforms.[3] Commons Select Committee

---

[3] M Russell, '"Never Allow a Crisis to Go to Waste": The Wright Committee Reforms to Strengthen the House of Commons' (2011) 64(4) *Parliamentary Affairs* 612.

chairs in the new Parliament were elected via secret ballot of the whole House, while other members were elected by their respective parties; and a backbench business committee was established to organise non-government business in Parliament. Both of these reforms had the potential to strengthen the role and influence of backbenchers; but they did not result from having a coalition government.[4]

So what happened in Parliament over the first 18 months of an unusually long first session?[5] Given that the Coalition had a comfortable majority in the Commons and a plurality in the Lords, what might have been expected was a relatively quiescent Parliament.

In fact, there was unprecedented rebelliousness.[6] Both Houses had a heavy parliamentary agenda: there was legislation on constitutional reform, Europe, localism, health and welfare reform, amongst other matters. By the end of October 2011 there had been well over 150 separate revolts in the Commons by government MPs, some of which were significant, such as votes on tuition fees and a referendum on the EU. That was more than any single parliamentary session since the end of World War Two, even if the session was an unusually long one. These rebellions took place in the first session following a change of government, when rebellions would generally be expected to be at their lowest. Most of the rebellious MPs were Conservative, but they represented a minority – perhaps a quarter – of the parliamentary party as a whole. By contrast, at the end of 18 months all Liberal Democrat backbench MPs had rebelled at least once, save one.[7] Still, in that same period the Coalition did not lose a division in the Commons. That was partly because of the Coalition's majority, and partly because members of the two parties rebelled on different matters: the Conservatives on constitutional issues, particularly Europe, and the Liberal Democrats on social issues.

In the Lords there were 25 defeats in the first 18 months. Serious defeats in the Lords included the Public Bodies Bill and the Parliamentary Voting and

---

[4] Although the Coalition deserves the credit for implementing them, which the outgoing Labour Government had failed to do. The Conservative manifesto contained a commitment to implement the Wright reforms; and Sir George Young, the new Leader of the House of Commons, did so at the start of the 2010 Parliament.

[5] In September 2010 the Government announced that the State Opening of Parliament would move from November 2011 to Easter 2012, meaning in effect that the first session of Parliament would be almost two years long. This was done ostensibly in anticipation of the (then) Fixed Term Parliaments Bill, which would establish a fixed, five-year parliamentary term. Following implementation of the bill a parliamentary term would then consist of five one-year sessions: extending the first session of the 2010–15 Parliament would avoid a final session of just a few months. Critics noted, however, that extending the first session had the benefit of giving the Coalition additional time to pass its demanding first session legislative programme: any bills that were not enacted within the session could not be carried over into the next session.

[6] This paragraph is based on the work of Phil Cowley and Mark Stuart: see www.revolts.co.uk and www.nottspolitics.org/2011/07/05/ten-things-we-know-about-coalition-mps

[7] The one MP who had not voted against the whip was David Laws. See P Cowley and M Stuart, 'The Independent View: And then there was one … (Unmasked! The only backbench Lib Dem MP 100% loyal to the Coalition)' *Lib Dem Voice* (18 November 2011), www.libdemvoice.org/the-independent-view-and-then-there-was-one-unmasked-the-only-backbench-lib-dem-mp-100-loyal-to-the-coalition-25914.html

Constituencies Bill (see chapter nine). And in spite of having a very long first parliamentary session, long debates in the Lords had put the legislative timetable under severe pressure. Defeats in the Lords are not uncommon, however. Discipline is difficult in a chamber where there is little scope for promotion. More importantly, since the removal of hereditary peers in 1997 no political party in the Lords has had an overall majority. That has made it more difficult for governments to pass their legislation through the upper house.

Under New Labour, the ratio of defeats to divisions was one in three: in 2010–11, the ratio was one in five. The Coalition would only lose a division in the Lords because of its greater plurality. The first 18 months suggested that the Government was only likely to lose a division if the Crossbenchers attended and voted in large numbers against the Government.

Many Conservative and Liberal Democrat interviewees voiced the suspicion that the Crossbenchers were beginning to vote more coherently as a group, and that they had become the swing vote in the Lords. Certainly, in terms of defeats, the Crossbenchers' vote in this period was a contributing factor in over three-quarters of all defeats in the Lords.[8] That was historically unusual: under New Labour the Crossbenchers' contribution to defeats was only significant in one defeat in five. Labour peers, aware of the Crossbenchers' potential role as the swing vote, 'courted' the Crossbenchers on key issues such as health reform. But the Crossbenchers were wary of being 'enlisted' by one party or another.

Arguably, however, the Crossbenchers' behaviour under the Coalition was consistent with past behaviour. Historically Crossbenchers had a record of voting slightly against the Government, their claim being that they voted against 'bad legislation'. They had the lowest rate of attendance, but often turned out for high profile issues; and their votes tended to be decisive on moral and civil liberties issues. So it remained to be seen whether the Crossbenchers' behaviour under the Coalition was a response to the legislative workload of the first 18 months, rather than a fundamental change.

So the first 18 months saw a busy, rebellious Parliament, but it was not yet unmanageable. The Government remained in control. Voting patterns, however, are only part of the picture. We need to look at Parliament in more detail to see how the Coalition worked. Here we will look at the two coalition partners both together and separately: first, to describe the mechanisms of interparty cooperation and coordination, mostly between the two frontbenches; and second, to describe the mechanisms established by each parliamentary party to influence and communicate with the frontbench. We give further, more in-depth examples of the impact of the Coalition on the legislative process in chapters nine and ten.

---

[8] Our thanks to Meg Russell and Meghan Benton for providing us with this analysis, an earlier version of which can be found in M Russell and M Sciara, 'Why does the Government Get Defeated in the House of Lords? The Lords, the Party System and British Politics' (2007) 2 *British Politics* 299.

Table 6.1 The Five Biggest Commons Rebellions, 2010–11

| Date | Bill or policy area | Conservative rebels | Lib Dem rebels | Total rebels |
|------|---------------------|---------------------|----------------|--------------|
| 24 Oct 2011 | EU membership referendum | 81 | 1 | 82 |
| 22 Oct 2011 | Protection of Freedoms Bill | 41 | 2 | 43 |
| 9 Dec 2010 | Tuition fees increase | 6 | 21 | 27 |
| 11 Jan 2011 | EU Bill (parliamentary sovereignty amendment) | 25 | 0 | 25 |
| 10 Nov 2010 | EU economic governance | 25 | 0 | 25 |

Source: www.publicwhip.org.uk

Table 6.2  The Five Biggest Government Defeats in the Lords, 2010–11

| Date | Bill | Conservative | | Labour | | Lib Dem | | Crossbenchers and others | | Government |
|------|------|-----|------|---|---|---|---|---|---|---------|
| | | For | Agst | F | A | F | A | F | A | majority |
| 14 Dec 2010 | Public Bodies Bill (Chief Coroner) | 141 | 0 | 0 | 178 | 20 | 4 | 4 | 95 | −112 |
| 19 Jan 2011 | PVSC Bill* (Isle of Wight constituency) | 75 | 28 | 0 | 123 | 45 | 14 | 2 | 31 | −74 |
| 14 Dec 2011 | Welfare Reform Bill (Under-occupancy) | 144 | 1 | 0 | 159 | 44 | 14 | 2 | 84 | −68 |
| 28 Mar 2011 | Public Bodies Bill (Youth Justice Commission) | 107 | 5 | 0 | 157 | 49 | 7 | 6 | 56 | −63 |
| 16 Feb 2011 | PVSC Bill (AV referendum turnout) | 122 | 27 | 0 | 183 | 74 | 1 | 19 | 66 | −62 |

* PVSC Bill – Parliamentary Voting System and Constituencies Bill
Source: www.ucl.ac.uk/constitution-unit/research/parliament/house-of-lords/lords-defeats

## COOPERATION AND COORDINATION

We saw in chapter four that at 'the Centre' – No 10, the Deputy Prime Minister's Office and the Cabinet Office – strong personal relationships were formed between ministers in both coalition parties. In Parliament, however, the picture was more complicated. There was cooperation at the top, with daily and weekly meetings between key parliamentary leaders and party whips. But at the 'bottom', backbenchers in the coalition parties responded to being in a coalition as separate parties. This was a business relationship, not a meeting of minds.

## The Coalition Agreement

The Interim Coalition Agreement (Interim Agreement) and the Programme for Government (PfG) together operated as a key focal point around which coalition cooperation and coordination took place. Interviewees sometimes distinguished between the Interim Agreement and the PfG (referring to the Coalition Agreement or Agreements), but since the majority of interviewees focused on the PfG, for simplicity's sake we will refer to that as 'the Coalition Agreement' unless otherwise stated. Parliamentarian interviewees in both parties talked of the Coalition Agreement as 'the bible' – but often in a resigned, unenthusiastic manner. It was a contract, the terms of which both parties felt obliged to adhere to; and on many issues this adherence was expected to be unquestioning, because the compromises reached were finely tuned on both sides. One Lib Dem minister said:

> Where we've had to go along with things in the Coalition Agreement which we never really liked, we're gritting our teeth and holding our nose, and we're doing it because it's an agreement. . . . How are we going to get them to agree to House of Lords reform, and vote for it, if we don't vote on other things that we don't like?

Backbenchers and interest groups alike spoke of how ministers always returned to the Coalition Agreement as their key point of reference. One interviewee said: 'If you press [ministers], they will say, "privately, I agree with you: we didn't want it – but the Coalition Agreements say otherwise"'. For some backbenchers, however, the Coalition Agreement did not compel obedience. According to one Conservative MP:

> None of us fought the election on the coalition manifesto, so various colleagues have worries about various things the Government are doing. The whips can't say to them, 'But you've got to vote for this because you won your seat, because this was part of the manifesto', which often sways people . . . we can just say, 'Well, it wasn't. I didn't sign up for this and I don't like it'.

Indeed, some MPs would argue that they were not rebelling *against* things they stood for at election, but rather in *favour* of things they stood for at election.

In the Lords, the status of the Coalition Agreement was ambiguous. Since the Agreement was not presented to the public prior to the election, some argued that the Salisbury-Addison convention did not apply. Crudely put, the convention was that the Lords would not substantially amend or wreck a government bill if it appeared in the Government's election manifesto.[9] At the end of the first 18

---

[9] The best analysis of the Salisbury-Addison Convention can be found in Joint Committee on Conventions, 'Conventions of the UK Parliament' HC (2005–06) 1212-1, www.publications.parliament. uk/pa/jt200506/jtselect/jtconv/265/265.pdf

months, the application of the convention to the Coalition Agreement remained an open question.[10]

There were two further matters, since 'Coalition agreements are the script, not the play'.[11] The first related to the interpretation and implementation of the Agreement. There were debates in both parties about whether the Agreement should be interpreted narrowly or more broadly – a narrow interpretation usually being demanded when the pledge originally came from the other party's manifesto. Witness one Lib Dem peer discussing the European Union Bill:

> [If] you look at the Coalition Agreement it does make some references to referenda on treaty change, which we would have accepted, reluctantly. . . . We agreed to add [it] . . . to the sacred list of things where there had to be a referendum. But we saw absolutely no reason whatsoever why that should then be extended to 56 other issues . . . that's why we felt perfectly free to be against it.

Dealing with areas where the Coalition Agreement was silent was also problematic. Both parties approached such areas on a case-by-case basis, but there was a general feeling that parliamentarians might be less committed on those issues that fell outside the terms of the Agreement. In short, the Coalition Agreement was a tool for the Government to assert and enforce discipline, but it had limits. As the parliamentary term continues, its importance and influence may wane.

## The Whips and Party Discipline

In the Commons, Patrick McLoughlin and Alastair Carmichael, the chief whips of the Conservative and Liberal Democrats, met daily with their teams.[12] Both parties' teams also met before the daily coalition whips' meeting to discuss internal issues and cooperation.[13] In the Lords, the respective parties' chief whips had adjoining offices, and were in contact two to three times a day; and the two parties' teams met together weekly. Finally, there were also weekly meetings for each coalition partner's Commons and Lords Whips to ensure coordination between the Houses.

Cooperation among the whips created few problems. Both parties' whips were pleased to have a decent working government majority in the Commons. As already noted, rebellions were numerous but remained small in scale, most of them involving MPs from only one of the two coalition partners. Having a

[10] See the evidence of the then Crossbenchers Convenor, Baroness D'Souza, www.publications. parliament.uk/pa/cm201011/cmselect/cmpolcon/528/528vw06.htm

[11] WC Müller and K Strøm, 'Coalition Agreements and Cabinet Governance' in K Strøm, WC Müller and T Bergman (eds), *Cabinets and Coalition Bargaining: The Democratic Life Cycle in Western Europe* (Oxford University Press, 2008) 159.

[12] In the Commons there were 14 Conservative whips, two of whom were unpaid; the Liberal Democrats had three official whips, and three unofficial whips (who were also unpaid). The three unofficial whips (Stephen Gilbert, Robert Smith and Tessa Munt) were appointed to lighten the new workload brought about by entering government.

[13] I Dale, 'In conversation with . . . Patrick McLoughlin' *Total Politics* (1 November 2011), www. totalpolitics.com/articles/268817/in-conversation-with-patrick-mcloughlin.thtml

coalition and a solid majority was a double-edged sword. Having a coalition with a majority worked for the whips and the frontbench – witness the comments of one government Commons whip:

> If there is likely to be a rebellion on the Tory side, usually over Europe, then there's a particular need for a Lib Dem presence, and likewise . . . if there are issues where the Lib Dems might be flaky.

But there was potentially a greater incentive for backbenchers to vote against the Government: they were safe in the belief that they could rebel without the Government losing the vote entirely.

Under the Coalition, everyday interaction between the frontbench and backbench continued as usual, but the job of the whips in both Houses became more demanding. Various mechanisms were established in both parties (see below) to ensure good lines of communication between frontbench and backbench. These mechanisms were useful, but they meant more discussion, and more meetings. Time became a precious resource. As one Liberal Democrat Lords whip said:

> One other thing we've learned about coalitions is that it means more meetings. What you really need is a pre-meeting to talk about what you're going to talk about; then the meeting; and then a post-meeting meeting; and then you meet with backbenchers to explain what you've achieved. That's half a day gone.

When enforcing discipline within the coalition parties, the government whips in both Houses acted as separate teams. Party discipline had to be tightened: in the Commons, the number of three-line whips increased for both government parties. This caused resentment, with backbenchers from both parties feeling that they were being whipped because of the other party's recalcitrance. And the whips' job was more difficult because there was less patronage available: there were fewer ministerial posts to offer because they had to be shared between two parties; and Select Committee posts were subject to election. Changes to electoral boundaries may become a potential future source of dissent, as individual MPs begin to assess the probability of re-election.[14]

However, the majority of government MPs followed the whip of their own accord: resentment had not yet crystallised into anything threatening to the Coalition. It may be that the various institutional arrangements established following the Coalition's formation channelled resentment into more effective or productive forums, as discussed below.

In the Lords, many peers had the familiar sense of being ignored by a new government. That neglect manifested itself in several ways: the small number of ministers appointed from the Lords; the poor quality of legislation arriving in the House; and the rise in appointments to the Lords. As in the Commons, there were attempts to increase discipline:

---

[14] The Parliamentary Voting Systems and Constituencies Act 2011 provided for the process of reducing the number of UK constituencies from 650 to 600 by 2015. If implemented, the impact of the boundary reforms will be to increase competition for seats. For more on this Act see ch 9.

[Discipline] was very loose in opposition – they would put out a whip saying it's a two-line whip or three-line whip or whatever. Now as a whip I ring round all my people every weekend . . . Very unpleasant especially when you've got people who are rebels . . . I get an earful. (Conservative Lords whip)

In short, party discipline tightened under the Coalition in both Houses of Parliament. That was natural: discipline – enforcement of the party line – always strengthens when going into government. But this did not mean that there was greater *cohesion* – that is, shared agreement between each party and within each party.

## Backbenchers: 'A Business Relationship'

Backbench MPs from both parties showed no enthusiasm for joint party meetings. They acknowledged the need for unified government, but they worried about distinctiveness. And ensuring distinctiveness meant differentiation and separation:

I talk to [the Lib Dem] ministers because I regard them as part of the Coalition Government, but I don't talk to their [backbench] . . . because they're trying to run a different political party . . . we've got to keep the flame of our parties alight . . . We're trying to differentiate ourselves. (Conservative MP)

A Liberal Democrat MP made a similar point:

I'm less keen on doing [bipartisan meetings] . . . we have to keep the distinctiveness between us as parties . . . We have to keep our complete separate identities as political parties, work together at ministerial level.

In the Lords, there was more interaction between the two government parties, because Conservative and Lib Dem peers had worked together closely in opposition during the 13 years of New Labour. So in 2010–11 there were bipartisan meetings to discuss key legislation such as the Parliamentary Voting System and Constituencies Bill and on the NHS reforms; and there were moves for more coordinated meetings between the chairs of Liberal Democrat and Conservative backbench committees. The behaviour of Labour peers in the first year also pushed the two coalition parties together. One Liberal Democrat peer said of the Labour Party:

The business over the AV [Alternative Vote] bill just strengthened that feeling that we're just going to beat these bastards. In the course of nine months, we've gone from a majority of Lib Dems wishing the maths had worked out better to our current position where we don't want anything to do with them, frankly.

### THE PARLIAMENTARY PARTIES

Having dealt with the machinery of coordination and cooperation between the parties, we now look at how unity and distinctiveness were managed within the parliamentary parties. In the sections that follow we first set out each parliamentary party's subjective experience of the Coalition and go on to examine key forums in which coalition problems were raised.

## The Liberal Democrat Parliamentary Party

Having formed a coalition, the parliamentary party was surprised at how little thought had been given to some of the consequences of that decision.[15] One such consequence was the loss of Short Money and Cranborne Money, money provided by the state for opposition parties but which is not available to parties in government. The negotiating team had not discussed this issue at all during negotiations, despite such funding coming to approximately £2 million, or a third of the Liberal Democrats' income.[16] In the weeks following coalition formation, talks between the two parties on how to resolve this funding crisis continued, but were terminated following the resignation of Lib Dem Chief Secretary to the Treasury, David Laws.

The loss of state funding did not pose much of a problem for the Conservatives, who were generously funded by private donors, but it had devastating immediate and long-term effects on the Lib Dems. Many of the staff in the Parliamentary Office who dealt with party policy had to go. The parliamentary party responded to this both by seeking personnel secondments from companies sharing an interest, and by relying more heavily on the researchers of Lib Dem MPs. A levy was placed on peers and ministers in order to fund additional parliamentary support.[17] Almost all Liberal Democrat interviewees complained of a crippling lack of resources.

Many Liberal Democrats also found it difficult to shift from opposition to being in government. As one Liberal Democrat special adviser stated: 'It is much harder than simply moving probing amendments. We're in government now, and so we deliver differently'. That transition was made more difficult by the Liberal Democrat leadership's adoption of the so-called 'three-point plan' for coalition relations, focusing in the first phase on unity rather than distinctiveness (see chapter eight). In the first phase, the Lib Dems would prioritise unity and cooperation over party differentiation; in the second phase at mid term the party would renew itself and its identity; and in the final phase – not before April 2015 – the Lib Dems would engage in explicit differentiation.[18] The first phase was meant to give the Liberal Democrats credibility in government, but it also increased tensions within the parliamentary party, who felt muzzled.

---

[15] For more on this see ch 3.

[16] T Bale and E Sanderson-Nash, 'A Leap of Faith and a Leap in the Dark: The Impact of the Coalition on the Conservatives and the Liberal Democrats' in S Lee and M Beech (eds), *The Cameron-Clegg Government: Coalition Politics in an Age of Austerity* (Basingstoke, Palgrave Macmillan, 2011).

[17] ibid.

[18] M d'Ancona, 'The Tories couldn't deliver the goods without the Lib Dems' *Telegraph* (15 January 2011), www.telegraph.co.uk/comment/columnists/matthewd_ancona/8262007/The-Tories-couldnt-deliver-the-goods-without-the-Lib-Dems.html

The decision to deal with the deficit more speedily than the Lib Dems had envisioned during their campaign was mostly a matter decided within the Executive. The impact of the 2010 Comprehensive Spending Review was delayed and staggered, so the parliamentary party and the wider party were able to stomach this. In contrast, the vote to raise university tuition fees led to great tensions within the parliamentary party, and in a serious failure of party management, Lib Dem MPs voted three different ways (see chapter ten).

Concern over the proposed NHS reforms, losing the AV referendum and then suffering losses in local government elections in May 2011 compounded Lib Dem regrets over the first year, and the decision to emphasise unity in government at the expense of party distinctiveness. As one Liberal Democrat minister said: 'Where we made a mistake in our first year . . . was in being more "coalition than the Coalition" . . . for things that we actually weren't desperately enthusiastic about'.

There was recognition from the Lib Dem frontbench that there needed to be greater engagement with the backbenchers. Witness one Lib Dem minister's remarks:

> Reflecting back, for the first nine months or so it felt it was my role to explain and justify the government's position to the party and to stakeholders – but it wasn't to broker agreement between the parties and the Government. But as a result of our experiences, the role has changed to a degree and has become more one of brokering agreement with the party.

This stance was not merely adopted because of the leadership's insistence on unity, though. It was also a product of the nature of the legislation coming through. Some of it was the product of compromise fought out in the Executive, and Lib Dem ministers were unable or unwilling to reopen debate again – so it was presented to backbenchers as a fait accompli. This did not sit well with backbenchers who were either used to being in opposition or at least used to debating issues in more depth. And so there was frustration (see chapters nine and ten). As already noted, almost every Lib Dem MP had rebelled at least once over this period, and that was unusual. The Conservative parliamentary party at least had a history of dissent – such as during John Major's time – but the Lib Dem parliamentary party did not. Contrary to its public image, it had long been the most highly disciplined and cohesive of the three main parties at Westminster. The Lib Dems were showing the strain of being in government.

So the first 18 months were marked by the realities of managing the transition from opposition, and attempting to find a balance between unity in government and maximising party distinctiveness. But although the Liberal Democrats were new to government, of the two coalition parties they developed the more sophisticated institutional arrangements to respond to the pressures of being in a coalition.

### Managing, Monitoring and Representation: The Liberal Democrat Parliamentary Party's Institutional Arrangements

*1. The Parliamentary Party Plenary Meeting*

The key forum for the parliamentary party remained the weekly plenary meeting of all 57 Liberal Democrat MPs, including those in the Government, plus special advisers (spads) and some peers (though there was also a separate meeting for Lib Dems in the Lords). There was a discussion of forthcoming business in the Commons and the Lords; a media report; a presentation; and a report from Nick Clegg, who almost invariably arrived late. Conservative ministers were occasionally invited to parliamentary party meetings in the Commons and the Lords when specific subjects were being discussed.

In theory, the plenary meeting was the sovereign parliamentary body, where tough decisions were made (eg on tuition fees). But as one Liberal Democrat MP noted, the parliamentary party meeting was 'not quite as important as before . . . now we are informed of decisions agreed by ministers'. One MP was more acerbic:

> There is a danger it's developing into a North Korean format of the great leader comes along . . . [tells] everyone they're wrong and then leaves. . . . Cabinet ministers in particular need to . . . appreciate the concerns of their colleagues and not instantly dismiss them. [For example] the date of the referendum, even where Lib Dems for six months or more were saying, 'This is awful, this is going to end in a crash if we don't do something about it'. And we were constantly told, 'It's going to be all right'.

*2. Representatives and Parliamentary Party Committees*

For the Lib Dems, being in coalition required ensuring that there were visible representatives of the party, as well as of the Government. Shortly after Vince Cable became Secretary of State for Business, Innovation and Skills, he stepped down as Deputy Leader of the Lib Dems in the Commons, and Simon Hughes MP was elected. In the Lords, Lord Alderdice was elected by Lib Dem peers to be their Convenor. This was partly a response to workload – both Cable and Lord McNally (Leader of the Lib Dems in the Lords) were now ministers; but it was also about the need to ensure an identifiable voice for the concerns of the backbench.

However, it was in the party's backbench committees that the impact of being in a coalition was most clear. The Liberal Democrats established their Parliamentary Party Committees (PPCs), which were to shadow government departments, in the early months of the Coalition.[19] They were a continuation of the Liberal Democrat policy teams that had existed in previous parliaments, but were modified to deal with being in a coalition.

---

[19] These were initially known as 'Backbench Committees', then 'Parliamentary Policy Committees', before finally being called 'Parliamentary Party Committees'.

Table 6.3  Liberal Democrat Parliamentary Party Committees, 2010–11

| Name of committee/department shadowed | Co-chairs of committees |
|---|---|
| Business, Innovation & Skills (BIS) + Treasury (merged) | Lorely Burt MP (Co-chair for BIS) <br> Lord Razzall (Co-chair for BIS) <br> Stephen Williams MP (Treasury) <br> Lord Newby (Treasury) |
| Communities & Local Government | Annette Brooke MP <br> Lord Tope |
| Constitutional & Political Reform (including Cabinet & House Business) | Mark Williams MP <br> Lord Tyler <br> Lord Maclennan (Cabinet Office) |
| Culture, Media & Sport | Don Foster MP <br> Baroness Bonham-Carter |
| Education, Families & Young People | Dan Rogerson MP <br> Baroness Walmsley |
| Energy & Climate Change (DECC) + Environment, Food and Rural Affairs (Defra) | Andrew George MP (DECC and Defra) <br> Lord Teverson (DECC) <br> Lord Greaves (Defra) |
| Health & Social Care | John Pugh MP <br> Lord Alderdice (May 2010–Summer 2011) <br> Baroness Jolly (from Summer 2011) |
| Home Affairs, Justice & Equalities | Tom Brake MP <br> Baroness Hamwee (Home Office) <br> Lord Thomas of Gresford OBE QC (MoJ) |
| International Affairs (FCO, Defence & DfID) | Martin Horwood MP <br> Baroness Falkner (FCO) <br> Lord Lee of Trafford (MoD) <br> Lord Chidgey (DFID) |
| Work and Pensions | Jenny Willott MP <br> Lord German |
| Transport | Julian Huppert MP <br> Lord Bradshaw |
| Northern Ireland | Stephen Lloyd MP <br> Lord Smith of Clifton |
| Scotland | John Thurso MP <br> Lord Maclennan |
| Wales | Roger Williams MP |
| Co-chairs | Tom Brake MP (convener) |

Sources: Personal interviews and T Grew, 'Lib Dems appoint backbench policy chiefs' *epolitix* (28 March 2011), www.epolitix.com/1832-blog/blog-post/newsarticle/lib-dems-appoint-backbench-policy-chiefs

The 14 PPCs each met weekly for roughly an hour. They were bicameral and jointly chaired, with one 'co-chair' coming from the Commons, the other from the Lords. Turnout varied, with anything between 5 and 20 attendees: this usually included a small number of MPs, a larger group of peers, plus whips, Lib Dem party representatives (from the Federal Policy Committee, the Local Government Association and the regional parties), and parliamentary researchers. The Liberal Democrat minister and/or spad attended the relevant PPC regularly. Conservative ministers attended PPC meetings by invitation.

The PPCs had a number of basic functions. They provided a link between frontbench and backbench, allowing the leadership to communicate with and coordinate backbenchers, and allowing backbenchers to make their concerns known to the leadership.[20] They were also a vehicle to ensure party cohesion and discipline: by organising and involving backbenchers in the policy process, there was less incentive for them to rebel. A co-chair position was also a form of patronage: it lay within the hands of Nick Clegg.

But the PPCs were also consciously developed in response to being in a coalition. Most obviously, the PPCs had a monitoring or 'watchdog' function: they ensured that Lib Dem pledges in the Coalition Agreement were being implemented fully, and damaging Conservative policies were minimised. One Liberal Democrat peer stated:

> I say to myself when we get these bills, 'Is it Liberal Democrat proof? Have we had involvement?' The reason you've got those co-chairs is so that when we get bills, they're not just dreamt up by policy wonks and Tories say, 'Oh that's fine. Sign it off'. It's so that it can be a coalition document. So that it can be coalition proof.

The PPCs also served as a vehicle for ensuring party differentiation. As one Lib Dem peer put it:

> We are always discussing 'what is the Lib Dem line?' . . . taking into account what the party says, what is set out in the Coalition Agreement, what is existing and future policy. If you were really to ask what is the purpose of these [PPCs], it's identity. We do not want to be merged.

Liberal Democrat distinctiveness was propagated in various ways in Parliament. A Liberal Democrat co-chair might speak on 'government' issues in a distinctly Lib Dem voice while a Liberal Democrat or Conservative minister would represent and speak for the Coalition. Similarly, a co-chair was sometimes 'fed' a particular line by a Liberal Democrat minister engaged in negotiations over policy.

One evolving function was that of policy development. For the Liberal Democrats, party policy has always been formulated through the Federal Policy Committee and ultimately the Party Conference, with growing input from the parliamentary party.[21] The Liberal Democrats were beginning to think about

---

[20] Cowley, *The Rebels* (n 1).

[21] A Russell, E Fieldhouse and D Cutts, 'De facto Veto? The Parliamentary Liberal Democrats' (2007) 78(1) *Political Quarterly* 89.

distinctive party policies, partly because they wanted to develop policy and implement it while still in government, but also to give the party a more distinctive voice.

Finally, PPCs were an attempt to make better use of scarce resources. Over one-third of their 57 MPs were in government, and lost to the backbench. The added loss of research and policy capacity meant that Lib Dem backbenchers were overstretched. Previously, backbench committees were composed solely of MPs; now the PPCs were made bicameral to increase their capacity.

In order to ensure greater consultation between the Liberal Democrats and the Government, a 'protocol for access' was agreed between Ed Llewellyn (Cameron's chief of staff) and Norman Lamb MP (Clegg's Chief Parliamentary and Political Adviser) in July 2010 (this is reproduced in Appendix six). This one-page document set out the need for cooperation and no surprises. It suggested advance notice of ministerial statements, access to briefing papers, and allowing Lib Dem co-chairs to attend ministerial meetings.

In practice, acceptance of this protocol was highly variable. Key was the attitude of the Secretary of State and his or her view of the Liberal Democrats: some were known to encourage consultation; others did not. For example, the protocol was followed closely in the Department for Culture, Media and Sport (DCMS) under Jeremy Hunt. Don Foster MP, co-chair of the DCMS PPC, had a departmental pass and regularly attended ministerial meetings, including those with officials. The principle of no surprises was closely followed, so that no major departmental announcements were made without first consulting Foster (and, to a lesser extent, Baroness Bonham-Carter, the other DCMS co-chair). Foster was heavily involved in the decision to sell the state-owned betting group the Tote to BetFred, a private bookmaker. Several interviewees described him as 'virtually a minister' in the department (see chapter five).

Andrew George, co-chair of the Department for Environment, Food and Rural Affairs (Defra) PPC, had a similar status in Defra, mostly because Caroline Spelman, the Secretary of State, insisted on Liberal Democrat involvement. However, it is worth pointing out that both DCMS and Defra were departments which had no Liberal Democrat ministerial representation: allowing the PPC co-chairs greater access was a means of ensuring that decisions and policies had Liberal Democrat input – although this input did not necessarily equate to influence.

That access and the promise of influence on ministers was sometimes a source of tension for co-chairs. With access came an implicit quid pro quo that the co-chair would be supportive in public. Witness the comment from one co-chair:

> It seems slightly false to be raising issues when I have a very easy way of asking the equivalent of a parliamentary question face-to-face . . . sometimes when my colleagues who are also co-chairs, put something out critical of the Government . . . I'm not yet sure in my own mind if that's the right thing to be doing. . . . But equally I'm conscious that if I don't, people have no idea what the victories are that Liberal Democrats have had.

But it was far more common for a PPC and its co-chairs to have a distant relationship with their department. A common complaint from Liberal Democrat interviewees was the lack of early consultation on key ministerial statements. One Lib Dem peer said:

> We expect to be consulted and play a part, and from time to time things happen which are completely unexpected. The best example I can give of that is the announcement . . . by the Home Secretary in response to the [UK] Supreme Court judgment on sex offenders . . . you had a feeling – what the hell are we meeting for once a week if we're not to be consulted on issues like this? All I could do on the day the statement was made . . . was to say I was ashamed.[22]

There was similar frustration over access to departments and ministerial meetings. Many co-chairs found it difficult to arrange meetings with ministers or secure adequate access to departments. By the summer of 2011, only 80 per cent of co-chairs had had one or more meetings with their respective Secretary of State. Many of the PPCs were struggling. They were overstretched, lacking basic administrative support. Others were too busy responding to events and firefighting to be useful. Some PPCs were simply sidelined. For instance, in health and the proposed NHS reforms, the Health PPC supported, rather than led, the party grassroots campaign.[23] One Lib Dem minister was critical, suggesting that the PPCs were trying to do too much: 'They don't know what they're for, and they don't do the job that they were set up to do. They may fill another need . . . but they're a complete muddle.' Tom Brake MP, co-chair of the Home Affairs and Justice PPC, convened a monthly meeting of all Lib Dem PPC co-chairs in October 2010 to discuss common issues. The co-chairs continued to meet through 2011, with a view to acting in a more coordinated manner and driving the party policy making process.[24]

Views differed on the access protocol, with some arguing that it was the bare minimum set of requirements that the relevant Secretary of State and department were expected to adhere to, others that close relationships cannot be legislated for. An audit of the protocol was completed by Norman Lamb and Lord Shutt by mid-2011, and found wide variance. The results were then discussed with Ed Llewellyn, which led to David Cameron in Cabinet reminding his Secretaries of State to be more inclusive.

Thus, the PPCs held the promise of being at once distinctive from the Executive, and able to influence it. In the first 18 months, however, they failed to deliver on

---

[22] This is a reference to the case of *R (F) v Secretary of State for the Home Department* [2010] UKSC 17, and the Home Secretary's response: see A Travis, 'David Cameron condemns supreme court ruling on sex offenders' *Guardian* (16 February 2011), www.guardian.co.uk/society/2011/feb/16/david-cameron-condemns-court-sex-offenders

[23] D Hall-Matthews, 'Planning, Positioning and Policy Process: Why Coalition has Tested Relationships between the Liberal Democrat Leadership and Grassroots' *Coalition at One Conference* (London, Institute for Government, 2011). It was also because the NHS reforms were laid out and agreed to prior to the establishment of the PPCs: see ch 10.

[24] See also ch 7.

this.[25] Their lack of explicit influence may have been due to the 'frontloading' of legislation in the first session; the PPCs may become more important as the Coalition continues. And there was one final problem: many Liberal Democrat interviewees argued that in order to have an impact on government, it was necessary to engage early, or 'upstream': by the time policies or legislation were announced in public, substantive change was difficult. However, if the parliamentary party was effective in securing change early, but in private, this meant that it lost the opportunity to signal to the public the extent of Lib Dem influence.

## THE CONSERVATIVE PARLIAMENTARY PARTY

Many Conservative MPs were angry at having 'lost' the 2010 election and being 'forced' into forming a coalition with the Liberal Democrats. Twenty of them understandably felt aggrieved at being passed over for ministerial posts now occupied by Liberal Democrats. But failing to win a majority and forming a coalition was not the only surprise. Shortly after the formation of the Coalition, Cameron announced that he wanted to allow frontbenchers as well as backbenchers full voting membership in the 1922 Committee (the 1922), traditionally the voice of the Conservative backbench. Membership of the 1922 is traditionally restricted to backbenchers when the Conservatives are in government, and Cameron's action was seen as an attempt to neuter the key forum of Conservative backbench MPs. Cameron won the vote, but this was viewed with great hostility. As a riposte, Graham Brady MP, a popular Conservative backbencher, was elected as 1922 Chairman, instead of the Prime Minister's 'preferred candidate' Richard Ottaway MP.

However, most Tory MPs seemed content to be back in government. The Coalition was accepted as being in the national interest. Many Conservative interviewees stressed the contingent, time-limited nature of the Coalition. One Conservative MP stated:

> It is a coalition for a particular purpose, for a defined time, and whose reason is for the good of the country. So, it is a defined relationship, it is not a developing friendship – and you put up with it.

Conservatives in the Lords agreed:

> It's been a bit of the tail wagging the dog . . . we've made concessions that are quite difficult to make. We have a joke in the Conservative Party that we need three hands because we need to go through the voting lobby sometimes holding our nose and covering our ears.

[25] For an example of how a PPC has influenced government legislation (albeit from a Liberal Democrat perspective) see A Brooke and G Tope, 'That's the Way to Do it! How Liberal Democrats made the Running on the Localism Bill' *Lib Dem Voice* (9 November 2011), www.libdemvoice.org/?p=25853&utm_source=tweet&utm_medium=twitter&utm_campaign=twitter

The debate between the Tory 'modernisers' (to which Cameron and most of the frontbenchers were seen to belong) and so-called 'mainstream' Conservatives continued (see chapter seven).[26] The right wing of the Party remained influential, however. Key associations such as No Turning Back, Cornerstone and the '92 Group formed a weekly steering meeting to bolster their influence in Parliament, and were instrumental in the election of 'mainstream' MPs to key positions such as the chairs of the 1922 subcommittees.[27]

The key issues testing the Conservatives were constitutional reform and Europe. Many Conservative MPs and peers grumbled about the Parliamentary Voting System and Constituencies Bill, but ultimately agreed to accept it because it was one of the Coalition's fundamental bargains. Although there was resentment, Conservative 'success' in the AV referendum and in the May 2011 local elections reduced complaints, but Lords reform may lead to further rebellions. While Lords reform was promised in the PfG, and previously in the Conservative manifesto, this was understood by Conservatives to be a 'third term' issue.[28]

Europe remained a divisive issue. In the Commons, one in five of all Conservative rebellions was on Europe, and they were double the average size of other Conservative rebellions.[29] Two of the largest rebellions in the first 18 months were on European issues (see Table 6.1). In July 2011, amidst concern that the UK would be funding further bailouts of Eurozone countries, Conservative MPs rebelled on a division to increase the amount that the IMF could potentially borrow from the UK, leading to a government majority of just 32. In October 2011, 81 Conservative MPs voted against a three-line whip in favour of a motion calling for a referendum on the UK's membership of the EU.[30] However, these rebellions might still have taken place had the Conservatives enjoyed a single-party majority government.

### Supporting the Minister: The Conservative Parliamentary Party's Institutional Arrangements

Institutionally the Conservatives seemed more relaxed about being in a coalition than the Lib Dems. That was partly a function of size: the Lib Dems had to reorganise themselves because of their stretched resources; but with six times as many backbenchers it was more difficult for the Conservatives to exercise centralised organisation. Another reason was the Conservatives' very different tradition of party democracy: once in power, it is the leadership who decides. So the Conservatives did not demonstrate the same concern with process. As

---

[26] T Bale, *The Conservative Party: From Thatcher to Cameron* (Cambridge, Polity, 2010); P Snowdon, *Back from the Brink: The Inside Story of the Tory Resurrection* (London, HarperPress, 2010).

[27] Bale and Sanderson-Nash, 'A Leap of Faith and a Leap in the Dark' (n 16).

[28] R Hazell, *The Conservative Agenda for Constitutional Reform* (London, Constitution Unit, 2011) 48–52.

[29] P Cowley, 'Ten things we know about Coalition MPs' *Ballots and Bullets Blog* (5 July, 2011), nottspolitics.org/2011/07/05/ten-things-we-know-about-coalition-mps

[30] N Watt, 'David Cameron rocked by record rebellion as Europe splits Tories again' *Guardian* (25 October 2011), www.guardian.co.uk/politics/2011/oct/24/david-cameron-tory-rebellion-europe

one Conservative peer responded to a description of the Lib Dems' parliamentary organisation: 'Oh no . . . we don't go in for that sort of thing . . . Very un-Conservative, that'.

## 1. The 1922 Committee Plenary Meeting

The key forum for the Conservative parliamentary party in the Commons remained the weekly 1922 Committee plenary meeting. The hour-long meeting involved weekly business and guest speakers. All Conservative Secretaries of State attended the 1922 plenary as guests at least once; and one or two Liberal Democrat ministers addressed the meeting briefly. It did not operate as a key forum for coalition issues. The plenary meeting was an information-sharing forum, a means of taking 'the temperature' of the party, with the 1922 executive officers meeting with the whips after the plenary meeting, and the Chairman meeting with the Prime Minister regularly. On rare occasions the committee might change the Conservative leadership's approach to an issue; but because of its size the plenary meeting remained unwieldy as a means of action and influence.

## 2. The 1922 Subcommittees

The 1922 Committee had five subcommittees. When the Conservatives were last in power, a subcommittee had shadowed every department. Following the 1997 general election, these subject backbench committees fell into desuetude. They were later revived but reorganised into broad subject groups.[31] In 2011 there were five subcommittees: Economic Affairs, Foreign Affairs, Home and Constitutional Affairs, Public Services, and Environment. The five chairs were elected by Tory backbenchers in the aftermath of David Cameron's attempt to assert his dominance over the 1922 Committee, and reflect the more vehemently Eurosceptic wing of the party.

Table 6.4  The Conservative 1922 Subcommittees, 2010–11

| Name | Chair |
| --- | --- |
| Economic Affairs (BIS, Treasury, DWP) | John Redwood |
| Foreign Affairs (FCO, DfID, MOD) | Edward Leigh |
| Home & Constitutional Affairs (DPMO, HO, MOJ, DCMS, SO, WO, NIO, DCLG) | Eleanor Laing |
| Public Services (Health, Education, Transport) | Andrew Percy |
| Environment (Defra, DECC) | Neil Parrish |

Source: L Zetter (ed), *Zetter's Political Companion*, April 2011 edn (London, Zetter's Political Services Ltd, 2011)

[31] P Norton, *Parliament in British Politics* (Basingstoke, Palgrave Macmillan, 2005) 125–7.

The subcommittees were similar in nature to the Lib Dem PPCs, though they were less systematised and more fluid. They met fortnightly, or more often if there were pressing issues. Attendance was highly variable: for instance, in one meeting on constitutional issues, there were fewer than 10 MPs present; for a meeting on the sale of forests with Caroline Spelman there were well over 100 in attendance.

The 1922 subcommittees had the same basic functions as other parliamentary backbench committees: primarily, they shared information and were a link between the backbench and frontbench. Conservative Secretaries of State appeared before the subcommittees to discuss upcoming policy and legislation, and to get feedback and ensure backbench cooperation. Each subcommittee chair met with their respective Secretaries of State on an ad hoc basis, but it was not systematic.

Graham Brady met with the subcommittee chairs on a regular basis to discuss best practices and 'progress', but there was no access protocol similar to that of the Lib Dems. That was thought unnecessary, because the Conservatives were the larger party; because Conservative ministers predominated in government; and again because Conservatives preferred to leave matters to the leadership. Still, some Conservative interviewees attested to the beginnings of a monitoring function: there was suspicion that their own frontbench could become too removed. They wanted to make sure Conservative pledges contained in the Coalition Agreement were being implemented. One subcommittee chair explained:

> The last thing [backbenchers] want is to have an executive which is out of touch. It is extremely important that ministers, whilst they're working with Liberal Democrats and in a coalition, still have a very, very keen focus on what the Conservative Party, the Conservative voter in the country, thinks and feels.

Moreover, Conservative interviewees argued that the 1922 subcommittees were intended to answer the historical problem of Conservative parliamentarians having no means of contributing to the party policy process – a particularly important matter, especially given the new 2010 intake eager to contribute. Previously, Conservative party policy while in government had been formulated by ministers, and indirectly through the civil service, with the parliamentary and extra-parliamentary party mostly being relegated to ratification:

> With a single-party government the government machine is informally a part of manifesto development because the forward-looking policy development work that's undertaken in departments very largely becomes the forward programme of the party seeking re-election. [In a] coalition government, all of that forward policy work is available to both parties. So if we are to go to the next election with two separate distinct manifestos, we need a separate process to do it. . . . The Backbench Policy committees will be a key part of that. (Conservative MP)

The policy making function answered the issue of distinctiveness. It was intended that Conservative ministers, the chairmen of the backbench committees and representatives of the national party working together (via the Conservative Policy Forum) would formulate new Conservative policy, with the process coordinated by Oliver Letwin. That was the theory; but the history of Tory policy making reveals that it tends to be done by a small group of people, rather than being the product of interaction between Central Office, the parliamentary party and the wider grassroots.

### 3. *The Association of Conservative Peers and Liaison Groups*

Conservatives in the Lords also had a weekly plenary meeting under the auspices of the Association of Conservative Peers, following roughly the same format as the 1922. It was an information-sharing forum, with ministers – Conservative and on occasion Liberal Democrat – discussing upcoming business and key issues. At the beginning of 2011, Baroness Shephard, chair of the Association of Conservative Peers, established 15 liaison groups to shadow government departments.

Table 6.5  **Association of Conservative Peer Liaison Groups, 2010–11**

| Name | Chair/Convenor |
| --- | --- |
| International Development | Viscount Eccles |
| Business, Innovation & Skills | Earl of Selborne |
| Cabinet Office | Lord Norton of Louth |
| Culture, Media & Sport | Viscount Eccles |
| Transport | Lord Ahmad of Wimbledon |
| Defence | Lord Selkirk of Douglas |
| Education | Baroness Perry of Southwark |
| Energy & Climate Change | Baroness O'Cathain |
| Environment, Food & Rural Affairs | Lord Gardiner |
| Foreign & Commonwealth Office | Lord Trimble |
| Health | Baroness Eccles of Moulton |
| Home Office | Lord Freeman |
| Justice | Lord Lucas |
| Treasury | Lord Hamilton of Epsom |
| Work & Pensions | Lord Boswell of Aynho<br>Baroness Stedman-Scott |

Source: L Zetter (ed), *Zetter's Political Companion,* April 2011 edn (London, Zetter's Political Services Ltd, 2011)

These groups were a modification of 'bill teams' which had existed under previous Conservative governments.[32] But they were also a response to the Coalition and the events of the second half of 2010. The leadership in the Lords realised that a more efficient and effective approach to business was necessary, given the small but significant number of government defeats in late 2010, and the heavy parliamentary workload promised over the first half of 2011. The liaison groups were also, perhaps, a response to the coordinated action of the Liberal Democrat PPCs.

The groups were highly variable in their scope, functions and effectiveness. The salient feature of the liaison groups was that their focus was on the minister and ministerial support – their key function was to ensure that in speaking on a bill the Conservative minister had support from two or three friendly peers. Generally speaking, membership of the liaison groups was small and fluid: most were reactive, meeting on an ad hoc basis.

Liaison group chairs were best understood as the equivalent of the Commons' Parliamentary Private Secretaries.[33] They acted as the eyes and ears of the minister in the Lords; they organised support for the ministers and they tested the temperature of the party. Liaison chairs occasionally met with the relevant Lords minister; more rarely with the Secretary of State, the ministerial team or the Commons subcommittee chairs. The functions of the chairs continue to evolve: one or two liaison group chairs have begun to take on a 'coalition' function, in that they have regular meetings with their Liberal Democrat peer co-chairs.

CONCLUSION

In the first 18 months following the May 2010 election, there was little sign that having a coalition at Westminster had led to a strengthening of Parliament or a concomitant weakening of the Executive. The Government remained firmly in control. They got all their business through, but with amendments to accommodate dissenters in one or other party (see chapters nine and ten). There were no splits in either coalition party, and (unlike previous UK coalitions) no party factions with an alternative leader.

There had been a busy and rebellious Parliament, but it was not yet unmanageable. In part, this was due to having a government majority in the Commons and greater government numbers in the Lords, which gave the Coalition sufficient leeway to pass legislation that was contentious for one coalition partner or the other. But it was also because the frontbenches of both parties worked closely together, and because parliamentarians accepted – or were resigned to – the Coalition. So for the frontbench coalition management had been successful.

Beyond the frontbench, backbenchers in both parties showed no enthusiasm for working together as a single unit: they acted and voted as separate parties.

---

[32] A bill team in this context is an informal group of government backbenchers who support a minister in the passage of legislation through Parliament.

[33] A Parliamentary Private Secretary (PPS) is an MP appointed by a government minister to act as their assistant in Parliament. PPSs are unsalaried, but are expected to vote with the Government.

Both parliamentary parties modified existing machinery and created new arrangements to respond to the demands of coalition. Party backbench committees offered the promise of influence, but they struggled to make headway. They also offered the promise of distinctiveness, and here both parties' committees seemed to have made some progress by becoming vehicles for producing party policy. This answered calls for distinctiveness from the party; but it was doubtful whether the wider public registered this.

For the Liberal Democrats, the first 18 months were marked by two matters: learning to work as a party of government; and shifting from a strategy of unity to one of distinctiveness. The parliamentary party had maintained its commitment to party democracy, and had not experienced serious intraparty dissent, perhaps because of all the intensive consultation and discussion; or, less happily, because the party had no time to pause and evaluate its performance. The more serious problem for the smaller party remained signalling to the public their distinctive contribution in government. The media seldom reported Liberal Democrat amendments in Parliament; and for the Lib Dem backbench committees, private influence was preferable to public rebellion.

For the Conservatives, on the other hand, going into government saw a reversion to type. The first 18 months were marked by a mix of increasing rebelliousness and continued deference to the Conservative leadership. Much of the rebelliousness focused on Europe, but was symptomatic of dissatisfaction with the leadership on a wider range of issues. The more strategic concern for the Conservatives was whether or not this dissatisfaction would impact upon the Conservatives' goal of achieving an overall majority in 2015.

# 7

# *The Political Parties*

## BEN YONG

[The] Lib Dems are in a speeding car. If we jump out now we know we're going to get mangled. Even if we're pretty confident that the car is aiming towards a brick wall, our chances are no worse if we stay in the car than if we jump out. (Liberal Democrat activist)

I N THIS CHAPTER we examine the general challenges presented by coalition for the political parties. In the previous chapter we saw how the unity/distinctiveness dilemma played out for the parties in Parliament: the frontbenches asserted unity, while the backbenches struggled to differentiate themselves. Here, we look more broadly at the relationships between leadership and party, and the longer term issues for the parties that arise as a result of being in a coalition.

The coalition parties have faced a number of challenges. An early obstacle was managing the transition to government and the loss of state funding: the impact of this was felt more strongly by the Lib Dems as a party relatively new to being in government. Then there were the challenges of internal party management: first, managing the relations between the party in government (ie, MPs and peers) with the party 'outside' Westminster (ie, party officials, activists and supporters), and then managing the pressures that being in a coalition placed upon internal party democracy; and second, ensuring and communicating each party's respective distinctiveness to the party faithful and to the electorate as a whole. And there was a final challenge: positioning for the next election. The 2010 hung parliament and the formation of a coalition at Westminster suggested that it could happen again.

As noted in earlier chapters, what counted as success often depended on the observer and their point of view. For the frontbench and leadership, success was about managing the expectations of the wider party. In this chapter, however, the focus is primarily on the understandings of the party membership in both the Conservatives and the Liberal Democrats. For them, success was measured in terms of distinctiveness; unity was secondary. Now in government, being in office was taken for granted by party members; what was important to them was showing influence and more specifically showing that party policy was being implemented.[1]

---

[1] K Strøm, 'A Behavioural Theory of Competitive Political Parties' (1990) 34(2) *American Journal of Political Science* 565.

## THE CONSERVATIVES: THE MORE THINGS CHANGE,
## THE MORE THEY STAY THE SAME

For the Conservatives, the formation of the Coalition was treated with some ambivalence. After 13 years in the wilderness, they were finally back in power. The Tories won 306 seats, and 36 per cent of the vote. They had won 95 new seats, 83 from Labour and 12 from the Lib Dems, and re-established their dominance in England, where they won 297 seats to Labour's 191 and the Liberal Democrats' 43.[2] The Conservatives were by far the largest party in the Commons.

And yet the aftermath of the 2010 election was somewhat bittersweet, with an ongoing debate about what the Election had meant. This debate reflected a continuing split within the Conservative Party between those espousing a focus on the core Tory vote and 'core' Tory values and issues (tax, immigration, Europe) – what some called 'mainstream' conservatism – and those who emphasised the need to reach out to the undecided and floating voters with more socially liberal policies – the so-called 'modernisers'.[3]

For many, particularly those at the mainstream end of the spectrum, the 2010 election campaign and David Cameron had been a failure. In spite of going into an election against an exhausted Labour government in its third term with a deeply unpopular incumbent Prime Minister, the Conservatives had been unable to secure a majority. They were now in government, but they were also locked into a five-year agreement with the Liberal Democrats. This had been due to a weak, ill thought through campaign which had been hijacked by the Lib Dems and 'Cleggmania'.

For those at the modernising end of the spectrum, the 2010 Election was a success: the percentage of those voting for the Conservatives had increased and there had been a large swing in the party's favour. Most importantly, the Tories were now back in power. If they had not succeeded in securing a single-party majority, that was because they had not modernised enough: while electors were tired of New Labour, they remained suspicious of the Conservatives and voted accordingly.[4] And going into a coalition with the Lib Dems could be seen as part of a long-term strategy for the party: it would increase the 'detoxification' of the Tory brand, and create a 'coalition' of progressive voters who would make it even more difficult for Labour to return to government. The Coalition, in other words, was seen as part of a broader strategy by Cameron to expand the Conservatives' control of the centre ground.[5]

The problem for the Conservative frontbench was very rarely their Lib Dem counterparts; it was members of their own party. As one interviewee said:

---

[2] P Dorey, 'Faltering Before the Finishing Line: The Conservative Party's Performance in the 2010 General Election' (2010) 5 *British Politics* 425.

[3] P Snowdon, *Back from the Brink: The Inside Story of the Tory Resurrection* (London, HarperPress, 2010); T Bale, *The Conservative Party: From Thatcher to Cameron* (Cambridge, Polity, 2010).

[4] Dorey, 'Faltering Before the Finishing Line' (n 2).

[5] Cameron also attempted to draw in former Labour MPs: BBC News, 'Labour's Alan Milburn accepts coalition role' (15 August 2010), www.bbc.co.uk/news/uk-politics-10977806

> Many of those in the Executive get along better with their counterparts than they do with their own party . . . [There is] a real problem of communication between those in government and those outside. (Conservative Party member)

It was difficult to determine how much of the intraparty conflict that played out over 2010 and 2011 would not have occurred but for the Conservatives being in a coalition. The debate about the direction of the party had been going on since at least 1997: perhaps what can be said is that had the Conservatives won a majority, the modernisers might have had to capitulate more often to those to the right of the party without the Lib Dem 'rump' in Parliament to fall back on. Having the Lib Dems on board gave the frontbench some freedom of movement in managing the Conservative right wing both inside and outside Parliament. More than one Conservative interviewee pointed to the alternative to coalition – minority government – and all the trouble that such a situation might have engendered:

> We couldn't [have made the cuts] . . . this last year if we'd been a minority government. And even if we'd had a majority of five . . . look at John Major's Government. Look at the nightmare it was. . . . What happens with a tiny majority, which is what John [Major] had, is that any group of five or six people can then determine policy. Because they say, 'We're going to vote against [the leadership]'. . . . It becomes impossible. You would need a really solid majority to get difficult legislation through. (Conservative peer)

### Changes in the Party Organisation

The party outside government underwent changes following the 2010 election. Conservative Campaign Headquarters (CCHQ) was reduced in size. This was not so much a result of the loss of state funding – unlike the Lib Dems and Labour, the Conservatives remained relatively flush thanks to private donations – but rather reflected established practice. Prior to a general election, Conservative Party staffing always rose exponentially, and was then sharply trimmed back post-election. In the aftermath of the 2010 election, key Conservative staffers were brought into government as special advisers or in some other capacity. Many interviewees seemed to think that CCHQ had been marginalised while the leadership was now busy operating the levers of power. One former Conservative Party staffer said: 'CCHQ isn't really doing much at all. Much of the staff have gone. It brings out dull press releases. It's supposed to be doing work for 2015'. But that was to ignore the work CCHQ was doing elsewhere: in addition to policy development, it was also engaged in election campaigning (by-elections, local government, London Mayor and Assembly etc) and, of course, fundraising.

By the beginning of 2011, a set of institutional arrangements had been established to develop party policy. This was driven by the concern that the parliamentary party and the wider party membership would become alienated from the frontbench, and by the concern that the Conservative Party needed a means of developing its own distinctive party policy over the 2010–15 parliamentary term (see chapter six). The Conservative Policy Forum (CPF), meant to be a means by which the rank-and-file could provide input into the development of party policy, was re-established in January 2011.[6] A quadripartite arrangement of the CPF, the 1922 subcommittees (discussed in chapter six), CCHQ and the Conservative leadership under the overall direction of Oliver Letwin was, in theory, to produce the 2015 manifesto. However, many Conservative interviewees expressed doubt about the arrangements. One activist noted:

> The Conservative Policy Forum's been re-launched and is actively seeking opinion from membership far and wide. Part of that is a PR exercise to keep them happy and make them feel they're involved, but they do hope to pick some gems up from the dross.

A Conservative peer, drawing on his experience in helping to draft a previous party manifesto, was similarly sceptical of greater party involvement in the drafting of policy:

> I was leading in [one] area . . . We literally sweated it out in a morning. . . . It was rather good, actually, but [there was] bugger all about policy groups or anybody else. So the fact that [the subcommittees] are or are not in existence is not by itself predictive of their role in actually setting things.

He continued:

> The Tories . . . don't really like organisation that much . . . it isn't quite the same dynamic [as in the Liberal Democrat Party], but I think the fact that you do need what I may term vehicles, and managed and controllable vehicles for the expression of controlled dissent, is quite an important part in this.

The peer's phrasing was apposite: this was about management rather than providing greater internal democracy. Nevertheless, the establishment of such arrangements suggested that the leadership recognised the anxieties of the party as a whole.

## Party Differentiation

Over the course of 2010–11, Conservative supporters continued to call for Tory rather than 'coalition' policies to be implemented. There was apparent reason to be anxious – membership numbers appeared to be dropping. The Conservative Party has rarely published figures revealing its total membership, as there is no legal requirement to do so;[7] but one unconfirmed report (widely cited) suggested that Conservative membership had dropped by 80,000 members from the 2005

---

[6] P Goodman, 'Good News about Manifesto Planning for the Next Election' *ConservativeHome* (12 January 2011), www.conservativehome.blogs.com/thetorydiary/2011/01/progess-in-forming-party-policy-for-the-next-election.html. The CPF's website can be found at www.conservativepolicy-forum.com

[7] House of Commons Standard Note, 'Membership of UK Political Parties' (2009), www.parliament. uk/briefing-papers/SN05125. This is also due the looser organisation of the Conservative Party.

figure of 257,000 to 177,000 in 2010.[8] It was, however, difficult to say whether this was as a result of entering into a coalition, or part of a more general long-term trend of declining party membership.[9]

One Conservative Party member interviewed just before the Alternative Vote (AV) referendum in May 2011 said:

> There's a very difficult mood in the Tory Party . . . The Prime Minister [will] be talking about the Tory Party in terms of the AV campaign but as of this Friday he'll revert to being Prime Minister talking about the Coalition. So that's the tension. The Tory MPs want to hear a Tory Prime Minister talking about the Tory Party and we're not getting it.

Concerns about party distinctiveness often took the form of concern about 'watered-down' Tory policies: over Europe, over human rights, over the management of the economy, and so on. This was often expressed on the widely read website *ConservativeHome*, run by Tim Montgomerie (former aide to Work and Pensions Secretary Iain Duncan Smith and a Eurosceptic favouring the 'core vote' approach) and funded by Conservative Lord Ashcroft.

This concern about watered-down policies and the need to present purely Conservative policy to the rank-and-file and to the wider public continued throughout 2011. For instance, prior to the Autumn Conference in early October 2011, two books were published by Tory MPs: *The Future of Conservatism: Values Revisited*, and *After the Coalition*.[10] *The Future of Conservatism* was edited by members of the 'older' guard within the Conservative Party, including David Davis MP, a former contender for the Conservative Party leadership, and Brian Binley, treasurer of the 1922 Committee. *After the Coalition* was written by five Conservative MPs from the new 2010 intake. Both books emphasised the Coalition's time-limited nature and the constraining effect it had had on the Conservative Party and its impact in government. And both books were an attempt to encourage a debate over the long-term future of the Conservative Party and party policy following 2015.

But anxieties over party differentiation were not limited to Conservatives at the mainstream end of the spectrum. One moderniser thought that coalition with the Lib Dems was a double-edged sword:

> It's a good thing the Tories have had to learn to compromise. But it's dangerous too, because the Lib Dems are getting all the fluffy stuff, and the tough stuff, deficit reduction, that's good Tory stuff. Which is fine in the short term and probably necessary, but in the long term, 2014–15, when we stand up and say 'vote for us alone' – there's a really difficult balancing act in how you take credit for stuff which is joint and how you say, 'the Lib Dems were wrong on this so vote for us' . . . the Tories need to own the good stuff and the bad. If they don't own the good stuff then it all comes to nothing. 2015 comes and all people see are Tories cutting, cutting, cutting.

---

[8] This figure comes from Tim Montgomerie, the influential Conservative editor of *ConservativeHome*: 'Tories voice fears over falling membership' *Guardian* (5 October, 2010), www.guardian.co.uk/politics/blog/2010/oct/05/tories-fears-falling-membership

[9] S Ingle, *The British Party System: An Introduction* (New York, Routledge, 2008).

[10] D Davis, B Binley and J Baron, *The Future of Conservatism: Values Revisited* (London, Biteback Publishing, 2011).

Something of this could be seen in the internal debates leading to 'the pause' in the NHS reforms: one reason the pause was initiated was because of fears of how the proposed reforms would impact on the Tory image (see chapter ten).

Cameron himself was to some extent constrained by his position as Prime Minister. It was his role to project unity as head of the Coalition, and so to a large extent he was unable to cater to the broader party membership's desire for a more explicitly Conservative PM. Who, then, was meant to speak for the Conservatives? Traditionally, the chairman of the Conservative Party was meant to speak to party concerns. Following the 2010 election Cameron appointed two Tories to the post: Baroness Warsi, who was also made Minister without portfolio in the Cabinet Office; and Andrew (later Lord) Feldman, former Chief Executive of the Conservative Party. Warsi had often appeared on the BBC's *Question Time* and, while a well-known face of the party, was often criticised for being a poor public performer; Feldman preferred to work behind the scenes. In September 2010 Cameron rectified this and appointed Michael Fallon MP as Deputy Chairman.[11]

In practice, however, Cameron showed himself to be a canny differentiator, intervening strategically to demonstrate that he was the key spokesman for the Conservative Party. For instance, shortly after the formation of the Coalition in late May 2010, Cameron reassured both Tory members and voters in a media blitz that he was still a Conservative PM delivering on issues that mattered to Conservatives.[12] Similarly, it was initially understood that both Cameron and Clegg would take a low profile approach to the AV referendum; and Cameron himself officially distanced himself from the official 'No' campaign (as opposed to the solely Conservative 'No' campaign).[13] However, pressure from the Conservative Party both inside and outside Parliament led Cameron and Chancellor George Osborne to become personally involved. This may in part have been a response to the Lib Dems' shift towards a more aggressive differentiation strategy as mandated by the March 2011 Lib Dem Conference.[14] Osborne made allegations about the funding for the 'Yes' campaign;[15] and Cameron made a late speech highly critical of AV (see chapter eight).[16]

One Conservative activist noted in an interview just before the AV referendum:

> The reason Cameron's got so heavily involved in the 'No' campaign is because it's reuniting Tory party MPs and activists back with him . . . So the AV campaign has been a good thing for Cameron and a disaster for Clegg. . . . [Cameron is] able to say, 'I told you I'd campaign against it. . . . I've been very prominent and probably on Thursday I can claim quite a big role in it'.

[11] T Bale and E Sanderson-Nash, 'A Leap of Faith and a Leap in the Dark: The Impact of the Coalition on the Conservatives and the Liberal Democrats' in S Lee and M Beech (eds), *The Cameron-Clegg Government: Coalition Politics in an Age of Austerity* (Basingstoke, Palgrave Macmillan, 2011).

[12] ibid, 243.

[13] BBC News, 'AV referendum: Cameron "not responsible for No to AV"' (3 May 2011), www.bbc.co.uk/news/uk-politics-13260010

[14] On this, see the Lib Dem section below.

[15] G Wilson, 'Osborne raps "dodgy" Yes to AV' *Sun* (13 April 2011), www.thesun.co.uk/sol/homepage/news/3524950/Osborne-raps-dodgy-Yes-to-AV.html

[16] 'No to AV' website, 1 May 2010, www.no2av.org/05/second-referendum-broadcast

The overwhelming vote against a change to the electoral system, and Cameron's late intervention in the 'No' campaign, boosted his position with the parliamentary party but also with the party outside Parliament. The Conservatives' relative success in local government elections – they gained 85 councillors and four councils (unusually for an incumbent party in government, and one imposing severe cuts, no less) – was a welcome boost for Cameron and his position within the party.

Table 7.1  English Local Government Results, May 2011

| Party | Councils | +/- | Councillors | +/- |
|-------|----------|-----|-------------|-----|
| Con | 157 | +4 | 5108 | +85 |
| Lab | 57 | +26 | 2459 | +857 |
| Lib Dem | 10 | -9 | 1099 | -747 |
| Other | 55 | -21 | 793 | -209 |

Source: BBC News, 'Vote 2011' (10 May 2011),
www.bbc.co.uk/news/uk-politics-12913122

Table 7.2  Scottish Parliament Election Results, May 2011

| Party | Total seats | +/- |
|-------|-------------|-----|
| SNP | 69 | +23 |
| Lab | 37 | -7 |
| Con | 15 | -5 |
| Lib Dem | 5 | -12 |
| Other | 3 | +1 |

Source: BBC News, 'Vote 2011', *BBC News* (10 May 2011),
www.bbc.co.uk/news/uk-politics-12913122

Pressure on Cameron to act had built up again by the end of 2011, particularly over Europe.[17] The parliamentary party rebelled more on European issues than on any other issue, and in the second half of 2011 there were two serious rebellions by Conservative MPs, both on Europe (see chapter six). The Eurozone crisis – the potential for sovereign debt default and its impact spreading throughout the Eurozone – had been simmering for much of 2010 and 2011. In December 2011, EU leaders had begun to negotiate a new agreement with rules limiting member governments' borrowing. Cameron refused to sign up to the agreement, on the

[17] Wintour and Watt, 'Why the Tory right no longer trusts David Cameron on Europe' *Guardian Blog* (9 December 2011), www.guardian.co.uk/politics/wintour-and-watt/2011/dec/08/davidcameron-debt-crisis?INTCMP=ILCNETTXT3487

basis that it would harm British interests. Cameron's decision was seen as heavily influenced by well coordinated Conservative Eurosceptics.[18] And while Liberal Democrats fumed, Cameron was once again secure in his leadership, ending the year stronger than ever before.[19]

## 2015: Coalition Redux?

Few Conservatives interviewed had given much thought to 2015, rightly noting that it was far too early to make predictions. Many Conservatives predicted greater fractiousness come 2014–15. One Conservative MP said:

> The last year is more likely to be much more fractious actually because at that point we'll have an election coming up, we'll all want to start differentiating ourselves and it will be much more difficult to find joint purpose.

Conservative interviewees thought it unlikely that there would be another coalition. Of course, this would depend very much on the circumstances at the time, but all Conservative interviewees emphasised the time-limited nature of the present Coalition. One Conservative MP interviewed in April 2011 said:

> It's such an abnormal time, because of this deficit which is always the elephant in the room. . . . That's always been the problem but come the next time, were there to be a coalition, hopefully that wouldn't be the same elephant in the room and therefore the dynamic would be quite different . . .

Few Conservative interviewees were willing to entertain the idea of pre-electoral pacts so early in the parliamentary term. Nick Boles, new Conservative MP for Grantham and Stamford, and founder of centre-right think tank Policy Exchange, had suggested pre-electoral pacts in the early months of the Coalition.[20] But he was rare in being a Conservative enthusiast for the Coalition anyway. The general position within the party was opposition to pre-electoral pacts, and a suspicion that the leadership of both parties might come to an informal agreement to allow one or the other partner to win. This suspicion was apparent at the Oldham East and Saddleworth by-election in mid-January 2011, where a by-election had been forced when the sitting Labour MP was found guilty of knowingly making false statements. Both coalition parties denied a pre-electoral pact, formal or informal.[21]

---

[18] I Martin, 'Can the Coalition survive David Cameron's veto?' *Telegraph* (10 December 2011), www.telegraph.co.uk/news/worldnews/europe/eu/8948425/Can-the-Coalition-survive-David-Camerons-veto.html

[19] T Clark, 'Cameron's approval rating outstrips his government's – poll' *Guardian* (25 December 2011), www.guardian.co.uk/politics/2011/dec/25/cameron-approval-rating-grows-poll

[20] See his *Which Way's Up? The Future for Coalition Britain and How to Get There* (London, Biteback Publishing, 2010).

[21] M White, 'David Cameron denies Oldham byelection pact claims' *Guardian* (6 January 2011), www.guardian.co.uk/politics/2011/jan/06/david-cameron-denies-oldham-byelection-pact

One hope expressed by some Conservative interviewees was the idea that the Conservative Party would absorb key members of the Liberal Democrats – most likely, the economic liberal wing. Absorption of a smaller party by the Conservative Party had happened in previous UK coalitions (see chapter two).[22] Said one Conservative MP:

> We won't go in with Tories and Lib Dems configured as they now are. The question is: whom should the Conservatives not oppose at the next election? The only way to make that viable is for some kind of merger to take place. But that merger should not lead to a change in the name or character of the Conservative Party. [We will] explain to Lib Dems that they will have influence and careers in the Conservative Party. But the Conservative Party needs to establish the terms on which this negotiation can be done.

This would be doubly beneficial for the Conservative Party: it would lead to an infusion of new blood and widen the appeal of the party; but it would also weaken the Liberal Democrats.

### THE LIBERAL DEMOCRATS: THE TRANSITION FROM OPPOSITION TO GOVERNMENT

The Liberal Democrats secured 23 per cent of the vote, and 57 seats in the House of Commons. They made a modest gain in terms of the share of the popular vote, but lost five seats. This was disappointing given 'Cleggmania': the sudden rush of attention from the media and public following Nick Clegg's performances during the leaders' debates in April 2010. But 2010 repeated the experience of 2005: once again the Lib Dems delivered a highly uneven performance, reflecting the fact that they had no truly safe seats or social base.

In fact, the Lib Dems gained eight seats, five from Labour and three from the Conservatives; but lost 13 seats, all but one of those going to the Conservatives. The results reflected the revival of the Conservatives in the South of England and the inability of Lib Dems to make significant inroads into Labour heartlands.[23] And there was at least one other factor that was often raised to explain the Lib Dems' relative failure at the 2010 election: the credibility gap. Many voters thought the Lib Dems could not win, and were worried that a vote for the Lib Dems would be a wasted vote.

Despite the disappointing electoral results, the Lib Dem party rank-and-file could not help but be jubilant: the formation of the Coalition meant that the Lib Dems were finally a party of government. Moreover, the party's adherence to party democracy was maintained, with ratification by the Federal Executive and parliamentary party, and a (constitutionally unnecessary) Special Conference.

---

[22] T Bale, 'The Black Widow Effect: Why Britain's Conservative–Liberal Democrat Coalition Might Have an Unhappy Ending', forthcoming in *Parliamentary Affairs*.
[23] D Cutts, E Fieldhouse and A Russell, 'The Campaign that Changed Everything and Still Did Not Matter? The Liberal Democrat Campaign and Performance' (2010) 63(4) *Parliamentary Affairs* 689.

The biggest immediate shock for the Lib Dems came after the formation of the Coalition: they had lost Short Money and Cranborne Money, the state funding for opposition parties.[24] The impact this had in Parliament is noted in chapter six, but there was also damage to the party outside Parliament. Most of the communications staff were made redundant after the 2010 election; equally as important was the loss of staff within the Liberal Democrat Policy Unit, because this affected the policy making ability of the Federal Party. For instance, previously a member of staff had worked within each of the Lib Dems' working policy groups as a 'rapporteur', providing administrative support; but following the 2010 election, Lib Dem working groups had to perform administrative tasks themselves.

The issue of funding for the coalition parties had been overlooked, and was in the process of being redressed when David Laws resigned as Chief Secretary to the Treasury over misinforming Parliament about his expenses. Attempts were made by Clegg to return to the issue of party funding in 2010–11, but additional state funding proved difficult to justify, given the Coalition's austerity programme.[25] This was in spite of a report on party funding by the Committee for Standards in Public Life, under whose recommendations the Lib Dems would have gained the most.[26]

The loss of staff coincided with a difficult transition into government. One Lib Dem staffer at Cowley Street (the location of the Liberal Democrats' national headquarters)[27] described the first three months:

> [The] ministers went into a little tent by themselves for three months. . . . They were fighting all these turf battles within the departments. There was this period when all these people just disappeared. They were suddenly surrounded by civil servants and Tories. There was a real feeling of alienation across the party. . . . For a month . . . no one talked to me at all. They went into government, and total radio silence. It wasn't deliberate. People literally didn't have a phone; offices weren't set up. There's still a bit of a legacy from this. There's still resentment.

## Changes in the Party Organisation

Entrance into government, and into a coalition, had more subtle effects on the Liberal Democrat Party. As with many small parties entering a coalition, there were competing pressures: pressures from 'above' to change and adapt to their situation; but also resistance from 'below' to avoid being too deeply transformed

---

[24] The Lib Dems, however (along with the Conservatives and Labour), did continue to receive policy development grants from the Electoral Commission.

[25] P Wintour, 'No extra state funding for political parties this parliament, says Clegg' *Guardian* (15 November 2011), www.guardian.co.uk/politics/2011/nov/15/no-extra-funding-parties-clegg

[26] See Committee on Standards in Public Life, *Political Party Finance: Ending the Big Donor Culture* (November 2011), www.public-standards.gov.uk/Library/13th_Report___Political_party_finance_ FINAL_PDF_VERSION_18_11_11.pdf

[27] The Lib Dems' national headquarters moved to Great George Street in Westminster, London in August 2011.

by the transition to government.[28] Before noting these pressures, it is worth recounting some of changes to the party that have taken place since 1997. For although entrance into government caused problems between those inside Parliament and those outside it, many of these problems already existed in nascent form.

As of 1997 the Lib Dems had become more professionalised and more leader-oriented.[29] The parliamentary party tripled in size between 1992 and 2005, from 20 MPs to 62 MPs – and with this came increased state funding; additionally, a much larger parliamentary party led to subtle changes in the relationships among the constituent parts of the party at the federal level.

Increased state funding meant that the Lib Dems were able to mount a more professional operation at Westminster and Cowley Street, including employing experts from outside the party, and merging press operations so that the leader now spoke for the party.[30] Moreover, a larger number of MPs and peers meant that the parliamentary party's influence within the Liberal Democrat party increased. Formally the parliamentary party had no power to determine policy – that was the prerogative of the Federal Policy Committee (FPC) and ultimately Conference – but in practice the parliamentary party had at the very least an informal veto over party policy, and even a de facto power to make policy, because of the parliamentary party's daily involvement in legislative policy making at Westminster.[31] In short, the Liberal Democrats were already undergoing professionalisation and rationalisation, which threatened to draw power away from the wider party towards a much smaller group. Entering a coalition might exacerbate the issue of preserving party democracy, but the problem predated the Coalition.

Problems had already emerged in the early months of the Coalition, such as the issue of 'transmission' between the frontbench, backbench, and the wider party. They were beginning to be solved through the adaptation of institutions, such as the establishment of the Parliamentary Party Committees (PPCs), explicitly seen as a means of preserving the Lib Dems' adherence to party democracy.[32] Initially the PPCs were a means for Lib Dem ministers to connect with the backbenchers from both Houses, but members of the Federal Policy Committee and Lib Dems from outside organisations (the Local Government Association, Student Associations, etc) were also invited to PPC meetings. There were complaints: FPC members were sometimes not clear on what their role was; non-parliamentary members were sometimes asked to leave meetings because of the confidential issues being discussed; and ministers privately wondered if

[28] K Deschouwer, 'Comparing Newly Governing Parties' in K Deschouwer (ed), *New Parties in Government: In Power for the First Time* (Abingdon, Routledge, 2008) 1–16, 10–11.

[29] AT Russell and E Fieldhouse, *Neither Left Nor Right? The Liberal Democrats and the Electorate* (Manchester, Manchester University Press, 2005); E Evans and E Sanderson-Nash, 'From Sandals to Suits: Professionalisation, Coalition and the Liberal Democrats' (2011) 13 *British Journal of Politics and International Relations* 459.

[30] Evans and Sanderson-Nash, 'From Sandals to Suits', ibid.

[31] A Russell, A Fieldhouse and E Cutts, 'De Facto Veto? The Parliamentary Liberal Democrats' (2007) 78(1) *Political Quarterly* 89.

[32] See ch 6.

members from the wider party should be there at all. But these were seen as temporary or teething problems: the commitment to internal party democracy was being maintained.

With so many senior Lib Dems now viewed primarily as representatives of the Coalition government, party members thought that it was necessary for other Lib Dem MPs to appear to be solely representatives of the party. For instance, when Vince Cable stepped down as deputy leader, Simon Hughes MP was elected in his place; and in mid-November 2010, Tim Farron MP was elected as President of the Lib Dems, his role being to act as 'a spokesperson for the party membership and to represent their views to the party leadership'.[33] Farron in particular played a key role in party differentiation. As Party President, previously a rather low-key role, Farron voiced the concerns of the broader party membership and appeared to advocate a strategy of equidistance from the two main parties.[34]

It is worth noting that Hughes and Farron were thought to come from the 'left' of the Lib Dems. Much was made of the 'split' between the Orange Bookers and Social Liberals in the first 18 months of the Coalition. The 'Orange Bookers' were those who had contributed to a 2004 book suggesting 'liberal' answers to long-standing problems – 'liberal answers' meaning choice and competition, and a shift away from the use of the state to solve issues.[35] Social Liberals, on the other hand, tended to see the state as a legitimate force for change.[36] These labels were crude: after all, Vince Cable, often perceived to be on the left of the party, contributed to the *Orange Book*; and Nick Clegg, often seen as being on the right, contributed to both the *Orange Book* and a later Lib Dem publication identified as Social Liberal.[37] But because many members of the Lib Dem frontbench were Orange Bookers (including Nick Clegg, Chris Huhne, David Laws and Ed Davey), this was seen as a potential source of division.

So the election of Hughes and Farron served to reassure the rank-and-file that their voice would be heard by the leadership. In practice, however, the matter was not so clear – as one Lib Dem activist noted, 'many Liberal Democrats are double-hatted and triple-hatted, which makes matters difficult'. Tim Farron, for instance, was not just Party President but also served on the Federal Executive Committee (FEC) and Federal Policy Committee (FPC). It made sense: the Party President could represent the wider membership to the leadership; but since he was sitting on the FEC and FPC he was also part of the leadership himself.

[33] BBC News, 'Tim Farron elected as Lib Dem president' (13 November 2011), www.bbc.co.uk/news/uk-11750362

[34] See, for instance, A Sparrow, 'Tim Farron: Labour "utterly dishonest" about state of economy' *Guardian* (18 November 2011), www.guardian.co.uk/politics/2011/nov/18/tim-farron-interview-andrew-sparrow?INTCMP=SRCH; and M Chorley, 'Lib Dem president accused of "slagging off the coalition"' *Independent* (1 January 2012), www.independent.co.uk/news/uk/politics/lib-dem-president-accused-of-slagging-off-the-coalition-6283807.html

[35] D Laws and P Marshall (eds), *The Orange Book: Reclaiming Liberalism* (London, Profile Books, 2004).

[36] The Social Liberals have their own website: see www.socialliberal.net.

[37] M Taylor et al, *Reinventing the State: Social Liberalism for the 21st Century* (London, Politico's, 2007).

The tuition fees debacle (see chapter ten) illustrated the difficulty of being a party of government, where painful trade-offs had to be made between the need to formulate policies attractive to voters and the realities of being in office. Such trade-offs could also be seen in debates over who determined policy within the party. One Lib Dem party member interviewed after the September 2011 Spring Conference noted:

> There is a bit of a split . . . between those who want to retain the ability of the Conference to decide issues in some detail; and those who recognise that it's not sensible for the Conference to decide detailed policy. . . . some motions do discuss things like the contractual requirements in GP contracts and so on. That's too detailed and ties the hands of the leaders too much, certainly in the context of a coalition but even in the context of single-party government.

It was not clear how this tension between the sovereign power of Conference and parliamentarians – particularly the leadership – could be resolved. Another Lib Dem activist argued that going into coalition had transformed the relationships between Lib Dem federal institutions and the wider party, which suggested further conflict over party policy in the future:

> The leadership of the party has got stronger, because they can implement policy. Whereas previously, you couldn't have Nick Clegg as Home Affairs Spokesman decide what the line was. [The] parliamentary party often . . . would determine that. The extra-parliamentary group is stronger than it was. Or at least more important because . . . the parliamentary party is reduced. Therefore what you're left with is the same constitutional powers of the extra-parliamentary party, the high profile and executivisation of the leadership . . . the leadership wants to ignore the party pretty much and crack on with delivering government. . . . The parliamentary party used to determine the policy. . . . Now . . . the parliamentary party, if it's told something, it's usually after the fact. It's pliant, because it's being whipped.

## Party Differentiation

The tensions of being in government, the weakening of the parliamentary party and the need to stay true to its activist roots could also be seen in the party debate over how the Lib Dems should differentiate themselves while in a coalition. There were strong differences of opinion about differentiation strategy between those in government and those outside, particularly Lib Dem activists.

Initially, the wider Lib Dem membership and many activists seemed willing to accept the stance the Lib Dem leadership had taken towards being in a coalition: that is, emphasising cooperation with the Conservatives and downplaying difference or conflict in the early stages of the Coalition, and engaging in party differentiation once good relations between the parties were established and the Coalition had stabilised. Thus the September 2010 Autumn Conference was a relatively quiet affair, with the party rank-and-file mostly approving of the leadership's actions. There was some ambivalence, as one Lib Dem activist suggested:

I was struck at conference in September [2010] at how people seemed to be in two minds. During Clegg's Q&A, he was asked whether he shouldn't be publicly disagreeing more. Huge round of applause. He said, 'no, we shouldn't – we have to show the Coalition can be stable'. Huge round of applause again.

The small group of party activists we interviewed wanted more active attempts at party differentiation from those in Parliament and in government. Talking about Richard Reeves (Nick Clegg's chief strategist) and his three-point plan (ie, unity and cohesion in the early years, followed by a progressive shift towards party differentiation in the later years of the Coalition),[38] one activist said:

The idea that you have to show that coalition works before you show how it works doesn't make sense . . . if you say, 'right now we'll show you how good coalition government is by not disagreeing on economic policy in [times] of crisis', that doesn't show how good coalition government is. It shows how far we're willing to sell out . . . you have to show from the beginning how it's working . . . you have to show the workings; you have to say this is what we thought, this is what they thought, this is what we compromised on, sometimes. Not all the time but sometimes.

And in spite of the establishment of all the subtle differentiation mechanisms noted in the previous section, issues such as tuition fees raised the question of what influence the Lib Dems might be having in government. As part of the party's attempt to show what its influence was, Cowley Street published a list of Lib Dem achievements in government in late December 2010: it listed 49 Lib Dem manifesto pledges which had been implemented.[39] This was later updated for the Spring Conference in March 2011: by this time, 106 pledges had been implemented.[40] The Lib Dems' most obvious 'policy win' was raising the income tax threshold, removing over a million people from the income tax system. But it was unclear whether publishing long lists of detailed policy impressed anyone other than the party faithful. Opinion polls suggested it was unclear that the wider public could discern the impact of the Lib Dems in government.[41]

There were conflicting reports regarding the impact on the Lib Dems of having entered into government. 2010 had seen a halt in the trend of declining party membership, which had dropped from 73,000 in 2001 to 59,000 in 2009. In 2010 membership rose to 65,000; but that was due to those joining during the 2010

---

[38] M d'Ancona, 'The Tories couldn't deliver the goods without the Lib Dems' *Telegraph* (15 January 2011), www.telegraph.co.uk/comment/columnists/matthewd_ancona/8262007/The-Tories-couldnt-deliver-the-goods-without-the-Lib-Dems.html

[39] *Liberal Democrats: Our Manifesto in Practice* (December 2010). For a discussion see H Duffett, 'The Liberal Democrat Manifesto in Practice' *Liberal Democrat Voice* (28 December 2010), www.libdemvoice.org/the-liberal-democrat-manifesto-in-practice-22566.html. Note that the December 2010 document was later modified in March 2011 to take into account further achievements in government.

[40] *Liberal Democrats: Our Manifesto in Practice* (March 2011), www.scribd.com/doc/50509263/Lib-Dem-Achievements-in-Govt-MARCH-2011-Red-indicates-new. This document modifies the document published in late December 2010. The document was not updated for the 2011 Autumn Conference.

[41] J Curtice, 'Shaping the Coalition' *Parliamentary Brief Online* (30 September 2011), www.parliamentarybrief.com/2011/09/shaping-the-coalition#all

election.[42] The Lib Dems' popularity in the polls steadily declined from formation in May 2010 until it reached single figures in late 2010.[43] In part this probably reflected the disappearance of the protest vote: voters disaffected with the Lib Dems were shifting their vote to other parties. But it was also a public backlash against the Lib Dems' actions in government, and the feeling that the Lib Dems had broken their pre-election promises – most obviously over tuition fees, but also over the 'U-turn' on dealing with the fiscal deficit, and growing wariness over proposed health reform.

By the March 2011 Spring Conference, the view of the wider membership had shifted towards the activists' view. At Conference, Lib Dems passed a motion on strategy, stating that Lib Dem ministers, MPs and peers should:

> . . . demonstrate to the wider public the specific contribution that we have made to the programme of the Coalition Government by identifying:
>
> a) Those policies which derive from the Liberal Democrat's existing and emerging policy platform.
> b) Those aspects of Government policy which Liberal Democrats have changed to be more consistent with our principles and beliefs.
> c) Those aspects of Government policy which originated from the Conservative party policy platform.[44]

In short, the wider party now wanted not just public evidence of the Lib Dems' contribution to government, but also a means by which they could distance themselves from unpopular policies – ie those they saw stemming from the Conservative Party. This was vital, for it seemed to members that even on 'coalition' policies the Lib Dems were shouldering a disproportionate amount of public blame. The Lib Dems were heading towards that strange stance which so many small parties in a coalition will take – what the Belgian Green Party called 'participposition'.[45]

The AV referendum campaign in late March–early May 2011 also hardened the view of Lib Dems both inside and outside Parliament that they needed to change their approach to being in government. The campaign stung Lib Dems: whereas Cameron's late intervention in early May 2011 won him plaudits from his party (both parliamentary party and the wider membership), Clegg was mostly sidelined in the campaign because he was seen as harmful to the chances of success.

The final result for the AV referendum was 68 per cent voting 'no' for electoral change and 32 per cent voting 'yes'.[46] That marked a low point for the Lib Dems

---

[42] The most recent data for Liberal Democrat membership appears to be here: Reports to Autumn Conference 2011 Birmingham (Autumn 2011), www.libdems.org.uk/siteFiles/resources/docs/conference/Reports%20to%20Conference%20Original%20Version.pdf

[43] See Appendix two.

[44] Liberal Democrat website, 'Carried with amendment: strategy, positioning and priorities' (13 March 2011), www.nickclegg.com/policy_motions_detail.aspx?title=Carried_with_amendment%3A_Strategy%2C_Positioning_and_Priorities&pPK=07a9d6af-9669-4fda-8560-5303c4e495f0

[45] Deschouwer, 'Comparing Newly Governing Parties' (n 28) 10.

[46] For the Liberal Democrats' own analysis of the AV referendum result see *Liberal Democrats Consultative Session Election Review May 2011*, www.libdems.org.uk/siteFiles/resources/docs/conference/Liberal%20Democrats%20Election%20Review%20.pdf

– it was another identifiable policy 'loss', but of equal concern were the results of the English local government elections. The Lib Dems lost almost 750 seats, mostly to Labour in the North, and to the Conservatives in the South (see Table 7.1). The Lib Dems also did very badly at the Scottish parliamentary elections, losing 12 of their 17 seats (see Table 7.2).

The leadership and the parliamentary party responded to Conference's March 2011 motion, most immediately on the NHS reforms (see chapter ten). The rest of 2011 saw attempts by key Lib Dems to assert their distinctiveness in relation to various issues: the August riots in England, banking reform, employment law reform, House of Lords reform and, of course, Europe. The Lib Dems' new aggressive stance on differentiation pleased activists and the broader membership, but it had no discernable impact on their opinion poll rating (see Appendix two).

## 2015: Coalition Redux?

A noticeable feature of interviews with Liberal Democrats was their consistency on most issues, but one matter on which they differed strongly was what would happen in 2015 and beyond. One Lib Dem staffer argued:

> I am absolutely sure that there will not be a Lib Dem-Con coalition after 2015. The party wouldn't stand for it again. The only way it might happen [would be] if the election result was exactly the same. The party would be absolutely desperate not to. The party does not want to be seen as the permanent junior branch of the Conservative Party. If there is *any* possibility of doing a deal with Labour rather than the Conservatives at the next election, that's what will happen.

But one Lib Dem minister expressed pessimism about a coalition with Labour:

> It's not about shared ideology, it's about shared obligation . . . you've built up enough trust in order to make that happen. . . . the Labour Party are obsessed with briefing against one another. I think they would be hell to be in coalition with . . . because you have to have high levels of trust and better behaviour in coalition. . . . They'd have to sort out their personal behaviour.

These two points of view demonstrate the gap between those Lib Dems 'inside' government and Parliament, and those within the wider party 'outside' Westminster and Whitehall. The minister's stance – quite typical of Lib Dem parliamentarian interviewees – stemmed from the experience of working in government and having to respond to a hostile Labour opposition on a daily basis. The staffer's focus was on the broader Lib Dem membership, and the belief that equidistance between the parties was the best means of ensuring future electoral success. One activist opined on the lack of strategic thinking about the future:

> My big fear is that you could have a situation in the next election . . . where the maths suggest the greater logic of a Labour Lib Dem [coalition] . . . [but] the well will have been poisoned because we have been attacking each other so unreasonably. . . . Clegg

never concedes that Labour are doing anything right and blames them . . . [We need to show] a willingness to work with both sides, showing that the point of coalition is not about agreeing but about negotiating, which we had better start doing soon – otherwise people will think it's extraordinary to be going with Labour when in fact it's absolutely normal if we go in with Labour next time.

The Lib Dems' position at the time of writing (December 2011) reflected the views of the broader membership: equidistance. This was agreed to at the March 2011 Spring Conference:

The Liberal Democrats will fight the next general election in Great Britain as an independent party without any pacts or agreements with any other party and presenting our manifesto as the clear and distinct basis for liberal government. . . .

The Liberal Democrats intend to enter the next general election campaign with no preference for potential future coalition partners.[47]

Thus there was consternation amongst Lib Dems in late November 2011, when Chancellor George Osborne announced in his Autumn budget statement that he would extend his austerity programme beyond 2015 because of lower growth. The Lib Dem Chief Secretary, Danny Alexander, later stated publicly that the Lib Dems would need to work with the Conservatives on plans for two years following 2015. This seemed to contradict the party's position determined by Conference in March 2011, and various Lib Dem figures, including Simon Hughes, deputy leader of the Liberal Democrat parliamentary party, were quick to reject the implications of Alexander's comments.[48]

By early 2012 the Liberal Democrats were reviewing how to deal with future negotiations, including how to appoint the negotiating team (and whether this should be limited to just MPs), and a revision of the triple lock procedure. The wider party was pushing back, insisting on adherence to greater party democracy.

The Lib Dems' dilemma was not assisted by Labour's oft-changing stance towards them: Labour oscillated between treating the Lib Dems as part of the Government; denigrating them as the weak link within the Government; or making appeals to the Lib Dems to break with the Conservatives and work with Labour. So, for instance, in December 2010 the newly elected Labour Party leader Ed Miliband persuaded eight former Lib Dem parliamentary candidates, including Richard Grayson, a former Liberal Democrat Policy Director, to take part in Labour's policy review process.[49] Over 2011, however, there were attempts from Labour to encourage the press to refer to the Coalition as the 'Conservative-led Government', downplaying the Lib Dems' role and emphasising the dominant role of the Conservatives.[50] In the

---

[47] 'Carried with amendment' (n 44).

[48] 'Liberal Democrats fear Conservative election grip' *Financial Times* (20 November 2011), www.ft.com/cms/s/0/cdf4050c-1b6a-11e1-85f8-00144feabdc0.html#axzz1hGCMzmE1

[49] BBC News, 'Ed Miliband asks Lib Dems to help draw up Labour policy' (13 December 2010), www.bbc.co.uk/news/uk-politics-11981011. Grayson himself was a Lib Dem to the 'left' of the party.

[50] J Murphy, 'Don't say Coalition, say Tory-led government, Labour's spin chief tells media' *Evening Standard* (18 January 2011), www.thisislondon.co.uk/standard/article-23915147-dont-say-coalition-say-tory-led-labours-spin-chief-tells-media.do

Parliamentary Voting Systems and Constituencies Bill debate in February and March 2011, relations between Labour peers and Lib Dem peers became poisonous. One Lib Dem peer said:

> Now that the Coalition has been going and Labour realise it's working, quite a lot of them are furious with us for 'betraying them'. So there's quite a lot of antagonism now and [the Parliamentary Voting Systems and Constituencies Bill] hasn't helped. I'm really furious at the way Labour have behaved on this. They're going to have to work really hard to re-build relations with us because . . . they've messed about and it's in no small measure aimed at us.

Labour again made overtures to the Lib Dems following David Cameron's use of the British veto at a Brussels summit in early December 2011, encouraging Lib Dems to break with the Conservatives over Europe.[51] These overtures were rejected by leading Lib Dems.[52] Labour's continually changing stance toward the Lib Dems suggested that they had not yet thought about positioning for the next election, or that the leadership was intent on securing a single-party majority.[53] This was in spite of evidence suggesting that it would still need to rely on third parties in order to secure a majority in the Commons.[54]

## CONCLUSION

Forming a coalition with the Lib Dems affected the Conservatives least: intraparty conflict, often stemming from a tension about whether to focus on the Conservative core vote over a broader voting public (crudely expressed in terms of a debate between 'mainstream' conservatism and modernisation), would have happened anyway under single-party government. What differed was the oft-raised concern regarding a lack of emphasis on Tory policies rather than coalition policies. There were attempts to address this by means of changes within the party organisation, giving greater 'voice' to the party outside the frontbench, but the Conservatives' traditional reliance on their leader remained strong: David Cameron came under pressure to assert party distinctiveness.

Entering a coalition had immediate, ongoing and long-term effects on the Lib Dems as a political party. Most immediately, there was the loss of state funding,

---

[51] D Alexander, 'Labour will make a big, open offer to the Lib Dems on Europe' *New Statesman* (13 December 2011), www.newstatesman.com/politics/2011/12/britain-europe-dems-british

[52] A Grice, 'Lib Dems laugh off Ed Balls' calls for a new coalition' *Independent* (22 December 2011), www.independent.co.uk/news/uk/politics/lib-dems-laugh-off-ed-balls-call-for-a-new-coali-tion-6280396.html?origin=internalSearch

[53] For a rare exception see M Sowemimo, 'The Next Hung Parliament: How Labour Can Prepare' (London, Compass, 2010), www.clients.squareeye.net/uploads/compass/documents/Hung_parliament_2011.pdf

[54] See eg J Curtice, 'British Gloom has yet to light Labour's hopes' *Parliamentary Brief* (7 December 2011), www.parliamentarybrief.com/2011/12/british-gloom-has-yet-to-lighten-labours-hopes#all; P Diamond and G Radice, *Southern Discomfort Again?* (London, Policy Network, 2011), www.policy-network.net/uploads/media/154/7134.pdf

which severely weakened the party as an effective organisation. More generally, there were ongoing issues stemming from entering into government: most obviously, dealing with the inevitable tension between efficient and effective government and the need to retain party democracy; and having to make tough decisions about whether to prioritise policy over votes, or vice versa. And finally, there was the problem of signalling distinctiveness, or impact in government. These pressures were reflected in shifts in power – sometimes intended, sometimes unintended – in the institutional structure of the party. The Lib Dems had exhibited considerable inventiveness in establishing differentiation mechanisms: these demonstrated potential to show distinctiveness to the party membership, but it was not clear that the Lib Dems had succeeded in communicating their distinctiveness to the wider public. The end of 2011 saw the Lib Dems still looking for an identifiable policy win.

Finally, none of the parties, including Labour, had yet come to grips with the possibility of another hung parliament in 2015. This was understandable: it was simply too early, and it was unclear whether or not another hung parliament would result from a general election. Both the Conservatives and Labour thought in terms of securing a single-party majority, and perhaps, failing that, a single-party minority. The Lib Dems, on the other hand, were caught in a dilemma. Many feared an ongoing relationship with the Conservatives, but could not see how they might cooperate with Labour. Coalition had broken the assumption that the two parties were natural allies; and Labour's aggressive behaviour in opposition had not helped build any kind of rapprochement. The end of 2011 saw no resolution to this dilemma.

# 8

# The Coalition and the Media

BRIAN WALKER

The media find it easy to have a default division. It used to be Europhile/Eurosceptic, Blair/Brown and now it's Tory/Lib Dem. (Nick Robinson, BBC)

## INTRODUCTION

IN ITS FIRST 18 months, the Coalition faced a basic problem that it never entirely resolved: Should it speak with a single voice, or with two voices? In unison was the obvious answer, particularly over the critical issues of financial and economic management. But how then should each party register political gains, especially if these were at the other's expense?

The unity/distinctiveness dilemma is a theme running through this book. Another is how to evaluate the performance of the Coalition. How successful it is deemed to have been will depend on the observer and their point of view. In this chapter we look at the Coalition Government's relations with the media from four different perspectives. We study first the Government's media operation, and how Whitehall sought to project the Coalition as unified and effective. Next we examine how the media reported on the Coalition, and whether it depicted it as unified or split. Finally we discuss the media strategies of the two coalition parties and their effectiveness, in particular in terms of the effect on their poll ratings.

The chapter describes how the Coalition survived critical media scrutiny but at the cost of compromising an image of pristine unity. This occurred particularly during three stress tests of their own making and two major developments at the end of 2011 beyond the Coalition's control; persistently low economic growth leading to an extension of the planned period of austerity by two years; and the fallout from the crisis over Europe and the euro which they had been desperate to avoid. The earlier stress tests of the first year we discuss in greater detail in chapters nine and ten. They were the Liberal Democrats' U-turn over their election pledge to abolish university tuition fees; the 'agreement to disagree' over the Alternative Vote (AV) for electing MPs; and 'the pause' to rethink the sweeping reforms to the National Health Service. We concentrate on the Tory press. We do so because although a section of it came under unprecedented scrutiny itself, it remained the largest part of the media, and, despite falling circulation, still greatly influenced the political agenda for politicians and broadcasters alike.

Political communication under a coalition was bound to be different than for single-party government. Prime ministerial spin had been viable under New Labour because 'what Tony wants' dictated all else. Gordon Brown's protestations of openness were undermined by the hostile private briefings of his communications aide Damian McBride. David Cameron could not behave like either of his Labour predecessors. Everything of importance had to go through the Coalition; he had to consult Nick Clegg.

As the media tested its fault lines, the image of unity gave way to a coalition of differences. Asserting Lib Dem distinctiveness may have stabilised Nick Clegg's leadership, but it encouraged the media in their instinctive hunt for 'splits'. David Cameron was a more reluctant differentiator, but pressure from his own right wing was becoming harder to resist, urged on by the Tory press.

Nevertheless, essential coalition solidarity held, due to the overriding importance of managing the economy, some shared values, and the knowledge that too much open division would threaten cohesion and even survival. For evidence, the chapter relies on the unfolding story of the Coalition as told by the media and discussed in interviews with senior journalists and media handlers in both parties and the civil service.

### THE MEDIA OPERATION FOR A COALITION

Governing by coalition required a fundamental recasting of the Downing Street media operation after 13 years of Labour spin and rebuttal had transformed into a barely controllable vortex. The precedent of the Brown years to appoint a civil servant to head the operation was not followed; there was to be a politically balanced media team led by a Conservative special adviser (spad). The Lib Dems did not object; they accepted that No 10 was Cameron territory. Six of the original media team were Conservative spads, two were Lib Dems. Andy Coulson was appointed director of communications, with Lena Pietsch, Nick Clegg's chief spokesperson, as his deputy. It was the high watermark of the influence of tabloid journalism in government. Even Blair and Brown, so close to Rupert Murdoch in government, had never gone as far as to appoint a former News International editor who had quit his chair under a cloud of uncertain size.

Lib Dem warnings of possible contamination fell far short of the veto they could surely have exercised over his appointment. Yet from accounts given by Conservative and Lib Dem professionals involved, Andy Coulson made the transition from party attack dog to coalition media chief smoothly.

Coulson's successors were eager to contrast the togetherness of coalition with the intrigue and suspicion of Labour. From the front lobby of No 10, doors that had once been slammed shut were thrown open along the corridor through No 11 to No 12, now Downing Street centre's communications suite. Walk along a short passage in No 12 and you came to the little panelled office where the Conservative, Lib Dem and civil service government spokespersons sat desk to desk. One of them noted: 'Initially when we had a phone call to make, tension rose and we'd go into a corner somewhere. But all that stopped and we now make phone calls quite openly'.

Every speech of the Prime Minister and Deputy Prime Minister was signed off by the other. When it came to party speeches there was no signing off, but they still saw them. Every morning the No 10 communications staff set the course of the day together, before splitting up to take their instructions at the strategy meetings held for Cameron and Clegg separately. In the late afternoon they reconvened as a joint team to reset for the morning papers and look ahead. This was the routine through which coalition presentation evolved. David Cameron gave his personal authority to new rules forbidding briefing against the other party; anyone caught breaking them would be sacked. But all this turned out not to be quite as impressive as it first seemed. Events showed that there was no bar on ministers flatly contradicting each other in public. And could aspersions on the other party always be avoided if you were explaining in private why your party's approach was better than theirs?

## AWAY FROM THE CENTRE: SPADS AND PARTY HQS

The Centre was supposed to coordinate the briefing role of the special advisers to ministers in the departments. Of more than 50 Conservative spads, almost half were on media work, whereas most of the 20-odd Lib Dems worked on policy as well. Both parties' HQ media staff supplemented their efforts, even though their staffing had been cut since the election, the Conservatives down from 30 to a dozen, the Lib Dems from 13 to 5. Typically they lined up loyal MPs for interview and provided rebuttal comment. None of their work, both insisted, amounted to briefing against the other coalition partner, except during the 'agreement to disagree' over the Alternative Vote campaign which got quite personal. The Lib Dems constantly complained of a lack of resources. For instance, party HQ had to offer political support to spad-less Lib Dem ministers such as the pensions Minister Steve Webb. Said a Lib Dem party source: 'We could not go to a Conservative spad for information, so the only source was Steve himself'. For a party comprised of young people, experience of government comms was practically non-existent compared to the 'powerhouses' of the two larger parties. The Lib Dem view was that by the time of the Coalition's first anniversary, the parties and the civil service still had not worked out a properly coordinated communications strategy. In October 2011, this was partly addressed by the appointment of six new Lib Dem spads working across departments.

## EARLY MEDIA ATTITUDES TO COALITION

How did the new order of government fare with those parts of the media holding a left, right and zero-sum view of the world? While they carried a variety of political news and views, all the tabloids except the pro-Labour *Daily Mirror* were their own brand of Tory. The *Daily Telegraph* and the *Daily Mail* presented an alternative Conservative agenda for economic growth and were suspicious of Cameron modernisation. The *Times* was the Tory modernisers' only consistent supporter. The *Guardian*, which controversially supported the Lib Dems in the election, leaned towards the higher deficit spending adopted by Labour. The *Independent* was the Lib Dems' only half-reliable friend.

For the right wing press, coalition was an affront to the established order. Newspapers that had backed the Conservatives for the 2010 election found that things were never to be same again. Four factors shaped change. First, the Lib Dems, whom the Tory press had largely ignored, were now a second centre of power. Second, the vigorous Toryism of both the *Daily Telegraph* and the Mr Angry of the press, the *Daily Mail*, was more than the Coalition could accept. Third, there was a perception in politics that newspapers' influence was being chipped away by falling circulation, the continuing dominance of television, and the growth of new media. The parties' publicity machines were now exploiting social media to break the papers' old monopoly on defining the story. The last change factor was the review of media ethics and regulation included in the Leveson inquiry into the *News of the World* phone hackling scandal.[1] This was likely to force them to tone down excesses of behaviour even in the rough and tumble of political journalism.

Politicians' fear of the tabloids was at last exposed. At the height of the phone hacking revelations in the summer of 2011, the admissions from MPs Simon Hughes and Tom Watson that politicians were 'scared of the barons of the media and their red-topped assassins'[2] echoed Tony Blair's valedictory warning of the 'feral media just tearing people and reputations to bits' and reducing government's ability to take decisions.[3]

## A BRIEF HONEYMOON

David Cameron and Nick Clegg's personal commitment to coalition unity immediately impressed the public, satisfied the wider Lib Dem Party (the Conservative rank-and-file were not consulted) and calmed the markets. 'It's now impossible to do "split" stories', declared the BBC's political editor Nick Robinson (somewhat

---

[1]  The Leveson Inquiry is discussed at www.levesoninquiry.org.uk

[2]  N Watt, 'Phone hacking: MPs "were too scared to testify in court" says MP' *Guardian* (9 September 2010), www.guardian.co.uk/media/2010/sep/09/phone-hacking-mps-scared-testify

[3]  BBC News, 'Blair on the media: full text' (12 June 2007), www.news.bbc.co.uk/1/hi/uk_politics/6744581.stm

rashly). Once the moment of euphoria was over, senior journalists of the left and right reflected on the nature of the Coalition Agreement:

> It's still the main document for the PM's official spokesman. Someone said it's treated like 'a mixture of the Koran and the Bible'. It's also looked at seriously by the civil service. Over time, it'll become frayed. (Patrick Wintour, Political Editor, *The Guardian*)

> There's always trouble when the Government do things that are not on that list. An example of that is Conservatives' abandonment of lower inheritance tax. The Lib Dems rather neatly regard the Agreement as the last word on what the Government would do. The tuition fees episode illustrates that this was a naïve view. Another example was forestry, hardly likely to be in any manifesto. A third example is NHS policy where both parties wanted to go further than they said in the Agreement. (Danny Finkelstein, Executive Editor, *The Times*)

Finkelstein was right. The Coalition's biggest tests were not over legitimacy ('the Government nobody elected') or the Agreement's status, but over fudges or unforeseen issues. The first year fell roughly into two parts: May to November, when the Coalition concentrated on establishing its credentials for government; and from then on, when they went through self-imposed stress tests in which party differences were laid bare.

## THE *TELEGRAPH* TARGETS THE LIB DEMS

But first, the *Daily Telegraph* performed a couple of stress tests of its own on the newcomers to power, the Lib Dems. Only three weeks into government, the sudden resignation of the Lib Dem Treasury Chief Secretary David Laws,[4] an apparent pillar of financial and personal rectitude, came as a result of a delayed action *Telegraph* scoop dug out from its voluminous files of MPs' expenses claims.[5] Although Laws' departure was essentially a throwback to the previous Parliament, it planted the notion that the Lib Dems were the Coalition's weak link with the public.

Then in December, hungry for new scoops after its MPs' expenses coup, the *Telegraph* made a minor scandal of the fact that seven Lib Dem ministers were guilty of saying one thing about their new Conservative colleagues in public and another in their surgeries, much less complimentary, to a brace of personable young women reporters posing as constituents. It was an odd use of undercover techniques and, to some, unethical and unnecessary in political journalism. Despite censure from the Press Complaints Commission, the *Telegraph* was unrepentant. The comments of Lib Dem Business Secretary Vince Cable in particular gave a rare insight into the reality of coalition relationships:

---

[4] See ch 4.

[5] H Watt and R Winnett, 'Treasury Chief David Laws, his second lover and a £40,000 claim' *Telegraph* (28 May 2010), www.telegraph.co.uk/news/newstopics/mps-expenses/7780642/MPs-Expenses-Treasury-chief-David-Laws-his-secret-lover-and-a-40000-claim.html

You can argue these things publicly, but then it becomes more difficult to get them to compromise ... there is a constant battle going on behind the scenes ... They know I have nuclear weapons, but I don't have any conventional weapons. If they push me too far then I can walk out of the Government and bring the Government down and they know that. So it is a question of how you use that intelligently without getting involved in a war that destroys all of us.[6]

## RESTIVENESS ON THE RIGHT

By no means was the media pressure felt only by the Lib Dems. Seldom had press support for a new Conservative Prime Minister been so heavily qualified. Cameron had failed to win the election. If he couldn't beat Brown, could he beat anyone? As the economy failed to grow, the Tory press increased pressure for a whole package of deeper cuts and lower taxes, a firmer grip on crime and immigration, a British referendum on repatriating powers from Brussels, and moves to reduce the role of the Strasbourg court over British human rights. Every coalition policy shift began to be labelled a U-turn: axing free school milk for the under-fives, imposing child benefit cuts on higher earners, withdrawing funding for sports partnerships, and selling off state-owned forests; this, despite the fact that most of them were not interparty disputes.

## WEAKNESSES UNDER ANDY COULSON

By the end of 2010, strategic and structural weaknesses at the Centre had been recognised, including the need to grip big themes that cut across parties and departments. Nick Clegg acquired a new civil service head of communications, James Sorene. The No 10 and Cabinet Office press operations were to become more integrated to achieve closer central control of the communications efforts of the Whitehall departments.

This was the outcome of a report produced in March 2011 by Matt Tee, the outgoing permanent secretary of Government Communications. It recommended replacing the old semi-independent Central Office of Information (COI) with a new Government Communications Centre, and the axing of more than half of the COI's 2,000 jobs.

The strategy deficit had been evident for some time under Andy Coulson. Coulson's strength had been his ability, as an Essex boy made good, to say at meetings what the *Daily Mail* and *Sun* leader columns would say. But it wasn't a strategy; it was an instinct. He lacked an evidential base. According to a former official close to the media operation, the disbandment of the strategic communications group

---

[6]    H Watt, R Winnett and H Blake, 'Vince Cable: "I could bring down the Government if I'm pushed"' *Telegraph* (20 December 2010), www.telegraph.co.uk/news/politics/liberaldemocrats/8215462/Vince-Cable-I-could-bring-down-the-Government-if-Im-pushed.html.

was one step too far and it had been a mistake to allow the planning grid, the weekly diary of government announcements and events, to become 'less forcibly managed'. In Labour's heyday under the long serving grid manager Paul Brown, who retired in March 2011, even cabinet ministers had had to toe the line of his quality control by providing announcements strong enough to make first or second leads in news programmes and help give strategic coherence to government policy. A less centralised approach might have seemed appropriate for a return to cabinet government, particularly under a coalition. But Coulson, the former official felt, had reduced media planning to the point where the Coalition was losing the initiative. Nor did he seem to have adequate control of the special advisers in the departments:

> Under Andy Coulson I don't think the political side of the house at No 10 was ever sure whether if somebody dropped a clanger, at [the Department of] Energy and Climate Change, say, did Andy Coulson as head spad for the Coalition ring up a Liberal Democrat spad and give them a bollocking? Or did it have to be a Liberal Democrat who did that? Coulson – I don't think – ever really got his head around the fact that while there is no political party called 'The Coalition', you do have to have a political voice which the civil service cannot voice for you, which is a differentiator between you and the Labour Party. You need to think about how you manage that voice.

Benedict Brogan of the *Telegraph* complained that Steve Field, the civil servant who was the Prime Minister's official spokesman under Coulson, lacked authority because he gave the impression that he was 'not in the room' when political decisions were taken. But Field's role was to brief on government policy, not on party positioning. Downing Street's riposte was that while there was a lot of day-to-day media, the Prime Minister felt that only a few big issues really mattered.

## NEW POLITICAL AND MEDIA STRATEGIES

For a new No 10 communications strategy, the timing of Coulson's resignation in the New Year over the mounting phone hacking scandal was fortuitous. Two conflicting jobs were separated: handling the day-to-day media cycle and devising a clearer political strategy to bring coherence to government messages. The top Conservative strategist Steve Hilton was freed up to concentrate on overall government as distinct from political strategy. Hilton was Cameron's conscience. The *Times*' Danny Finkelstein described his function in Hilton language:

> 'Why the hell are you doing this job, Dave? You might be out in three years' time anyway, so why don't you bloody well do something?' His great power is to counter the polls, the focus groups and the civil servants, and ask why we are doing this.

Craig Oliver, the replacement for the former Tory tabloid editor, was a very different creature. A former ITN journalist and editor of the BBC's Election 2010 coverage, Oliver's television background marked a significant shift in media priorities away from newspapers in the digital age. The gap in strategic planning was filled by the complementary appointment of Andrew Cooper, founder of the polling company Populus who in earlier years had 'knocked around with Dave' and was noted for his fearlessness in telling evidence-based truth to power.

Cooper was drafted in belatedly to achieve for the Conservatives what the late Philip Gould had done for New Labour.[7] Cameron and George Osborne had recognised that the fits and starts of the past year were a drift back to the negative image of the election campaign. Cooper was to give a sense of internal coherence to what the party would stand for up to May 2015, and to the values voters associated with Cameron. This, it will be noted, was a strategy for Cameron and the Conservatives, not the Coalition. Cooper's intensive private polling and focus group work (funded by the Conservative Party, not by the Government), was aimed at producing results that convinced the public that the Coalition was doing all it could to mitigate pain and build trust. This applied to the spending cuts but also to immigration and the aftermath of the summer riots of 2011.

Where did the Lib Dems fit in? Shoulder to shoulder, if Cooper had his way, with nothing much to say about party differentiation. The original strategy of his nominal Lib Dem deputy, Richard Reeves, was complementary. His three-point plan recommended: first, establishing the Lib Dems' credibility in government; second, freshening up their appeal in the mid term; and third, explicitly differentiating themselves from the Conservatives as a distinct party in the next general election, but not before April 2015. Although the Lib Dems drastically foreshortened the timetable after only 10 months in government, the Conservatives preferred to play it long and limit differentiation in the interests of both the Lib Dems and the Coalition, as they saw it.

A key Cooper argument was that wider public opinion was more important than party opinion at this stage. And the Conservatives, bluntly, knew so much more about public opinion than the Lib Dems, even about Lib Dem supporters, partly because the Conservatives had 'a hundred times more resources' to find out what the voters thought. Furthermore, Cooper was no fan of the Lib Dems' political reform agenda. In his view they were wrong to insist on the AV referendum so early in the Parliament, and Lords reform might remain beached in spite of its inclusion in the Coalition Agreement (see chapter nine). Cooper's friend and supporter of Conservative modernisation, Danny Finkelstein of the *Times*, took the low view of Lib Dem strategy even further:

> The Lib Dems have strangely little idea of what the voters think, partly to do with a shortage of party resources. They often get it locally. But no party would have had an immigration amnesty for the election or made a mess of AV and then turned to Lords reform as the next issue.

### STRESS TEST FOR THE LIBERAL DEMOCRATS: TUITION FEES

For the right wing press, targeting the Lib Dems was not only ideologically agree-able; it also reflected changing public opinion. While poll ratings for both parties soon fell after the initial honeymoon, the Conservatives steadied at around the late 30 per cent level of the general election, but the Lib Dems plummeted to a morale shattering 9 per cent by the end of 2010, as many voters felt betrayed at their joining the Coalition. Labour's gain to a level just ahead of the Conservatives was almost entirely at the Lib Dems' expense. As an Ipsos Mori analysis pointed out, dissatisfaction with the Lib Dems was also increasing dissatisfaction with the Coalition itself[8] (see Appendix two for further poll analysis).

Yet if the papers were remorseless, for the most part the Lib Dems were authors of their own misfortune. The university tuition fees debacle showed what can happen when a party in opposition makes a promise, tries and fails to change its terms, and is then ultimately unable to keep it in government (see chapter ten). Lib Dems later confessed to a PR disaster; they should have concentrated on the fact that the new fee repayments system would be more progressive than the old, rather than obsessing over the party processes that had locked them into trouble. The verdict of the BBC's Political Editor Nick Robinson was more polite than many, but damning just the same:

> Because the leadership were arguing for a policy the leadership didn't believe in and had tried to change, they probably thought the public already knew they had no intention of doing it and didn't really believe in it. But the public didn't know that. I think the Lib Dems have got to be a bit careful of self-pity on this. When a party stares into a lens to say one thing and does the opposite, you get a bad press. It's not a competence problem, like if only they had only spun it better.

### STRESS TEST FOR BOTH PARTIES: AV REFERENDUM

By May 2011 it had become clear that the Lib Dems' insistence in the 'agreement to disagree' on bringing forward a referendum on the Alternative Vote early in the Parliament and on the same day as English council elections, had more disagree-ing about it than they bargained for. Their friendly coalition partners had become the 'ruthless' Conservatives once more (see chapter nine). Election mode was back in full swing and the Lib Dems suffered yet again. The AV referendum cam-paign being a cross-party campaign with a Labour split, coalition cohesion was all but suspended.

Senior Lib Dems accused Cameron and the Conservative campaign manager George Osborne of telling lies about the horrors of AV. Lib Dem Secretary of State

---

[8]  S Pope and H Cleary, 'The Coalition's balancing act' *politics.co.uk* (16 May 2011), www.politics.co.uk/comment-analysis/2011/5/16/analysis-the-coalition-s-balancing-act

for Energy and Climate Change Chris Huhne did so across the cabinet table. The verdict of the LSE's Robin Archer at the time was apt:

> The AV referendum campaign is a disgrace. The Yes campaign is bad. The No campaign is worse. Both are so keen to use the brightest colours and stir the most visceral emotions that they have not just exaggerated or obfuscated the issues but have built their arguments around claims that are either willfully misleading or completely fictitious.[9]

Attacks on 'Calamity Clegg' from the anti-AV press – Labour-leaning as well as Tory – went with the grain of public opinion expressed by the 2 to 1 majority that voted against changing first past the post. And it was not unfair to ask if the Lib Dems were trying to rig the system in favour of permanent coalition, leaving themselves perpetually in power.

## CLEGG: 'FROM HERO TO ZERO'

During both stress tests – over the AV referendum and the tuition fees U-turn – the media did not take the lead or create the climate. But to the Lib Dems, media efforts to match their earlier MPs' expenses scoops felt like harassment. A senior party media handler described the onslaught for much of the Coalition's first year:

> The press coverage of Clegg's social mobility strategy launched in April 2011 focused on just one thing: that Clegg had benefited from an internship in his father's bank. What happened then was a familiar pattern, that insinuations were amplified and up to a score of BBC staffers keep ringing up to ask if there was any truth behind the hints, terrified in case they missed a story which was only a hare set by the Tory press. Another example came in February when the political gossip blogger Guido Fawkes and others asked why Scottish Secretary Mike Moore was absent for a division, linking this to wild rumours of a black dominatrix and his forthcoming resignation. This is a party that has been in crisis communications mode since the first leaders' debate.

For a less experienced Lib Dem spad, self-criticism verged on self-pity:

> The Tory press want to kill us and they hate themselves for having to keep us alive . . . Tuition fees are going to haunt us for five years. The charge is we lied over tuition fees and people can grasp that. We don't have many friends: The *Mail*, *Sun* and *Telegraph* don't like us, the *Mirror* hates us, the *Guardian* feel betrayed . . . We are phenomenally overstretched and overworked.

## THE LIB DEMS FIGHT BACK

After the AV disaster and with their support flatlining at around 10 per cent, the Lib Dems longed for a run of success. Nick Clegg had begun to assert Lib Dem

---

[9] R Archer, 'A disgraceful referendum campaign has obscured the real case for AV' *LSE Blog* (1 May 2011), www.blogs.lse.ac.uk/politicsandpolicy/2011/05/01/av-campaigns-disgraceful

distinctiveness more boldly in public as early as January 2011 by 'lifting the relationship with the Conservatives onto . . . a more business like arrangement . . . and to let the public know more about the process by which we reach agreement'. But any impact he might have hoped for was lost in the tuition fees debacle and the AV referendum defeat. Coinciding with the Coalition's first anniversary in May, it was time for a relaunch. As a senior adviser close to Clegg put it:

> People want to hear a clearer voice from the Lib Dems. It is very dangerous to seem gagged by the Tories. You can win all the battles you like behind closed doors but winning them outside is very difficult. Yet on future relations within the Coalition, we will not be forced apart. You will not hear a word about a plan B. This doesn't mean there aren't difficulties in language over, say, immigration and the Home Office. But in the long term we will stick together. Neither party will get any credit if we don't.

### STRESS TEST FOR BOTH PARTIES: NHS REFORMS

This time differentiation yielded results, although some were exaggerated. Reneging on a previous Cabinet consensus, Nick Clegg warned in spring 2011 that unless there were 'substantial, significant changes' to the mammoth Health and Social Care Bill provisions on handing commissioning powers to GPs and extending private provision of services, he would tell Lib Dem MPs and peers to join Labour in voting them down.[10] After registering Clegg's speech, Cooper and Oliver went jointly to tell Cameron to report their own findings that proposed reforms were not working with professional and public opinion. While this was in the interests of the Coalition, it was also a partisan Conservative move to trump Clegg's initiative. Cooper saw a risk to the Conservatives if they allowed the Lib Dems to monopolise on compassion. He was all too aware of the potential for the Lib Dems to claim at the next election that the Conservatives were planning to privatise the NHS and that they had stopped it. That the Conservative strategists could not allow.

As a result of the NHS 'listening exercise', or 'pause', recommended by Cooper, Nick Clegg leapt in first by declaring victory for 13 Lib Dem objectives, a partisan claim that incensed Tory backbenchers.[11] But Cooper's tactics had bought time to make changes that may have saved the bill and both parties' faces. As the BBC's Nick Robinson commented:

> The media find it easy to have a default division. It used to be Europhile/Eurosceptic, Blair/Brown and now it's Tory/Lib Dem. Actually, over the NHS it was as much that Cameron thought Lansley had got it wrong as Clegg. We can be over-absorbed with the Lib Dems.

---

[10] 'Nick Clegg threatens to block NHS reforms' *Guardian* (8 May 2011), www.guardian.co.uk/politics/2011/may/08/nick-clegg-veto-nhs-reforms. See also ch 10.

[11] P Hennessey and L Donnelly, 'Clegg: NHS U-turn is big win for Lib Dems' *Telegraph* (11 June 2011), www.telegraph.co.uk/news/politics/nick-clegg/8570422/Clegg-NHS-U-turn-is-big-win-for-Lib-Dems.html

Downing Street even made a virtue of the competition between the parties by claiming victory for the Coalition:

> Clegg didn't sound off. His people briefed. Political parties always brief around the margin. It would be different if the PM and the DPM openly disagreed. This hasn't happened over the NHS. There had been no support for the reforms from the professional bodies to start with, but at least we ended up with a hearing. To us, that was major success, but the mainstream media reported it as a U-turn. Success for our communications isn't always about success in the media.

## THE COURSE OF LIB DEM DIFFERENTIATION

As a political positioning technique, Lib Dem differentiation proved to be a double-edged sword, creating as much hostility among Conservatives as approval on their own side and promoting the theme of 'split' stories, the very outcome the Coalition had set out to avoid. Messages could be confusing; some differentiation was clearly choreographed between the two leaderships, while some was obviously about outright disagreement. It was one thing for Clegg to commend positive Lib Dem contributions, but quite another to list Conservative measures the Lib Dems had blocked, including pledges to cut inheritance tax, replace Trident in the parliamentary session, build more prisons and reform the Human Rights Act.[12] These claims inevitably drew return fire. David Cameron publicly declined to accept a Lib Dem moderating role. A browse through the Constitution Unit's archive of media coalition coverage reveals the range and depth of coalition clashes large and small.[13]

While positioning was a natural function of political activity, more often than not it was the impact of the clash that lingered while the later compromise barely registered. At the September 2011 Lib Dem party conference Clegg declared: 'Let me say something really clear about the Human Rights Act. In fact I'll do it in words of one syllable: It is here to stay'. Less than a fortnight later, Tory Home Secretary Theresa May told the *Telegraph*, 'I'd personally like to see the Human Rights Act go'.[14] That same month, Chris Huhne told *Prospect* magazine:

> If the cut in the top rate of tax is just a way of helping the Conservatives' friends in the City to put their feet up, then forget it. They are simply not going to get the votes in the House of Commons.[15]

---

[12] R Winnett, 'Nick Clegg to boast of blocked Conservative policies' *Telegraph* (11 May 2011), www.telegraph.co.uk/news/politics/nick-clegg/8505968/Nick-Clegg-to-boast-of-blocked-Conservative-policies.html

[13] See the Constitution Unit coalition government webpage, www.ucl.ac.uk/constitution-unit/research/coalition-government

[14] P Hennessey, 'Home Secretary: scrap the Human Rights Act' *Telegraph* (1 October 2011), www.telegraph.co.uk/news/politics/8801651/Home-Secretary-scrap-the-Human-Rights-Act.html

[15] J Macintyre, 'Huhne attacks Tories "helping their friends in the City"' *Prospect* (11 September 2011), www.prospectmagazine.co.uk/2011/09/huhne-attack-osborne-50p-rate

And David Cameron's first headline response to the summer riots of 2011, 'criminality pure and simple', contrasted with Nick Clegg's call for compassion for 'those who slip through the cracks'.

Political profit and loss accounts were issued by opposing sides: lists of what the Lib Dems had prevented and gains they'd made which both the Lib Dem and the Tory right could equally identify but which the Lib Dems boasted about and the Tory right deplored.[16] There were even doubts about the authenticity of differentiation which the media were quick to expose. Clegg, unaware of an open mike, blurted out a hidden truth when he told Cameron after a joint public meeting: 'if we keep doing this we won't find anything to bloody disagree about in the bloody debates' (in the next election campaign).[17] That, many thought, was the real Nick Clegg speaking.

From thinking comfortably of the Coalition as 'almost a technical and managerial government' in which the partners 'express their values', No 10 became resigned to the media 'seeing everything through coalition lenses: who's won, who's lost, the general observation on any government. Since tuition fees they now have splits defined. It's a very easy story to write but quite difficult to counter.' This perceptive verdict on their own efforts was the inevitable result of the Coalition shifting from the early emphasis on principles that both parties held in common, to a significant increase in the areas of disagreement. Lib Dem victories were too slight or their claims too premature to be wholly convincing. Eventually from a senior Lib Dem source came advice against pushing differentiation too far. Olly Grender, the senior Lib Dem who was acting deputy head in No 10 communications, had reservations, as she explained before she was appointed:

> I think differentiation works best after you've done it. Differentiation for the Lib Dems will always be how you protect those on lowest income, raising of the 10k threshold, although the Tories will say they would have done that anyway. What is critical is that in two years' time Nick stands up and says, 'we got care for the elderly through, we got the pupil premium through, what is happening to the five year olds that we first introduced this policy for? That is my social mobility proved'. You have to put your time and energy into proof points, and not on a public image that is not going to be turned round in one-off interviews.

There were signs that this advice struck home. In October 2011, a report Downing Street had commissioned from venture capitalist Adrian Beecroft leaked, which made the radical recommendation that the concept of unfair dismissal of workers should be scrapped in order to increase business competitiveness. Vince Cable promptly declared the report a 'non- starter', even before it was published.[18] Because the incident exposed poor political management and coalition differences so starkly

---

[16]  See Tim Montgomerie's 'Concession-O-Meter', www.conservativehome.blogs.com/thetorydiary/2010/11/a-stock-take-of-conservative-and-liberal-democrat-compromises.html

[17]  Channel 4 News, 'Clegg in "too close to Tories for comfort" gaffe' (24 March 2011), www.channel4.com/news/clegg-in-too-close-to-tories-for-comfort-gaffe

[18]  E Rigby and K Stacey, 'Cable rejects scrapping unfair firing law' *Financial Times* (26 October 2011), www.ft.com/cms/s/0/5b46e9f2-0003-11e1-ba79-00144feabdc0.html#axzz1jok5D0bu

on a matter linked to the deficit reduction strategy, reports circulated that it was time to ease up on differentiation in the interests of cohesion.[19] A senior Lib Dem source was quoted as saying: 'We have to be careful about the briefers. We cannot have people in Downing Street briefing against each other. We are not going to be like Blair and Brown'.[20] Practice, it seemed, had not lived up to early promise.

## TRUE BLUE MEDIA VERSUS THE MODERNISERS

The Beecroft report had wider significance. David Cameron was reported to have rejected it for going too far and the *Financial Times* reported that Cameron's own strategy adviser Steve Hilton claimed that the Chancellor had also blocked the report because it 'risked retoxifying the Tory brand over reducing employment rights'.[21] The episode, minor in itself, was evidence of the profound arguments going on across party lines about the pace of public sector reform and the size of the state. In the end, a coalition compromise was struck, allowing firms with fewer than 10 employees to pay workers off without being taken to an employment tribunal and requiring workers in larger firms to go to arbitration before going to tribunal.

The Beecroft report touched a nerve with the media champions of the right, who often accused Cameron of using the Lib Dems as an alibi for avoiding radical action.[22] The most persistent Tory media critic of the Coalition, Tim Montgomerie, editor of the website *ConservativeHome*, was a pacemaker for pushing Cameron towards the 'growth strategy' of deeper cuts and lower taxes required to save the nation. By the end of the first year he had reached his logical conclusion:

> The Tory leader should have listened to his members at the time of the Coalition negotiations. He should have formed a minority government, governed for a few months, laid out his programme and then asked the people to vote again. Sadly, but understandably, Cameron did not choose that path. He chose the yellow Europhile bird in the hand and formed Britain's first coalition government since the war. That government is looking unable to deliver both the ambitious growth agenda that Britain needs and the Conservative agenda that – whatever some commentators may say – is what the majority of voters want.[23]

[19] N Watt, 'Nick Clegg vetoes Conservative donor's idea to help firms sack workers' *Guardian* (8 November 2011), www.guardian.co.uk/politics/2011/nov/08/nick-clegg-vetoes-work-reform

[20] Wintour and Watt, 'Rethink on managing coalition after Nick Clegg rejects No 10 report' *Guardian Blog* (8 November 2011), www.guardian.co.uk/politics/wintour-and-watt/2011/nov/08/liberal-conservative-coalition-nickclegg

[21] G Parker and E Rigby, 'Cameron's anger at claim of Osborne rift' *Financial Times* (8 November 2011), www.ft.com/cms/s/0/308fccbe-0a3b-11e1-92b5-00144feabdc0.html#axzz1jok5D0bu

[22] For example, *Times* columnist Rachel Sylvester wrote on 31 May 2011: 'The Lib Dems' anger is an act. Off stage, the coalition is still cosy. In fact, it may even survive a Tory majority' (a minority view). 'From rose garden romance to secret love' *Times* (31 May 2011), www.thetimes.co.uk/tto/opinion/columnists/rachelsylvester/article3045004.ece

[23] T Montgomerie, 'Afraid of being right' *Spectator* (30 July 2011), www.spectator.co.uk/essays/7127203/afraid-of-being-right.thtml

The sharp rebuff from Danny Finkelstein of the *Times* revealed the gap between the Tory right and the Cameron modernisers:

The honest answer to Tim is I don't understand what he means. In my opinion this Government is introducing very radical educational reforms, a massive deficit reduction plan, reducing the size of the state, reforming the welfare system, choice programmes of public service reform. What more do these people want?

The *Daily Telegraph* shared some of Montgomerie's analysis. In his column Deputy Editor Benedict Brogan began to strike a note of disillusion:

A ministry full of radical promise got off to an audacious start across a range of fronts, but is now in retreat, frightened of taking risks, riven by internal disputes and desperate to appease its Lib Dem junior partner.[24]

But Brogan was in a dilemma. As he put it later:

It isn't evident that Cameron's best effort to reposition the Conservatives towards the centre has succeeded, that he has put together a 44 per cent [electoral] offer. If you believe that, you can see Cameron keeping his options open for some sort of understanding with the Lib Dems at the next election. That's not to say the Conservatives can never win a majority but it's unlikely under this leader at this time and maybe never. Maybe voting has become too fragmented.

And secondly – or perhaps really firstly – there were paying readers to consider:

From the outset, our readers were very enthusiastic about the Coalition – politicians pulling together for the common good and so on. Even though our readers take issue with them on many matters – for example, high speed rail, red tape, Europe, higher rate tax – they remain broadly in favour of it. And we have a mind to that.

## EUROPE AND THE DEFICIT: BASIC CHALLENGES TO THE COALITION

It was events in the last few weeks of 2011 that subverted basic assumptions upon which the Coalition had been based. These were the hope that deficit reduction would wind down in time for the 2015 election and the belief that tensions and divisions over Europe had been contained by the Coalition agreement.

In the Chancellor's autumn statement in November 2011, due to faltering economic growth and worsening prospects, the period for eliminating the structural financial deficit was extended to 2017, two years beyond the limit of the Programme for Government (PfG) and the fixed term of the Parliament. The Tory press joined the Chancellor in the diversion of ridiculing Labour for wanting to solve a borrowing crisis by borrowing more. The reality was that, at a stroke, hopes had been blighted for campaigning at the next election on a modest economic upswing. A chorus of Lib Dem objections greeted the commitment made by the Lib Dem

---

[24] B Brogan, 'Retreat – and recrimination – is in the air' *Telegraph* (17 June 2011), www.telegraph.co.uk/news/politics/8583102/Retreat-and-recrimination-is-in-the-air.html

Treasury Chief Secretary Danny Alexander to join the Conservatives in making a further £30 billion of cuts after the next election. Nick Clegg and the Lib Dems claimed credit for alleviating measures such as higher spending on building projects, a 5.2 per cent rise in state benefits, more child care help and a scheme to ease youth employment.[25] But how could the parties credibly differentiate on the core issue for the 2015 election campaign when they were locked into such a plan?[26]

For all the attention paid to the Lib Dems, it was the Conservatives who produced the most dramatic piece of differentiation so far: David Cameron's shock veto in December 2011 against a proposed new EU treaty to advance economic and political integration and forestall future crises over the euro. Cameron's tactics were clearly influenced by the largest ever rebellion of 81 Conservative MPs a few weeks earlier, in favour of holding a referendum and making an early bid to repatriate powers from Brussels.[27] Terms favoured increasingly by many Tory MPs and urged on by the stridently Eurosceptic press far exceeded those in the PfG, which only provided for a referendum in the unlikely event of a move to transfer more powers from London to Brussels rather than in the opposite direction. Downing Street frankly admitted that Cameron had breached the Coalition Agreement in order to placate his troops:

> Mr Cameron's pledge to repatriate power from Brussels was not official government policy . . . We have a coalition government and some of the things that Conservative members of the Government are saying reflect Conservative Party policy and some things reflect the Government's policy.[28]

At the fateful Brussels summit on 8 December 2011, it was becoming clear that the emerging Franco-German terms for a new EU treaty to create a new fiscal union for Eurozone members and aspirants had implications for Britain and the City that were anathema to the bulk of the Conservative Party. On behalf of the pro-EU Lib Dems, Nick Clegg had approved in advance Cameron's terms to protect British financial services from tighter Brussels regulation and a financial transactions tax. But when the French and German leaders rejected them in the small hours, Cameron vetoed the treaty idea after consulting Chancellor George Osborne but not Clegg.[29] After appearing to accept the veto at first, Clegg changed tack under party pressure and launched what was described in the media as an

---

[25] A Grice, 'An age of austerity just might benefit the Tories' *Independent* (3 December 2011), www.independent.co.uk/opinion/commentators/andrew-grice/andrew-grice-an-age-of-austerity-just-might-benefit-the-tories-6271550.html

[26] P Wintour, 'Spending cuts bind coalition partners?' *Guardian* (30 November 2011), www.guardian.co.uk/politics/2011/nov/30/spending-cuts-bind-coalition-partners

[27] See P Cowley and M Stuart, 'The Conservative Euro revolt: 10 points to note' *Ballots & Bullets* (25 October 2011), www.nottspolitics.org/2011/10/25/the-conservative-euro-revolt-10-points-to-note

[28] J Kirkup, 'Tory demands on EU powers are impossible for Coalition, says Nick Clegg' *Telegraph* (25 October 2011), www.telegraph.co.uk/news/worldnews/europe/eu/8849273/Tory-demands-on-EU-powers-are-impossible-for-Coalition-says-Nick-Clegg.html

[29] For a contemporary analysis of Cameron at the summit see 'The moment, behind closed doors, that David Cameron lost his EU argument last night' *Economist* (9 December 2011), www.economist.com/blogs/bagehot/2011/12/britain-and-eu-1

attack on Cameron's decision, telling him that the veto was 'bad for Britain . . . I made it clear it was untenable for me to welcome it'.[30] But healing moves were afoot straight away. Clegg stopped short of criticising Cameron personally. Although he was notably absent as the Prime Minister reported on the summit to the Commons, he later declared that there was no threat to the Coalition. However much the veto dismayed the Lib Dems by isolating Britain from the rest of the EU, it disarmed Cameron's Conservative and media critics and gave him a modest bounce in the polls.

In purely coalition terms, the key move in consequence of the veto was the disappearance of any chance of a 'seize the moment' referendum on any new EU treaty. This would have produced a far more ruinously divisive campaign than the AV fiasco. Arguably, it averted an existential coalition crisis. The autumn statement and the EU veto established the Lib Dems in their niche as the pro-EU party in favour of five more years of deficit reduction. To the veteran pollster Sir Robert Worcester, they also confirmed that Cameron had Clegg in a 'death hug'.[31]

## VERDICTS ON DIFFERENTIATION

Did anyone benefit from a year of ventilating important differences in public? It could be argued that the Coalition was over the worst, as many of their first year crises had been the product of inexperience and the legacy of opposition. Lib Dem resilience had been tempered by the experience of power. On the other hand, Lib Dem differentiation tactics had antagonised right wing opinion in Parliament and played into the hands of the media for whom 'split' stories were the default. The polls reported a resounding negative, with the Lib Dem initiators of differentiation and the Coalition itself coming off worst. In April 2011 a Populus poll for the Institute of Government found that, compared with single-party government, coalitions were considered weaker (68 per cent), more indecisive (73 per cent), less responsive to the public (57 per cent), and more confused about what they stand for (80 per cent).[32]

Nick Clegg's public reputation failed to improve. There was little evidence that distinctive Lib Dem policies had much impact. Despite their continuing challenge to NHS reforms, only 30 per cent thought they had influenced NHS policy.[33] Overall the results showed that the Conservatives were broadly stuck where they had been in May 2010 but within distance of Labour and even sometimes slightly ahead. These spurts provided ammunition to the right wing, some of whom argued that the Lib Dems were holding the Government back and that the Conservatives would

[30] Nick Clegg on BBC1's *Andrew Marr Show* (11 December 2011), www.news.bbc.co.uk/1/hi/programmes/andrew_marr_show/9659858.stm

[31] P Toynbee, 'Nick talks pure Cameronomics' *Guardian* (20 September 2012), www.guardian.co.uk/commentisfree/2010/sep/20/clegg-talks-pure-cameronomics

[32] Poll details in A Paun, *One Year On: The First Year of Coalition Government* (London, Institute for Government, 2011).

[33] ibid.

be better off going it alone. An alternative view was that the public was losing faith in all three main parties due to the continuing economic crisis.

## THE UNCERTAIN EFFECTS OF THE DIGITAL REVOLUTION

Is our concentration on Tory newspapers overdone and out of date? The grip of News International had loosened. Digitisation was diversifying media power. UK newspaper sales declined by 25 per cent between 2007 and 2009. The *Telegraph*'s dropped from 1 million in 2002 to 636,000 in 2011. However, Benedict Brogan was still claiming a leading role for newspapers as he questioned the appointment of the TV man Craig Oliver as Andy Coulson's successor:

> For someone of his seniority it's strange he doesn't understand that the broadcasters have their daily agenda set by the newspapers. I'm sure he's very good at TV but he doesn't know anything about political journalism.

A senior Conservative source dismissed these concerns. Oliver's appointment was 'a sign of the times':

> I think the press is becoming less and less influential anyhow. Circulations are dropping like mad. We see newspapers more and more as a means of getting on television. If you get the splash in the *Daily Telegraph*, *Guardian* or the *Times* you stand a very good chance of getting it onto TV.

The expansion of 24-hour news broadcasting consolidated radio and television as the main fora for political news and debate at the expense of Parliament. The Coalition, like its predecessors, tried to fill unlimited airtime with more announcements than the parliamentary timetable could cope with, even after adjustments to make proceedings more topical and responsive to public concerns. Apart from exploring differences within the Government, the existence of the Coalition made no difference to broadcast political reporting, which remained based on newsworthiness. Audience debate programmes such as BBC1's popular weekly *Question Time* required a different approach from the News. In order to represent the coalition parties, the minister of one party tended to be balanced by an independent minded backbencher or peer of the other party. This was done to provide full scope for the coalition parties' distinctiveness.

## WILL THE LEVESON INQUIRY CHANGE THE TERMS OF TRADE
## BETWEEN POLITICIANS AND THE MEDIA?

Conservative media handlers were nervous that phone hacking cases might come to court and embarrass David Cameron at the next election. More might come out about the 14 private meetings he admitted holding with News International executives in the Coalition's first year (Nick Clegg had 20 with the chiefs of various media). Most hobnobbing became restricted to the usual lower level contacts with journalists. The Prime Minister's aides feared rough treatment from the likes of the *Mail* and the *Telegraph*, which resented the inclusion of statutory control of the press in the Leveson Inquiry's terms of reference. The code of conduct for journalists might become stricter on definitions of intrusion and harassment. Perhaps the *Telegraph* would think twice before carrying out any more sting interviews of the kind that threatened Vince Cable's ministerial career. But overall the political parties were unlikely to have an easier time, as was already evident in the coverage of Liam Fox's resignation as Defence Secretary.[34]

## CONCLUSION

Chapters four and five depicted a government that was remarkably unified and harmonious in terms of how the Coalition operated in Whitehall. This chapter has painted a more turbulent picture. Despite the government press machine presenting government policy as coordinated and unified, with the coalition partners discussing their differences but then resolving them, that was not how it always appeared in the media. This was partly because the press thrives on stories of government splits; and partly because the coalition partners sometimes accentuated their differences, under pressure from their party to do so. Inevitably the image of unity was compromised, and no media strategy run by party servants or officials could impose a corrective. In the age of Twitter it had become impossible to restrain comment or rebuttal. And for most of the media it seemed too much to hope that they might report open debate within government without doing so in terms of splits. Public perceptions of coalition remained negative, with the Coalition perceived as weak, indecisive, and unclear about what it stood for.

The unity/distinctiveness dilemma was particularly acute for the Liberal Democrats. Reports began to circulate that for them, 2012 would be a year of even greater differentiation, partly in the hope that this might make them look good compared with Labour.[35] This was in spite of the fact that at the end of 2011 there was little to show for Lib Dem differentiation except a proliferation of 'split' stories which did nothing to improve their poll results. Remarkably perhaps, the Conservatives barely suffered – although they did not significantly gain, given that they had received, at best, lukewarm and heavily qualified support from their traditional media supporters.

But even the severest media critics baulked at coalition dissolution. For one thing, they were bound to fear contagion from political turbulence in the

---

[34] 'Liam Fox statement: oh no, not another victim' *Guardian* (19 October 2011), www.guardian.co.uk/politics/blog/2011/oct/19/liam-fox-statement-another-victim

[35] R Sylvester, 'Nick Clegg might not look sad much longer' *Times* (17 January 2012), www.thetimes.co.uk/tto/opinion/columnists/rachelsylvester/article3288630.ece; B Brogan, 'How will the Coalition cope with a year of living fractiously?' *Telegraph* (18 January 2012), www.blogs.telegraph.co.uk/news/benedictbrogan/100130578/how-will-the-coalition-cope-with-a-year-of-living-fractiously

Eurozone. For another, although opposition to the Coalition's economic policy was growing, there was no corresponding increase in public support for the idea that Labour would do any better or that the Conservatives could win an election outright. And it had to be recognised that the Coalition was retaining the political initiative and functioning well enough as a government. As we saw in chapters four and five, most disagreements were not between the coalition parties, because many of the problems of government transcended them.

Cameron and Clegg remained personally committed not to split over Europe or anything else if they could possibly help it. The pair played a 'hard cop, soft cop' routine where their values were different but the outcomes were compatible. Commons rebellions increased but had so far avoided threatening the Coalition majority when it counted. Thanks to the phone hacking scandal, David Cameron may finally have achieved his initial ambition of keeping the media at a greater distance. But one senior journalist fired a parting shot: 'Cameron has had had an easy time. That may change. If the economy tanks, all bets are off'.

# 9

# *Case Study I: Constitutional Reform*

## ROBERT HAZELL

Part of the problem with this wretched Bill is that it is trying to organise things to suit the requirements of this Coalition. (Bill Cash MP, in House of Commons debate on the Fixed Term Parliaments Bill, 13 July 2011)[1]

The Bill is a fine example of what coalition politics produces – a document delivered by two parties, working together despite their differing traditional outlooks on the EU. (Tim Farron MP, President of the Liberal Democrats, on Second Reading of the European Union Bill, 7 December 2010)[2]

## INTRODUCTION

T HIS CHAPTER TAKES a number of case studies from the constitutional reform programme to illustrate the internal and external workings of the Coalition Government in its first 18 months. The case studies exemplify the range of possibilities that coalition partners can adopt when trying to splice together different policies from their respective manifestos. These include: adopting one party's policy (eg the European Union Bill, which was Conservative policy); adopting the other party's policy (eg fixed term parliaments, a Lib Dem policy); a compromise between the two parties' positions (eg reducing the size of the House of Commons); establishing a commission to propose a way forward (eg on a British bill of rights); or acknowledging that there is no half-way house, and allowing an agreement to disagree (the Alternative Vote (AV) referendum, on which the parties campaigned on opposing sides).

Each of the case studies is then used as a prism to show how the Coalition worked: in implementing the Coalition Agreement; in negotiating within the Executive; in getting its proposals through Parliament; in handling relations with the political parties; and with the media. They illustrate the crucial importance of the Coalition Agreement, and how faithfully it was followed. But they also illustrate that however faithful the Government was to the Agreement, the two parties could not always deliver their supporters in Parliament; especially in the House of Lords.

---

[1] Hansard HC Deb, 13 July 2011, vol 531, col 361.
[2] Hansard HC Deb, 7 December 2010, vol 520, col 219.

The case studies presented are all from the Government's constitutional reform programme. For the Liberal Democrats, being able to implement their long held ambitions for constitutional reform was one of the reasons why they entered the Coalition. But the Conservatives also had extensive plans for constitutional change. So the chapter opens by presenting the whole of the constitutional reform programme, and explaining the respective contributions of the Conservatives and the Liberal Democrats. It then goes on to analyse five key measures within it: the AV referendum; reducing the size of the House of Commons; fixed term parliaments; the EU Bill; and a British bill of rights.

## THE CONSTITUTIONAL REFORM PROGRAMME

Constitutional reform was generally believed to have been the Liberal Democrats' contribution to the Coalition Government's agenda. The Conservatives certainly did not see themselves as constitutional reformers, and our interviews with Conservative ministers and backbenchers confirmed that. But before the election their reform agenda was as extensive as the Liberal Democrats'. The Constitution Unit's pre-election briefing on the Conservative agenda for constitutional reform ran to a dozen chapters.[3] There was also a surprising amount of common ground. It was not just the Orange Book economic liberals who found a great deal of compatibility between the two manifestos: the process was also helped on the other side by the Conservatives' unacknowledged plans for constitutional reform.[4] Most of their plans were for further constitutional change, as can be seen from the list of their manifesto commitments in Table 9.1 below.

The strongest common ground ideologically was the parties' shared commitment to decentralisation and localism. The big Conservative constitutional changes were to reduce the size of Parliament (Commons and Lords); introduce a British bill of rights; legislate to require referendums for future EU Treaties; introduce English votes on English laws; and hold referendums on elected mayors in all major cities. The 'referendum lock' for EU Treaties might be thought anathema to the Liberal Democrats, but they had their own, more radical commitment to 'an in/out referendum the next time a British government signs up for fundamental change in the relationship between the UK and the EU'.[5] Both parties also had to address the unfinished business of Labour's constitutional reforms: strengthening the autonomy of the House of Commons (the Wright Committee reforms); further reform of the House of Lords; and devolution, where a response was needed to the demands from all three devolved assemblies for further powers, and to the West Lothian Question.

[3] R Hazell, *The Conservative Agenda for Constitutional Reform* (London, Constitution Unit, 2010).

[4] 'Orange Booker' is a term used to describe those who contributed to a 2004 book suggesting 'liberal answers' to longstanding problems – 'liberal answers' meaning choice and competition, and a shift away from the use of the state to solve issues. See D Laws and P Marshall (eds), *The Orange Book: Reclaiming Liberalism* (London, Profile Books, 2004).

[5] Liberal Democrat manifesto 2010, 67.

As a clear indication of the Liberal Democrats' strong commitment to constitutional reform, in government Nick Clegg took the lead on the whole constitutional reform programme. It was the only subject for which he took direct responsibility. Eighty staff from the Constitution Directorate in the Ministry of Justice moved across to the Cabinet Office to support him in that role. But our analysis suggests that by the end of the Coalition Government, Clegg may have delivered more of the Conservative package of constitutional reforms than his own. In particular, he failed on the AV referendum; and he is likely to fail on Lords reform, the Lib Dems' second biggest priority.

Table 9.1 sets out the main constitutional reform items in the Coalition's Programme for Government (PfG).[6] It is inevitably a crude score card, listing all the reforms as if they were equal, when some are clearly more important than others. The table shows where a commitment in the PfG came from: the Liberal Democrat manifesto (column 2), the Conservative manifesto (column 3), or both. Of the 18 items listed, 14 were in the Conservative manifesto, and nine in the Lib Dem manifesto. So just on this crude scoring basis, the Conservatives did better than the Lib Dems in shaping the Government's reform agenda.

**Table 9.1  Origins of the Main Constitutional Reform Proposals in the Programme for Government, and their Prospects of Success**

| Programme for Government | LD | C | Result | Lib Dem manifesto | Conservative manifesto |
|---|---|---|---|---|---|
| Referendum on AV | o | | x | Introduce proportional voting system, preferably STV | Retain first past the post |
| Reduce House of Commons to 600 MPs | o | ● | √ | Reduce to 500 MPs if elected by STV | Reduce to 585 MPs |
| Introduce referendum on further Welsh devolution | ● | o | √ | Give Welsh Assembly primary legislative powers | Will not stand in the way of Welsh referendum on further legislative powers |
| Implement Calman Commission in Scotland | ● | o | √ | Implement Calman on new powers to Scotland | White Paper on how to deal with Calman |
| Fixed term parliaments | ● | | √ | Fixed term parliaments | Make royal prerogative subject to greater parliamentary control |
| Legislate so that future treaties are subject to 'referendum lock' | | ● | √ | Hold in/out referendum next time UK signs up for fundamental change in relations with EU | Amend ECA 1972 so that future Treaties are subject to referendum lock |

[6] We will refer to the PfG as 'the Coalition Agreement' unless otherwise stated.

| | | | | | |
|---|---|---|---|---|---|
| Hold referendums on elected mayors in 12 largest English cities | | ● | √ | | Give citizens in England's 12 largest cities chance of having an elected mayor |
| Wholly or mainly elected second chamber | ● | ○ | x | Elected House of Lords | Build consensus for a mainly elected second chamber |
| Commission on British bill of rights | ○ | ● | x | Protect Human Rights Act | Replace Human Rights Act with UK bill of rights |
| Commission on West Lothian Question | | ● | x | | English votes on English laws |
| Right of recall of MPs | ● | ● | √ | Power of recall in the event of serious wrongdoing | Power of recall triggered by proven serious wrongdoing |
| Prevent misuse of parliamentary privilege | | ● | x | | Introduce a Parliamentary Privilege Act |
| Implement Wright Committee reforms for House of Commons | | ● | √ | | Establish Backbench Business Committee |
| Speed up individual electoral registration | | ● | √ | | Swiftly implement individual voter registration |
| 200 all postal primaries | | ● | x | | All postal primaries |
| Petitions to force issues onto Parliament's agenda | | ● | √ | | Petitions to force issues onto Parliament's agenda |
| Reform of party funding | ● | ● | x | Seek agreement on comprehensive reform to include donations cap | Cap donations at £10k, limit spending through electoral cycle |
| Statutory register of lobbyists | ● | ○ | √ | Statutory register of lobbyists | Legislate if lobbying industry does not regulate itself |

Key:
● = manifesto commitment fully incorporated into Programme for Government
○ = manifesto commitment only partially incorporated
√ = delivered, or likely to be delivered
x = not delivered, or unlikely to be delivered

Column 4, headed 'Result', indicates whether the commitment is likely to be delivered or not. It cuts both ways in terms of whether the parties might regard the result as a success. So the AV referendum failed; but the Conservatives would regard that as a success. The Commission on a British Bill of Rights seems likely to fail; the Lib Dems might not regard that as failure. It also requires some educated guesswork about future results, and not everyone will agree with the forecasts. But the provisional analysis of this scorecard suggests that by the end of the Parliament Nick Clegg will have delivered eight of the Conservative commitments for constitutional reform, but only five of his own. He will get little credit from the Conservatives for this, because they do not see themselves as constitutional reformers. The risk is that he will be damned by his own side for his failures, and ignored by the Conservatives for his successes. Some Whitehall interviewees felt that Clegg should not have taken responsibility for the constitutional reform programme: it took up a lot of his time in the first year, which was already hugely pressured, and he had no one to blame if it failed.

## THE AV REFERENDUM AND REDUCING THE SIZE OF THE HOUSE OF COMMONS

David Laws claims the credit for linking the Conservative plan to reduce the size of the House of Commons with the Liberal Democrat plan for a referendum on the voting system.[7] In government the Coalition linked these two reforms together in one bill, the Parliamentary Voting System and Constituencies (PVSC) Bill. This was to ensure that the Conservatives would vote for the AV referendum in Part 1 of the bill, and the Lib Dems for the reduction in the size of the House of Commons in Part 2. Both proposals involved a compromise from the parties' original manifesto commitments; but in Conservative minds agreeing to hold a referendum on AV was a far bigger concession. In the coalition negotiations it was the deal-breaker, and it was the last item to be agreed, with great reluctance on the Conservative side.[8] The Conservatives were staunch supporters of first past the post, and feared that if the AV referendum were carried, it would be a stepping stone towards proportional representation, and end their hopes of ever gaining an overall majority.

For the Liberal Democrats, agreeing to a reduction in the size of the House of Commons was less unpalatable, since their own manifesto had contained a commitment to reduce the Commons by a quarter to 500 seats, compared with the Conservative manifesto cut of a tenth, to 585. But the Lib Dem reduction was linked to a switch to Single Transferable Vote, a proportional voting system with multimember constituencies. The parties compromised in the Coalition Agreements on a reduction from 650 to 600 seats. Despite the Lib Dems having supported a reduction in their manifesto, this was always seen as a Conservative proposal; perhaps

---

[7] D Laws, *22 Days in May* (London, Biteback Publishing, 2010) 100.

[8] ibid, 101–5; R Wilson, *Five Days to Power* (London, Biteback Publishing, 2010) 162–4.

because the Conservatives stood to gain more in terms of electoral advantage.[9] In both the Interim Coalition Agreement and the PfG the two proposals were linked together:

> We will bring forward a Referendum Bill on electoral reform, which includes provision for the introduction of the Alternative Vote in the event of a positive result in the referendum, as well as for the creation of fewer and more equal sized constituencies. We will whip both Parliamentary parties in both Houses to support a simple majority referendum on the Alternative Vote, without prejudice to the positions parties will take during such a referendum.[10]

In government Nick Clegg took the lead on both proposals, as part of his overall responsibility for the constitutional reform programme, supported by his Conservative junior minister in the Cabinet Office, Mark Harper MP, designated Minister for Political and Constitutional Reform. They pushed ahead at top speed, with intensive discussions as they turned the proposals into a bill. Unusually, not much discussion took place in Cabinet Committee, because the policy was settled so early on. One senior Cabinet official said:

> That was almost before the entire cabinet committee structure was even set up, so I think that was a very top-down policy. Most detail of that was done by the PM, DPM; Mark Harper [Clegg's Conservative Minister of State] was obviously much involved, Tom McNally [Lib Dem Minister in the Ministry of Justice], Danny Alexander. In some sense that's a bad example for normal coalition running; that was such a sui generis bill because it was so early on, and it was so critical to get it in.
>
> Decision-making in the very early stages of coalition on the PVSC Bill was complex but not difficult. We had to help ministers understand complicated subjects and work out what their political instincts were and where the grounds were for compromise. Trust levels then were much lower than they are now . . . Even at an early stage they cracked through it . . .

The Lib Dems were anxious to hold the AV referendum as early as possible, and the Conservatives knew they had to get legislation through early if the boundary reviews for 600 new constituencies were to be completed and implemented by 2015. The bill was introduced after just 10 weeks in government, on 22 July 2010, with no White Paper and no consultation. It was very tightly whipped: the Government could not afford any concessions, lest the combined package unravel. They pushed the bill through as fast as they could, but the committee stage in the Commons lasted five days on the floor of the House, and in the Lords the committee stage lasted an unprecedented 17 days, after an extraordinary filibuster by Labour peers, with occasional crossbench support.

---

[9] One early estimate was that the reduction and consequential boundary changes might lose the Liberal Democrats 14 seats, the Conservatives 15 and Labour 18: see L Baston, 'Boundary changes: how could they affect the UK?' *Guardian* (6 June 2011), www.guardian.co.uk/politics/datablog/2011/jun/06/boundary-change-constituency-lewis-baston. Of the 31 seats to go in England, it was estimated that the Lib Dems would lose 5 seats, the Conservatives 7 and Labour 18: A Lewis, 'YouGov/Sun – CON 37, LAB 41, LDEM 10' *UK Polling Report* (13 September 2011), www.ukpollingreport.co.uk/blog/archives/4007

[10] PfG, ch 24.

The bill was the subject of critical reports from the new Political and Constitutional Reform Committee in the Commons, the Welsh Affairs Committee, and the Lords Constitution Committee.[11] All three committees lamented the rushed timetable and the absence of any consultation. They also questioned why the two parts of the bill had to be taken together, when Part 2 demanded much more detailed scrutiny. But despite these critical reports, no major amendment was accepted by the Government in either House. This was the bill our interviewees had in mind when they said that while coalition government requires compromise within the Executive, that can sometimes leave no room for further compromise in Parliament, lest the carefully crafted package is unpicked.

The brutal whipping left very sore feelings in Parliament, especially on the Conservative benches. When interviewed, Conservative MPs and peers swore that they would not swallow any further Lib Dem constitutional reforms. But within the Government the hard pounding to ensure passage of the bill left a very different impression. A senior Cabinet Office official said:

> The passage of the PVSC Bill was a major piece of glue. Both sides knew they could fight alongside each other under serious enemy fire and win, and win on something where neither side wanted the other bit of that bill. That builds a very high level of trust. By the time you've slept next to your fellow peer in the House of Lords or paraded time after time through the lobby in the House of Commons it does build something – you start to feel on the same side.

The tensions in Parliament were as nothing compared with the bitter feelings unleashed during the subsequent referendum campaign. The Coalition Agreements allowed the Conservatives and Lib Dems to campaign on opposite sides. There was dirty campaigning on both sides, with wild exaggerations of the positive or negative effects of AV. Nick Clegg stayed out of the campaign, because he was not regarded as an asset by the 'Yes' side; but David Cameron did an unexpected broadcast for the 'No' campaign in which he argued that 'AV would be wrong for Britain. It is obscure, unfair and expensive. It will mean that people who come third in elections can end up winning. It will make our politics less accountable'.[12] This led Chris Huhne to complain noisily in Cabinet about a breach of faith, and during the last weeks before the referendum relations seemed badly strained.[13]

---

[11] See Political and Constitutional Reform Committee, 'Parliamentary Voting Systems and Constituencies Bill' HC (2010–11) 437; Welsh Affairs Committee, 'The Implications for Wales of the Government's Proposals on Constitutional Reform' HC (2010–11) 495; and Select Committee on the Constitution, 'Parliamentary Voting Systems and Constituencies Bill: Report' HL (2010–11) 58.

[12] 'Second Referendum Broadcast' No to AV (1 May 2011), www.no2av.org/05/second-referendum-broadcast.

[13] See: BBC News, 'AV vote won't split coalition, say Clegg and Cameron' (1 May 2011), www.bbc.co.uk/news/uk-13251734; BBC News, 'AV Referendum: Huhne confronts Cameron at Cabinet' (3 May 2011), www.bbc.co.uk/news/uk-politics-13269677; A Stratton and P Wintour, 'AV dragged coalition to edge of a precipice' *Guardian* (5 May 2011), www.guardian.co.uk/politics/2011/may/05/av-dragged-coalition-to-edge; and P Wintour, 'Liberal Democrats vent fury at David Cameron as party suffers election rout' *Guardian* (6 May 2011), www.guardian.co.uk/politics/2011/may/06/liberal-democrats-david-cameron-election.

In the May 2011 referendum, AV was convincingly defeated by 68 per cent to 32 per cent. The Lib Dems blamed the result on the failings of the 'Yes' campaign; but in truth the referendum could never have been won on such a short timescale. The Constitution Unit had warned since June 2010 that the referendum would be defeated if so little time was allowed for public information and education.[14] The filibuster in the Lords gave the Lib Dems an excuse to call off the referendum and blame the Labour Party for the delay. One of Clegg's advisers had wanted to postpone the referendum to 2014, and some on the Lib Dem backbenches also urged delay; but the leadership had convinced themselves that the sooner the referendum was held, before the budget cuts began to bite, the greater its chances of success. Ironically some Conservatives had a better sense of the likely outcome, as reflected by this Conservative adviser, interviewed before the AV referendum:

> On the timing the Lib Dems were mad. There was as we told them a much better chance of winning it at the end of the Parliament when the pain of the cuts was beginning to recede. Conservative MPs weren't happy but the Lib Dems absolutely insisted. They weren't clear what their arguments were.

## FIXED TERM PARLIAMENTS

The Liberal Democrats have long supported fixed term parliaments. The Labour Party also supported fixed terms in their 2010 manifesto. But the Conservatives have never done so. They saw nothing wrong in the Prime Minister advising the Queen when to dissolve Parliament, even if that enabled the incumbent Government to choose a date for the next election which maximised their electoral advantage. But both Lib Dems and Conservatives were keen to demonstrate that coalitions need not be unstable or short lived, and anxious to buttress the new Coalition against destabilising no confidence motions. So the Interim Coalition Agreement of 11 May 2010 stated:

> The parties agree to the establishment of five-year fixed term parliaments. A Conservative-Liberal Democrat Coalition Government will put a binding motion before the House of Commons in the first days following this agreement stating that the next general election will be held on the first Thursday of May 2015. Following this motion, legislation will be brought forward to make provision for fixed term parliaments of five years. This legislation will also provide for dissolution if 55% or more of the House votes in favour.

If the aim of the proposals was to introduce stability and certainty, initially they had the opposite effect. The Government never put a motion before the House to set the date of the next election. They were advised that such a resolution would

---

[14] R Hazell, *The Conservative-Liberal Democrat Agenda for Political and Constitutional Reform* (London, Constitution Unit, 2011) 19–20. For the Liberal Democrats' own analysis of why the referendum was lost, see Liberal Democrats Consultative Session, *May 2011 Election Review* (August 2011).

be redundant if followed by legislation to achieve the same effect.[15] But there were several confused and angry parliamentary debates in May and June 2010. There was confusion over the difference between a no confidence motion and a dissolution motion;[16] and criticism of the 55 per cent threshold for dissolution, which aroused particular suspicion because the government parties had 56 per cent of the seats.[17]

Eventually Nick Clegg announced on 5 July 2010 that the Coalition Government had revised the proposals, to raise the threshold for a mid-term dissolution, and to clarify the difference between a voluntary dissolution and a hostile no confidence motion. A majority of two-thirds would be needed to dissolve parliament, as opposed to the 55 per cent first suggested; but votes of no confidence would still require only a simple majority.[18]

Apart from this initial wrinkle, developing the policy on fixed term parliaments raised further difficulties within the Executive. Although the bill was very short, it raised big questions of constitutional principle. Should any discretion be retained for the Prime Minister? Could this Parliament bind its successors? Could it require a two-thirds super-majority? Should there be a cooling off period? On the first question, the civil service took care to brief the Prime Minister separately about the significant amount of power that he was being asked to relinquish, even though the policy was being crafted by the Deputy Prime Minister. One senior Cabinet official said: 'we thought he needed to understand that this was a very major change where he personally was going to give up power'.

The policy was settled reasonably easily within government; but the bill did not have an easy passage through Parliament. The Fixed Term Parliaments Bill was introduced very early, on 22 July 2010, the same date as the PVSC Bill. Labour did not oppose its Second Reading, but several Conservative backbenchers voiced their opposition to the change. Jacob Rees-Mogg MP opposed on the traditional Tory ground that it would undermine the monarchy; while Richard Shepherd MP opposed on the more democratic ground that governments already had five years under the Parliament Act 1911, so long as they retained the confidence of MPs.[19]

At the committee stage the Conservative William Cash MP tabled a series of amendments, and forced three divisions: on removing the provision for a two-thirds majority; removing the 14-day cooling off period after a successful no confidence motion; and requiring each new Parliament to choose whether to apply

---

[15] There was also concern about the status and effect of a resolution if the PM decided to ignore it and seek dissolution anyway.

[16] A no confidence motion is normally a hostile motion, which if passed requires the Government to resign or seek a dissolution. A dissolution motion is a novelty, which would normally be moved by the Government.

[17] Jack Straw MP in Hansard HC Deb, 7 Jun 2010, vol 511, col 25; Hansard HL Deb, 27 May 2010, vol 719, cols 136–244.

[18] Hansard HC Deb, 5 July 2010, vol 513, col 23. The two-thirds threshold for a voluntary dissolution was taken from the equivalent provisions in the devolution legislation.

[19] Hansard HC Deb, 13 September 2010, vol 515, cols 675 and 694.

the terms of the bill. Half a dozen Conservative MPs voted against the Government on each amendment.[20]

Following critical reports from two Select Committees, the debates in the House of Lords were even more sceptical.[21] The Government had expended a lot of political capital in forcing through the PVSC Bill, and the Lords were not going to be rolled over again. Labour peers insisted that the proper length of a fixed term was four years, not five. The sunset clause moved by William Cash MP was re-introduced by the crossbench peer Lord Pannick QC, and with strong crossbench support it was agreed to by 190 to 184 on 10 May 2011. Lib Dem peers argued strongly against; but six dissident Conservatives tipped the balance. As a result, fixed term parliaments would need to be approved following each election with an affirmative resolution in each House.

In the Commons the amendment was removed on 13 July, with nine Conservatives and one Lib Dem MP voting against. William Cash MP said that the bill was 'trying to organise things to suit the requirements of this coalition', and in the Conservative/Lib Dem relationship 'the tail was wagging the dog'.[22] The Lords reinstated the amendment, and eventually a compromise was reached on a semi-sunset clause. This required the Prime Minister in 2020 to establish a committee to review the operation of the Act and to make recommendations for its amendment or repeal, if appropriate.

The bill had come to the Lords in January, but did not receive Royal Assent until September 2011. Its troubled passage illustrated two themes running through this book. The first was that even if the Coalition reached agreement fairly easily on a policy within the Executive, that agreement cannot necessarily be delivered in Parliament. The second was that in Parliament the House of Lords was likely to present more difficulties for the Government than the Commons. That did not bode well for future legislation on constitutional reform, in particular the Government's plans for reform of the House of Lords.

## THE EUROPEAN UNION BILL

In terms of coalition dynamics, the EU Bill was the mirror image of the Fixed Term Parliaments Bill. It was a Conservative proposal, with much less attraction for the Liberal Democrats. The Lib Dems accepted the Conservative proposals in the PfG, but then ran into trouble with their supporters in Parliament, particularly in the House of Lords.

The EU Bill was a sop to the Eurosceptic wing of the Conservative Party. After the Lisbon Treaty in 2007, Cameron pledged that a future Conservative government

---

[20] Hansard HC Deb, 24 November 2010, vol 519, col 312; Hansard HC Deb, 1 December 2010, vol 519, col 835.

[21] Commons Political and Constitutional Reform Committee, 'Fixed Term Parliaments Bill' HC (2010–11) 436, and Lords Constitution Committee, 'Fixed Term Parliaments Bill' HL (2010–11) 69 [46].

[22] Hansard HL Deb, 13 July 2011, vol 729, cols 361 and 369.

would prohibit, by law, any further transfer of power to the EU without a referendum. They would also legislate to make it clear that ultimate authority rests not with the EU but with the Westminster Parliament. So the Conservative manifesto stated:

> We will amend the 1972 European Communities Act so that any proposed future Treaty that transferred areas of power, or competences, would be subject to a referendum – a 'referendum lock' . . . We will introduce a United Kingdom Sovereignty Bill to make it clear that ultimate authority stays in this country, in our Parliament.[23]

The difficulty for the Liberal Democrat negotiators was that their manifesto had also proposed an EU referendum, albeit of a more fundamental kind. It stated: 'Liberal Democrats therefore remain committed to an in/out referendum the next time a British government signs up for fundamental change in the relationship between the UK and the EU'.[24] The only compromise they achieved in the PfG was to soften the commitment to introduce a UK Sovereignty Bill. The wording about the referendum lock remained the same as in the Conservative manifesto:

> We will amend the 1972 European Communities Act so that any proposed future treaty that transferred areas of power, or competences, would be subject to a referendum on that treaty – a 'referendum lock'. We will examine the case for a United Kingdom Sovereignty Bill to make it clear that ultimate authority remains with Parliament.[25]

As with fixed term parliaments, the proposals raised some fundamental constitutional issues. Would a future government and Parliament be bound by the new law? Which Treaties would be caught by the referendum lock? What would a sovereignty bill actually say, and what legal effect would it have? The policy lead lay with the Foreign Secretary William Hague. But Nick Clegg was heavily involved, and the Conservatives took great care to involve the Liberal Democrats. One Cabinet Office official noted:

> There was initial nervousness amongst the Lib Dems, with Hague and David Lidington [Conservative, Minister for Europe] being in the lead, and both being known eurosceptics. But the FCO went to great pains to involve ministerial colleagues, and they had detailed discussion about the scope of the bill, the referendum lock, what would be caught by it, whether a future Act of Parliament would be required, etc. There were two discussions in the [Cabinet's] European Affairs Committee . . . The FCO bill team were very careful to involve Chris Huhne [deputy chair of the European Affairs Committee]; and to ensure there was collective agreement to the Government's response to Lib Dem amendments in Parliament. In coalition terms, it was handled exceptionally well.

The bill was introduced in November 2010. It contained a (rather meaningless) sovereignty clause in place of a separate sovereignty bill. But the main challenge for the draftsman was how to capture those transfers of power to the EU which would be subject to the referendum lock, without making all Treaty changes (for

---

[23]  Conservative manifesto 2010, 113–14.
[24]  Liberal Democrat manifesto 2010, 67.
[25]  PfG (20 May 2010), ch 13.

example, future Accession Treaties) subject to referendum. So the bill exhaustively specified a detailed list of 26 Treaty changes or Article 48(6) decisions which would require a referendum.

In the Commons the Liberal Democrats were quietly supportive. Tim Farron MP, the Lib Dem party President, commented in the Second Reading debate that the bill was 'a fine example of a coalition product: it is a sensible compromise'. Farron continued hopefully:

> Despite our differing traditional outlooks on the EU, the Coalition has come together, found common ground and drawn a line – obviously – under the European constitutional question once and for all.[26]

The Commons debates were dominated by eurosceptic Conservative MPs trying to strengthen the sovereignty clause and tighten the referendum lock. The Lib Dems remained largely silent, but in divisions supported the Government. Whipping was very tight; like the PVSC Bill, this was a carefully crafted compromise on which the Government could not concede an inch. As one of the business managers explained:

> There are some issues where you know that the slightest deviation from the agreed line is going to cause difficulties on one side or the other. And a classic example of that is the European stuff. We know that if we deviate in any way from the basis of the Coalition Agreement and the position which has been carefully stitched together, then the whole thing unravels. So we cannot allow any movement on that . . . it reduces flexibility when you're in areas where there is a high level of party engagement.

In the Lords it was a different story. The whip runs more lightly, and the Lords debates from March to June 2011 coincided with the AV referendum, which added to the strain on Lib Dem loyalties. The Government was defeated on four amendments. On two of them Lib Dem rebels made the difference between defeat and victory. The biggest rebellion of 19 Lib Dem peers was on a sunset clause, rather similar to the Lords amendment to the Fixed Term Parliaments Bill, which would have limited the referendum lock to the current Parliament. One of the rebels explained to us the limits of the doctrine dictating that governing parties had to support what was in the Coalition Agreement, as well as the limits on whipping senior figures in the Lords:

> And then the argument becomes, but why should they if it's not in the Coalition Agreement . . . One prime little example of that was the Europe bill, where there was reference in the Coalition Agreement but not very precise reference to what the bill actually said. And so, several of us simply worked on the basis that we would not be whipped on that . . . we got away with it because we were too senior to discipline . . . [and we] persuaded at least half a dozen very senior Conservatives to take the same line.

The four government defeats were subsequently reversed in the Commons, so that the bill was eventually passed in July 2011 with just four government

---

[26] Hansard HC Deb, 7 Dec 2010, vol 520, cols 217 and 219.

amendments. Perhaps the last word should rest with Stephen Gilbert MP, a Lib Dem backbencher who intervened during the Commons debates. He warned that the referendum lock might inhibit the Government's power to act in times of crisis, and risked aggravating any situation before positive steps could be taken. Although the Treaty changes talked of in late 2011 to introduce greater fiscal discipline into the Eurozone did not trigger a UK referendum under the EU Act 2011, his words may yet prove hauntingly prescient.[27]

## THE BRITISH BILL OF RIGHTS

This next case study illustrates the advantage gained by one party by insisting on tight wording in the Coalition Agreements; and the use of a commission to try to resolve the differences between the two parties. Formally there was little difference between the parties. Both the Liberal Democrats and the Conservatives had a commitment to introduce a British bill of rights;[28] as indeed had the Labour Party.[29] But the Coalition Government's policy represented a compromise by the Conservatives, because their commitment had been to repeal the Human Rights Act and replace it with a British bill of rights which might soften some of the more stringent requirements of the European Convention on Human Rights (ECHR): in the shorthand, 'ECHR minus' rather than 'ECHR plus'.[30] Since 2006 Cameron had gained favour with the tabloids by announcing that the Conservatives would repeal the Human Rights Act, but it remained ambiguous whether this would include resiling from aspects of the ECHR.

The PfG made it quite clear that any British bill of rights must be firmly ECHR plus:

> We will establish a commission to investigate the creation of a British Bill of Rights that incorporates and builds on all our obligations under the European Convention on Human Rights, ensures that these rights continue to be enshrined in British law, and protects and extends British liberties.

This was a clear victory for the Liberal Democrats, as one Lib Dem spad recognised:

[27] For a view that Cameron's demands at the EU summit in December 2011 were formulated with a view to avoiding triggering the referendum requirement in the EU Act 2011, see P Yowell, 'EU Act: Law and Politics' *UK Constitutional Law Group*, www.ukconstitutionallaw.org/2012/01/19/paul-yowell-eu-act-2011-law-and-politics

[28] The Lib Dems have long supported a British bill of rights, as part of a written constitution. In their 2010 manifesto, responding to the threat to the Human Rights Act, they adopted a more defensive position, pledging to 'ensure that everyone has the same protections under the law by protecting the Human Rights Act'.

[29] The Brown Government had done work on a British bill of rights, issuing a Green Paper in 2009 titled *Rights and Responsibilities: Developing our Constitutional Framework* (March). For a much more detailed analysis see Joint Committee on Human Rights, 'A Bill of Rights for the UK?' HL HC (2007–08) HL 195-I HC 150-I.

[30] For an explanation of Conservative policy and its genesis see Hazell, *The Conservative Agenda for Constitutional Reform* (n 3) 63–64.

> We did very well in the coalition negotiations to get the formula of wording that we did, which basically says ECHR plus, which is a situation we're perfectly happy with. This is more of a problem for their side to be honest; we had a good line in the Coalition Agreement which gave them almost no wriggle room. Our people don't really care if there's a bill of rights or not, as long as the Human Rights Act isn't watered down and we don't pull out of the ECHR.

In government the policy lead was given to Conservative Ken Clarke, as Justice Secretary: human rights did not transfer across to Nick Clegg with the rest of the constitutional reform programme. But for the Lib Dems this did not present a cause for concern: Ken Clarke was seen as a staunch defender of human rights, who had been publicly scathing about the Conservative commitment to repeal the Human Rights Act.[31] He got on very well with his Lib Dem junior minister, Lord McNally, and our Whitehall interviewees noted that there were far more tensions between Ken Clarke and the Tory Home Secretary Theresa May than there were between Clarke and his Liberal Democrat colleagues.

This helps to explain why Ken Clarke was in no hurry to establish a commission on a British bill of rights. But in February 2011 things warmed up. First there was a Commons debate on prisoner voting rights, when MPs strongly opposed the ECHR's rejection of a blanket ban in *Hirst*.[32] A week later the Home Secretary proclaimed that she was 'appalled' at a year-old judgment from the Supreme Court giving people a right to appeal against being kept forever on the sex offenders register.[33] Pressed about this at Prime Minister's Questions, Cameron told Parliament that the judgment flew 'completely in the face of common sense'. He added that a bill of rights commission would be 'established imminently because I think it's about time we started making sure decisions are made in this Parliament rather than in the courts'.[34]

There followed intense negotiations between the coalition partners regarding the commission's terms of reference, timetable and membership. Because of the wording of the Coalition Agreement the Lib Dems started from a strong position, and the terms of reference made no mention of repealing the Human Rights Act, nor of resiling from any of the obligations of the ECHR. Indeed they opened by repeating word-for-word the Coalition Agreement:

> The Commission will investigate the creation of a UK Bill of Rights that incorporates and builds on all our obligations under the European Convention on Human Rights, ensures that these rights continue to be enshrined in UK law, and protects and extends our liberties. It will examine the operation and implementation of these obligations, and consider ways to promote a better understanding of the true scope of these obligations and liberties . . . It should consult, including with the public, judiciary and

---

[31] J Chapman, 'Ken Clarke brands Cameron's bill of rights "xenophobic"' *Daily Mail* (28 June 2006), www.dailymail.co.uk/news/article-392891/Ken-Clarke-brands-Camerons-rights-xenophobic.html

[32] *Hirst v United Kingdom (No 2)* (2005) (App no 7402/5/01) [2005] ECHR 681.

[33] *R (F) v Secretary of State for the Home Department* [2010] UKSC 17. For the Home Secretary's response see A Travis, 'David Cameron condemns supreme court ruling on sex offenders' *Guardian* (16 February 2011), www.guardian.co.uk/society/2011/feb/16/david-cameron-condemns-court-sex-offenders

[34] Hansard HC Deb, 16 February 2011, vol 523, col 955.

devolved administrations and legislatures, and aim to report no later than by the end of 2012.

On the subject of membership there was a standoff, with each party packing the commission. The Lib Dems nominated four human rights experts and advocates (Lord Lester QC, Baroness Kennedy QC, Prof Philippe Sands QC, Judge David Edward), and the Conservatives four known critics of the Human Rights Act (Jonathan Fisher QC, Martin Howe QC, Anthony Speaight QC, and Michael Pinto-Duschinsky). Sir Leigh Lewis, the chair, may struggle to find common ground between these fiercely opposed teams.

It might be thought that establishing the commission would take the heat out of the issue. But fierce skirmishing continued between the parties. For a while it even seemed as if Cameron wanted to break ranks and set up a second commission, to prepare a separate Conservative policy for their 2015 manifesto.[35] This would have been a real vote of no confidence in the Coalition's commission. Whenever a human rights issue was in the headlines, the PM criticised the Human Rights Act, and Lib Dems leapt to its defence. So after the August riots, Cameron attacked the chilling effect of human rights laws, and Nick Clegg wrote in their defence in the *Guardian*.[36] A fresh outbreak of hostilities occurred during the party conferences in October, with the *Daily Mail* running the headline "'I want to scrap the Human Rights Act, but Clegg won't let me" says the PM'.[37] Eager to exploit public hostility to the Human Rights Act, the Conservatives were keen to maintain party differentiation on the issue, even if it involved ignoring collective cabinet responsibility and undermining the Government's own commission.

## CONCLUSIONS

These five case studies illustrate some common themes running throughout this book. Although both the Conservatives and the Liberal Democrats had big commitments to introduce constitutional changes, there were significant differences between them on individual items. In resolving those differences there was a lot of give and take on both sides. The biggest compromise was on the AV referendum, which was neither side's first choice. The Lib Dems compromised on reducing the size of the House of Commons, which went against their electoral interests, while

---

[35] M Savage and F Gibb, 'Tories ready for a fight on human rights "interference" from Europe' *Times* (17 February 2011), www.thetimes.co.uk/tto/news/politics/article2916641.ece; Editorial, 'Coalition politics: Conflict of Tory loyalties' *Guardian* (22 February 2011), www.guardian.co.uk/commentisfree/2011/feb/22/coalition-politics-human-rights-editorial

[36] See D Cameron, 'Speech on the fight-back after the riots' *New Statesman* (15 August 2011), www.newstatesman.com/politics/2011/08/society-fight-work-rights for the full text of Cameron's speech; N Clegg, 'Human beings need human rights – in Britain as well as Libya' *New Statesman* (25 August 2011), www.newstatesman.com/politics/2011/08/society-fight-work-rights

[37] J Slack, 'I want to scrap the Human Rights Act, but Clegg won't let me' *Daily Mail* (3 October 2011), www.dailymail.co.uk/news/article-2044530/David-Cameron-I-want-scrap-Human-Rights-Act-Nick-Clegg-wont-let-me.html

the Conservatives conceded over fixed term parliaments. The Lib Dems conceded over the EU Bill, and the Conservatives over the requirement for any British bill of rights to be ECHR plus.

Contrary to the stereotype that coalition government must be weak, slow and indecisive, the two parties resolved their differences with extraordinary speed and decisiveness. They did so using a combination of the formal and informal machinery described in chapter four. So the EU Bill was discussed twice in Cabinet's European Affairs Committee, chaired by William Hague, with Chris Huhne (deputy chair) and Nick Clegg closely involved. By contrast, the PVSC Bill was brokered informally, with most of the details resolved by the Prime Minister and Deputy PM, assisted by Mark Harper, Lord McNally and Danny Alexander. That was partly because the brokering occurred in the first weeks of the Government, before Cabinet Committee structures were fully established. But later on much of the detail on Lords reform was also brokered directly between the PM and DPM, before anything went formally to the Home Affairs Committee or was discussed in the cross-party group.

Once the policy had been settled, the coalition partners showed extraordinary unity and discipline in defending the compromises struck, however much they might privately disagree with them. Whipping was very tight on the PVSC Bill and the EU Bill. To symbolise the coalition parties' commitment to the 'other' part of the bill, Mark Harper led on Part 1 of the PVSC Bill in the Commons (on the AV referendum), and Lord McNally spoke on the 'Conservative' Part 2 in the Lords. The Government displayed exemplary collective cabinet responsibility, with the only lapse being the Prime Minister's outbursts against the Human Rights Act, which appeared at times to undermine his own Government's commission.

The fourth thing to note is that despite the Government's iron clad discipline, their compromise proposals did not have an easy passage through Parliament. Conservative backbenchers hated the AV referendum and disliked fixed term parliaments; while the Liberal Democrats had reservations about the EU Bill. But, as explained in chapter six, they rebelled on different issues. The Government suffered no defeats in the House of Commons, but had much more difficulty in the Lords. The PVSC Bill was almost blocked in the Lords by the 17-day filibuster, severely delaying the rest of the legislative programme; and the Fixed Term Parliaments Bill was almost emasculated by the sunset clause. However faithful the Government's commitment to collective responsibility and to defending the compromises they had agreed, they could not always deliver their supporters in Parliament.

A final theme running through the book is the difficulties that face the junior coalition partner. The Liberal Democrats had entered the Government expressly to deliver their long held plans for constitutional reform, and put their leader in charge. Surely they held the trump cards? And yet even here the Conservatives proved dominant. They were the larger party, with the longer manifesto, and many more of their ideas for political and constitutional reform entered the PfG than items from the Lib Dems.[38] And, if the score card in Table 9.1 proves correct, at the end of this Government more of the Conservatives' ideas for constitutional reform will have been implemented.

It is true that the AV referendum was an own goal by the Lib Dems. But a better resourced junior partner, with better informed advisers, might not have made such a disastrous strategic error. It is also true that Table 9.1 assumes that Lords reform will make no further progress. But if that judgement proves correct, it will again be because of Conservative dominance. If the Government decide not to proceed with the Lords reform bill published in draft in July 2011, or introduce a bill, which then fails to pass, it will be because there is not a majority for the bill in either House. The reason will be that the Conservative backbenchers have had enough of constitutional reform; on this issue, the dominant partner has gone on strike.

---

[38] Four times as many, according to the analysis in Appendix one. Of the 27 items on Political Reform in the PfG, 21 derived from the Conservative manifesto, 5 from the Lib Dems', and 3 were shared. But not all the items are of equal weight: many of the Conservative reforms were relatively minor.

# 10

# Case Studies II: Tuition Fees, NHS Reform, and Nuclear Policy

## PETER WALLER AND BEN YONG

Whether or not it was the right decision that we came to in the end is almost irrelevant. You know, we broke a pledge, we're hated for it. (Senior Lib Dem, on tuition fees)

It's probably the best thing that happened to us, from a political point of view. (Lib Dem activist, on the NHS reforms)

It was only ever an economics issue for him. (Official, on Chris Huhne and nuclear policy)

## INTRODUCTION

THIS CHAPTER DISCUSSES three case studies on events that caused – or in the third case was expected to cause – significant difficulties for the coalition partners in their first 18 months. These are: the student tuition fees saga, which was one of the main 'agree to disagree' areas of the Programme for Government (PfG) and caused major difficulties for the Liberal Democrats, who split three ways when voting on the issue; the health service reforms, which were not initially seen as likely to cause a major headache for the Coalition, but then proved highly contentious and forced a rethink, partly driven by external pressure; and the coalition policy on nuclear power, which was identified in the PfG as a potential area for formal disagreement but proved in practice remarkably problem-free for the Coalition.

Each case study is used to illustrate how the Coalition managed contentious issues: in negotiating, and then implementing, the Coalition Agreement; in getting its proposals through Parliament; and in handling relations with the political parties. Discussion of the three case studies is based largely on published sources and we did not request interviews on them as specific topics. But all three issues came up in a number of the interviews we conducted, and those interviews provided verification of the published sources.

CASE STUDY ONE: STUDENT TUITION FEES

Student fees were a source of considerable tension for the Coalition Government, and for the Liberal Democrats in particular. Fees were undoubtedly the subject that created the greatest sense of betrayal amongst those who voted for the Lib Dems in the 2010 election. Yet this was a train crash which could have been predicted given the implausibility of the Liberal Democrat manifesto policy, and especially given the economic situation. It is ironic that the political party most expected to have thought ahead to the compromises needed to form a coalition should have found themselves with a flagship policy which was unlikely to ever be deliverable. Time will tell whether and when the electorate will forgive them for doing so. At the time of writing, that moment had not yet come.

## Why were Tuition Fees an Issue?

What was possible to fund for free in the 1960s when only about 10 per cent of the population went to university was no longer possible when the aim was for more than 40 per cent to attend. Progressively, students came to be expected to contribute more and more to the costs of their higher education; initially with loans replacing grants for living costs, and then with the introduction of tuition fees in the late 1990s, rising to an annual charge of £3,000 in 2006. But analysis conducted at the time showed that there would still be a funding gap in the medium term, so the Labour Government asked Lord Browne in November 2009 to chair an independent review to look at higher education funding and student finance.

## Student Fees and the General Election

Going into the 2010 election, both the Tories and Labour were distinctly non-committal on student fees and kept their options open. The Tory manifesto simply stated that it would 'consider carefully' the recommendations of the Browne report. In contrast, the Liberal Democrats had a longstanding commitment to abolishing tuition fees which remained in place despite a failed attempt in early 2009 by the leadership to overturn the policy on grounds of affordability. The manifesto accordingly made no mention of the Browne report, but made a commitment to:

> Scrap unfair university tuition fees for all students taking their first degree, including those studying part-time, saving them over £10,000 each. We have a financially responsible plan to phase fees out over six years, so that the change is affordable even in these difficult economic times, and without cutting university income. We will immediately scrap fees for final year students.[1]

---

[1] Liberal Democrat manifesto 2010, 39.

The National Union of Students (NUS) made student fees an election issue and asked parliamentary candidates to sign a pledge not to increase fees; over 400 Liberal Democrat candidates signed up.[2] There were numerous photographs of senior Lib Dems making the pledge, and the party did well in university constituencies.

### The Programme for Government – and the Run-up to Publication of the Browne Report

The PfG recognised the problems faced by the Liberal Democrats while continuing to keep the Coalition's options open. It stated:

> We will await Lord Browne's final report into higher education funding, and will judge its proposals against the need to:
>
> – increase social mobility;
> – take into account the impact on student debt;
> – ensure a properly funded university sector;
> – improve the quality of teaching;
> – advance scholarship; and
> – attract a higher proportion of students from disadvantaged backgrounds.
>
> If the response of the Government to Lord Browne's report is one that Liberal Democrats cannot accept, then arrangements will be made to enable Liberal Democrat MPs to abstain in any vote.

Within days it became clear that not all Liberal Democrats would be satisfied with the option of abstaining. On 28 May 2010, former party leader Sir Menzies Campbell said:

> I have never voted against my party in the past but . . . I signed a pledge, and I would find it very difficult not to reflect that pledge in my vote. I would find it very difficult, impossible, to vote for and very difficult, I think, on an issue of this kind simply to abstain.[3]

But before the Browne report was published, Vince Cable, who had taken responsibility for this particular poisoned chalice as Secretary of State for Business, Innovation and Skills, began to recognise publicly the need for students to pay more of the costs of their education. In a speech on 15 July 2010 he said:

> I do not yet know where we shall come out but no one should be under any illusion that there will be any other than deep cuts in government spending on universities. . . . The reality is we are going to have to develop a model in which the balance of funding for higher education in England combines less public support and more private investment from those who benefit most from it.[4]

---

[2] As did many Labour candidates.

[3] BBC News, 'Ex-Lib Dem leader Campbell would rebel on tuition fees' (28 May 2010), www.bbc. co.uk/news/10174915

[4] The transcript of the speech is available at www.bis.gov.uk/news/speeches/vince-cable-higher-education

One important aspect of the problem facing Cable was that the overall spending output of his department was dominated by university funding. Had he not gone along with increased student fees, he would have had to either contemplate university closures or eliminate all other spending by his department. Neither option would have been any more palatable.

### The Browne Report – and Reaction

The Browne report was published on 12 October 2010 and effectively recommended no limit on tuition fees.[5] Vince Cable immediately signed up to the significantly higher fees but suggested that the Government would impose a cap. The Government announced their detailed proposals on 3 November, making clear that they expected most student fees to be set at £6,000 per annum, though with provision for some universities to charge £9,000. Measures were put in place to protect those from poorer backgrounds – an issue of real importance to the Liberal Democrats. And, of course, the Coalition kept stressing that fees would be paid initially by the Government and would only need to be repaid when graduates began to earn significant salaries.

But these detailed arguments got lost in the noise created by the large student demonstrations – with many parents supporting the students' arguments – which made it appear that many young people would face a lifetime of debt. Much of the focus was on the Lib Dem 'betrayal', which shifted the blame onto the Liberal Democrats while the Tory Party was able to stand on the sidelines. As the necessary parliamentary vote approached, the possibility arose that Liberal Democrat ministers, not just backbenchers, might exercise their entitlement in the PfG to abstain. This raised the bizarre possibility of a Secretary of State being unwilling to vote in support of his own proposals. Vince Cable told the BBC on 1 December 2010:

> My own personal instinct, partly because I'm the secretary of state responsible for universities and partly because I think the policy is right, my own instincts are very much to vote for it but we want to vote as a group. . . . We want to support each other, we try to agree these things as a group as other parties do. But as I say my position is somewhat different but I'm willing to go along with my colleagues [if they decide to abstain].[6]

Before the vote took place on 9 December 2010, however, the Lib Dems had agreed that all those in ministerial posts would vote in favour of the fee increase. But the party split down the middle on the issue, with 28 voting for, 21 against and 8 abstaining or absent. The Coalition survived the split and won the vote by 21 votes overall. Had all the Lib Dems abstained – the course of action provided for in the PfG – the vote would have been lost.

---

[5] The Browne Report, fully titled *Securing a Sustainable Future for Higher Education: An Independent Review of Education Funding and Student Finance*, can be found at www.bis.gov.uk/assets/biscore/corporate/docs/s/10-1208-securing-sustainable-higher-education-browne-report.pdf

[6] BBC News, 'Vince Cable may abstain from vote on tuition fees' (1 December 2010), www.bbc.co.uk/news/uk-politics-11874406

Our interviewees recognised that this was a defining moment in the history of the Coalition. One Lib Dem spad said:

> Tuition fees were a complete disaster in PR terms for all sorts of reasons. Whether or not it was the right decision that we came to in the end is almost irrelevant. You know, we broke a pledge, we're hated for it. That condemned us. We were seen as the patsies of the Tories.

And a Lib Dem MP who abstained in the vote noted:

> The whips had to oblige the payroll vote to go through in favour and half a dozen of us, me included, did what the Coalition Agreement said we should do which was abstain. But frankly we're all over the place and the public don't remember the 20 odd who voted against . . . they just remember that we split three ways. And if there's a lesson in all of that it is that whatever you decide to do, you have to do it together.

### Conclusions

The tuition fees saga illustrates some typical features of how coalition works; in other respects, however, it was highly unusual. Typical was the resort to an independent commission, albeit one established by the previous Government, to resolve a difficult policy issue. Typical also was the unity and discipline shown by the coalition partners within the Executive once they had a taken a difficult decision on the policy. Vince Cable showed complete loyalty in defending the decision, and David Willetts (Conservative Minister of State for Universities and Science) took his full share of responsibility for the policy.

What was unusual was that in Parliament the Liberal Democrats showed a complete lack of discipline, splitting three ways. Despite Willetts' defence of the policy, the press focused solely on the Lib Dems' difficulties, making the tuition fees saga a political disaster for the Liberal Democrats. A policy that had proved attractive in the run-up to the election – and which helped distinguish them from the two larger parties – led to widespread accusations of betrayal and reinforced a sustained slump in the opinion polls.

Was the train crash avoidable? The Lib Dem leadership had been worried about the potential costs of the commitment before the election, but were outvoted by the party's Federal Policy Committee. The Liberal Democrat manifesto in 2015 will no doubt be much more cautious about distinctive or populist policies which may simply not be deliverable in government.

### CASE STUDY TWO: THE NHS REFORMS

Reform of the National Health Service was not initially seen as likely to cause friction between the coalition partners – and in contrast to the other case studies in this chapter, no one thought there might be a need for the PfG to contemplate an 'agreement to disagree' on the issue. But as the complex nature of the NHS reforms revealed itself, it became one of the most publicised and polarising of the Coalition's policies.[7] A notable feature was the role of opinion of those outside Parliament and of 'NHS professionals' in causing a rethink.

## The NHS and the General Election

In the lead-up to the 2010 general election, the Conservatives were careful to signal that they would not alter the fundamentals of the NHS. Indeed, David Cameron had talked of the NHS as his 'number one priority'.[8] This was part of the modernisers' long-term strategy of detoxifying the Tory brand. So in the Conservative manifesto there was a pledge to increase spending in real terms for the NHS. But the manifesto also made clear that the Conservatives would engage in structural reform and decentralise the health service: so GPs were to be given budgeting responsibilities; independent health boards were to be created; and administrative costs were to be reduced by a third.[9]

In their manifesto, the Liberal Democrats made clear the importance of the NHS, but made no specific guarantee to protect it from cuts. Their focus was on more localised health care – such as the abolition of Strategic Health Authorities and the establishment of democratically accountable local health boards.[10]

## The Coalition Agreements

The Interim Coalition Agreement published on 11 May 2010 contained a single line devoted to the NHS and health: a commitment (from the Conservative election manifesto) that funding for the NHS should increase in real terms each year. Thereafter followed negotiations for the more detailed PfG, mostly led by Conservative Oliver Letwin and Lib Dem Danny Alexander. The NHS section was apparently done last, and took a long time to negotiate, with Andrew Lansley (Conservative Secretary of State for Health) and Paul Burstow (who became Liberal Democrat Minister of State in the Department of Health) having little input, if any, and officials from the Department of Health not being consulted at all.

---

[7]  Of course, the reforms only relate to England: the devolved administrations in Scotland and Wales now have responsibility for the 'National' Health Service – so 'NHS reform' should be understood to mean '*English* health reform'.

[8]  BBC News, 'David Cameron says NHS at heart of Tory manifesto' (4 January 2010), http://news.bbc.co.uk/1/hi/8438965.stm

[9]  R Page, 'The Emerging Blue (and Orange) Health Strategy: Continuity or Change?' in S Lee and M Beech (eds), *The Cameron-Clegg Government: Coalition Politics in an Age of Austerity* (Basingstoke: Palgrave Macmillan, 2011) 89–104.

[10]  ibid.

The PfG devoted three pages to the NHS, consisting of 30 pledges. It emphasised commonality between the parties – such as the commitment of both parties to an NHS that was free at the point of use and available to everyone based on need. A key pledge placed strategically at the beginning of the NHS section was to 'stop the top-down reorganisations of the NHS', but a careful reading of the entire set of pledges shows a general commitment to the decentralisation of the health service, and to ensuring greater accountability. Two-thirds of the NHS section could be crudely identified as either coming from the Conservatives' election manifesto or previous Conservative Party policy documents, and one-third from the Liberal Democrats' election manifesto or previous party policy documents.[11] In practice, the two parties' policies were sometimes shoehorned together in the PfG to produce proposals which were neither quite of either party, nor internally inconsistent.

There were subtle differences between the coalition parties on the NHS.[12] Broadly speaking, while both parties emphasised decentralisation, for the Conservatives this was to be characterised by greater involvement of the private sector and the market. Decentralisation for the Liberal Democrats, in contrast, was to be driven by greater localisation and democratic accountability. But this was complicated by the fact that some key Liberal Democrats (particularly those on the frontbench) straddled this divide in being avowedly pro-market. These differences would manifest themselves as the two parties began to engage with the Health and Social Care Bill (Health Bill), which was meant to establish a legislative framework for the reforms.

## White Paper: *Equity and Excellence*

In July 2010, the Coalition published a White Paper titled *Equity and Excellence: Liberating the NHS*.[13] This laid out the Government's proposals for NHS reform, and was to be followed by the Health Bill in January 2011. *Equity and Excellence* proposed a major restructuring of the NHS, including: the decentralisation of NHS decision-making, greater competition for services and greater patient choice; the establishment of GP commissioning consortia with their own budgets to buy care services; the abolition of Strategic Health Authorities and Primary Care Trusts, to be replaced by a new NHS Commissioning Board; and the transformation of the foundation trust regulator, the Monitor, into an economic regulator to promote competition between providers.[14] These reforms were to be completed

---

[11] In particular, *Renewal: Plan for a Better NHS* (September 2008), www.conservatives.com/News/News_stories/2008/09/Our_plan_for_a_better_NHS.aspx

[12] See, for instance, M Birtwistle, 'Should health services be commissioned by technocrat or democrat?' *MHP Blog* (11 May 2011), www.mhpc.com/blog/should-health-services-be-commissioned-technocrat-or-democrat

[13] Department of Health, *Equity and Excellence: Liberating the NHS* (2010), www.dh.gov.uk/en/Publicationsandstatistics/Publications/PublicationsPolicyAndGuidance/DH_117353

[14] There is a useful explanation of the current structure of the NHS (at the time of writing, 2011) and the proposed structure in the Commons Library Research Paper 'Health and Social Care Bill', www.parliament.uk/briefing-papers/RP11-11

by the end of 2014. The only way to reconcile the White Paper with the PfG was to argue that the restructuring was bottom-up rather than top-down.

The marked extent to which the White Paper departed from the agreed PfG – Primary Care Trusts had disappeared, for example, while much of public health was to be transferred to local government – led to one of only two meetings of the Coalition Committee (the Cabinet Committee established to act as the final arbiter on the PfG) in the first 18 months.[15]

At this point, the Liberal Democrats were still finding their way in government, and the more immediate issues for them were the Spending Review and tuition fees. Concerns about the proposed reforms were growing within the parliamentary party; but there were much more widespread worries expressed by various interest groups in the health sector, notably on the speed of the reforms, accountability, the emphasis on competition for service provision, and perhaps above all the need to find £20 billion in 'efficiency savings' by 2014–15 (which was separate from the reforms, but threatened to have a far more visceral impact on the NHS).[16] There were critical discussions about the White Paper at the Liberal Democrat Autumn Conference in September 2010, which alerted the party leadership to potential problems. But it was not until the Health and Social Care Bill was published in late January 2011 that Liberal Democrat dissatisfaction with the reforms began to crystallise.

## The Health and Social Care Bill

The Health Bill went before Cabinet in the winter. It was a mammoth bill, larger than the founding 1946 Act, containing over 300 clauses and 24 schedules. It was signed off by all, including Nick Clegg and Paul Burstow. Burstow in particular, as the Liberal Democrat representative in the Department of Health, had been carefully consulted and involved in the details of the bill.

The bill was introduced in the House of Commons in January 2011. There were fairly nondescript exchanges, with Labour being hostile, Conservative MPs favourable, and very few Liberal Democrat MPs present. In the second reading division on the bill on 31 January, it passed with a comfortable majority. No coalition MPs voted against, though Liberal Democrat MP Andrew George – who sat on the Commons Health Select Committee – abstained.

However, opposition to the NHS reforms both inside and outside Parliament was growing and manifested itself at committee stage, where the bill was examined in detail between 8 February and 31 March 2011. The Public Bill Committee for the Health Bill had a membership of 26 MPs, with a government majority of 11 Tories and three Liberal Democrats. It was the longest committee stage for a bill since 2002, with 28 sittings and over 100 divisions. Although opposition

---

[15] See ch 4.
[16] Commons Library Research Paper, 'Health and Social Care Bill' (n 14). See also Page, 'The Emerging Blue (and Orange) Health Strategy: Continuity or Change?' (n 9).

amendments were tabled, all were defeated, and voting took place largely along party lines.

Concerns were also steadily growing in the Liberal Democrat Party, which resulted in a motion at the March 2011 Spring Conference. A pro-reform motion proposed by the party leadership was voted through, but with two major amendments, representing a clear defeat for the leadership. Conference voted in support of an amendment to make clear that it:

> regrets that some of the proposed reforms have never been Liberal Democrat policy, did not feature in our manifesto or in the agreed Coalition Programme, which instead called for an end to large-scale top-down reorganisations.

In the same amendment, the Lib Dem Conference called on Lib Dem politicians to work to amend the Bill in Parliament and denounce the prospect of an increasingly market-based NHS. The second major amendment focused on local democratic accountability, and the role of local councillors in the new NHS.[17] The Spring Conference marked a turning point in the Liberal Democrats' approach to the proposed NHS reforms: from this point onwards, Liberal Democrat criticism of the Health Bill became explicit and outspoken.


### 'The Pause'

On 6 April 2011 the Department of Health initiated a 'Listening Exercise' for two months, to 'pause, listen, reflect and improve' on the Health Bill – hence becoming informally known as 'the pause'. An independent advisory panel, the NHS Future Forum, was tasked with seeking feedback on the proposals, particularly from the health professions. The pause was remarkable as the legislation was still in Bill Committee stage – at which point any government would expect to be clear on the thrust of their policy.

The pause was initiated because of nervousness within government over the growing opposition to the proposed reforms – discontent not just from the parties but also from the various professional bodies in the health sector. Lansley had had great difficulty explaining and reconciling the complex and often conflicting nature of the reforms, and ensuring that the reforms did not get entangled with the programme to secure £20 billion in efficiency savings over the 2010–15 parliamentary term. Put differently, the pause was an attempt to reassert control over 'the narrative' surrounding the NHS reforms.[18] It signalled that responsibility for key decisions on presentation – and therefore to some extent substance – had shifted from Andrew Lansley and Paul Burstow in the Department of Health to

---

[17] Details of the motion can be found in the March 2011 Federal Conference Report, 13–16, www.nickclegg.com/siteFiles/resources/PDF/2011%20March%20Sheffield%20Report.pdf

[18] See, for instance, the following poll, which showed that concern about the NHS had increased sharply by May 2011, falling behind the economy and unemployment: www.ipsos-mori.com/research-publications/researcharchive/2795/EconomistIpsos-MORI-Issues-Index-May-2011.aspx

No 10 and the DPM's Office; and from this time on there was more supervision from the centre of government generally. In May 2011, for instance, Sean Worth, the health special adviser in the No 10 Policy Unit, was moved to the Department of Health to help Lansley.[19] No 10 was beginning to reassert control over the departments after a long period of being hands-off.[20]

The pause was seized upon by Liberal Democrats, who saw the need to respond to the motions made at the 2011 Spring Conference, and because of the party's steadily declining electoral support. This reflected the perceived need to move away from an emphasis on coalition unity towards greater party differentiation (see chapters seven and eight). Norman Lamb MP, for instance, Nick Clegg's 'chief political adviser', threatened publicly in early April 2011 to quit if a number of changes were not made to the bill. And shortly after the 'no' result on the Alternative Vote referendum became clear, Nick Clegg announced that the Liberal Democrats would block the reforms unless significant changes were made to the Health Bill.[21] One Liberal Democrat interviewee said of the NHS reforms: 'It's probably the best thing that happened to us, from a political point of view.'

The NHS reforms also posed a dilemma for the Conservatives. Few were happy with Lansley's lacklustre performance over this period, but nonetheless Conservative backbenchers, out of loyalty and conviction, argued for the retention of their preferred policies: competition and economic regulation of the NHS.[22] Others – the 'modernisers', or those within 'Team Cameron' – were worried about the public reaction to the health reforms ('the NHS is not safe with the Conservatives'), as it threatened the long-term strategy of detoxification (see chapter eight). One Conservative special adviser argued:

> NHS reform was fundamentally off on the wrong tack and was creating a massive political problem for the Government and the Conservative Party. What we needed to do was buy time, go back to first principles and find out what was the problem to which the reforms were the solution.

So Clegg's open criticisms were choreographed, or at least signed off, by the Conservatives at the Centre.[23] One Liberal Democrat parliamentarian who was closely involved in the process argued: 'It was actually quite a safety first strategy for them to stick close to Nick Clegg's position through that period – and Nick actually did get more leverage as a result.' The pause allowed the Conservatives to retreat on an unpopular platform without seeming divided internally. So while

[19] A Porter, 'David Cameron sends his own spin doctors to help Lansley with NHS reforms' *Telegraph* (6 May 2011), www.telegraph.co.uk/news/politics/8498648/David-Cameron-sends-his-own-spin-doctors-to-help-Lansley-with-NHS-reforms.html

[20] This could be seen, for instance, in the decision to reconfigure the No 10 Policy Unit: see ch 5.

[21] 'Nick Clegg threatens to block NHS reforms' *Guardian* (8 May 2011), www.guardian.co.uk/politics/2011/may/08/nick-clegg-veto-nhs-reforms

[22] Wintour and Watt, 'Coalition's divisions over future of NHS deepen into open warfare' *Guardian Blog* (19 May 2011), www.guardian.co.uk/politics/wintour-and-watt/2011/may/18/andrewlansley-nhs?INTCMP=ILCNETTXT3487

[23] N Watt, '"NHS reform is safe" – Andrew Lansley makes private plea for Tory support' *Guardian* (13 June 2011), www.guardian.co.uk/politics/2011/jun/13/nhs-reform-andrew-lansley

the public perception may have been that the pause and the changes that followed were the product of a coalition 'split' over the NHS, in one sense the two parties were united by the competing considerations driving their respective parties in calling for a temporary halt to the reforms.

In June 2011, David Cameron agreed to a number of recommendations suggested during the pause. These to some extent watered down the original proposed reforms, and included: making clear that the primary duty of Monitor was not to promote competition; widening the membership of the GP-led consortia; the creation of clinical senates; relaxing the initial 2013 deadline for completion of the reforms; prohibiting the Government from seeking to increase the role of the private sector as an end in itself; and ensuring that the Health Secretary would remain ultimately accountable for the NHS.[24] Nick Clegg would separately claim to his party that the Liberal Democrats had been successful in meeting 11 of the 13 changes demanded by the Spring Conference.[25]

### The Health and Social Care Bill Returns to Parliament

Following the pause, the Health Bill was sent back to the Commons. Over 1,000 amendments were submitted by the Government, and although the vast majority of these were simply name changes, some were intended to implement the recommendations agreed by Cameron, Lansley and Clegg.[26] The final Commons vote on the bill in September was won by the Government by 316 votes to 251, a reduced majority compared to the second reading. Four Lib Dem MPs voted against the bill.

### The 2011 Autumn Conference

In the run-up to the Liberal Democrats' 2011 Conference, there was speculation as to whether the party membership would push for further changes to the proposed reforms. In practice, the Autumn Conference was far less fractious than the Spring Conference. Nick Clegg claimed again that the Liberal Democrats in government had brought real change to the Health Bill; and Paul Burstow argued that it was not the case that the Government had stopped listening to concerns. Two parliamentarians were less sanguine. John Pugh, co-chair of the Lib Dem Health backbench committee, described NHS reforms as a 'huge strategic mistake' which would damage both coalition parties. Lib Dem Baroness Shirley Williams

---

[24] N Watt, 'NHS reforms: Cameron accepts "substantive" changes to health bill' *Guardian* (14 June 2011), www.guardian.co.uk/society/2011/jun/14/nhs-reforms-cameron-accepts-substantive-chages

[25] N Watt, 'Nick Clegg under fire over health reform "victory"' *Guardian* (12 June 2011), www.guardian.co.uk/politics/2011/jun/12/nick-clegg-health-reform

[26] V Macdonald, 'Heath Bill is "biggest upheaval in NHS history"' *Channel 4 News* (6 September 2011), www.channel4.com/news/debate-on-nhs-health-and-social-care-bill

conceded that some positive changes had been made to the proposals since the Government's listening exercise began, but also vowed to scrutinise the bill intensely in the Lords, and press for further changes.

Liberal Democrat rebels, led by Dr Evan Harris, failed to force a vote on the party's policy towards the reforms, falling short of the two-thirds majority necessary. A debate on the NHS went ahead, but members could not vote on the issue at all. A successful vote against the plans might have been construed by Liberal Democrats in the Lords as providing them with a mandate to oppose the bill.

### The Health and Social Care Bill in the House of Lords

The bill then moved to the Lords. The second reading stage, which began on 11 October 2011, saw two of the largest Lords votes for over a decade, with over 100 peers speaking and almost 600 peers voting. Various key amendments were tabled, intended to delay the bill from passing in the current parliamentary session. But these amendments were defeated by government peers and Crossbenchers.

In early November the Coalition Government initiated a 'mini-pause' on the issue of the Secretary of State's constitutional responsibility for the NHS until January 2012.[27] That was to allow time for a negotiated compromise on the controversial issue, and to avoid a predicted rebellion by Lib Dem peers and Crossbenchers. It was also intended to avoid further delay to the passage of the bill: the responsibility of the Secretary of State was only one of many controversial aspects of it. Fifteen days were set aside in December for the committee stage, in which the bill was examined line by line. That was an unusually long time, but it was necessary to meet the concerns of both Lib Dem and Crossbench peers.

At the time of writing, it was still not clear whether the Health Bill would become law. There was still the Health Bill's Report stage to navigate, at which time all amendments to the bill would be considered. That was expected to begin in early February 2012. However, the Health Bill was only one of a number of large bills before Parliament. Major concessions seemed likely, because the deadline for the enactment of legislation was late March 2012. After this time any bills not accepted by Parliament would be lost, because it would not be possible to carry them forward into the next parliamentary term.[28]

### Conclusion

The NHS reforms raised questions about the drafting process of the Coalition Agreements. The reforms did not feature in the Initial Coalition Agreement of

[27] R Ramesh, 'NHS bill clause put on hold to stave off revolt by Liberal Democrat peers' *Guardian* (2 November 2011), www.guardian.co.uk/society/2011/nov/02/nhs-bill-clause-hold-lords

[28] M D'Arcy, 'Turbulent times ahead for peers' *BBC: Mark D'Arcy's Blog* (14 December 2011), www.bbc.co.uk/news/uk-politics-16177521; see also 'May Day for the Queen's Speech' *PoliticsHome* (3 January 2012), www.politicshome.com/uk/article/42900/may_day_for_the_queen.html

11 May, and it was this Agreement that the two parliamentary parties signed up to upon entering the Coalition. So it was understandable that Liberal Democrats who disagreed with the reforms could say that they had not been properly consulted. Whitehall experts were also not consulted, and the Department of Health struggled to turn the contradictions in the PfG into a workable policy.

The formal coalition machinery was put to full use, with the departures from the PfG being discussed in the Coalition Committee and Home Affairs Cabinet Committee. Paul Burstow as the Lib Dem minister in the Department of Health was fully involved; and his Lib Dem colleagues initially remained loyal and unified. But the unnecessarily complex and contentious nature of the reforms and the legislation to implement them left the coalition parties open to criticism from all sides. For the Lib Dems, difficulties first emerged in Parliament, and then at the Liberal Democrat Conference in spring 2011. It was at this point that Nick Clegg felt obliged to publicly distance himself and insist on changes to the reform package. The Conservative leadership was happy to allow the smaller party to engage in party differentiation. It gave them leeway to strategically retreat on a set of policies that were potentially explosive for their own party identity, and without explicitly criticising one of their own.

### CASE STUDY THREE: NUCLEAR POWER

In the immediate aftermath of the election, nuclear power seemed likely to be a particularly difficult issue for the coalition parties. It was one where the Coalition Agreement had set out the opposing positions of the two parties, and allowed the Lib Dem spokesperson to speak against government policy. But in the first 18 months it did not cause major divisions: it was 'the dog that didn't bark'.

In their respective manifestos for the 2010 election, the Labour and Conservative parties were broadly supportive of new nuclear investment while the Liberal Democrats remained opposed. The key sentences of the three manifestos were:

> We have taken the decisions to enable a new generation of nuclear power stations . . . [Labour][29]

> [We will be] clearing the way for new nuclear power stations – provided they receive no public subsidy [Conservative][30]

> [We] reject a new generation of nuclear power stations; based on the evidence nuclear is a far more expensive way of reducing carbon emissions than promoting energy conservation and renewable energy [Lib Dem][31]

[29]  www.labour.org.uk/uploads/TheLabourPartyManifesto-2010.pdf
[30]  www.media.conservatives.s3.amazonaws.com/manifesto/cpmanifesto2010_lowres.pdf
[31]  www.network.libdems.org.uk/manifesto2010/libdem_manifesto_2010.pdf

## The Programme for Government

On the face of it the position of the coalition partners was irreconcilable – the Tories were in favour of new nuclear build and the Lib Dems were opposed. But the two parties nevertheless managed to find a way through. The amount of text devoted to the issue in the PfG was far more extensive than either partner had included in their manifesto. The full text read as follows:

> Liberal Democrats have long opposed any new nuclear construction. Conservatives, by contrast, are committed to allowing the replacement of existing nuclear power stations provided that they are subject to the normal planning process for major projects (under a new National Planning Statement), and also provided that they receive no public subsidy.
>
> We will implement a process allowing the Liberal Democrats to maintain their opposition to nuclear power while permitting the Government to bring forward the National Planning Statement for ratification by Parliament so that new nuclear construction becomes possible. This process will involve:
>
> – the Government completing the drafting of a national planning statement and putting it before Parliament;
> – specific agreement that a Liberal Democrat spokesperson will speak against the Planning Statement, but that Liberal Democrat MPs will abstain; and
> – clarity that this will not be regarded as an issue of confidence.[32]

At the time, this aspect of the PfG – which was apparently drafted by Chris Huhne, who was about to become the Lib Dem Secretary of State in the Department of Energy and Climate Change (DECC), and by Oliver Letwin for the Tories – came in for much sceptical comment. As with student fees, it seemed a nonsense for the Lib Dems to be free not to support a policy coming from a department headed by a Lib Dem Secretary of State.

But in practice, the drafting was quite astute. It gave the Lib Dems a conscience vote, in that they could abstain in Parliament without threatening the Government's parliamentary majority, because the Labour Party would find it difficult to vote against nuclear, given their manifesto position. Moreover, though not explicitly discussed in the PfG, the distinction between the respective positions of the parties was perhaps less marked in the manifestos than assumed: the Lib Dem opposition to nuclear was based on the potential cost of the technology, and they had not coupled this with opposition on environmental grounds; and the Tory support for new nuclear had the caveat that no public subsidy should be involved.

[32] www.direct.gov.uk/prod_consum_dg/groups/dg_digitalassets/@dg/@en/documents/digitalasset/dg_187876.pdf

### What Happened in Practice?

There was some initial nervousness in DECC as to whether the willingness to embrace nuclear power in the PfG would translate into actual support in government. But it soon became apparent that both coalition partners were clear that if industry wanted to invest in new build then government would facilitate the necessary regulatory approvals. One official noted:

> The Secretary of State's position, as he explained it, was that he has always been deeply sceptical of the true costs of nuclear and believes they have always been glossed over, so he was doubtful whether nuclear would in practice be delivered if government had a no subsidy policy. But he was equally clear that he had no theological objection to nuclear power. So it was only ever an economics issue for him.

This message was reiterated to the industry by both the Secretary of State and by Charles Hendry as Energy Minister. Chris Huhne also made his position clear to the Lib Dem 2010 Conference:

> There is an important place for new nuclear stations in our energy mix as long as there is no public subsidy. . . . And I say again there will be no subsidy to nuclear, for a very clear reason: it is a mature technology, not an infant needing nurture.

That said, it was clear that everything that the Government was doing was being watched closely by various NGOs who were opposed to nuclear and were very willing to go to court for judicial review if the Government made any procedural misjudgements. One concern was that 'subsidy' had never been precisely defined and so was open to different interpretations, including the possibility that market mechanisms which penalised carbon extensive generation might be seen as a subsidy to low carbon generation. So the Secretary of State defined the term in a statement to Parliament in October 2010:

> I would like to take this opportunity to reconfirm the government's policy that there will be no public subsidy for new nuclear power. To be clear this means that there will be no levy, direct payment or market support for electricity supplied or capacity provided by a private sector new nuclear operator unless similar support is also made available more widely to other types of generation. New nuclear power will, for example, benefit from any general measures that are in place or may be introduced as part of wider reform of the electricity market to encourage investment in low carbon generation.[33]

### Fukushima – Impact in Germany but not in the UK

The Japanese tsunami in March 2011 led to major safety concerns at the nuclear power plant at Fukushima, and was briefly thought to have derailed the Coalition's support for new nuclear build in the UK. The German Government reacted

---

[33] Hansard HC Deb, 18 October 2010 col 42-6WS.

within a couple of months by deciding to halt all nuclear energy generation in Germany. In the UK, the Coalition responded by commissioning a safety report on the implications from the nuclear safety regulator which in due course made only moderate recommendations for changes, none of which undermined the case for new nuclear build. The report attracted little publicity. The dog, even though provoked, had failed to bark again.

### Conclusion

Despite the seeming irreconcilability of the two parties' positions on nuclear power, the drafting of the PfG was an astute compromise. Chris Huhne as the Secretary of State faithfully implemented the compromise, which was to facilitate new nuclear build if the economics were right. He allowed development of the regulatory framework and identification of potential new sites. A Lib Dem loyalist could have taken a different stance, especially post-Fukushima. But as in other policy areas, the Liberal Democrats showed themselves disciplined and loyal to the PfG.

### OVERALL CONCLUSIONS

These case studies deal with very different subjects, but some overall lessons can be drawn. First is the crucial importance of the wording of the Coalition Agreement, with a stark contrast between the health service reforms and nuclear policy. The NHS section of the PfG contained serious internal contradictions, starting with the pledge to stop top-down reorganisations, and with unresolved inconsistencies between Conservative and Lib Dem commitments which had been thrown together. By contrast, the section on nuclear power acknowledged the differences between the two parties' policies, and proposed a careful way forward which allowed the Lib Dems significant differentiation. It may have helped the drafting, and subsequent implementation, that Chris Huhne was involved in drafting that section of the PfG, while Andrew Lansley had very little involvement in framing the health section.

The second lesson is similar to one in the previous chapter: however hard the coalition partners might have strived to reach agreement in government, that agreement could become unpicked in Parliament. That was clearly the case with the NHS reforms, where the first signs of trouble emerged during committee stage in the House of Commons, before the Lib Dem party conference; and the bill encountered even more trouble in the House of Lords. It was also the case with tuition fees, with the Liberal Democrats splitting three ways on the crucial vote. It was not the case with nuclear power; but one reason why that policy did not cause any political difficulty for the Coalition in its first 18 months may be that it was not subjected to any parliamentary test.

The third lesson marks a difference from the previous chapter. There we found that the parties had shown remarkable unity and discipline in defending the compromises that had been agreed. In two of the case studies in this chapter the Liberal Democrats broke ranks. They did so over tuition fees, in a very messy way, with only eight abstaining as the Coalition Agreement had provided for. They broke ranks strongly and publicly over the health service reforms, with a resolution by party conference to amend the Health Bill, followed by Clegg announcing that the Lib Dems would block the bill unless it was changed. But in coalition terms the health service revolt may have been licensed dissent: the Conservatives would probably have been forced to modify their proposals themselves even under single-party government.

The fourth lesson is that the Conservatives proved dominant in terms of the policy outcome. This was most clearly the case with tuition fees and nuclear power: the Conservatives got the policy outcome they wanted. Given the Liberal Democrats' rejection of new nuclear power stations in their manifesto, they might have been surprised to find their own Secretary of State paving the way. On the health service the score card is mixed: initially the Conservatives seemed dominant, but subsequently the Lib Dems clearly had an influence, and a strong one, in moderating the proposals.

This leads to the final point, which is the extent to which the Liberal Democrats paid a heavier price than the Conservatives for implementing coalition policies. On tuition fees the Lib Dems took almost all the flak; they had abandoned one of their flagship policies. But in any coalition the smaller party will need sacrifice more of its key policies than the larger party. It is also more vulnerable to claims of betrayal, because its defeats are more visible; whereas the quiet retreat of the Tories on their health reforms could be balanced against the fact that across government as a whole the Tories remained largely dominant.

Paradoxically, the minority party in a coalition might actually benefit from not having the Secretary of State role in any area of significant importance to them. It might be expected that having a Lib Dem Secretary of State at the Department for Business, Innovation and Skills (BIS) was better for the Lib Dems than having a junior ministerial role at the Department of Health, in that the Lib Dem influence on the outcome would be much stronger. But if the Tories had been in charge of BIS, the Lib Dems would have been able to achieve some visible concessions as the student fees policy was developed, and this might have been seen by the press as the Lib Dems losing out, but still putting up a fight. Additionally, the party in Westminster would not have been so obviously split between those who felt they must vote against the policy on principle and those who felt constrained to support a Lib Dem Secretary of State.

This observation applies equally – though as a mirror image – to the NHS issue. The press presentation of the issue was of a Tory retreat and a victory – even if a minor one – for the Lib Dems. Had Vince Cable been Secretary of State, the policy proposals from the Department of Health might not have been very different; but No 10 might have been less inclined to intervene when they became unpopular, and the Lib Dem opposition in Westminster might have been less strident.

As we have noted throughout the book, the unity/distinctiveness dilemma is more acute for the junior partner in a coalition. The junior partner has the greater problem in making its overall contribution to the government visible to the press and the electorate. It is always going to lose more arguments than it wins and will have to make more concessions on policy issues. But one advantage it does have – and one that is denied to the senior partner – is that it will usually have some scope for portraying itself on a limited number of issues as managing to achieve concessions; particularly when there is scope – as there was in relation to the health service reforms – for its campaigning to take place at least partially in public. In such circumstances, the junior partner can not only make a difference, but also be seen to be making a difference.

For that approach to be viable, however, it can only really be employed where the senior partner is visibly in charge of the issue concerned. Campaigning against policies that are being fronted by one's own party makes the party seem divided, which always sends a negative message. But that constraint does not apply when the issues can be identified with the larger party, as was the case in the NHS debate.

# 11

# *Lessons for the Future*

## ROBERT HAZELL

Prepare for all possible outcomes . . . the other lesson is, don't assume the future is a reflection of the past. (Cabinet Secretary Sir Gus O'Donnell, September 2011)

### INTRODUCTION: THE LIMITS OF GENERALISATION

I T IS NOT easy to generalise from the experience of the first 18 months of the UK's Coalition Government. All coalitions are unique in terms of their historic and political context. They depend critically on the parliamentary arithmetic, which determines the balance of power between the parties in government, and between government and opposition; and on the ideological compatibility of the partners. A coalition between two parties whose parliamentary strength is in the ratio of 5:1 (the approximate ratio between Conservative and Lib Dem MPs in May 2010) is very different from a coalition with a ratio of 10:1, 15:1 or 20:1. A coalition between a centre-right and a centre party is very different from a 'grand coalition' of left and right; or from a 'rainbow coalition' including nationalist or extremist parties. The other determining factors are the personalities involved, particularly of the party leaders, and the degree of trust that exists between them and senior figures around them.

But although it is early days, it is still possible to draw some early conclusions from the experience of the UK's Coalition Government and its first 18 months in office. Coalition government is a learning process, as seen clearly in a country like New Zealand, where each coalition has built on the experience of its predecessors. Our book is a contribution to that learning process. The first part of this final chapter covers the remainder of this Parliament, and the second looks at wider lessons for future coalition governments in future Parliaments.

### LESSONS FOR THE REMAINDER OF THE 2010 PARLIAMENT

The most important thing to say is that the Coalition made a very strong start. The omens were not good. As we saw in chapter two, coalitions tend to be less stable than single-party majority government. In Britain's strongly majoritarian political culture, coalitions have been seen as particularly undesirable: unstable, short lived, quarrelsome, producing weak and ineffective government.[1] David Cameron before the 2010 election gave voice to the traditional fears, saying: '[With] a permanent hung Parliament – a permanent coalition – we would never have strong and decisive government'.[2] But in its first 18 months the Coalition defied these gloomy expectations. Despite his misgivings, Cameron proved to be a natural coalition leader, quickly developing a trusting relationship with Nick Clegg and his senior colleagues. For their part, the Liberal Democrats dedicated the first year of the Coalition to demonstrating that they could be loyal and effective partners in government. In Parliament the Coalition proved very stable, being undefeated in the House of Commons, and suffering fewer defeats in the Lords than its single-party government predecessor. And in the first year the new Government took a series of remarkably bold decisions, starting with the ambitious deficit reduction strategy. This led many critics to say that, far from being weak and ineffective, the Coalition was being too bold, doing too much and too fast.

So at the end of the first 18 months the Coalition Government had demonstrated that, contrary to the British stereotype, coalition government could be stable, harmonious and decisive. The questions addressed in the first part of this chapter are: How long can this last? What do the partners need to do to make it last? How can they renew the Coalition mid term? And how will it end?

### How Long will it Last? Fixed Terms and Mid-Term Renewal

The Fixed Term Parliaments Act 2011 states that the next election will be on 7 May 2015. The Coalition introduced fixed terms in order to buttress the stability of the Government, and to avoid the debilitating speculation that occurs in the second half of every Parliament about when the Prime Minister will call the next election. The legislation helps to provide greater stability, and the likelihood is that the Government will last to 2015. There is only limited provision for mid-term dissolution in two circumstances: following a no confidence motion, if no alternative government can be formed within 14 days; or following a resolution of two-thirds of the House of Commons. These are high thresholds which are likely to be reached only in a major political crisis.

Such a crisis could be triggered by the economy, which dwarfs all of the Government's other difficulties. It was in part the economy that brought the Coalition together in the first place, and it is by the Government's response to the problems of the economy that voters will judge whether the Coalition has succeeded or failed. As one Lib Dem special adviser (spad) noted:

---

[1] This may no longer be the perception in Scotland and Wales. But the surveys on public attitudes to coalition do not contain regional breakdowns that might confirm this.

[2] T Dunn and S Hawkes, 'Cameron warning on coalition course' *Sun* (27 April 2010), www.thesun.co.uk/sol/homepage/news/election2010/2949044/Cameron-warning-on-coalition-course.html

> I think this Coalition came together because of the economy . . . there was a genuine,
> genuine threat of a crisis after the General Election last year. People really were worried
> that we would go into economic meltdown.

A Cabinet Office official made the same point:

> The fiscal position created that sense of common purpose which was very obvious from
> different ministers on both sides right from the start. The platform was burning brightly
> and fiercely and they felt a strong common need to go in and get on with things.

Eighteen months on, the platform was still burning, and economic meltdown
seemed even closer.

Economic recovery is key to the success or failure of the Coalition, and all else
has been subordinate to that. This may create growing tensions between the coalition partners, especially if their strong initial consensus around the deficit reduction strategy starts to fray. The tensions spilt over into the parties' different
attitudes towards Europe. But despite occasional differences of emphasis between
Cable and Osborne, there was no demand in the first 18 months from the Lib
Dems for a Plan B. And if the Government does start to change its tack, the shift
may come as much from the Chancellor as from the Business Secretary.[3] As with
the NHS service reforms, the Conservatives will be as anxious to save their skins as
their Lib Dem partners.

## Mid-Term Renewal

How does a government renew itself mid-term, and refresh its appeal to the voters? Traditionally through new policies, and new faces. The Coalition will need
new policies as it exhausts its original agenda: in May 2011 it reported that it was
well on the way to completing two-thirds of the commitments in the original
Programme for Government (PfG).[4] The difficulty is that with no new money,
there is very little room for policy initiatives of the traditional kind, involving
increased spending. The Conservatives may seek to redouble public service
reforms; but as they found with the NHS reforms, the Lib Dems may react strongly
against creeping privatisation.

In spring 2011 there was talk of developing a mid-term review, a revised and
updated PfG with a new set of policies to carry the Coalition through the second
half of the Parliament. Conservative minister Letwin and Lib Dem cabinet minister Alexander were asked to think about how this might be worked up. The original idea of a new programme, 'Coalition 2.0', was soon shelved. The Liberal
Democrats felt uncomfortable about getting even deeper into bed with the
Conservatives, at a time when they wanted to start emphasising their policy distinctiveness. And senior Lib Dems were not confident that they could get a revised

---

[3] The November 2011 autumn statement contained a little nod towards Plan B, with the Lib Dems
claiming credit for its emphasis on quick infrastructure investments.
[4] See www.number10.gov.uk/wp-content/uploads/coalition-one-year-on.pdf

coalition agreement through the party's triple lock procedure. But the plan was still to produce a mid-term review showing how the existing Programme would be fulfilled. The Liberal Democrat spring conference in 2012 was to discuss the party's priorities for the mid-term review, aiming for a negotiated agreement with the Conservatives for debate at the autumn conference. A possible forerunner was the Liberal Democrat Policy Paper *Facing the Future: Policy Development Agenda*, produced for the Party Conference in September 2011.[5] It was designed to identify gaps in policy and to set the framework for party policy making for the rest of the Parliament, with a long section on Liberal Democrat values. However, it was very light in terms of specific policies. This illustrates another difficulty regarding mid-term coalition agreements: that in the second half of a Parliament, coalition partners do not want the other party to start borrowing their ideas.

The other way to refresh a government is by introducing new faces. A summer reshuffle is a tradition in British government, and Tony Blair made nine changes in his first Cabinet in July 1998. By comparison Cameron has been very restrained. In the first 18 months two limited reshuffles were forced upon him following the resignation of David Laws in May 2010 and Liam Fox in October 2011, which led to minimal changes.[6] There was no summer reshuffle in 2011.[7] Cameron faces a cohort of Conservative backbenchers hungry for promotion. But because the Lib Dems hold one-fifth of ministerial posts, and because Cameron is publicly committed to promoting more women, only a handful of male backbenchers have a chance.

The Deputy Prime Minister provides a further constraint, because he must be consulted and he nominates all the Lib Dem ministers. Clegg's dilemma is the opposite of Cameron's. He has drawn down most of his limited pool of ministerial talent in the Commons. When they come to the first reshuffle, the Lib Dems might consider appointing more ministers from the Lords, where they have much more experience and depth of talent on their backbench than in the Commons. The Lib Dems might also like to consider appointing some 'bridging' ministers, so that they can cover more than one department. It is a common practice for Associate Ministers in New Zealand to monitor more than one department. There were two Conservative bridging ministers in the UK Coalition's first 18 months of government, but no Lib Dems.[8]

---

[5] Liberal Democrat Party, *Facing the Future: Policy Development Agenda* (8 January 2011), www.libdems.org.uk/siteFiles/resources/docs/conference/100%20-%20Facing%20the%20Future.pdf

[6] The only other replacements followed the resignation of two Lords ministers: Pauline Neville-Jones as Security Minister in May 2011, and Angela Browning as Crime Prevention Minister in September 2011. Both were in the Home Office.

[7] Cameron let it be known that there would be no summer reshuffle. See M Crick, 'Will Lansley swap jobs with Hammond?' *BBC Newsnight Blogs* (27 April 2011), www.bbc.co.uk/blogs/newsnight/michael-crick/2011/04

[8] Ed Vaizey (Minister for Culture and Communications) in the Department for Culture, Media and Sport (DCMS) and the Department for Business, Innovation and Skills, and Nick Herbert (Minister for Policing and Criminal Justice) in the Home Office and Ministry of Justice. Vaizey took on his role in the DCMS only after Business Secretary Vince Cable lost his media responsibilities in January 2011.

## How Can the Partners Make it Last? The Conservatives

The Conservatives are in a strong position. The Coalition provided them with a comfortable majority of 83 in the Commons, and a working majority in the Lords. The PfG incorporated the most important Conservative policies, in particular on deficit reduction. Of the Liberal Democrats' unpalatable policies the most unpalatable was the Alternative Vote (AV) referendum, which went down to a crushing defeat. And the Lib Dems took all the flak on the decision to increase tuition fees, which was a Conservative, not a Lib Dem, policy.

Conservative support held up well in the polls in 2010 and 2011. The Liberal Democrats did disastrously, seeing their ratings slump from the 24 per cent they polled in the May 2010 election to around 12 per cent by the autumn. The greatest risk for the Conservatives is that the Lib Dems become so disenchanted that they decide to quit the Coalition, leaving the Conservatives in a minority government. This might coincide with a Lib Dem split, or change of leader. To minimise this risk the Conservatives need to keep hugging the Lib Dems close, and killing them with kindness. They can afford to be generous, and have understood this well: making the odd policy concession, allowing them a distinctive voice, giving them their share of ministerial announcements and photo opportunities, while knowing that it will be hard for the Lib Dems to recover.

This does not necessarily harm the Conservatives with the public. The only downside is with the Tory party faithful. On some issues, it has suited Cameron to have the Lib Dems hold him nearer to the centre ground. But as the next election approaches, Cameron's centrist stance may come under challenge from the right wing of the party, seeking sharper demarcation. No serious leadership challenger is yet in sight; but votes on European issues could see Maastricht style rebellions, threatening the Government's majority.

## How Can the Partners Make it Last? The Liberal Democrats

The Liberal Democrats face far greater difficulties. Improving their effectiveness in government through more systematic coordination of Lib Dem ministers, or increasing the number of special advisers, now seems almost irrelevant. Their big challenge is to show that they are making a difference, on issues that the voters notice and care about. Their differentiation strategy in Year Two, evidenced over demanding a rethink of the NHS reforms, or their different approach to the Human Rights Act or the summer riots, yielded no change in their poll ratings. By the end of 2011 these had remained stubbornly at around 12 per cent for over a year.

The difficulty for the Lib Dems is that the party's differentiation strategy is too subtle for most voters. In September 2011 only 36 per cent thought that the party had made the Government more 'moderate and centrist', and only 26 per cent believed that the party had managed to get 'real Liberal policies put into action'.[9] The Lib Dems are indelibly tarnished by their *volte face* over university tuition fees (see chapter nine) and their support for the deficit reduction strategy, and it is going to be very difficult to overcome that.

The prospect of losing their seats is going to cause growing unease amongst Lib Dem MPs. Were they to poll only 15 per cent at the next election, three-quarters of Lib Dem MPs risk losing their seats. If they were to poll only 12 per cent, four-fifths of their seats would be at risk.[10] Around 10 Lib Dem seats will go because of boundary changes. The Liberal Democrats face a crunch vote in Parliament in October 2013 when the House of Commons has to approve the orders making the change. That will give the Liberal Democrats major leverage. But if they decided as a party to renege on their previous support for reducing the Commons by 50 seats and the consequent boundary changes (see chapter eight), it would probably spell the end of the Coalition. If only some Lib Dem MPs were to rebel, it would not threaten the Government, because it seems unlikely that many Tory MPs would join them.

Parties facing serious electoral defeat may change their leader to offer a fresh image. Nick Clegg might decide to stand down anyway, especially if he seems unlikely to be re-elected in Sheffield. His most likely successor is the party's President Tim Farron MP; or, if he avoids criminal conviction, Chris Huhne MP, who narrowly lost the leadership election in 2007. It is possible that Clegg could stand down as leader but remain within the Government, as the Free Democratic Party's leader did in Germany following disastrous election results in May 2011 (he remained Foreign Minister). The other risk for the Lib Dems is a party split, between 'coalition Liberals' and the rest. On three previous occasions member-ship of a coalition has split the Liberal Party (see chapter two). The historical result of those previous splits has been that the coalition Liberals were gradually absorbed by the major coalition partner, the Conservatives.

## The Endgame: How Might the Coalition Dissolve?

Some commentators assert that the coalition partners must dissolve the Coalition early in order to fight the next election as two separate parties. This goes against the usual practice in Europe, and in Westminster systems such as Scotland and New Zealand. It is true that coalitions may fracture early; but they seldom do so simply to enable the parties to campaign separately at the next election. In Scotland in 2003 and in 2007 the Labour/Liberal Democrat coalition governed right through to election day, while Labour and the Lib Dems fought the election as separate parties (see chapter two).

[9] YouGov poll, reported in J Curtice, 'Shaping the Coalition' *Parliamentary Brief* (30 September 2011).
[10] If they were to poll 12 per cent they would probably hold a dozen seats; at 10 per cent they would retain only half a dozen. Information kindly supplied by Colin Rallings, Plymouth, Lewis Baston, ERS, and Anthony Wells at YouGov. All stress that the estimates are strongly subject to local factors, which could cushion Lib Dem losses.

It is true that on both occasions they envisaged forming another coalition, so they had reason not to fight each other too bitterly. Similarly in New Zealand, most coalitions have governed through to election day. The proportional voting system increases the likelihood of hung parliaments, and so the possibility of coalitions continuing. The difference at Westminster may be that the 2010 hung parliament and coalition are regarded as a one-off, reducing the incentives for the coalition partners to cooperate as the election approaches.

It is perfectly feasible that the Conservative-Lib Dem Coalition will last through to May 2015, but that the parties will differentiate themselves electorally in the last year or so. That may make it more difficult for the parties to agree government policy from 2014 onwards, leading to policy stasis and a thin legislative programme in the last session. The Conservatives will campaign for an overall majority next time, while the Liberal Democrats will hope for another hung parliament, and stress the moderating influence they had, saving the country from Conservative excess.

If the Coalition does dissolve earlier, it will be because the Lib Dems decide to leave. Lib Dem MPs facing electoral wipeout may feel the need to distance themselves from the Coalition in order to save their seats. They may be mistaken in thinking that this will improve their electoral chances, but if the prospects look grim they may feel that they have nothing to lose. They can put pressure on Clegg to leave the Coalition at the weekly meetings of the parliamentary party, or put down resolutions at party conference. Clegg could resist, possibly creating a split; but ultimately he would have to bow to the party's will, or resign.

Liberal Democrat departure from the Coalition need not bring down the Government. The Lib Dems could continue to support the Government on a confidence and supply basis, under the kind of agreement that supported the Lib-Lab Pact in 1977–8. They would be unlikely to benefit electorally unless they could show a *casus belli* which had caused them to leave the Government, on an issue which attracted major public support (eg the introduction of charges for using the NHS). If the only reason for leaving is the hope of achieving a more distinct profile outside the Government than inside, the public are likely to be bemused, and the Lib Dems may not achieve their aim. Government gives politicians a much higher profile than opposition, especially for the third party. For the Conservatives, it would obviously weaken the Government to lose their majority; but it might strengthen the Conservative case for seeking an outright majority at the next election.

Finally, there is the question of electoral pacts. For the Lib Dems these may be a lifeline; for the Conservatives, an insurance policy.[11] Liberal Democrats whom we interviewed were vehemently against any pre-electoral agreements, for fear of being branded permanent partners of the Conservatives. But some might change their tune if the alternative is annihilation. Electoral pacts could run the whole spectrum of cooperation, from unofficial pacts at local level to official collaboration at national level. Unofficial pacts are more likely. The Conservatives could decide not to field a

---

[11] One Conservative who promoted the idea of further cooperation with the Liberal Democrats was Nick Boles MP. See N Boles, *Which Way's Up? The Future of Coalition Britain and How to Get There* (London, Biteback Publishing, 2010).

candidate, or not to fight very hard in certain key constituencies, such as Nick Clegg's constituency in Sheffield, or Vince Cable's in Twickenham. It might be easier for them to agree such deals in Labour/Lib Dem marginals in the north of England, where the Conservatives have no hope of winning, than in Conservative/ Lib Dem marginals in the south. In 2010 the Conservatives won 12 seats from the Lib Dems; in 2015 they will hope to take more.

Electoral pacts would be more valuable for Lib Dem MPs in the South; how valuable would depend on how far the Conservatives were willing to go. In the 1918 coupon election, the Conservatives did not field any candidates against coupon Liberals, and the Liberals did not stand against coupon Conservatives. The coupon was a letter of endorsement jointly signed by David Lloyd George and the Conservative leader Andrew Bonar Law, issued to candidates who supported Lloyd George's Coalition. One hundred and fifty-nine Liberal candidates received the coupon, and 127 were elected, so endorsement almost guaranteed election. But the gains from electoral pacts can be short lived. The split from the Asquith Liberals ultimately proved fatal for the Liberal Party; and in 1922 Conservative backbenchers rebelled en masse against the Coalition. In New Zealand electoral pacts have similarly proved a double-edged sword. In 2009 electoral pacts enabled the election of MPs from two minor parties, but demonstrated the fundamental weakness of the arrangement at the same time, since those who benefitted from pacts owed their place in Parliament to the dominant party.

## LESSONS FOR FUTURE PARLIAMENTS

In the second part of this chapter we look at lessons for future coalition governments in future Parliaments. This might be in 2015, or 2020, or much further ahead. But whenever it happens, people will look back and ask, what can we learn from the experience of the 2010 Coalition? So we set out here some general lessons which might have application in the future. We consider separately the roles of all the main actors in the political parties, government, Parliament, and the civil service.

Our recommendations address a central question: how do you make coalition government work? But as we noted in chapter one, how well coalition 'works' will depend on the observer and their point of view. Different observers will have different measures of success. By addressing our recommendations to different actors, we must acknowledge that there are tensions between some of the recommendations that follow. Politics is frequently a zero-sum game, in which not everyone can win. So when we offer lessons to the smaller party on how they can maximise their influence, it may be at the expense of the larger party; and vice versa. And when we offer recommendations to backbenchers on how they can maximise their influence, it may be at the expense of the frontbench. There will also be tensions between maintaining the overall stability and harmony of the Coalition, and maximising the influence of the different players within it. So not all of the recommendations that follow are mutually compatible.

## Lessons for the Political Parties

We have divided this first set of recommendations chronologically into three sections. These are: the run-up to the election; the negotiations following the election; and the first months of the new government.

### Before the Election

One crucial lesson from 2010 is to write a manifesto which is not just geared towards single-party majority government. Parties need to have half an eye on the possibility of negotiations following the election, whether for a coalition or minority government. Some manifesto pledges can be drafted as non-negotiable, red line commitments which are deal-breakers; others in vaguer terms, as bargaining chips which can be traded in subsequent negotiations. The main cautionary note is to beware of making excessively firm commitments which might subsequently have to be modified, as the Lib Dems found to their cost with their pledge to abolish tuition fees. A secondary one is to recognise the possible advantage that comes from a detailed manifesto with a lot of commitments. One reason why the 2010 PfG was 75 per cent Conservative but only 40 per cent Lib Dem was that the Conservative manifesto contained over 550 pledges, and the Lib Dem manifesto well over 300 (see Appendix one).

Following on from the 2010 experience, party manifestos will be scrutinised more closely, by the media and public, for clues as to which party might align with which. The Conservatives and Labour will state that they are still aiming for single-party majority government. The Lib Dem manifesto will be analysed particularly closely for signs that they are closer to the Conservatives. The Lib Dems will also be pressed much harder than last time about their preferred partner, but are likely to stick to the same formula – that they will negotiate first with the party with the most votes and the most seats.

A second lesson for the parties prior to the election is to maintain good relations with the leaders and senior members of other parties, because they might become part of the negotiations. The range of possible negotiating parties next time might include the nationalist parties, and minor parties like the Greens, UKIP and the BNP. A third lesson is to select the party's negotiating team in advance and rehearse them. The team leader needs to analyse the other parties' manifestos, as the Conservatives did in 2010, so that they open the negotiations on the front foot, in full command of the issues and the agenda. A fourth lesson is to have clear procedures for reporting lines during the negotiations (to the leader; to the shadow Cabinet?), and for ratification of any agreement.[12]

Labour got many of these things wrong in 2010. It is true that some items in their manifesto had been drafted with an eye to winning cross-party support

---

[12] In early 2012 the Liberal Democrats were reviewing how to prepare for future negotiations, including how to appoint the negotiating team, and a revision of the triple lock procedure.

(eg the commitment to a referendum on AV). But the party had not selected a negotiating team; they had not rehearsed; they started at a disadvantage because of Brown's poor relationship with Clegg; and they had not thought through reporting lines, or ratification of any agreement by the parliamentary party. The eyewitness accounts testify to how poorly prepared they were.[13]

## During the Negotiations

The main thing the parties to any future negotiation should consider allowing themselves is more time. 2010 was exceptional in two respects. The markets were unusually nervous, following the economic crisis in Greece; and the UK media were impatient for a result, being used to new governments being formed within 24 hours. So the parties were under extreme pressure to reach a rapid conclusion. It is to be hoped that in future five days is regarded as the minimum that is required for negotiations, rather than the norm. In Germany the average time for negotiations is 20 days. In other Westminster systems, such as Scotland and New Zealand, negotiations also take longer: typically 10 to 14 days. Government does not appear to suffer as a result.

One fact that is sometimes overlooked is that it did take two weeks to produce the more detailed PfG (from 5 to 20 May). What was unusual about the UK negotiations was the publication of an interim agreement after five days. This might set a precedent for future negotiations; or in calmer times, the parties might proceed all the way to a full agreement.

Extra time might allow the negotiators greater opportunity to consult the civil service (discussed below); and to consider a range of ancillary matters which might otherwise be overlooked. These could include ensuring that there is a process for determining issues on which the Coalition Agreement is silent, which needs to go in the procedural section of the Agreement. Or it could include a more general 'right to disagree' clause of the kind adopted by the coalitions and confidence and supply agreements in New Zealand (see chapter two). Other ancillary matters to negotiate, especially for smaller parties, are additional resources for the party to support its role in government: how many special advisers there will be, how they will be deployed, and whether state funding will continue to support the party in Parliament.

The parties might consider allowing more input from the civil service. The civil service was kept out of the room during the five days of negotiation between 5 and 9 May 2010. Cabinet Office officials were involved in the subsequent negotiations to produce the PfG on 20 May, but Whitehall departments were excluded. Secretaries of State were discouraged from consulting their officials and departments were given only 12 hours to comment on their sections of the final draft.[14]

---

[13] R Wilson, *5 Days to Power: The Journey to Coalition Britain* (London, Biteback Publishing, 2010) 22–26.

[14] Information supplied by the negotiators and their advisers.

The reason again was speed: to maintain momentum and not lose goodwill. But the experience in Scotland suggests that the civil service can offer a lot more support if the parties will allow it. In 2003 Scottish civil servants were in the room, maintaining a cumulative record of agreements reached, and helping to draft the programme for government. They were also there to provide information, evidence and advice. Again, good government did not suffer; the Scottish Permanent Secretary Sir John Elvidge gave a detailed account of how his officials were closely involved while remaining scrupulously neutral between the parties.[15]

The negotiators also need time to carry the wider party with them. In 2010 practices varied widely. The Liberal Democrats were bound by the 'triple lock' to consult the parliamentary party and the Federal Party Executive, because in the first instance the agreement needed 75 per cent approval from both. The parliamentary party met three times and was shown the text of the Interim Coalition Agreement. To be safe the Lib Dems also organised a special party conference, which met and approved the Interim Agreement on 16 May 2010.[16] By contrast, the Conservative 1922 Committee met only twice, and was not shown the Interim Agreement; and the Parliamentary Labour Party did not meet at all. The other political parties may not wish to adopt such strong internal party democracy as the Lib Dems; but the pressure next time will be for more involvement, not less. It also helped the Liberal Democrat leadership through all the tribulations of the Coalition that the party voted strongly to endorse it in the first place.

In 2010 the Conservatives and Liberal Democrats deliberately put to one side any discussion of division of office until they had agreed on division of policy. As a result the division of ministerial posts was dealt with in a rush at the end, between Cameron and Clegg. Several Lib Dems think that they lost out at this stage:

> I think at the end of that they had completely exhausted themselves. Precious little thought really went into the machinery of the Coalition which was part two of it. And by part three of it, which was bums on seats, Nick did this completely on his own with Cameron . . . I think we got a completely duff deal. (Liberal Democrat minister)

The Lib Dem minister may be unrealistic about what his party could have achieved; and others may disagree with his negative assessment of the outcome. What is undeniable is that the division of office was negotiated in an even greater rush than the division of policy.[17] Given that reshuffles are harder in a coalition, it is all the more important to get the allocation and placing of ministers right at the start. It does not have to be done in a mad rush. The formation of a new government can and should be a more orderly process, as it is in other countries, including

---

[15] J Elvidge, *Northern Exposure: Lessons from the First Twelve Years of Devolved Government in Scotland* (London, Institute for Government, 2011) 15–17.

[16] The special conference, requiring a two-thirds majority, was the second part of the triple lock. Failing that, the third part was a postal ballot of all the members, also requiring a two-thirds majority.

[17] Coalition complicated the allocation of ministerial posts. One offer had to be withdrawn, and some ministerial appointments in the Lords were afterthoughts, added (and made unpaid) when it became clear that a department needed a Lords minister.

Westminster systems. Time spent planning properly at this stage is not time wasted.[18]

### In the First Year of Government

The rush in May 2010 was also driven by the tradition that the first main item of parliamentary business has to be the debate on the Queen's Speech. This is the traditional test of confidence in the new Government, expressing support for the Government's legislative programme for the first session. But the first item of business could be an investiture vote, in which the Commons affirms confidence in the new Prime Minister.[19] That is what happens in Scotland and Wales, with the election by the legislature of the First Minister, formally confirming who can command confidence. And if the coalition partners have just negotiated a coalition agreement for the next five years, it makes more sense for Parliament to be invited to endorse the entire coalition agreement. That could also help to end the sterile argument often heard in the media that the coalition agreement had no legitimacy because no one had voted for it. If Parliament voted formally to support the coalition agreement as part of the Queen's Speech debate, Parliament would be formally endorsing the Coalition and its policy programme. But the parties will need to make that clear to Whitehall the moment they enter government, if that is what they want to happen. Whitehall will be all prepared for a Queen's speech debate within one or two weeks of a new government taking office.

Political parties also need to be aware that newly appointed ministers will be intensely busy in the first few months of a new government. There was a feeling in 2010, especially amongst the Liberal Democrats, that they had 'lost' their leading figures (see chapter seven). So parties need to plan in advance how communication between the party in government and the party outside will be maintained. It may help to keep some senior figures in the party outside the Government, to maintain liaison, and to provide a distinctive voice for the party. The Liberal Democrats achieved this by keeping outside the government Simon Hughes MP, former party president and from June 2010 deputy leader of the party, and Tim Farron the MP, the Party President since November 2010.

### Lessons for the Smaller Party in Government

Smaller parties in a coalition can be a lot smaller than the Liberal Democrats were in 2010; they might have half a dozen MPs, or less. And there can sometimes be more than one small party in a coalition. Whatever their size, the key strategic

---

[18] P Riddell and C Haddon, *Transitions: Preparing for Changes of Government* (London, Institute for Government, 2009); P Riddell and C Haddon, *Transitions: Lessons Learned* (London, Institute for Government, 2011).

[19] ibid.

problem is to maintain the party's distinctiveness while being an effective partner in a unified government. It is no coincidence that smaller coalition partners tend to do worse at elections than the larger partner.[20] The smaller the party, the greater the problem of maintaining the party's visibility. The key to maintaining visibility is to choose distinctive portfolios, and distinctive policies by which the party will be remembered.

There is likely to be a trade-off between maximising visibility to the public and maximising a party's influence within government. In the academic literature this is linked to the choice between maximising votes, office and policy.[21] Maximising public visibility is achieved by leading departments with a high public profile: the Treasury, Foreign Office (but both are likely to claimed by the larger party), Home Office, Health, Education. The next best way to be visible is to lead departments closely connected with the party's own policy priorities, such as the Department of Energy and Climate Change (DECC) for the Lib Dems (or, in a possible future government, the Greens). In terms of maximising influence, the smaller party could aim to have a watchdog minister in every front-line department (but only if the numbers permit); or choose central departments which are less visible, but have strong cross-government influence and control (such as the Cabinet Office or Treasury).

In 2010 the Liberal Democrats eschewed leading a high profile department (for example, Clegg taking the Home Office); but they pursued a combination of the other three strategies. With 16 ministers, they were able to place a watchdog minister in almost every Whitehall department. In so doing they clearly went for breadth rather than depth. In terms of the departments they chose to lead, they chose departments close to their own policy priorities, with Chris Huhne in DECC, Vince Cable in the Department for Business, Innovation and Skills, and Nick Clegg leading the constitutional reform programme.[22] And they achieved strong cross-government influence with Danny Alexander as Chief Secretary to the Treasury, leading the deficit reduction programme, and Nick Clegg having a major cross-government role in the Cabinet Office and chairing the Cabinet's Home Affairs Committee.

The Liberal Democrats had very little time to think about the allocation of portfolios, because of the haste with which the Government was formed. But in making the choices they did, they opted in effect for a strategy of maximising their influence within government rather than maximising their visibility to the public. They did the same in relation to their policy priorities. Constitutional reform and climate change are close to the hearts of the Lib Dems, but the polls have long shown they are of much less concern to the general public. Other key Lib Dem

---

[20]   R Miller and J Curtin, 'Counting the Costs of Coalition: The Case of New Zealand's Small Parties' (2011) 63 *Political Science* 107–8.

[21]   K Strøm, 'A Behavioural Theory of Competitive Political Parties' (1990) 34(2) *American Journal of Political Science* 565.

[22]   Climate change and constitutional reform were clear Lib Dem priorities. Business, Innovation and Skills (BIS) were less so; Vince Cable was given BIS because he couldn't be Chancellor.

priorities, such as the pupil premium in schools, or raising the tax threshold to £10,000, have not achieved sufficient visibility to be strongly associated with the Liberal Democrats. The iconic policies with which the Lib Dems were most closely associated in 2010–11 were the deficit reduction programme, the increase in student tuition fees, and the AV referendum. In the first two cases the Lib Dems were perceived to have broken their promises and betrayed their supporters by acquiescing to Conservative policy, and in the third case were perceived to have spectacularly failed on one of their own policies. In all three cases the association was a negative one.

So the message for smaller parties has to be to think carefully about your priorities; think hard about what is achievable; and what you want to demonstrate at the end that you have achieved. Aim high, but aim for tangible achievements. It is not impossible for the smaller partner to be associated with high profile policies. The Labour/Lib Dem Coalition in Scotland became known for two iconic policies: the abolition of up-front tuition fees, and the introduction of free personal care for the elderly. Both were Lib Dem priorities which were reluctantly accepted by the larger coalition partner. Both are now looking increasingly unaffordable: it is easier to identify popular wins at a time of growing budgets than at a time of cutbacks in spending.

The final matter that smaller parties need to focus on is support structures. The watchdog model, spreading ministers as widely as possible across departments, can leave them feeling very isolated. One Lib Dem minister felt the isolation and lack of support very keenly: 'I think it's been a terrible mistake to send people on their own into a department behind enemy lines, as it were, with no support mechanism at all'. It is not just a question of resources; the support they need is psychological as well as practical. So the remedy lies in establishing support networks: regular meetings of the entire ministerial team (something the Lib Dems were not good at organising, at least initially); assigning nominated staff in the Leader's office to be the contact point and support person for each minister out in departments; perhaps creating an intranet for isolated ministers to seek and provide support to each other, where they can post questions and offer advice.

The smaller the party, the greater the need for additional resources.[23] Small parties should demand one special adviser for each of their ministers, and two for their cabinet ministers. This would provide a bit more capacity for junior ministers to cover policies outside their immediate portfolio, and to feel less isolated. If no more special advisers can be made available, then the smaller party should stipulate that their junior ministers are supplied with additional policy advisers by the civil service. This needs to be formally agreed at the start: if it is left to the discretion of individual departments the response is likely to be no.

---

[23] Commenting on this section, an overseas expert also said that the smaller the party, the greater the risk of exhaustion. All governments ultimately become exhausted, but small parties risk early exhaustion if they try to take on too much. Smaller coalition partners need to have a realistic sense of what is achievable, and to husband their efforts accordingly.

The resources needed to support the leader of the smaller party will depend on what role they wish to play. If they lead a major department they will automatically have the resources of a Secretary of State. They will want some additional special advisers, especially if they are going to attempt to monitor policy across the whole of government. To play a full cross-government role, the leader's office needs to be the size of Clegg's as it had become by 2011, with five Private Secretaries and five spads (plus four more spads outposted to No 10). An alternative model, as floated in chapter four, is for the Deputy Prime Minister to be supported directly by No 10, sharing all the support systems available to the Prime Minister, but with separate Private Offices. But there was little enthusiasm for that amongst most of our interviewees.

Smaller parties also need to think about support structures for their party in Parliament. Most state funding (Short Money in the Commons, Cranborne Money in the Lords) is channelled only to the opposition parties, and withdrawn from parties in government. Chapters six and seven related how severe the impact of this sudden withdrawal was on the Lib Dems. A party that wishes to retain state funding must negotiate for this as part of the coalition agreement. It can point to the fact that in most countries with state funding the norm is for funding to be available to all parties represented in Parliament, and not just opposition parties.[24] But the parties' cautious response to the 2011 report of the Committee on Standards in Public Life reveals the continuing difficulties that face anyone who tries to make the case for an increase in state funding of political parties in the UK.[25]

One final issue is Michels' 'iron law of oligarchy': the phenomenon that political parties, no matter how democratic, will develop oligarchic tendencies.[26] Going into coalition may exacerbate that tendency towards oligarchy and away from internal party democracy. For the Lib Dems there were competing pressures: pressures to change and adapt to their new status; but there was also resistance to being too deeply transformed by the transition to government.[27] It is important to recognise that as the party's public face becomes more complex and differentiated, there may be greater demands for expertise (eg press officers, policy experts) and greater coordination between the party in government and the party outside. The party's central office may need to be strengthened as the linchpin between the party in government and the wider party.[28]

---

[24] K-H Nassmacher, 'The Funding of Political Parties in the Anglo-Saxon Orbit' in R Austin and M Tjernström, *Funding of Political Parties and Election Campaigns* (Sweden, International Institute for Democracy and Electoral Assistance, 2003).

[25] Committee on Standards in Public Life, *Political Party Finance* (November 2011), www.public-standards.gov.uk/Library/13th_Report___Political_party_finance_FINAL_PDF_VERSION_18_11_11.pdf

[26] R Michels, *Political Parties* (New York, The Free Press, 1962).

[27] K Deschouwer, 'Comparing Newly Governing Parties' in K Deschouwer (ed), *New Parties in Government: In Power for the First Time* (Abingdon, Routledge, 2008) 1–16, 10–11.

[28] N Bolleyer, 'The Organisational Costs of Public Office' in Deschouwer (ed), *New Parties in Government*, ibid, 17–44.

## Lessons for the Larger Party in Government

The larger party faces far fewer challenges than the smaller party or parties. It is less likely to suffer at the next election from having been in coalition. It is leading the Government, and has a higher profile, so its distinctive identity is less likely to be eclipsed. It has larger resources, often much larger, to support the party in government and in Parliament. But leading a coalition is not the same as leading single-party government, and there are some lessons to be learned from the 2010 experience.

Cameron was exemplary as a coalition leader in the first 18 months. Within government he developed an effective balance between the formal and informal machinery whereby the parties consulted and deliberated with each other. The informal machinery was so effective that the high level Coalition Committee hardly ever met. Issues were brokered first through the informal groups described in chapter four, and then were taken formally through the cabinet machinery for final collective decision. The golden rule was 'no surprises'. Some Liberal Democrat junior ministers might have felt marginalised in their departments; but collectively Lib Dem ministers could not complain (and have never done so) that they were not properly consulted. Nevertheless the formal dispute machinery of the Coalition Committee was there in the background should it ever need to be deployed.

So the lesson for future coalitions is to use the Cabinet Committee system for formal collective deliberation and decision-making. But supplement it with informal forums where the parties can broker things first. Compromises and coalition deals are best done bilaterally, in smaller groups such as the weekly meetings of the PM and DPM, the Quad, and Letwin/Alexander. These precise groupings need not be replicated, but every coalition will need regular meetings of the PM/ DPM. And because they are both so busy, every coalition needs regular meetings of their proxies. Mrs Thatcher famously said, 'Every Prime Minister needs a Willie'. It could equally be said that 'Every coalition needs an Oliver': a negotiator, a facilitator, someone who commands the Prime Minister's complete confidence and the trust of the other party, who oils the coalition wheels and keeps them turning. This need not necessarily be a minister: in some coalitions the Letwin/ Alexander role is performed by chiefs of staff.[29]

One other imaginative move was to outpost four of the Lib Dem spads to No 10. This helped to break down the sense of two opposing camps, and certainly helped to ensure no surprises, especially on the media side. It is another small example of the emotional intelligence displayed by Team Cameron towards their Lib Dem partners. Lord Strathclyde, Leader of the Conservatives in the House of

---

[29] For example, in Helen Clark's three New Zealand coalitions from 1999 to 2008, this role was performed by her chief of staff, Heather Simpson, working with her opposite number Andrew Ladley (1999–2005); in Scotland's Labour/Lib Dem Coalition the role was taken by Jim Wallace's senior special adviser, Sam Ghibaldan.

Lords, gave up one of his special advisers to support his Lib Dem counterpart, Lord McNally. Conservative Education Secretary Michael Gove authorised additional support for his Lib Dem junior minister Sarah Teather. Cameron consistently went out of his way to be generous to the smaller party. He understood that he could afford to be: as the junior partner the Lib Dems struggled to keep up and are more likely to suffer electorally. And in turn Nick Clegg and his colleagues responded by being extraordinarily loyal and steadfast in their support for the Coalition.

The larger party must be sensitive to the needs of the smaller party, be generous towards them, and give them their moments in the sun. The Lib Dems were given their share of announcements, and allowed occasionally to speak with a different voice. And when they were down they had to be helped back up. So at key moments, such as the May 2011 elections and AV referendum, Cameron was generous in victory. The Conservatives must have been privately delighted; but publicly they did not show it.

Cameron was also generous in allowing the Liberal Democrats additional special advisers. Both parties quickly came to regret Cameron's pre-election pledge to reduce their numbers: coalitions need more special advisers, not fewer. So the numbers were gradually increased from 71 to 81, until by the end of 2011 the Conservatives had 58 and the Lib Dems had 23.[30] Although in the first 18 months the spads did not appear to play a significant role as coalition brokers, they have the potential to do so. Just as the PM and DPM need proxies to negotiate on their behalf, so do their busy ministers. Spads are an additional channel of communication; they can save ministers' time in establishing the scope for agreement, or work out the details of agreements made. They can also help to maintain a connection with the party and outside groups.

A future coalition government should raise any ceiling on the numbers of spads, and be willing to explain why they need more.[31] They should also think carefully about their allocation. One reason why spads did not play a greater role as coalition brokers was that in departments they operated in separate, one-party silos. Coalition brokerage works better in integrated units such as those in No 10. So a new coalition might consider giving each department three special advisers, enabling both parties to have at least one in each department, and providing more support for the junior partner. If that level of additional support is unacceptable, then they should consider cross-posting spads, like the Lib Dem spads in No 10. And if it is not possible for junior ministers from the smaller party to be allowed their own spads, the Government should consider allowing them additional civil service support.

---

[30] Cabinet Office, Written Ministerial Statement on Numbers and Costs of Special Advisers (9 December 2011), www.cabinetoffice.gov.uk/sites/default/files/resources/LIST_AND_COSTS_9_DECEMBER_0.pdf. The statement records 21 Lib Dem spads, but lists only four of the additional six Lib Dem spads agreed in late 2011.

[31] There is no statutory limit. The only constraint is the practice of regularly publishing detailed lists of the numbers and costs of special advisers: ibid.

All this generosity to the junior coalition partner inevitably generated resentment in the Prime Minister's own party. If there was criticism of Cameron, it was for neglecting his own side. The leader of a coalition must look after his own party as well as the junior partner. There will be disappointed members of the shadow Cabinet who did not get the jobs they expected, because they were displaced by the coalition partner. There will be others who do not get any ministerial position for the same reason. They need to be given consolation prizes, which is harder now that Select Committee chairmanships are no longer part of the whips' patronage. But there is some scope to appoint unpaid ministers, subject to the statutory maximum of 95 office holders in the House of Commons.[32] And there are Task Forces, tsars, and ambassadorships: senior positions in the party which can be offered to soften the blow for those who lost out.

The backbenchers and the wider party also need constant reassurance that the Prime Minister is on their side. There will always be suspicion that the larger party has compromised its ideals and conceded too much to the junior partner. *ConservativeHome* and guardians of the party flame in the media watch closely for signs of betrayal. So the Prime Minister needs to reassure his backbenchers, talk to the backbench committees, and invite people round to No 10. And he needs to signal that his heart is with the party stalwarts, even if the Coalition sometimes holds him back. A good example is the continued sniping at the Human Rights Act, discussed in chapter eight. The European Convention on Human Rights is safe, thanks to tight wording in the PfG. But from time to time Cameron allowed himself an indignant outburst to show which side he was really on.[33] Other examples are his response to the 2011 riots ('criminality pure and simple'), and uncoded words in his Mansion House speech on Europe ('we sceptics').[34] It is less necessary for the larger party constantly to remind the public of its distinctive identity, but the party faithful always need encouragement.

## Lessons for the Parties in Parliament

For the backbenchers in the coalition parties, seeing their leaders go into government is a moment of triumph, but also one of loss. After working closely together for years in the trenches of opposition, the leaders suddenly disappear into Whitehall. And the troops go too, because with the withdrawal of Short and Cranborne Money the staff who support the party in Parliament can no longer be paid. So the backbenchers must regroup, and find new ways of organising and of managing with fewer resources.

---

[32] House of Commons Disqualification Act 1975.

[33] J Slack, 'I want to scrap the Human Rights Act but Clegg won't let me, says PM' *Daily Mail* (3 October 2011), www.dailymail.co.uk/news/article-2044530/David-Cameron-I-want-scrap-Human-Rights-Act-Nick-Clegg-wont-let-me.html

[34] Hansard HC Deb, 11 August 2011, vol 531, col 1052; 'David Cameron: we Eurosceptics are only trying to help' *Economist* (14 November 2011), www.economist.com/node/21538516

One answer is to create an effective system of backbench committees. The main decisions are whether to combine MPs and peers in a single network; and how many committees to create – is there to be one for every Whitehall department, or fewer committees covering broader policy areas? In 2010 the Conservatives and the Liberal Democrats set about this in different ways. The Liberal Democrats, with fewer than 40 backbench MPs, joined forces with the 90 Lib Dem peers to create a combined network of 12 party policy committees, led by a co-chair from each House. The Conservatives moved more slowly. With over 200 backbench MPs they re-established five subcommittees of the 1922 Committee in the Commons, and in the Lords the Association of Conservative Peers was left to create a separate set of committees.

The next question is to be clear about the purpose of these committees: what are they trying to achieve? Are they mainly cheerleaders for government policy? Are they seeking to influence government policy? Or are they developing policy for the next election, and maintaining the party's distinctive brand? The Liberal Democrats saw the main purpose of their party policy committees as being to influence government policy. To that end they negotiated a protocol to maximise their chances of influencing policy, by giving them access to departments and official information (see Appendix six). Chapter six showed that experience was patchy, with only a few committees able to use the protocol to the fullest extent. But access and early involvement are crucial, if backbenchers are really going to help shape policy at the formative stage rather than criticise it once introduced in Parliament. And there is a trade-off: because of the need for confidentiality, only a few trusted backbenchers will gain significant access (typically just the chair), and the rest of the committee will be left in the dark. The other trade-off is that if the chair does succeed in influencing policy at the formative stage, that can seldom be publicised: victories behind the Whitehall curtain cannot be trumpeted, and the party's distinctive contribution remains unknown.

Whitehall caution is understandable. Because the Lib Dem party policy committees included not only MPs and peers but also party researchers and other party experts, they were not leak-proof. Backbench committees have to operate in different modes, depending on their purpose. When trying to influence government policy at the formative stage, they have to play the Whitehall game, be trustworthy and willing to keep Whitehall's secrets. When gathering ideas to develop party policy for the next election, they will want to be as open as possible, involving NGOs, think tanks and outside policy experts, not just the parliamentary group. And when maintaining the party's distinctive brand, they will want to cry their wares as loudly as possible, both in Parliament and outside. So they need leaders capable of operating in all these different modes, and explaining to the group which mode they are operating in at any one time.

The committees could press for two small procedural changes at Westminster to make their lives easier. One is the practice whereby opposition spokesmen are given advance notice of ministerial statements 45 minutes before they are delivered. The chairs of backbench committees could be extended the same courtesy, on the same understanding – that if the courtesy is breached the privilege would be withdrawn. The second is a more difficult issue. Westminster procedure is largely geared to a two-party system. The Government is deemed to speak with one voice, with a presumption that the minister speaks for both coalition parties. This means fewer opportunities for government backbenchers in the subsequent debate to express their parties' distinctive slant on the issue. It is not something that can formally be provided for: in the Commons, the Speaker and his Deputies need to be additionally sensitive to the different strands of opinion in the House; in the Lords it is more difficult because the House is self-regulating.

## Lessons for the Civil Service

For the civil service, planning for a possible future coalition begins well before the next election. First, there are the pre-election contacts with opposition parties; then the election period; and then negotiations between the parties in the event of a hung parliament. Now that we have fixed term parliaments, pre-election contacts could be authorised 12 months ahead of the next election: so from May 2014. (A mid-term collapse of the Coalition could of course trigger an earlier election, but there is no point in authorising pre-election contacts starting now.) In principle there should be a level playing field, with the parties in government being treated the same way as the opposition parties. They should be given the same opportunity to explain their plans and priorities post-2015, and the civil service should respond in the same limited way, answering factual questions but not offering direct policy advice. This could be done by the Permanent Secretary in each department; or the Permanent Secretary could appoint a transition team, possibly with a nominated contact for each of the parties.[35] The difficulty arises when ministers in government seek advice towards the end of the Parliament which can help them formulate continuing policy. This may be perfectly legitimate: policy does not artificially stop in 2015. Coalition ministers with one eye to the election may also seek to commission advice for their eyes only. If that happens the civil service should generally respond by treating the request under the more limited rules for pre-election contacts, dealing with it through that channel, and explaining why it has done so.

As the election approaches both parties in government will go into election mode. Some of the mutual trust and understanding that has underpinned the Coalition may begin to dissolve. Officials must be prepared for that, and try to ensure continuing due process in terms of the business of government, even if ministers cease to cooperate in other ways. Media handling may prove particularly difficult, and Whitehall should circulate early guidance to all press officers

---

[35] Riddell and Haddon, *Transitions: Lessons Learned* (n 18).

and special advisers regarding the election rules, and the distinction between party and government communications.[36]

The Cabinet Office should also organise press briefings ahead of the election regarding the procedures to be followed in the event of a hung parliament. In 2009 that was left to private briefings organised by the Institute for Government and the Constitution Unit, but it is really a government responsibility. The *Cabinet Manual* is now available to explain the conventions and processes to be followed, and the Cabinet Office needs to publicise the rules as widely as possible, organising briefings for the print, broadcast and foreign media.[37] It could also explain ahead of time the role of the civil service during and after the election. Cabinet Secretary Sir Gus O'Donnell was unfairly criticised in 2010 for facilitating the negotiations between the political parties and enabling the Coalition to be formed. But Gordon Brown as Prime Minister had authorised the civil service to support the negotiations, and it was helpful for the Cabinet Office to host the talks. It was the parties that decided to form a coalition, not the Cabinet Secretary.

Because this practice is new territory for the civil service, still regarded with suspicion by some politicians as a 'civil service takeover', it would be sensible to set out in advance the different support roles that the civil service might be called upon to play. Assistance can include purely logistical forms of support (rooms, phones and computers, food and drink); being in the room as note takers, and drafters of the agreement; being outside the room as providers of information, analysis and advice. In Scotland the civil service has played all three roles.[38] But in London in 2010 the political parties kept civil servants out of the room during the initial five-day negotiations. For the subsequent 10-day negotiation of the PfG the Cabinet Secretariat were more closely involved, helping with drafting and bits of advice; but Whitehall departments were not.

The important thing to get across to both the political parties and the media is that this is a menu, from which the parties can select as much or as little as they choose. It is not the civil service taking control. And there is no pre-determined outcome. Indeed it would be helpful to remind the parties and the media that the outcome might be a minority government, as well as a majority or minority coalition; that coalitions do not necessarily include the largest single party; that everything is ultimately up to the parties to decide; and that the talks will last as long as the parties decide, not the civil service. As in 2010, it would be useful for the civil

---

[36] One breach occurred during the Oldham East and Saddleworth by-election in February 2011, when the Lib Dem local government minister Andrew Stunell MP issued a party press release hailing a government scheme to reuse empty homes. The scheme was officially unveiled the following week. The Cabinet Secretary investigated and said that Stunell had apologised for his mistake. See Wintour and Watt, 'Minister apologises after sailing close to the wind on byelection rules' *Guardian Blog* (13 January 2011), www.guardian.co.uk/politics/wintour-and-watt/2011/jan/13/oldham-east-and-saddleworth-liberaldemocrats

[37] The Cabinet Office's *Cabinet Manual*, published in October 2011, explains the process of government formation. This is discussed in ch 3.

[38] For a detailed account see J Elvidge, *Northern Exposure* (London, Institute for Government, 2011) 14–17.

service to do scenario planning for all possible contingencies, and to factor in the minor parties (SNP, DUP, Plaid Cymru, Greens, UKIP, BNP) as possible participants in some of the talks, depending on the electoral outcome. The contingency planning also needs to include negotiations being conducted in parallel. It requires a lot of advanced preparation; if the Cabinet Office does not have sufficient capacity, it might consider drafting in a retired senior civil servant to help lead the exercise.[39]

The rest of this section assumes that another coalition government is formed: not necessarily Conservative/Lib Dem, not necessarily with a 5:1 ratio in Parliament. In many coalitions the junior partner is a lot smaller; and there can be more than two partners in a coalition. But again, without getting too stuck on the experience of 2010, there are some general lessons for the civil service to bear in mind. The first is to appreciate that the smaller the junior partner, the more support (relatively) it will need if it is to be effective. Is the larger party willing to see this additional support being provided? The issue may have been covered in the coalition negotiations. If not, the civil service may need to raise it. Junior ministers given a watching brief over a whole department will need more support than is normally provided to a junior minister. The Permanent Secretary will need to enquire whether the Secretary of State is willing to authorise additional resources to support the broader role. If there are not enough spads, one solution is to allow civil servants to play a more political role in being ministers' policy advisers: as happened in 2010 in the Department for Education to provide additional support for Lib Dem junior minister Sarah Teather, and in the Department of Heath for Lib Dem junior minister Paul Burstow.

A second lesson is to understand the need for more 'process' in a coalition: more meetings to build up trust, and explore the sensitivities of the different partners; meetings to broker coalition deals; meetings with backbenchers of both parties; and sometimes even 'pre-meeting' and 'post mortem' meetings. So business can take longer. Ministers from the smaller party will be under particular pressure, because they have to attend disproportionately more meetings for their numbers and resources.

A third issue is to be prepared for backbench representatives seeking access to the department and sometimes to official information. This may be on an informal basis, arranged through the minister; and the authorisation to talk to backbenchers and disclose information will come from the minister. But there may be a protocol encouraging departments to grant access; if there is, officials should observe the spirit of the protocol.

## CONCLUSIONS

We do not know when the UK might next have a coalition government, or what form it might take. But whenever it happens, with whichever partner(s), there are

[39] For the 2010 election Sir Gus O'Donnell appointed Alex Allan, one of the Cabinet Office Permanent Secretaries, to lead the contingency planning.

some general lessons to be derived from the 2010 experience. We don't try to summarise them all here; we merely highlight a few of the positive examples that the 2010 Conservative-Liberal Democrat Coalition offers in terms of how to make coalition government work.

New Zealand had distilled the essentials into two basic principles: good faith, and no surprises. The 2010 Coalition enshrined these in its procedural agreement. The partners developed both formal and informal machinery to ensure that the principles were observed. Integrated units helped to foster mutual understanding. Cabinet Committees enabled formal sign-off by both coalition partners, but any sensitive policy was brokered informally first.

Trust and good personal relations were not taken for granted. They were worked for, by the party leaders and all around them. From his first 'big, open and comprehensive offer', Cameron continued to show generosity towards his Lib Dem colleagues. They responded in kind, with loyalty and commitment to upholding the unity of the Coalition. That commitment will be increasingly tested in the years to come, possibly to destruction. But in terms of how it started out, the Conservative/Lib Dem Government showed that coalition government need not be quarrelsome, weak and indecisive. In its first 18 months it set a model of harmonious and unified government which may prove hard to follow.

# Appendix 1

## *Party Breakdown of the Coalition Agreements*

As part of our research we analysed the two coalition agreements, to see how much of each derived from Conservative policies, and how much from the Liberal Democrats. On 10 May 2010 the parties produced their Interim Coalition Agreement (Interim Agreement), a document of some 3,000 words and 90 pledges. Ten days later, the Coalition published its Programme for Government (PfG), setting out the Government's plans in much greater detail in a document of 16,000 words and 400 pledges.

With the help of a number of interns (in particular, Patrick Graham, Chris Appleby, Ashley Palmer and Robbie Fergusson) we carried out two separate analyses of these agreements, each from a different starting point. The first analysis started from the parties' respective 2010 election manifestos, and asked how many pledges in each of them made it into the Interim Agreement, and then the PfG. That analysis produced some simple figures estimating how much of each party's manifesto had made it into the two agreements. In our interim report, published in June 2011, we stated that approximately 75 per cent of the Liberal Democrat manifesto appeared in the PfG, as compared with only 60 per cent of the Conservatives'.

Later examination, however, showed that we had not applied the same level of rigour in coding the two parties' manifestos. By using different coders, the treatment of the Conservative manifesto was stricter than the treatment of Lib Dem pledges. If we had treated the Conservative manifesto in the more generous terms applied to the Lib Dems', we would have concluded that a greater percentage of the Conservative manifesto made it into the PfG.

Moreover, that analysis only showed how much of the coalition parties' respective manifestos made it into the two coalition documents. It ignored the fact that the Conservative manifesto was much longer (approximately 550 pledges) than the Lib Dem manifesto (well over 300 pledges). Put differently, it took no account of the *proportion* of the PfG that could be considered 'Conservative' or 'Lib Dem'. That was addressed in our later analysis, which shows that the proportion of the coalition agreements which can be classified as Conservative is higher, because of the larger size of the Conservative manifesto.

Finally, the outcome of the initial analysis focuses solely on what the Conservatives and Lib Dems gained as separate parties. The blunt results may be subject to misinterpretation, and ignore the possibility that some agreement pledges could be *both* Conservative *and* Lib Dem; that some pledges might be compromises; and that some pledges may come from outside the manifestos altogether (as the second analysis shows, this comes to over 10 per cent of the PfG).

Learning from the problems that arose from the first analysis, a second, more nuanced analysis was done in the second half of 2011. This took a different approach, starting from the Interim Agreement and PfG and estimating what percentage of each document could be categorised as 'Conservative', 'Lib Dem', 'both', 'compromise' or 'neither'. This produced a different set of figures. The PfG was roughly 75 per cent Conservative in its content and 40 per cent Liberal Democrat: a victory for the Conservatives.

Neither analysis was perfect. There were difficulties in counting (what counts as a pledge?) and subjective coding (how much of the pledge needs to be there for it to count as included?). But examining the coalition agreements is one means of measuring the relative success of the coalition parties. A full analysis setting out our pledge by pledge analysis is available on the Constitution Unit website:

www.ucl.ac.uk/constitution-unit/research/coalition-government

THE COALITION AGREEMENTS CATEGORISED BY PARTY CONTRIBUTION

In the second, more nuanced analysis we studied the pledges in both the Interim Agreement and the PfG against the two parties' 2010 election manifestos and traced them back to either the manifestos or some other party policy document. We then classified Interim Agreement and PfG pledges according to their origin and nature: Conservative or Lib Dem; from both parties; representing a compromise between the two parties; or from neither manifesto. So, for instance, a PfG pledge found in the Conservative manifesto would be classed as 'Conservative'; a PfG pledge found in a Lib Dem policy document would be classed as 'Lib Dem (non-manifesto)'. As before, we note that many of the pledges in the two documents were simply lifted word-for-word from the parties' manifestos or some party policy document.

There are a number of caveats to be made. First, there is the issue of consistency. The two parties' manifestos are quite different in style. The Conservative manifesto tends towards specificity, especially in terms of implementation; the Lib Dem manifesto less so. This meant that there were various challenges: determining whether or not a pledge in the PfG was 'Conservative' in origin was often straightforward because of the Conservative manifesto's specificity; the difficulty often lay in determining whether or not a pledge in the PfG could be said to be 'Lib Dem' because of the broadly worded nature of Lib Dem pledges.

Secondly, this analysis does not take into account the relative significance attached to different policies by the two parties. For example, the Conservatives predominated in the Political Reform section of the PfG; but, having secured a commitment to a referendum on voting reform, conceding a series of smaller Tory policies may have seemed a price worth paying for the Lib Dems.

A third caveat is that such an analysis may lead people to infer that the Conservatives 'won' on the basis of the number of their pledges appearing in the

Interim Agreement or the PfG. But that is not necessarily so: it may be that the Lib Dems were happy to insert Conservative pledges that they had been considering themselves, or which also fit with their party's values. Put differently, identifying a pledge by its origin as Conservative or Lib Dem does not necessarily mean that that pledge represents a 'win' only for that party. It may be a 'win' for both parties.

However, this approach, which produced more nuanced results, allows for greater discussion, and so following the overviews we provide short commentaries on key sections.

## Overview

The analyses of the Interim Agreement presented in Tables A1.1 and A1.2 reveal a very high degree of overlap between the two parties; 40 per cent of the pledges had featured in both parties' election manifestos in some form. The Conservatives came only slightly ahead of the Liberal Democrats: including items (manifesto and non-manifesto) classified as 'both', the Interim Agreement was roughly 70 per cent Conservative and 60 per cent Lib Dem.

Table A1.1  The Interim Coalition Agreement by Proportion (%)

| Section | Con | LD | B | C | N |
|---|---|---|---|---|---|
| Deficit Reduction | 33.3 | | 66.7 | | |
| Spending Review | 25.0 | 25.0 | 37.5 | 12.5 | |
| Tax Measures | | 50.0 | 33.3 | 16.7 | |
| Banking Reform | 25.0 | | 75.0 | | |
| Immigration | 50.0 | 50.0 | | | |
| Political Reform | 20.0 | 20.0 | 40.0 | 20.0 | |
| Pensions & Welfare | 71.4 | | 28.6 | | |
| Education—Schools | 100.0 | | | | |
| Education—Higher Education | 50.0 | | | 50.0 | |
| Relations with the EU | 37.5 | 25.0 | 25.0 | 12.5 | |
| Civil Liberties | 8.3 | 66.7 | 25.0 | | |
| Environment | 31.6 | 10.5 | 52.6 | 5.3 | |

Con   Conservative
LD    Liberal Democrat
B     both
C     compromise
N     neither party

Note:  Cells shaded grey indicate where the majority of pledges lay.

Table A1.2 Interim Coalition Agreement Pledge Backgrounds

| Section | Policy background | | | | | | | | Total |
|---|---|---|---|---|---|---|---|---|---|
| | Manifesto | | | | Non-manifesto | | | | |
| | Con | LD | B | C | Con | LD | B | N | |
| Deficit Reduction | 2 | | 4 | | | | | | 6 |
| Spending Review | 2 | 2 | 3 | 1 | | | | | 8 |
| Tax Measures | | 3 | 2 | 1 | | | | | 6 |
| Banking Reform | 2 | | 6 | | | | | | 8 |
| Immigration | 1 | 1 | | | | | | | 2 |
| Political Reform | 2 | 2 | 4 | 2 | | | | | 10 |
| Pensions & Welfare | 2 | | 2 | | 3 | | | | 7 |
| Education – Schools | | | | | 1 | | | | 1 |
| Education – Higher Education | 1 | | | 1 | | | | | 2 |
| Relations with the EU | 3 | 2 | 2 | 1 | | | | | 8 |
| Civil Liberties | 1 | 8 | 3 | | | | | | 12 |
| Environment | 5 | 2 | 10 | 1 | 1 | | | | 19 |
| | | | | | | | | | |
| Totals | 21 | 20 | 36 | 7 | 5 | 0 | 0 | 0 | 89 |
| Percentages | 23.6 | 22.5 | 40.4 | 7.9 | 5.6 | 0 | 0 | 0 | - |

## Deficit Reduction

This was a very important section of the document, given the state of the economy, and it featured first in the Interim Agreement. Two-thirds of this section could be found in both parties' manifestos, and the remaining third was drawn from the Conservative manifesto. These proportions shifted only slightly in the PfG. The Lib Dems had already acceded to Conservative policy on the speed of deficit reduction.

## Spending Review – NHS, Schools, and a Fairer Society

This section was vaguer and cut across different policy areas, which in the PfG were given their own sections. Again, there was a high level of overlap, with 38 per cent of pledges coming from both manifestos, and an equal proportion (one-quarter of the total) coming from each of the parties alone. The two parties compromised over the Trident nuclear deterrent (a pledge shifted to the Defence section of the PfG). The NHS received only one mention in this section, a commitment to an increase in real spending. The NHS section in the Programme contained 30 pledges, and was dominated by the Tories.

## Tax Measures

This section was dominated largely by the Lib Dems; half of the policies here were taken directly from their manifesto. A further third were taken from both parties' platforms, and they reached a compromise on tax allowances for married couples. The proportions here remained relatively unchanged in the PfG.

## Banking Reform

This section witnessed the highest levels of agreement between the two parties, with three-quarters of the policies in this area coming from both of their manifestos, and the remaining quarter originating in the Tory manifesto. There was a shift towards the Tories when the final agreement was published, but the emphasis on unity between the coalition partners remained.

## Immigration

The two pledges in this section were shared equally between the two parties. The section was later expanded, but it remained equally apportioned between the coalition partners.

## Political Reform

Compared to the final PfG, where 27 pledges on this topic featured, this section was quite small. It was also reasonably equally shared out, with one-fifth coming from each party, two-fifths shared between both, and a further fifth of compromise. The compromises covered the AV referendum – which had been a major bone of contention during the negotiations – and the West Lothian question.

## Pensions & Welfare

This was a solidly Conservative section. In the PfG it was split into Jobs & Welfare, and Pensions & Older People. Almost three-quarters of the policy content here was Conservative.

**Education – Schools**

Only one pledge – a Conservative policy – was included in this section of the Interim Agreement, compared to 18 in the PfG, where the Conservatives again dominated.

**Education – Higher Education**

Here, the Conservatives predominated – of the two pledges, one came directly from their manifesto, and the other was a compromise between the two parties on the outcome of the as yet unpublished Browne Review.

**Relations with the EU**

Very similar in size and content to the equivalent section in the PfG, two-fifths of the pledges here came from the Conservatives, one-quarter from the Lib Dems, and a quarter again came from both. The remaining pledge consisted of a compromise on European criminal justice integration.

**Civil Liberties**

The Lib Dems held sway with two-thirds of the pledges here, and this section retained much of its shape when it went into the PfG.

**Environment**

This section witnessed a relatively high level of unity, with a little over half of the pledges coming from both manifestos, plus 32 per cent from the Conservatives, and 11 per cent from the Liberal Democrats. The parties reached a compromise on the divisive question of new nuclear power stations.

**Overview**

Table A1.3 suggests that the PfG was a strongly Conservative document. Including items counted as 'both', its content was roughly 75 per cent Conservative and 40 per cent Lib Dem. Fifty-three per cent of the policies were uniquely of Conservative origin, and only 23 per cent were Lib Dem. This may be explained simply by the fact that the Conservatives had a larger reserve of policy ideas when the agreement was being hammered out. The analysis also reveals a sizeable degree of ideological overlap between the two parties, as 20 per cent of policies came directly from both parties' manifestos. Areas of compromise accounted for 3 per cent of the total PfG. Of the 31 sections in the PfG, two were dominated by the Lib Dems, seven were split evenly between the parties, and in the remaining 22 the Conservatives dominated.

Table A1.4 sets out in more detail the origins of pledges from the PfG. Over 10 per cent of all PfG promises came not from the respective parties' manifestos but from party policy documents. In the commentary that follows we do not discuss every policy area, but highlight the more interesting or surprising results.

Table A1.3 The Programme for Government by
Proportion (%)

| Section | Con | LD | B | C | N |
|---|---|---|---|---|---|
| Banking | 45.4 | | 54.5 | | |
| Business | 61.9 | 28.6 | 9.5 | | |
| Civil Liberties | 7.1 | 57.1 | 28.6 | 7.1 | |
| Communities & Local Government | 59.3 | 22.2 | 18.5 | | |
| Consumer Protection | 66.7 | 33.3 | | | |
| Crime & Policing | 52.7 | 26.3 | 15.8 | 5.3 | |
| Culture, Olympics, Media & Sport | 33.3 | 33.3 | 33.3 | | |
| Defence | 57.2 | 14.3 | 14.3 | 14.3 | |
| Deficit Reduction | 30.0 | 10.0 | 60.0 | | |
| Energy & Climate Change | 34.7 | 21.7 | 39.1 | 4.3 | |
| Environment, Food & Rural Affairs | 50.0 | 16.7 | 33.3 | | |
| Equalities | 57.2 | 42.9 | | | |
| Europe | 44.4 | 22.2 | 22.2 | 11.1 | |
| Families & Children | 78.9 | 7.7 | 15.4 | | |
| Foreign Affairs | 70.0 | | 30.0 | | |
| Government Transparency | 46.2 | | 53.9 | | |
| Immigration | 28.6 | 28.6 | 28.6 | | 14.3 |
| International Development | 50.0 | 33.3 | 16.7 | | |
| Jobs & Welfare | 90.9 | | 9.1 | | |
| Justice | 55.5 | 22.2 | 22.2 | | |

Table A1.3  (*cont.*)

| Section | Con | LD | B | C | N |
|---|---|---|---|---|---|
| National Security | 100.0 | | | | |
| NHS | 60.0 | 36.7 | 3.3 | | |
| Pensions & Older People | 28.6 | 28.6 | 42.9 | | |
| Political Reform | 70.4 | 7.4 | 11.1 | 11.1 | |
| Public Health | 75.0 | | 25.0 | | |
| Schools | 44.5 | 16.7 | 27.8 | 11.1 | |
| Social Action | 85.7 | | 14.3 | | |
| Social Care & Disability | 80.0 | 20.0 | | | |
| Taxation | 22.2 | 44.4 | 22.2 | 11.1 | |
| Transport | 50.0 | 16.7 | 33.3 | | |
| Universities & Further Education | 42.9 | 14.3 | 28.6 | 14.3 | |

Note: Numbers may not add to 100% due to rounding up.

Table A1.4   The Programme for Government Pledge Backgrounds

| | Policy background | | | | | | | | |
|---|---|---|---|---|---|---|---|---|---|
| | Manifesto | | | | Non-manifesto | | | | |
| Section | Con | LD | B | C | Con | LD | B | N | Total |
| Banking | 3 | | 6 | | 2 | | | | 11 |
| Business | 8 | 6 | 2 | | 5 | | | | 21 |
| Civil Liberties | 1 | 8 | 4 | 1 | | | | | 14 |
| Communities & Local Government | 14 | 6 | 4 | | 2 | | 1 | | 27 |
| Consumer Protection | 5 | 3 | | | 1 | | | | 9 |
| Crime & policing | 9 | 5 | 3 | 1 | 1 | | | | 19 |
| Culture, Olympics, Media & Sport | 4 | 4 | 4 | | | | | | 12 |
| Defence | 3 | 1 | 1 | 1 | 1 | | | | 7 |
| Deficit Reduction | 3 | 1 | 6 | | | | | | 10 |
| Energy & Climate Change | 7 | 5 | 9 | 1 | 1 | | | | 23 |
| Environment, Food & Rural Affairs | 8 | 3 | 6 | | 1 | | | | 18 |

| | | | | | | | | | |
|---|---|---|---|---|---|---|---|---|---|
| Equalities | 1 | 3 | | | 3 | | | | 7 |
| Europe | 4 | 2 | 2 | 1 | | | | | 9 |
| Families & Children | 10 | 1 | 2 | | | | | | 13 |
| Foreign Affairs | 7 | | 3 | | | | | | 10 |
| Government Transparency | 5 | | 6 | | 1 | | 1 | | 13 |
| Immigration | 2 | 2 | 2 | | | | | 1 | 7 |
| International Development | 9 | 6 | 3 | | | | | | 18 |
| Jobs & Welfare | 6 | | 1 | | 4 | | | | 11 |
| Justice | 2 | 1 | 2 | | 3 | 1 | | | 9 |
| National Security | 3 | | | | 2 | | | | 5 |
| NHS | 14 | 8 | 1 | | 4 | 3 | | | 30 |
| Pensions & Older People | 2 | 2 | 3 | | | | | | 7 |
| Political Reform | 18 | 2 | 3 | 3 | 1 | | | | 27 |
| Public Health | 2 | | 1 | | 1 | | | | 4 |
| Schools | 7 | 3 | 5 | 2 | 1 | | | | 18 |
| Social Action | 6 | | 1 | | | | | | 7 |
| Social Care & Disability | 3 | 1 | | | 1 | | | | 5 |
| Taxation | 1 | 4 | 2 | 1 | 1 | | | | 9 |
| Transport | 5 | 2 | 4 | | 1 | | | | 12 |
| Universities & Further Education | 2 | 1 | 1 | 1 | 1 | | 1 | | 7 |
| | | | | | | | | | |
| Totals | 174 | 80 | 87 | 12 | 38 | 4 | 3 | 1 | 399 |
| Percentages | 43.6 | 20.1 | 21.8 | 3.0 | 9.5 | 1.0 | 0.8 | 0.3 | - |

## Civil Liberties

This was a strong policy area for the Lib Dems, and the majority (57 per cent) of pledges came directly from their manifesto, while only one policy (7 per cent) was uniquely Tory. Twenty-nine per cent of policies came from both parties' manifestos. On the divisive question of the Human Rights Act, the parties reached a deal whereby the Act would form the basis for any future British bill of rights. While it was classified as a compromise here, it could be viewed as a notable Lib Dem victory, given their longstanding support for the Human Rights Act.

## Crime & Policing

This section was Conservative-dominated, as just over half of the policies here came from the Tories and slightly over a quarter from the Lib Dems. Sixteen per cent could be traced to both manifestos. The parties reached a compromise on drug banning policy.

## Defence

This was another section in which the Conservatives dominated. Over half of the policy content was uniquely Tory, as compared with only one policy from the Lib Dems, and one policy from both parties. On the divisive question of the UK's nuclear deterrent, the parties were able to reach a compromise.

## Deficit Reduction

The 2010 election campaign might have led people to presume that this would be a largely Conservative section of the PfG. In fact, as the table reveals, sixty per cent came from both parties' manifestos. The remainder came more from the Conservatives (three) than the Lib Dems (only one), but the high level of unanimity here is worth noting.

## Europe

In this potentially controversial section the Conservatives won out. Four policies here came from their manifesto, compared to two from the Lib Dems. A further two policies came from both parties, and they compromised on European criminal justice integration.

## Foreign Affairs

The Conservatives dominated in this section, with seven-tenths of it coming directly from their manifesto. The Lib Dems could not claim any pledges as their own, though there was some overlap between the parties as the remaining three-tenths could be found in both manifestos.

## Immigration

The policies in this section were shared out equally between the parties: one-third from the Tory manifesto, one-third from the Lib Dems, and one-third from both.

## Jobs & Welfare

This was a heavily Tory dominated section of the PfG, reflecting their deep-seated desire to overhaul the welfare system; over nine-tenths came from the Conservative manifesto or their recent policy discussions.

## Health Service

There was a reasonably equitable distribution of policies in this section, the biggest in the entire Programme. Both parties had seemed open to quite radical NHS reform in their manifestos. Sixty per cent of the section was based on Conservative policy, 37 per cent came from the Lib Dems, and 3 per cent of pledges could be found in both manifestos. The number of pledges on the NHS in the PfG was far greater than in the Interim Agreement, which contained only one pledge on the NHS and no mention of structural reforms.

## Political Reform

Surprisingly, given the perception of the Liberal Democrats as the party of constitutional reform, this section was largely Tory. Seventy per cent was Conservative policy, only 7 per cent was Lib Dem, and 11 per cent was taken from both manifestos. This section also saw the largest number of compromises between the parties: on the future direction of devolution, the West Lothian question, and the AV referendum. In the Interim Agreement, the section on political reform had been much smaller, and more equitably distributed.

## Schools

Forty-five per cent of pledges in this section – greatly expanded since the Interim Agreement – were based on Tory policy, while the Lib Dems could lay claim to 17 per cent, and 28 per cent came from both manifestos.

## Taxation

This section proved to be a rare case of Lib Dem dominance, as it had been in the Interim Agreement. Four of the pledges here came solely from the Liberal Democrat manifesto, compared to only one from the Tories.

## Universities & Further Education

In the final section of the PfG the Conservatives prevailed: 43 per cent of the policies here were uniquely Tory. The Lib Dems failed to get any of their manifesto policies into this section, though one of the pledges here was Liberal Democrat-inspired. The parties compromised on the Browne Report on the future of higher education funding. Like the Schools section, this section was larger than in the Interim Agreement, and had become more Conservative in terms of policy content.

# Appendix 2

## Opinion Polls on the Coalition and the Political Parties, 2010–11

### BRIAN WALKER

Despite their preference for single-party government before the May 2010 election,[1] according to a YouGov-*Sun* poll 60 per cent of British public opinion rallied round the Coalition on its formation.[2] Ipsos MORI and YouGov both revealed that around half of the public approved of the first round of budget cuts in June.[3] However, the October 2010 spending review saw the real beginnings of a marked change of opinion. By December 2010, 47 per cent of those polled by the ICM-*Guardian* agreed that the decision to form a coalition was wrong, compared with 43 per cent who thought that it was right.[4] The Government consistently struggled in the polls throughout 2011, though it is worth noting the effect on the Coalition's approval ratings of David Cameron's EU veto in December 2011 (see Figure A2.1 Government Approval Ratings, June 2010–December 2011).

Indeed, negativity was a growing feature of the polls on the three main parties, their leaders and the Coalition itself, as the British public expressed increasing dissatisfaction with the political leadership on offer and mounting anxiety over the state of the economy.

On voting intentions, support for the Lib Dems plummeted by 18 points in the first eight months of the Coalition, reaching a low of 9 per cent in December 2010 and barely climbing into double figures thereafter. All three parties were basically flatlining for most of 2011, with Labour consistently but not convincingly ahead by a few points, often within the three-point margin of error.[5] See Figure A2.2 Voting Intentions Polling Results, June 2010–December 2011.

[1] J Vowles, 'Making a Difference? Public Perceptions of Coalition, Single-Party, and Minority Governments' (2010) 29(3) *Electoral Studies* 370.

[2] YouGov, *YouGov/The Sun Survey Results* (13 May 2010), www.cdn.yougov.com/today_uk_import/YG-Archives-Pol-Suntopical-100513.pdf

[3] Ipsos MORI, *Ipsos MORI Post Budget Reaction Poll Topline Results* (28 June 2011), www.ipsos-mori.com/Assets/Docs/Budget%20Reaction%20Topline.PDF; YouGov, *The Economy* (20 December 2011), www.cdn.yougov.com/cumulus_uploads/document/7645cvwcdc/YG-Archives-Trackers-Economy-201211.pdf

[4] J Glover and N Watt, 'Coalition Government support is dramatically down, poll shows' *Guardian* (26 December 2010).

[5] BBC News, 'Poll Tracker' (4 January 2012), www.bbc.co.uk/news/uk-politics-13248179

On whether the party leaders were doing a good or a bad job, all three had slipped into negative ratings by the end of 2010 (according to YouGov). Almost a year later, in the 15–16 December 2011 poll, the Conservative Prime Minister David Cameron (at 44 per cent 'well' and 50 per cent 'badly') fared best and consistently ahead of Labour leader Ed Miliband (at 28 per cent 'well' and 59 per cent 'badly'), leaving the Lib Dem leader and Deputy Prime Minister Nick Clegg trailing (at 18 per cent 'well' and 73 per cent 'badly' – a deficit of 55 points).[6] See Figure A2.3 Party Leaders Polling Results, May 2010–December 2011.

On the economy, the Coalition polled quite strongly from the outset, until around the last quarter of 2010. By January 2011, however, public confidence in the Coalition's economic policies had weakened and failed to recover fully. For the rest of the year, between 30 and 40 per cent of people believed the Coalition was handling the economy well (31 per cent as of early December 2011), while between 50 and 60 per cent claimed the opposite (reaching a high of 60 per cent in November).[7] See Figure A2.4 Government and Economy Polling Results, June 2010–December 2011.

The Conservatives could take some comfort from the fact that the weakening enthusiasm for the Coalition could be attributed almost entirely to the collapse of Liberal Democrat support, as disenchanted Labour supporters who had voted for the Lib Dems in the election deserted them for breaking their promises and betraying their principles. Labour's recovery, the fastest for an opposition for many years, gave them a modest lead over the Conservatives which was mainly at Lib Dem expense. However much voters disapproved of the severity of budget cuts (62 per cent, according to an ICM-*Guardian* poll in September 2011)[8] and the handling of the economy generally, the Conservatives were also encouraged that people persistently doubted that Labour had a better plan for managing the economy – although the gap was narrowing. Relative preference for one main party's economic management over another's was of limited relevance at the early stage of the electoral cycle, especially as confidence in the state of the UK economy was low.

On whether the Lib Dems had made a difference by the time of the Coalition's first anniversary, more than 50 per cent of both Conservative and Lib Dem voters agreed that they had. But two-thirds thought that the partners had disagreed on important policies and that the Lib Dems had had little effect on significant policies such as those on the NHS, university funding, and tax and spend. Only 37 per cent thought the Lib Dems had softened the blow of the harsher effects of the Government's deficit reduction plan.[9] With Labour and the Conservatives largely

[6] YouGov, *The Party Leaders* (22 December 2011), www.cdn.yougov.com/cumulus_uploads/document/1qhe1gcvmq/YG-Archives-Trackers-Leaders-221211.pdf

[7] YouGov, *The Economy* (20 December 2011), www.cdn.yougov.com/cumulus_uploads/document/7645cvwcdc/YG-Archives-Trackers-Economy-201211.pdf

[8] ICM Research, *ICM Poll for the Guardian* (26 September 2011), www.icmresearch.com/wp-content/blogs.dir/1/files/2011/09/2011_sept_guardian_poll.pdf

[9] Populus, *Coalition One Year On* (19 April 2011), www.instituteforgovernment.org.uk/pdfs/one_year_on_poll_results.pdf

becalmed, both parties were equally in contention for government following the 2015 election.

Speculating on that 2015 election at the end of the Coalition's first 18 months, another coalition led by either party seems possible, unless the Lib Dems are wiped out altogether. Very tentative forecasts, based on uniform swings and the proposed constituency boundary changes, would see the Lib Dems losing at least 10 notional seats in new constituencies; depending on whether the Tories or Labour were to gain a larger overall share of the vote, the Lib Dems could be reduced to between 5 and 15 seats on their projected 10 per cent share of the vote. To remain part of the government-forming equation they would need to increase their vote share to around 18 per cent, giving them around 31–43 seats in the new Parliament.[10]

[10] Information kindly supplied by Colin Rallings, Plymouth, Lewis Baston, ERS, and Anthony Wells at YouGov. All stress that the estimates are strongly subject to local factors.

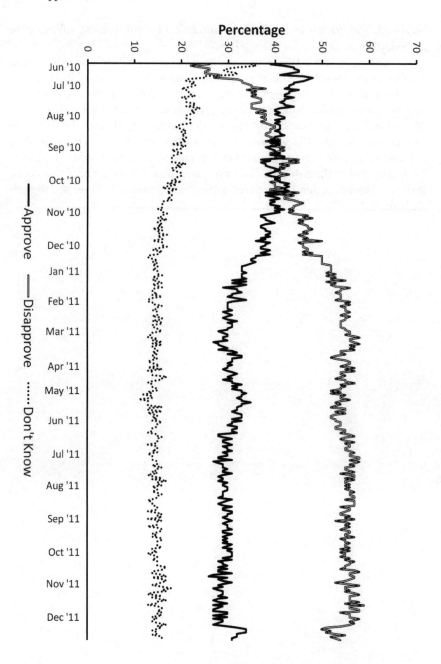

Figure A2.1  Government Approval Polling Results, June 2010–December 2011

Source: Yougov data: http://cdn.yougov.com/cumulus_uploads/document/t83oattrq3/YG-Archives-Pol-Trackers-Approval-231211.pdf, pp 1–7

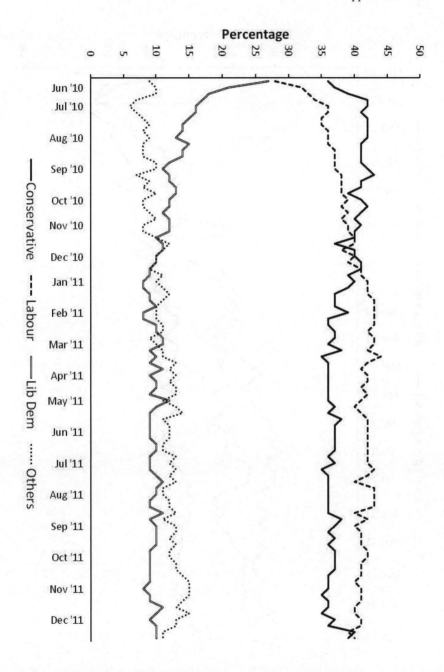

Figure A2.2  Voting Intentions Polling Results, June 2010–December 2011
Source: BBC poll of polls: www.bbc.co.uk/news/uk-politics-13248179

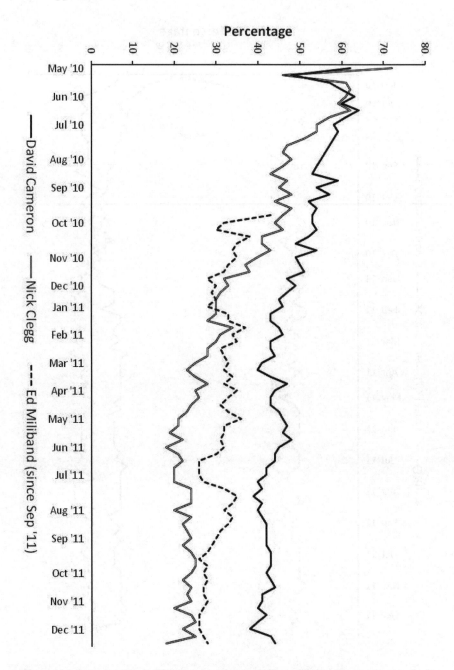

Figure A2.3 Party Leaders Polling Results, May 2010–December 2011

Source: Yougov data: http://cdn.yougov.com/cumulus_uploads/document/1qhe1gcvmq/
YG-Archives-Trackers-Leaders-221211.pdf, pp 1–6

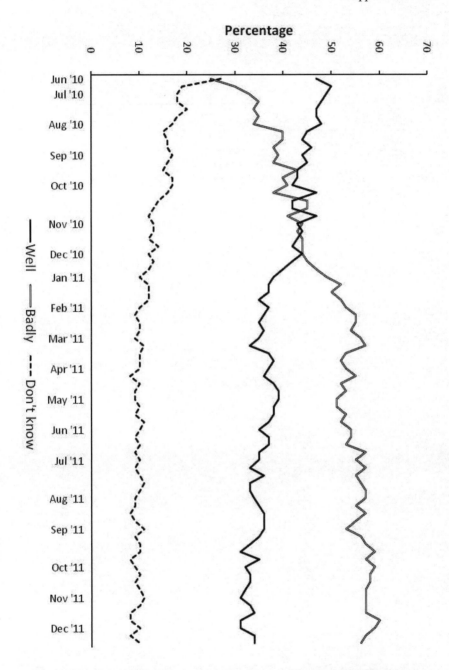

Figure A2.4 Government and Economy Polling Results, June 2010–December 2011

Source: Yougov data: http://cdn.yougov.com/cumulus_uploads/document/7645cvwcdc/
YG-Archives-Trackers-Economy-201211.pdf, pp 10–11

# Appendix 3

# *Coalition Government Chronology, 2010–11*

2010

May
*The Coalition begins life riding a wave of public enthusiasm, although it encounters its first difficulties when Lib Dem Cabinet minister David Laws resigns three weeks into the job, and the scale of the budget deficit becomes clear.*

5 May      General election held.

11 May      Gordon Brown resigns; David Cameron becomes Prime Minister and forms coalition with the Liberal Democrats.

12 May      Coalition Cabinet confirmed, 5 places for Lib Dems.

13 May      Initial Coalition Agreement published; first Cabinet meeting takes place.

14 May      Announcement of all ministers and members of the Government.

19 May      Nick Clegg's first major speech as DPM outlines that the Coalition will make the House of Lords fully elected, scrap ID cards, curb CCTV and defend the Human Rights Act.

20 May      Publication of the more detailed Programme for Government.
Over 100 Conservative MPs defy Cameron and vote against changes to the 1922 Committee that would open it to ministers too.

21 May      Publication of Coalition Agreement for Stability and Reform.

24 May      Chief Secretary David Laws announces first set of government cuts totalling £6 billion.

25 May      Coalition's first Queen's Speech (outlines 23 new bills).

29 May      David Laws resigns as Chief Secretary to the Treasury over expenses claims; Danny Alexander takes his place.

June
*The Coalition produces its first budget.*

2 Jun      Clegg's first PMQs; pledges vote for MPs on electoral reform.

22 Jun      Emergency Budget delivered by George Osborne.

July
*The Coalition's planned NHS reforms are outlined, and bills for parliamentary and electoral reform are introduced.*

4 Jul        Coalition promises to safeguard spending on health and overseas aid.
12 Jul       Health White Paper *Equity and Excellence: Liberating the NHS* published.
22 Jul       Fixed Term Parliaments Bill introduced.
             Parliamentary Voting System and Constituencies Bill introduced.
23 Jul       Conservative MPs' unhappiness with Coalition exposed when David Davis MP refers to Government as the 'Brokeback Coalition'.

August
*Parliament in recess.*

13 Aug       Local Government Secretary Eric Pickles announces abolition of the Audit Commission.
16 Aug       Clegg says renewing Trident is too expensive.

September
*Party conference season begins. Ed Miliband is elected leader of the Labour Party, defeating his brother and favourite candidate, David.*

18–22 Sep    Liberal Democrat Party Conference 2010.
25 Sep       Ed Miliband is elected new Labour leader.
26–30 Sep    Labour Party Conference 2010.

October
*The Spending Review outlines the cuts to be made by each department in the coming years.*

3–6 Oct      Conservative Party Conference 2010.
20 Oct       Spending Review published (covering funding for departments up to 2014–15).
28 Oct       Public Bodies Bill introduced (House of Lords).

November
*Tuition fee demonstrations end in scenes of violence and destruction outside Conservative Party HQ in London.*

9 Nov        Protests held against proposed rise in tuition fees.
11 Nov       EU Bill introduced.
30 Nov       Police Reform & Social Responsibility Bill introduced.

December
*£9,000 tuition fees are passed despite opposition from students. The Lib Dems are split three ways, with supporters, opponents and abstainers.*

9 Dec        Tuition fees debate held in House of Commons.
13 Dec       Localism Bill introduced.

20 Dec     Business Secretary Vince Cable caught in a *Telegraph* 'sting' saying he might leave the Government if pushed too far.

21 Dec     Cable reported to have said he was 'declaring war' on Rupert Murdoch over BSkyB bid. He is subsequently stripped of responsibility for media regulation, but remains Business Secretary.

## 2011

### January
*A poor result in the Oldham East and Saddleworth by-election causes consternation amongst Lib Dems about the direction they are taking.*

13 Jan     Oldham East and Saddleworth by-election held, with Labour maintaining its seat and the Lib Dems coming a distant second.

18 Jan–    House of Lords filibuster on Parliamentary Voting System and
1 Feb      Constituencies Bill.

19 Jan     Health and Social Care Bill introduced.
           Ed Miliband's head of communications sends letter to broadcasters asking them to stop using the term 'Coalition' and to use 'Tory-led government' instead.

21 Jan     Andy Coulson resigns as PM's head of communications.

### February
*Parliamentary Voting System and Constituencies Bill is passed just in time for the referendum to be held on 5 May.*

5 Feb      Cameron gives 'muscular liberalism' speech about multiculturalism.

9 Feb      Launch of 'Project Merlin': coalition negotiations with banks to cut bonuses and lend more to business. Former Lib Dem Treasury spokesman Lord Oakeshott resigns, criticising the Government's banking policy.

16 Feb     Parliamentary Voting System and Constituencies Act passed.

### March
*Britain and France lead the NATO air campaign in Libya, while at home trade unions lead the growing anti-cuts movement.*

4 Mar      Barnsley by-election: Labour hold their seat, Lib Dems finish sixth.

11 Mar     Opinion poll puts support for Lib Dems in single figures.

11–13 Mar  Liberal Democrat Spring Conference: motion passed condemning NHS reforms.

18 Mar     Cameron announces plan to send planes to Libya.

23 Mar     Second Coalition Budget announced.

26 Mar     Large protests against Government cuts take place.

29 Mar     AV referendum campaign begins.

## April

*Controversy surrounding the proposed NHS reforms continues.*

4 Apr　　　Coalition agrees to slow pace of health reforms after public criticism.

6 Apr　　　Health Listening Exercise – 'the Pause' – launched, runs until 31 May 2011.

10 Apr　　Norman Lamb MP threatens to quit as Nick Clegg's Permanent Private Secretary over NHS reforms.

14 Apr　　David Cameron makes controversial speech on cutting migration.

## May

*A month of heavy setbacks for the Lib Dems as they lose the AV referendum, and poll very badly in English local, Scottish Parliament and Welsh Assembly elections. Clegg says that this must be a turning point for the Lib Dems and the Coalition.*

5 May　　　AV referendum is defeated by 68% to 32%, on a turnout of 42%.

　　　　　　SNP win majority in Scottish Parliament and promise referendum on Scottish independence.

　　　　　　Labour win 30 seats in 60-seat Welsh Assembly.

　　　　　　Local government elections held in England: Labour gain 857 council seats and the Conservatives 85, while the Lib Dems lose 747.

17 May　　House of Lords reform draft bill and White Paper published.

26 May　　House of Lords Reform Bill introduced (House of Lords).

## June

*The Coalition start to backpedal over NHS reforms.*

7 Jun　　　Cameron gives conciliatory speech outlining five changes to plans for health reform.

## July

*News International and the phone hacking scandal dominate the headlines as serious questions are asked regarding Cameron's close relations with the Murdochs.*

4 Jul　　　Outcry after reports that the *News of the World* hacked into the voicemails of 13-year-old murder victim Milly Dowler.

　　　　　　Andy Coulson is arrested. Questions asked regarding David Cameron's decision to employ Coulson.

13 Jul　　News International withdraws its bid for control of BSkyB.

19 Jul　　EU Act passed, providing for referenda in the event of future treaty changes.

28 Jul　　Government announces rise in public sector pension contributions.

August
*London and other major English cities are affected by widespread rioting; a debate over social policy and policing ensues. The Eurozone debt crisis deepens, reinforcing Osborne's commitment to spending cuts.*

| | |
|---|---|
| 15 Aug | Cameron launches review of coalition social policy to deal with 'broken society'. Clegg publicly refuses to reconsider police spending cuts. |
| 17 Aug | Lib Dem Lords Mackenzie and Carlile criticise the Government's heavy-handed response to the riots. |
| 26 Aug | Nick Clegg states that he will not allow the Human Rights Act to be repealed by the Government. |
| 30 Aug | Speeding case file of Lib Dem Secretary of State for Energy and Climate Change Chris Huhne sent by Essex police to the Crown Prosecution Service; PM and DPM prepare for possible Lib Dem reshuffle in Cabinet. |
| 31 Aug | Downing St announces intention to reject anti-abortion amendment to the Health and Social Care Bill tabled by Conservative MP Nadine Dorries. |

September
*At the Lib Dem Conference Clegg insists that the party remains distinct from the Conservatives and is influencing the Government; he simultaneously stresses the Lib Dems' commitment to the Coalition and its policies, particularly spending cuts.*

| | |
|---|---|
| 6 Sep | 20 prominent economists call on the Government to abolish the 50p tax rate; Vince Cable claims that this will not happen. |
| | Lib Dem chief executive Chris Fox announces that he will stand down, citing a lack of party funding. |
| 7 Sep | Nadine Dorries MP challenges David Cameron in PMQs, claiming that the Lib Dems have an undue influence over coalition policy. |
| 10 Sep | William Hague states that he would prefer to distance the UK further from aspects of the EU, but has had to compromise on the issue with Lib Dems. |
| 12 Sep | Vickers Report published, proposing banking reforms to be instituted by 2019. |
| 13 Sep | Boundary Commission for England's review of parliamentary constituencies is released, causing concern amongst Lib Dem MPs that they will lose out as a result of the planned changes. |
| 14 Sep | Several trade unions announce plans to strike over public sector pension reforms at the TUC Conference. |
| 15 Sep | Fixed Term Parliaments Act passed. |
| 17–21 Sep | Liberal Democrat Party Conference 2011. |
| 25–29 Sep | Labour Party Conference 2011. |

October

*The Conservative Conference is marred by a row between Theresa May and Ken Clarke over the Human Rights Act. This is quickly overshadowed by the Liam Fox scandal.*

2–5 Oct    Conservative Party Conference 2011.

11 Oct    Cabinet Secretary Gus O'Donnell announces he will retire at the end of the year; plans are drawn up to separate the Cabinet Secretary from the Head of the Civil Service.

Health and Social Care Bill has Second Reading in the Lords, where it survives attempts to delay and block it.

14 Oct    Defence Secretary Liam Fox resigns after a scandal erupts around the activities of his close friend and self-styled adviser, Adam Werrity.

In the reshuffle that follows, Phillip Hammond is moved from Transport to Defence; Justine Greening becomes Transport Secretary. No Lib Dem ministers are affected.

15 Oct    Anti-capitalist activists set up camp outside St Paul's Cathedral as part of the global Occupy movement.

24 Oct    81 Conservative MPs (and 1 Lib Dem) vote in support of a referendum on EU membership, against the Government.

November

*The Eurozone crisis worsens. The Chancellor publishes his Autumn Statement.*

15 Nov    Home Secretary Theresa May's position is challenged as news breaks that UK border checks had been waived as part of her pilot scheme.

29 Nov    Chancellor's Autumn Statement announces a raft of new public sector investment projects.

December

*The Coalition enters a tense period after the PM uses the British veto at a Brussels summit on resolving the Eurozone crisis.*

9 Dec    David Cameron vetoes an EU-wide treaty change after unsuccessfully demanding protection for the British financial sector.

16 Dec    Feltham and Heston by-election: Labour retains its seat, Lib Dems finish third, only 88 votes ahead of UKIP.

19 Dec    Nick Clegg announces that the next Queen's Speech will include plans for an elected upper chamber, with PM's support.

# Appendix 4

## *Coalition Agreement for Stability and Reform*

**May 2010**

**Introduction**

This document sets out how we expect our Coalition Government to operate in practice and the basis upon which the Conservative and Liberal Democrat Parliamentary Parties will jointly maintain in office Her Majesty's Government.

It reflects the agreements reached by our Parliamentary Parties. We expect it to endure for the duration of the present Parliament. The Government will put a motion before the House of Commons in the first days of the Government stating its intention that, subject to Her Majesty The Queen's consent, the next General Election will be held on 7 May 2015, to be followed by legislation for fixed term Parliaments of five years. The passage of the legislation will be subject to a whip in the Parliamentary Parties in both Houses.

There is no constitutional difference between a Coalition Government and a single party Government, but working practices need to adapt to reflect the fact that the UK has not had a Coalition in modern times.

The Coalition Parties will work together effectively to deliver our programme, on the basis of goodwill, mutual trust and agreed procedures which foster collective decision making and responsibility while respecting each party's identity.

Close consultation between the Prime Minister and Deputy Prime Minister, other Ministers and members of the Conservative and Liberal Democrat Parties in both Houses will be the foundation of the Coalition's success. In the working of the Coalition, the principle of balance will underpin both the Coalition Parties' approaches to all aspects of the conduct of the Government's business, including the allocation of responsibilities, the Government's policy and legislative programme, the conduct of its business and the resolution of disputes.

## 1. Composition of the Government

1.1 The initial allocation of Cabinet, Ministerial, Whip and Special Adviser appointments between the two Parties was agreed between the Prime Minister and the Deputy Prime Minister.

1.2 Future allocation will continue to be based on the principle that the Parliamentary Party with fewer MPs will have a share of Cabinet, Ministerial and Whip appointments agreed between the Prime Minister and the Deputy Prime Minister, approximately in proportion to the size of the two Parliamentary parties. The Prime Minister, following consultation with the Deputy Prime Minister, will make nominations for the appointment of Ministers. The Prime Minister will nominate Conservative Party Ministers and the Deputy Prime Minister will nominate Liberal Democrat Ministers. The Prime Minister and the Deputy Prime Minister will agree the nomination of the Law Officers.

1.3 Any changes to the allocation of portfolios between the Parliamentary Parties during the lifetime of the Coalition will be agreed between the Prime Minister and the Deputy Prime Minister.

1.4 No Liberal Democrat Minister or Whip may be removed on the recommendation of the Prime Minister without full consultation with the Deputy Prime Minister.

1.5 The appointment of further Members of the Privy Council will be made following full consultation between the Prime Minister and Deputy Prime Minister.

## 2. Collective Responsibility

2.1 The principle of collective responsibility, save where it is explicitly set aside, continues to apply to all Government Ministers. This requires:

(a) an appropriate degree of consultation and discussion among Ministers to provide the opportunity for them to express their views frankly as decisions are reached, and to ensure the support of all Ministers;
(b) the opinions expressed and advice offered within Government to remain private;
(c) decisions of the Cabinet to be binding on and supported by all Ministers;
(d) full use being made of the Cabinet Committee system and application of the mechanisms for sharing information and resolving disputes set out in this document.

There are certain standard exceptions to the principle of consultation – the Chancellor's Budget judgements, quasi-judicial decisions and opinions of the Law Officers in particular. Budget judgements will require consultation with the Chief Secretary; when the Prime Minister is consulted the Deputy Prime Minister should also be consulted.

## 3. Functioning of the Government

3.1 The establishment of Cabinet Committees, appointment of members and determination of their terms of reference by the Prime Minister has been and will continue to be agreed with the Deputy Prime Minister. The Deputy Prime Minister will serve, or nominate another member of the administration to serve, on each Cabinet Committee and sub-committee. The existence and composition of Cabinet Committees and sub-committees will be published.

3.2 Consistent with the civil service code, all civil servants have a duty to support the Government as a whole. Special advisors may support an individual Minister in relation to their Government activities, but must at all times act in the interests of the Government as a whole. The private offices of individual Ministers, including the Prime Minister and Deputy Prime Minister, have a particular responsibility to their Minister.

3.3 The general principle will be that the Prime Minister and Deputy Prime Minister should have a full and contemporaneous overview of the business of Government. Each will have the power to commission papers from the Cabinet Secretariat.

3.4 The Prime Minister, with the agreement of the Deputy Prime Minister, has established a Coalition Committee which will oversee the operation of the Coalition, supported by the Cabinet Secretariat. It will be co-chaired by the Prime Minister and the Deputy Prime Minister, with equal numbers of members drawn from the two Coalition Parties.

3.5 Unresolved issues may be referred to the Coalition Committee from any other Cabinet Committee by either that Committee's chair (who will be a member of one Coalition Party) or its deputy chair (who will be a member of the other Coalition Party).

## 4. Policy and Legislative Programme

4.1 The principal policies of the Government are set out in the Coalition Programme for Government, of which the first part is the Agreement of 11 May, and the second part is 'The Coalition: our programme for government' of 20 May.

## 5. Support for the Government in Parliament

The Government Chief Whip and Deputy Chief Whip will consult and co-operate with each other to ensure the delivery of the Government's programme. Parallel arrangements will operate in respect of the Government Chief Whip and Deputy Chief Whip in the House of Lords.

5.1 The two Parties will aim to ensure support for Government policy and legislation from their two Parliamentary Parties, except where the Coalition Programme for Government specifically provides otherwise. If on any future occasion any other exceptions are required they must be specifically agreed by the Coalition Committee and Cabinet. Ministers will be responsible for developing and maintaining a constructive dialogue with Members of both Parliamentary Parties.

5.2  As a general rule, the same whip will be applied by both parties to their members. This includes legislation agreed as part of the Coalition Agreement. Any exceptions will be explicitly agreed by the parties, including exceptions identified in the Agreement of 11 May. In all circumstances, all members of both parties will be expected to support the Government on all matters of confidence.

5.3 The Chief Whip of the Conservative Party will serve as Government Chief Whip and the Chief Whip of the Liberal Democrats will serve as Deputy Chief Whip.

5.4 Each of the Parliamentary Parties will be responsible for their own internal arrangements for ensuring effective Parliamentary support for the Government on all issues covered by this Agreement.

5.5  Neither Parliamentary Party will support proposals brought before Parliament other than by the Government unless considered and agreed by both parties. The two Parties may agree in the Coalition Committee or in the Parliamentary Business Committee occasions on which issues will be subject to a free vote, which will normally be the case for Private Members' Bills

## 6. Public Appointments

On the issue of public appointments, the Prime Minister will consult with and have regard to the views of the Deputy Prime Minister.

# Appendix 5

## *Letter from Cabinet Secretary Sir Gus O'Donnell on Coalition Government*

**4 June 2010**

Dear Colleagues,

The Prime Minister has thanked staff in a number of departments for their support in managing the smooth transition to the new Government. I too would like to pass on my appreciation for the hard work and professionalism of all those who have been a part of ensuring a smooth transition to the new Government.

I would like to take this opportunity to set out some of the principles that should guide our future work with this administration.

The role of the Civil Service is to serve the Government of the day. This is of course no different for a coalition government, with majority and minority partners. At this time of transition it is vital that all staff are mindful of our core values as civil servants – integrity, honesty, objectivity and impartiality – in order to support the government effectively to deliver its programme. Applying these core values in all we do and sticking to the formal procedures of collective decision making will make a significant contribution to making the coalition work.

### Cabinet Committee Clearance

Both coalition parties are represented on all Cabinet Committees and collective agreement through the Cabinet Committee clearance process is therefore of additional importance, as one means of making the coalition work.

The civil service should contribute to the success of this process by ensuring that:

- Standard 6 day clearance times are rigorously applied (save for unavoidable exceptions, e.g. to meet parliamentary deadlines) to ensure that there is time for necessary departmental and coalition consideration as part of the process;
- Minsters have strong briefing for any committee they attend; and

- Ministers' diaries are managed to ensure personal attendance at committee meetings. The attendance of either a departmental deputy or political deputy will be at the discretion of committee chairs. With the exception of the Privy Council and parliamentary business, Cabinet Committee business takes precedence over all other commitments. Private offices and officials should make early contact with the Cabinet Secretariat to discuss policy and clearance well in advance of that clearance being sought.

The Cabinet Secretariat will shortly be publishing revised guidance on clearing policy through Cabinet and Cabinet Committees.

### Escalation

All ministers and civil servants should consider the decisions of Cabinet Committees as binding unless:

- the chair and the PM (in consultation with the deputy chair and DPM) agree an issue is sufficiently serious it should be referred to full Cabinet;
- either the chair or deputy chair of the Committee conclude an issue raises coalition issues and is sufficiently serious to be referred to the Coalition Committee;
- the principle of collective responsibility has been explicitly set aside; or
- Treasury ministers invoke their right to have a matter referred to full Cabinet on public expenditure grounds.

Escalation should be very much the exception. If agreement cannot be reached at one meeting it is normally preferable to refer it to the next (on the basis of further information or analysis by officials) or to a small group of ministers to consider and report back.

### Parliamentary Handling

The coalition necessarily results in a wider range of views on Government, as well as opposition, backbenches which will require effective parliamentary handling.

The Civil Service should contribute to the smooth running of Parliament and respond to its demands in performing its constitutional role to hold the executive to account by:

- meeting set timescales on all correspondence and the laying of papers;
- maintaining a high level of accuracy and relevance when responding to PQs or Member's letters;
- ensuring Parliamentary Branches provide a prompt, high quality service to Parliament and their departmental colleagues;
- anticipating and managing the possible slower passage of legislation; and

- providing a good and timely service to Select Committees to facilitate their working.

## Working with the Coalition Agreement

The Coalition Agreement is the programme for the new Government which sets out its aims and objectives on key areas of policy for the next five years, with the over-riding priority being that of tackling the budget deficit. The Coalition Government was agreed collectively through the Coalition Committee, and departments should consider this an agreed position. However it should not be taken as clearance for further policy. Inevitably, as the policies within the agreement are worked up, they will often require further detailed cross-Whitehall consideration before they can be implemented.

I think it would be helpful for departments to adopt a requirement for submissions to ministers to include a section on "coalition considerations" under which officials should set out how the coalition has been taken into account in framing the advice. This should also include an evaluation of the proposals against the Coalition Agreement setting out whether they:

- accord with the Coalition Agreement;
- are at odds with the Coalition Agreement;
- are not covered by the Agreement; or
- are in an area covered by the Agreement but on a new issue.

In thinking about coalition issues, officials should consider the importance both sides of the coalition attach to a "no surprises" culture. In the same way officials may advise ministers that they should engage with a colleague whose departmental position conflicts with a proposed policy, civil service advice can flag the need to engage on a point of party political difference relevant to the functioning of the coalition. Permanent Secretaries may also advise ministers that an issue should be taken to the Coalition Committee.

For policy areas where the Coalition Agreement sets out "an agreement to disagree" it will be particularly important that Civil Service advice is confined to objective analysis and facts.

## Conduct of the Civil Service

Coalition Government requires a culture of openness and collaboration. Departments should review their procedures, board configuration and processes for circulating information to support such a culture. Private Office staff will have a key role in support of Coalition Government.

Access by the current administration to papers of the pre-1997 Conservative administration, including when ministers are considering any Freedom of Information cases, should be given to current Conservative Ministers only.

All staff should seek prompt advice from line managers where they are unsure about any new ways of working or the dividing line between internal government deliberation and party political competition.

Needless to say, I would be especially grateful if senior teams in all departments could ensure they have developed guidance and are providing leadership around the Civil Service's role in supporting coalition government.

Gus O'Donnell

# Appendix 6

## *Guidance on Liaison between Departments and Coalition Backbenchers, July 2010*

*This document was published in the* Times *on 26 April 2011. See www.thetimes. co.uk/tto/news/politics/article2998505.ece*

An important requirement for the smooth operation of the Coalition will be regular and open communication between Ministerial teams in departments and backbench Members of Parliament.

The aim should be to foster a continuing dialogue, avoid surprises and ensure that difficult decisions are arrived at through appropriate consultation, with colleagues in both Coalition parties understanding how decisions have been made and why.

To that end, the Liberal Democrats have established Parliamentary Groups covering the work of Government departments, each with co-chairs from Commons and Lords. Some groups cover more than one department. (The Conservatives will have their own arrangements to ensure an equivalent level of communication, especially with departments with a Liberal Democrat Secretary of State.)

Clearly, the precise arrangements will be a matter for each Parliamentary Group and the relevant Secretary of State to decide between them, and will vary department to department. The general principal however, is the more two way contact, the better.

The following elements will contribute to effective communication:

– making sure that the co-chairs of the Parliamentary Groups are alerted, through the Special Adviser, to major forthcoming Ministerial speeches or announcements (such as Written Ministerial Statements), and given the opportunity to contribute to them and comment on drafts, and vice-versa;

– involving the co-chairs in the policy-making process to the maximum extent possible, subject to the requirements of confidentiality;

– making sure that Ministerial colleagues are alerted to any major concerns Parliamentary colleagues in either of the Coalition parties may have about policy proposals or announcements in good time;

– ensuring that the Parliamentary group is given a list of the key Departmental contacts: Ministers, Special Advisers, Parliamentary Private Secretaries and Whips; and that those individuals make themselves available to the co-chairs;
– inviting the co-chairs to attend weekly Ministerial meetings;
– providing policy guidance to the co-chairs, through Special Advisers, on the content of speeches and articles, to assist in maintaining coherence with the Coalition's programme;
– establishing a regular meeting, say monthly, of both Lib Dem and Conservative backbenchers with an interest in the portfolio with the Minister to discuss relevant issues.

# Appendix 7

## No 10 Policy and Implementation Unit: Who's Who, Summer 2011

| Name | Role in Policy Unit | Previous background |
|---|---|---|
| Paul Kirby | Head of Policy | Partner in KPMG, seconded to work for George Osborne before the election to audit Conservative plans |
| Kris Murrin | Head of Implementation | Social psychologist. Founded What If? training. Associate of PM's Delivery Unit 2001–6 |
| Paul Bate | Health and Social Care | Former McKinsey consultant. PM's Delivery Unit 2003–6, on health policy. Director of management consultancy Delivery 2020 |
| Tim Luke | Business and Enterprise | Analyst with Lehman Brothers |
| Michael Lynas | Big Society | Accountant with Bain & Co. Seconded to work for Francis Maude before the election, helping plan for government |
| Ben Moxham | Energy and Environment | BP's alternative energy team. Riverstone private equity, founded by former head of BP Lord Browne |
| Chris Brown | Education, Children and Families | Civil service economist. Private Secretary to Chief Secretary to Treasury |
| Susan Acland-Hood | Home Affairs and Justice | Civil service Private Secretary to Gordon Brown on Justice and Home Affairs |
| Richard Freer | Defence | Ministry of Defence civil servant. Head of Defence Policy, Cabinet Office. Private Secretary to Gordon Brown on Defence |

| Miles Gibson | Infrastructure, Planning and Transport | Treasury official, worked in Department of Communities and Local Government and as Private Secretary in No 10 |
| --- | --- | --- |
| Hugh Harris | Welfare | Deputy Director, Welfare in Cabinet Office Strategy Unit |

# Appendix 8

## *Glossary*

| | |
|---|---|
| *1922 Committee* | Backbench committee comprising all Conservative MPs, excluding the frontbench when the party is in government. |
| *Association of Conservative Peers* | Group comprising all Conservative members of the House of Lords. |
| *Coalition Committee* | Formal Cabinet Committee dedicated to resolving issues and disputes between the two coalition parties, co-chaired by David Cameron and Nick Clegg. |
| *Coalition Operation and Strategic Planning Group* | Cabinet working group which is subordinate to the Coalition Committee and comprises Oliver Letwin (Con), Danny Alexander (LD), Francis Maude (Con), and Lord (Jim) Wallace (LD). |
| *Cranborne Money* | State funding given to opposition parties (and Crossbenchers) in the House of Lords. (See also 'Short Money'). |
| *Departmental business plan* | Three-year plans for Whitehall departments with objectives and targets, to increase their transparency and accountability. |
| *Diary Secretary* | Secretary based in the minister's Private Office responsible for the ministerial diary arrangements. |
| *Director General* | The second most senior civil servant in a government department, junior only to the Permanent Secretary. |
| *Economic and Domestic Affairs Secretariat* | Cabinet Office body which supports and services the Cabinet Committees on economic and domestic policy. |
| *Federal Policy Committee* | Liberal Democrat party body responsible for producing policy papers to be debated at conference and, officially, for drawing up the party's General Election manifestos in consultation with the parliamentary party. It is elected biannually at conference. |
| *Grid, the* | The schedule of forthcoming government media announcements, coordinated by No 10. |

| | |
|---|---|
| *Parliamentary Private Secretary* | MP appointed by a government minister to act as their unpaid assistant, and to be their eyes and ears in the House of Commons. |
| *Parliamentary Under-Secretary* | A Parliamentary Under-Secretary of State is an MP or peer from the governing party who is appointed to assist a Secretary of State or other government minister. They are the most junior in the ministerial hierarchy, ranking below Secretary of State and Minister of State. |
| *Permanent Secretary* | The senior civil servant within a government ministry charged with running the department (the full title is Permanent Under-Secretary of State). |
| *Policy and Implementation Unit* | Formerly the No 10 Policy Unit, this body exists to advise and support both the PM and DPM, and comprises civil servants and outsiders formerly in the private sector. |
| *Private Office* | Ministerial office staffed by civil servants responsible for such tasks as handling correspondence, organising the minister's diary and liaising with departments and officials on behalf of the minister. Usually headed by a Principal Private Secretary or a Private Secretary, depending on the minister's seniority in government. |
| *Quad, the* | Informal but important coalition decision-making group comprising David Cameron, Nick Clegg, George Osborne and Danny Alexander. Sometimes includes other ministers with a relevant policy concern, when it is known as the 'Quad plus'. |
| *Short Money* | State funding given to opposition parties in the House of Commons, based upon seats and votes won at the last election, and usually used for research and staffing support for frontbench spokesmen. |
| *Special adviser (spad)* | Temporary political adviser appointed to assist a government minister in a wide range of policy and media work. |

# Bibliography

## Books and Journal Articles

RB Andeweg and A Timmermans, 'Conflict Management in Coalition Government' in K Strøm, WC Müller and T Bergman (eds), *Cabinets and Coalition Bargaining: The Democratic Life Cycle in Western Europe* (Oxford University Press, 2008) 269–300.

H Back, HE Meier and T Persson, 'Party Size and Portfolio Payoffs: The Proportional Allocation of Ministerial Posts in Coalition Governments' (2009) 15(1) *Journal of Legislative Studies* 10–34.

T Bale, *The Conservative Party: From Thatcher to Cameron* (Cambridge, Polity, 2010).

T Bale, 'I Don't Agree with Nick: Retrodicting the Conservative-Liberal Democrat Coalition' (2011) 82(2) *Political Quarterly* 244–50.

T Bale, 'The Black Widow Effect: Why Britain's Conservative–Liberal Democrat Coalition Might Have an Unhappy Ending', forthcoming in *Parliamentary Affairs.*

T Bale and E Sanderson-Nash, 'A Leap of Faith and a Leap in the Dark: The Impact of the Coalition on the Conservatives and the Liberal Democrats' in S Lee and M Beech (eds), *The Cameron-Clegg Government: Coalition Politics in an Age of Austerity* (Basingstoke, Palgrave Macmillan, 2011) 237–50.

C Bentham, 'Liberal Democrat Policy-Making: An Insider's View, 2000–2004' (2007) 78(1) *Political Quarterly* 59–67.

R Blackburn, R Fox, O Gay and L Maer, *Who Governs? Forming a Coalition or Minority Government in the Event of a Hung Parliament* (London, Hansard Society & Study of Parliament Group, 2010).

T Blair, *A Journey* (London, Hutchinson, 2010).

V Bogdanor, *Coalition Government in Western Europe* (London, Heinemann, 1983).

V Bogdanor, *Multi-Party Politics and the Constitution* (Cambridge University Press, 1983).

V Bogdanor, *The British Constitution in the Twentieth Century* (Oxford University Press, 2004).

V Bogdanor, 'The Liberal Democrat Dilemma in Historical Perspective' (2007) 78(1) *Political Quarterly* 11–20.

V Bogdanor, *The New British Constitution* (Oxford, Hart Publishing, 2009).

V Bogdanor, *The Coalition and the Constitution* (Oxford, Hart Publishing, 2011).

N Boles, *Which Way's Up? The Future of Coalition Britain and How to Get There* (London, Biteback Publishing, 2010).

N Boles, M Pack and P Snowdon, 'Right Alignment' (2011) 17(4) *Public Policy Research* 189–200.

N Bolleyer, 'The Organisational Costs of Public Office' in K Deschouwer (ed), *New Parties in Government: In Power for the First Time* (Abingdon, Routledge, 2008) 17–44.

J Boston, *Electoral and Constitutional Change in New Zealand: An MMP Source Book* (Palmerston North, Dunmore, 1999).

J Boston, 'Multi-Party Governance: Managing the Unity-Distinctiveness Dilemma in Executive Coalitions' (2010) *Party Politics*, 20 December, 1–20.

J Boston and D Bullock, 'Experiments in Executive Government under MMP in New Zealand: Contrasting Approaches to Multiparty Governance' (2009) 7(1) *New Zealand Journal of Public and International Law* 39–76.

J Boston and A Ladley, 'The Efficient Secret: The Craft of Coalition Management' (2006) 4(1) *New Zealand Journal of Public and International Law* 55–90.

J Boston, S Levine, E McLeay, N Roberts and H Schmidt, 'The Impact of Electoral Reform on the Public Service: The New Zealand Case' (1998) 57(3) *Public Administration* 64–78.

D Brack, 'Leaders & Led – Liberal Democrat Leadership: The Cases of Ashdown & Kennedy' (2007) 78(1) *Political Quarterly* 78–89.

D Brack, 'Political Economy' in K Hickson (ed), *The Political Thought of the Liberals and Liberal Democrats since 1945* (Manchester University Press, 2009) 102–19.

J Brand, *British Parliamentary Parties: Policy and Power* (Oxford, Clarendon Press, 1992).

A Brazier, *Law in the Making: Influence and Change in the Legislative Process* (London, Hansard Society, 2008).

A Brazier and S Kalitowski, *No Overall Control? The Impact of a Hung Parliament on British Politics* (London, Hansard Society, 2008).

I Budge and H Keman, *Parties and Democracy: Coalition Formation and Government Functioning in Twenty States* (Oxford University Press, 1990).

D Butler, *Coalitions in British Politics* (London, Macmillan, 1978).

D Butler, *Government without a Majority: Dilemmas for Hung Parliaments in Britain,* 2nd edn (Basingstoke, Macmillan, 1986).

D Butler and G Butler, *British Political Facts,* 10th edn (Basingstoke, Palgrave Macmillan, 2010).

P Cairney, 'Coalition and Minority Government in Scotland: Lessons for the United Kingdom?' (2011) 82(2) *Political Quarterly* 261–9.

G Clark and S Kelly, 'Echoes of Butler? The Conservative Research Department and the Making of Conservative Policy' (2004) 75(4) *Political Quarterly* 378–82.

AS Cohan, 'The Open Coalition in the Closed Society: The Strange Pattern of Coalition Formation in Ireland' (1979) 11(3) *Comparative Politics* 319–38.

B Connaughton, 'Politico-Administrative Relations under Coalition Government: The Case of Ireland', paper presented at the 10th Annual NISPAcee Conference Cracow, 2002, www. unpan1.un.org/intradoc/groups/public/documents/nispacee/unpan003676.pdf

J Connelly, 'Vote Blue, Go Green, What's a Little Bit of Yellow in Between?' in S Lee and M Beech (eds), *The Cameron-Clegg Government: Coalition Politics in an Age of Austerity* (Basingstoke, Palgrave Macmillan, 2011) 118–33.

G Cook, A Lent, A Painter and H Sen, 'In The Black Labour: Why Fiscal Conservatism and Social Justice Go Hand-in-Hand', Policy Network, London, 2 December 2011.

D Corry, 'Power at the Centre: Is the National Economic Council a Model for a New Way of Organising Things?' (2011) 82(3) *Political Quarterly* 459–68.

P Cowley, *Revolts and Rebellions: Parliamentary Voting under Blair* (London, Politico's, 2002).

P Cowley, *The Rebels: How Blair Mislaid his Majority* (London, Politico's, 2005).

P Cowley, 'The Parliamentary Party' (2009) 80(2) *Political Quarterly* 214–21.

P Cowley, 'Political Parties and the British Party System' in R Heffernan, P Cowley and C Hay (eds), *Developments in British Politics 9* (Basingstoke, Palgrave Macmillan, 2011) 91–112.

P Cowley and M Stuart, 'Still Causing Trouble: The Conservative Parliamentary Party' (2004) 75(4) *Political Quarterly* 356–61.

P Cowley and M Stuart, 'Where has All the Trouble Gone? British Intra Party Parliamentary Divisions during the Lisbon Ratification' (2010) 5(2) *British Politics* 133–48.

B Criddle, 'More Diverse, Yet More Uniform' in D Kavanagh and P Cowley (eds), *The British General Election of 2010* (Basingstoke, Palgrave, 2010) 306–28.

J Curtice, 'So What Went Wrong with the Electoral System? The 2010 Election Result and the Debate about Electoral Reform' (2010) 63(4) *Parliamentary Affairs* 623–8.

J Curtice, 'Shaping the Coalition', *Parliamentary Brief*, 30 September 2011.

D Cutts, E Fieldhouse and A Russell, 'The Campaign that Changed Everything and Still Did Not Matter? The Liberal Democrat Campaign and Performance' (2010) 63(4) *Parliamentary Affairs* 689–707.

RJ Dalton, 'The Decline of Party Identifications' in RJ Dalton and MP Wattenberg (eds), *Parties without Partisans: Political Change in Advanced Industrial Democracies* (Oxford University Press, 2000).

E Damgaard, 'Cabinet Termination' in K Strøm, WC Müller and T Bergman (eds), *Cabinets and Coalition Bargaining: The Democratic Life Cycle in Western Europe* (Oxford University Press, 2008) 310–26.

L de Winter, 'Political Parties and Government Formation, Portfolios and Policy Definition' in KR Luther and F Müller-Rommel (eds), *Political Parties in the New Europe* (Oxford University Press, 2002) 143–68.

M Debus, 'Portfolio Allocation and Policy Compromises: How and Why the Conservatives and the Liberal Democrats Formed a Coalition Government' (2011) 82(2) *Political Quarterly* 293–304.

D Denver, 'The Results: How Britain Voted' (2010) 63(4) *Parliamentary Affairs* 588–606.

K Deschouwer, *New Parties in Government: In Power for the First Time* (Abingdon, Routledge, 2008).

P Diamond and G Radice, *Southern Discomfort: One Year On* (London, Policy Network, 2011).

P Dorey, 'Faltering before the Finishing Line: The Conservative Party's Performance in the 2010 General Election' (2010) 5(4) *British Politics* 402–35.

P Dunleavy, 'Facing Up to Multi-Party Politics: How Partisan Dealignment and PR Voting have Fundamentally Changed Britain's Party Systems' (2005) 58(3) *Parliamentary Affairs* 503–32.

P Dunleavy and RAW Rhodes, *Prime Minister, Cabinet and Core Executive* (Basingstoke, Macmillan, 1995).

K Dyson and T Saalfeld, 'Actors, Structures and Strategies: Policy Continuity and Change under the German Grand Coalition (2005–09)' (2010) 19(3) *German Politics* 269–82.

C Eichbaum and R Shaw, 'Enemy or Ally? Senior Officials' Perceptions of Ministerial Advisers before and after MMP' (2006) 58(1) *Political Science* 3–23.

J Elvidge, 'Northern Exposure: Lessons from the First Twelve Years of Devolved Government in Scotland' (London, Institute for Government, 2011).

E Evans, 'Two Heads are Better than One? Assessing the Implications of the Conservative-Liberal Democrat Coalition for UK Politics' (2011) 63(1) *Political Science* 45–60.

E Evans and E Sanderson-Nash, 'From Sandals to Suits: Professionalisation, Coalition and the Liberal Democrats' (2011) 13(4) *British Journal of Politics and International Relations* 459–73.

S Fielding, 'Labour's Campaign: Things Can Only Get . . . Worse?' (2010) 63(4) *Parliamentary Affairs* 653–66.

J Fischer and A Kaiser, 'Hiring and Firing Ministers under Informal Constraints' in K Dowding and P Dumont (eds), *The Selection of Ministers in Europe: Hiring and Firing* (New York, Routledge, 2009).

J Fleischer, 'A Dual Centre? Executive Politics under the Second Grand Coalition in Germany' (2010) 19(3) *German Politics* 353–68.

M Flinders and A Kelso, 'Mind the Gap: Political Analysis, Public Expectations and the Parliamentary Decline Thesis' (2011) 13 *British Journal of Politics and International Relations* 249–68.

R Fox, 'Five Days in May: A New Political Order Emerges' (2010) 63(4) *Parliamentary Affairs* 607–22.

M Gallagher and P Mitchell (eds), *The Politics of Electoral Systems* (Oxford University Press, 2008).

J Garry, 'The Demise of the Fianna Fáil/Labour "Partnership" Government and the Rise of the "Rainbow" Coalition' (1995) 10(1) *Irish Political Studies* 192–9.

R Grayson, 'Social Liberalism' in K Hickson (ed), *The Political Thought of the Liberals and Liberal Democrats since 1945* (Manchester University Press, 2009).

J Green, 'Strategic Recovery? The Conservatives under David Cameron' (2010) 63(4) *Parliamentary Affairs* 667–88.

O Grender and K Parminter, 'From "My Vote" to "The Real Alternative": Selling the Liberal Democrats' (2007) 78(1) *Political Quarterly* 108–16.

C Haddon and Z Gruhn, 'The Opposition' in A Paun (ed), *One Year On: The First Year of Coalition Government* (London, Institute for Government, 2011).

M Hasan and J Macintyre, *Ed: The Milibands and the Making of a Labour Leader* (London, Biteback Publishing, 2011).

R Hazell, *The Conservative Agenda for Constitutional Reform* (London, Constitution Unit, 2010).

R Hazell, *The Conservative-Liberal Democrat Agenda for Political and Constitutional Reform* (London, Constitution Unit, 2011).

R Hazell and A Paun (eds), *Making Minority Government Work: Hung Parliaments and the Challenges for Westminster and Whitehall* (London, Constitution Unit, 2009).

K Heidar and RA Koole, *Parliamentary Party Groups in European Democracies: Political Parties behind Closed Doors* (London, Routledge, 2000).

P Hennessy, *The Prime Minister: The Office and its Holders since 1945* (London, Allen Lane, 2001).

K Hickson (ed), *The Political Thought of the Liberals and Liberal Democrats since 1945* (Manchester University Press, 2009).

K Hickson, 'The End of New Labour? The Future of the Labour Party' in S Lee and M Beech (eds), *The Cameron-Clegg Government: Coalition Politics in an Age of Austerity* (Basingstoke, Palgrave Macmillan, 2011) 251–66.

D Hough, 'Breaking the Mould: Forming and Maintaining the Conservative-Liberal Democrat Coalition' (2011) 82(2) *Political Quarterly* 240–3.

S Ingle, *The British Party System: An Introduction* (New York, Routledge, 2008).

RW Jones and R Scully, 'Welsh Devolution: The End of the Beginning, and the Beginning of . . .?' in A Trench (ed), *The State of the Nations 2008* (Exeter, Imprint Academic, 2008).

R Katz and P Mair (eds), *How Parties Organize: Change and Adaptation in Party Organizations in Western Democracies* (London, Sage, 1994).

D Kavanagh and P Cowley, *The British General Election of 2010* (Basingstoke, Palgrave Macmillan, 2010).

D Kavanagh and A Seldon, *The Powers behind the Prime Minister: The Hidden Influence of Number Ten* (London, HarperCollins, 1999).

A King, 'Modes of Executive-Legislative Relations: Great Britain, France and West Germany' (1976) 1 *Legislative Studies Quarterly* 11–36.

EJ Kirchner and D Broughton, 'The FDP in the Federal Republic of Germany: The Requirements of Survival and Success' in EJ Kirchner (ed), *Liberal Parties in Western Europe* (Cambridge University Press, 1988).

M Laffin, 'Coalition-Formation and Centre-Periphery Relations in a National Political Party: The Liberal Democrats in a Devolved Britain' (2007) 13(6) *Party Politics* 651–68.

M Laver and KA Shepsle, *Making and Breaking Governments: Cabinets and Legislatures in Parliamentary Democracies* (Cambridge University Press, 1995).

D Laws, *22 Days in May* (London, Biteback Publishing, 2010).

D Laws and P Marshall (eds), *The Orange Book: Reclaiming Liberalism* (London, Profile Books, 2004).

JM Lee, GW Jones and J Burnham, *At The Centre of Whitehall: Advising the Prime Minister and the Cabinet* (Basingstoke, Macmillan, 1998).

S Lee and M Beech, *The Cameron-Clegg Government: Coalition Politics in an Age of Austerity* (Basingstoke, Palgrave Macmillan, 2011).

C Lees, 'Coalition Dynamics and the Changing German Party System' (2010) 28(3) *German Politics and Society* 119–32.

C Lees, 'The Grand Coalition and the Party System' (2010) 19(3) *German Politics* 312–31.

C Lees, 'How Unusual is the United Kingdom Coalition (and What are the Chances of it Happening Again)? (2011) 82(2) *Political Quarterly* 279–92.

KR Luther and F Müller-Rommel, *Political Parties in the New Europe: Political and Analytical Challenges* (Oxford University Press, 2002).

P Lynch, 'Governing Devolution: Understanding the Office of First Ministers in Scotland and Wales' (2006) 59(3) *Parliamentary Affairs* 420–36.

I McLean, '"England Does Not Love Coalitions": The Most Misused Political Quotation in the Book' (2012) 47(1) *Government and Opposition* 3–20.

P Mair, 'Party Organizations: From Civil Society to the State' in R Katz and P Mair (eds), *How Parties Organize: Change and Adaptation in Party Organizations in Western Democracies* (London, Sage, 1994) 1–22.

J Major, *John Major: The Autobiography* (London, HarperCollins, 2010).

R Malone, *Rebalancing the Constitution: The Challenge of Government Law-Making under MMP* (Wellington, Institute of Policy Studies, 2008).

P Mandelson, *The Third Man: Life at the Heart of New Labour* (London, HarperPress, 2010).

LW Martin and G Vanberg, *Parliaments and Coalitions: The Role of Legislative Institution in Multiparty Governance* (Oxford University Press, 2011).

R Michels, *Political Parties* (New York, Free Press, 1962).

B Miller and WC Müller, 'Managing Grand Coalitions: Germany 2005–09' (2010) 19(3) *German Politics* 332–52.

R Miller and J Curtin, 'Counting the Costs of Coalition: The Case of New Zealand's Small Parties' (2011) 63(1) *Political Science* 106–25.

P Mitchell, 'Ireland: From Single-Party to Coalition Rule' in K Strøm and WC Müller (eds), *Coalition Governments in Western Europe* (New York, Oxford University Press, 2000).

W Müller and T Meyer, 'Meeting the Challenges of Representation and Accountability in Multi-Party Governments' (2010) 33(5) *West European Politics* 1065–92.

W Müller and K Strøm, 'Coalition Agreements and Cabinet Governance' in K Strøm, WC Müller and T Bergman (eds), *Cabinets and Coalition Bargaining: The Democratic Life Cycle in Western Europe* (Oxford University Press, 2008) 159–99.

W Müller, T Bergman and K Strøm, 'Coalition Theory and Cabinet Governance: An Introduction' in K Strøm, WC Müller and T Bergman (eds), *Cabinets and Coalition Bargaining: The Democratic Life Cycle in Western Europe* (Oxford University Press, 2008) 1–50.

F Müller-Rommel, 'The Centre of Government in West Germany: Changing Patterns under 14 Legislatures (1949–1987)' (1988) 16(2) *European Journal of Political Research* 171–90.

K-H Nassmacher (eds), 'The Funding of Political Parties in the Anglo-Saxon Orbit' in R Austin and M Tjernström, *Funding of Political Parties and Election Campaigns* (Sweden, International Institute for Democracy and Electoral Assistance, 2003).

P Norton, 'The Organisation of Political Parties' in SA Walkland (ed), *The House of Commons in the Twentieth Century* (Oxford, Clarendon Press, 1979).

P Norton, 'The Parliamentary Party and Party Committees' in A Seldon and S Ball (eds), *Conservative Century: The Conservative Party since 1900* (Oxford University Press, 1994) 97–144.

P Norton, 'The United Kingdom: Exerting Influence from Within' in K Heidar and RA Koole (eds), *Parliamentary Party Groups in European Democracies: Political Parties behind Closed Doors* (London, Routledge, 2000) 39–56.

P Norton, 'Part 1: Cohesion' (2003) 9(4) *Journal of Legislative Studies* 57–72.

P Norton, *Parliament in British Politics* (Basingstoke, Palgrave Macmillan, 2005).

P Norton, 'The Con-Lib Agenda for the "New Politics" and Constitutional Reform' in S Lee and M Beech (eds), *The Cameron-Clegg Government: Coalition Politics in an Age of Austerity* (Basingstoke, Palgrave Macmillan, 2011) 153–67.

E O'Halpin, 'Partnership Programme Managers in the Reynolds/Spring Coalition 1993–1994: An Assessment', DCU Business School Research Papers Series (Paper No 6), Dublin University Business School, Ireland (1996).

E O'Malley, 'Government Formation in 2007' in M Gallagher and M Marsh (eds), *How Ireland Voted in 2007: The Full Story of Ireland's General Election* (Basingstoke, Palgrave Macmillan, 2008).

E O'Malley, 'Constructing and Maintaining Irish Governments' in K Dowding and P Dumont (eds), *The Selection of Ministers in Europe: Hiring and Firing* (New York, Routledge, 2009).

M Oaten, *Coalition: The Politics and Personalities of Coalition Government from 1850* (Petersfield, Harriman House, 2007).

DM Olson, 'Cohesion and Discipline Revisited: Contingent Unity in Parliamentary Party Group' (2003) 9(4) *Journal of Legislative Studies* 164–78.

J Osmond, *Crossing the Rubicon: Coalition Politics Welsh Style* (Cardiff, Institute of Welsh Affairs, 2007).

R Page, 'The Emerging Blue (and Orange) Health Strategy: Continuity or Change?' in S Lee and M Beech (eds), *The Cameron-Clegg Government: Coalition Politics in an Age of Austerity* (Basingstoke, Palgrave Macmillan, 2011) 89–104.

GWR Palmer and M Palmer, *Bridled Power: New Zealand's Constitution and Government,* 4th edn (Oxford University Press, 2004).

R Palmer, 'Coalition and Minority Government in Wales: Lessons for the United Kingdom?' (2011) 82(2) *Political Quarterly* 270–8.

A Paun (ed), *One Year On: The First Year of Coalition Government* (London, Institute For Government, 2011).

A Paun, 'United We Stand? Governance Challenges for the United Kingdom Coalition' (2011) 82(2) *Political Quarterly* 251–60.

T Quinn, J Bara and J Bartle, 'The UK Coalition Agreement of 2010: Who Won?' (2011) 21(2) *Journal of Elections, Public Opinions, and Parties* 295–312.

A Rawnsley, *Servants of the People: The Inside Story of New Labour* (London, Hamish Hamilton, 2001).

A Rawnsley, *The End of the Party* (London, Viking, 2010).

RAW Rhodes, 'From Prime Ministerial Power to Core Executive' in RAW Rhodes and P Dunleavy (eds), *Prime Minister, Cabinet and Core Executive* (Basingstoke, Macmillan Press, 1995).

RAW Rhodes and D Marsh, 'Policy Networks in British Government: A Critique of Existing Approaches' in RAW Rhodes and D Marsh (eds), *Policy Networks in British Government* (Oxford, Clarendon Press, 1992).

P Riddell and C Haddon, *Transitions: Preparing for Changes of Government* (London, Institute for Government, 2009).

P Riddell and C Haddon, *Transitions: Lessons Learned* (London, Institute for Government, 2011).

R Rogers and RH Walters, *How Parliament Works*, 6th edn (Harlow, Longman, 2006).

A Russell, 'Political Strategy' in K Hickson (ed), *The Political Thought of the Liberals and Liberal Democrats since 1945* (Manchester University Press, 2009) 147–62.

A Russell, 'Inclusion, Exclusion, or Obscurity? The 2010 General Election and the Implications of the Con-Lib Coalition for Third Party Politics in Britain' (2010) 5(4) *British Politics* 506–24.

A Russell and E Fieldhouse, *Neither Left Nor Right? The Liberal Democrats and the Electorate* (Manchester University Press, 2005).

A Russell, E Fieldhouse and D Cutts, 'De Facto Veto? The Parliamentary Liberal Democrats' (2007) 78(1) *Political Quarterly* 89–98.

M Russell, *House Full: Time to Get a Grip on Lords Appointments* (London, Constitution Unit, 2011).

M Russell, '"Never Allow a Crisis to Go to Waste": The Wright Committee Reforms to Strengthen the House of Commons' (2011) 64(4) *Parliamentary Affairs* 612–33.

M Russell and M Benton, *Selective Influence: The Policy Impact of House of Commons Select Committees* (London, Constitution Unit, 2011).

M Russell and M Sciara, 'Why does the Government get Defeated in the House of Lords? The Lords, the Party System and British Politics' (2007) 2 *British Politics* 299–322.

M Russell and M Sciara, 'The Policy Impact of Defeats in the House of Lords' (2008) 10 *British Journal of Politics and International Relations* 571–89.

M Russell and M Sciara, 'Independent Parliamentarians En Masse: The Changing Nature and Role of the Crossbenchers in the House of Lords' (2009) 62(1) *Parliamentary Affairs* 32–52.

T Saalfeld, 'Germany: Stable Parties, Chancellor Democracy, and the Art of Informal Settlement' in WC Müller and K Strøm (eds), *Coalition Governments in Western Europe* (Oxford University Press, 2000).

T Saalfeld, 'Institutions, Chance and Choices' in K Strøm, WC Müller and T Bergman (eds), *Cabinets and Coalition Bargaining: The Democratic Life Cycle in Western Europe* (Oxford University Press, 2008) 327–68.

M Schmidt, *Political Institutions in the Federal Republic of Germany* (Oxford University Press, 2003).

AF Seldon and S Ball, *Conservative Century: The Conservative Party since 1900* (Oxford University Press, 1994).

A Seldon and G Lodge, *Brown at Ten* (London, Biteback Publishing, 2010).

B Seyd, *Coalition Government in Britain: Lessons from Overseas* (London, Constitution Unit, 2002).

B Seyd, *Coalition Governance in Scotland and Wales* (London, Constitution Unit, 2004).

MJ Smith, *The Core Executive in Britain* (Basingstoke, Macmillan, 1999).

P Snowdon, *Back from the Brink: The Inside Story of the Tory Resurrection* (London, HarperPress, 2010).

M Sowemimo, *The Next Hung Parliament: How Labour Can Prepare* (London, Compass, 2011).

K Strøm, 'A Behavioral Theory of Competitive Political Parties' (1990) 34(2) *American Journal of Political Science* 565–98.

K Strøm and WC Müller (eds), *Coalition Governments in Western Europe* (Oxford University Press, 2000).

K Strøm, WC Müller and T Bergman, *Delegation and Accountability in Parliamentary Democracies* (Oxford University Press, 2003).

K Strøm, WC Müller and DM Smith, 'Parliamentary Control of Coalition Governments' (2010) 13 *Annual Review of Political Science* 517–35.

K Strøm, WC Müller and T Bergman (eds), *Cabinets and Coalition Bargaining: The Democratic Life Cycle in Western Europe* (Oxford University Press, 2008).

M Stuart, 'The Formation of the Coalition' in M Beech and S Lee (eds), *The Cameron-Clegg Government: Coalition Politics in an Age of Austerity* (Basingstoke, Palgrave Macmillan, 2011) 38–55.

M Taylor et al, *Reinventing the State: Social Liberalism for the 21st Century* (London, Politico's, 2007).

P Taylor-Gooby and G Stoker, 'The Coalition Programme: A New Vision for Britain or Politics as Usual?' (2011) 82(1) *Political Quarterly* 4–15.

MA Thies, 'Keeping Tabs on Partners: The Logic of Delegation in Coalition Governments' (2001) 45(3) *American Journal of Political Science* 580–98.

A Trench (ed), *The State of the Nations 2008* (London, Imprint Academic, 2008).

R Vandervorst, 'Parliamentarians' Perspectives on Proportional Representation: Electoral System Change in New Zealand' (2003) 55 *Political Science* 19–38.

L Verzichelli, 'Portfolio Allocation' in K Strøm, WC Müller and T Bergman (eds), *Cabinets and Coalition Bargaining: The Democratic Life Cycle in Western Europe* (Oxford University Press, 2008) 237–68.

J Vowles, 'Making a Difference? Public Perceptions of Coalition, Single-Party, and Minority Governments' (2010) 29(3) *Electoral Studies* 370–80.

P Warwick, *Government Survival in Parliamentary Democracies* (Cambridge University Press, 1994).

R Wilson, *5 Days to Power: The Journey to Coalition Britain* (London, Biteback Publishing, 2010).

D Wring and S Ward, 'The Media and the 2010 Campaign: The Television Election?' (2010) 63(4) *Parliamentary Affairs* 802–17.

B Yong, 'New Zealand's Experience of Multiparty Governance' in R Hazell and A Paun (eds), *Making Minority Government Work* (London, Institute for Government and Constitution Unit, 2009).

L Zetter (ed), *Zetter's Political Companion*, April 2011 edn (London, Zetter's Political Services Ltd, 2011).


## Blogs and Online Newspaper Articles

D Aitkenhead, 'David Willetts: "Many more will go to university than in my generation – we must not reverse that"' *Guardian G2* (20 November 2011), www.guardian.co.uk/politics/2011/nov/20/david-willetts-university-student-loans-debt

D Alexander, 'Labour will make a big, open offer to the Lib Dems on Europe' *New Statesman* (13 December 2011), www.newstatesman.com/politics/2011/12/britain-europe-dems-british

R Archer, 'A disgraceful referendum campaign has obscured the real case for AV' *LSE Blogs* (1 May 2011), www.blogs.lse.ac.uk/politicsandpolicy/2011/05/01/av-campaigns-disgraceful

L Baston, 'Boundary changes: how could they affect the UK?' *Guardian* (6 June 2011), www.guardian.co.uk/politics/datablog/2011/jun/06/boundary-change-constituency-lewis-baston

BBC News, 'Blair on the media: full text' (12 June 2007), www.news.bbc.co.uk/1/hi/uk_politics/6744581.stm

BBC News, 'David Cameron says NHS at heart of Tory manifesto' (4 January 2010), news.bbc.co.uk/1/hi/8438965.stm

BBC News, 'Lib Dems will not back early cuts, says Nick Clegg' (13 March 2010), www.news.bbc.co.uk/1/hi/uk_politics/8565722.stm

BBC News, 'Election: Cameron makes offer to Lib Dems on government' (7 May 2010), www.news.bbc.co.uk/1/hi/8667938.stm

BBC News, 'Full Text: Conservative-Lib Dem Deal' (12 May 2010), www.news.bbc.co.uk/1/hi/8677933.stm

BBC News, 'Ex-Lib Dem leader Campbell would rebel on tuition fees' (28 May 2010), www.bbc.co.uk/news/10174915

BBC News, 'Cameron "unsure of government's form" as he met Queen' (29 July 2010), www.bbc.co.uk/news/uk-politics-10794180

BBC News, 'Labour's Alan Milburn accepts coalition role' (15 August 2010), www.bbc.co.uk/news/uk-politics-10977806

BBC News, 'Vince Cable may abstain from vote on tuition fees' (1 December 2010), www.bbc.co.uk/news/uk-politics-11874406

BBC News, 'Ed Miliband asks Lib Dems to help draw up Labour policy' (13 December 2010), www.bbc.co.uk/news/uk-politics-11981011

BBC News, 'AV vote won't split coalition, say Clegg and Cameron' (1 May 2011), www.bbc.co.uk/news/uk-13251734

BBC News, 'AV Referendum: Huhne confronts Cameron at Cabinet' (3 May 2011), www.bbc.co.uk/news/uk-politics-13269677

BBC News, 'AV referendum: Cameron "not responsible for No to AV"' (3 May 2011), www.bbc.co.uk/news/uk-politics-13260010.

BBC News, 'Vote 2011' (10 May 2011), www.bbc.co.uk/news/uk-politics-12913122

BBC News, 'Tim Farron elected as Lib Dem president' (13 November 2011), www.bbc.co.uk/news/uk-11750362

BBC News, 'Poll Tracker' (4 January 2012), www.bbc.co.uk/news/uk-politics-13248179

M Birtwistle, 'Should health services be commissioned by technocrat or democrat?' *MHP Blog* (11 May 2011), www.mhpc.com/blog/should-health-services-be-commissioned-technocrat-or-democrat

B Brogan, 'Retreat – and recrimination – is in the air' *Daily Telegraph* (17 June 2011), www.telegraph.co.uk/news/politics/8583102/Retreat-and-recrimination-is-in-the-air.html

B Brogan, 'How will the Coalition cope with a year of living fractiously?' *Daily Telegraph* (18 January 2012), www.blogs.telegraph.co.uk/news/benedictbrogan/100130578/how-will-the-coalition-cope-with-a-year-of-living-fractiously

A Brooke and G Tope, 'That's the way to do it! How Liberal Democrats made the running on the Localism Bill' *Lib Dem Voice* (9 November 2011), www.libdemvoice.org/?p=25853&utm_source=tweet&utm_medium=twitter&utm_campaign=twitter

D Cameron, 'Speech on the fight-back after the riots' *New Statesman* (15 August 2011), www.newstatesman.com/politics/2011/08/society-fight-work-rights

Channel 4 News, 'Clegg in "too close to Tories for comfort" gaffe' (24 March 2011), www.channel4.com/news/clegg-in-too-close-to-tories-for-comfort-gaffe

J Chapman, 'Ken Clarke brands Cameron's bill of rights "xenophobic"' *Daily Mail* (28 June 2006), www.dailymail.co.uk/news/article-392891/Ken-Clarke-brands-Camerons-rights-xenophobic.html

M Chorley, 'Lib Dem president accused of "slagging off the coalition"' *Independent* (1 January 2012), www.independent.co.uk/news/uk/politics/lib-dem-president-accused-of-slagging-off-the-coalition-6302007.html

T Clark, 'Cameron's approval rating outstrips his government's – poll' *Guardian* (25 December 2011), www.guardian.co.uk/politics/2011/dec/25/cameron-approval-rating-grows-poll

N Clegg, 'Human beings need human rights – in Britain as well as Libya' *New Statesman* (25 August 2011), www.newstatesman.com/politics/2011/08/society-fight-work-rights

G Cook, A Lent, A Painter and H Sen, 'In the black Labour: why fiscal conservatism and social justice go hand-in-hand' (London, Policy Network, 2 December 2011), www.policy-network.net/publications/4101/-In-the-black-Labour

P Cowley, 'Ten things we know about Coalition MPs' *Ballots and Bullets Blog* (5 July 2011), www.nottspolitics.org/2011/07/05/ten-things-we-know-about-coalition-mps

P Cowley and M Stuart, 'A Coalition with wobbly wings: Backbench dissent since May 2010' *Ballots and Bullets Blog* (7 November 2010), www.revolts.co.uk/Wobbly%20Wings.pdf

P Cowley and M Stuart, 'The Conservative Euro revolt: 10 points to note' *Ballots and Bullets Blog* (25 October 2011), www.nottspolitics.org/2011/10/25/the-conservative-euro-revolt-10-points-to-note

P Cowley and M Stuart, 'The Independent View: And then there was one . . . (Unmasked! The only backbench Lib Dem MP 100% loyal to the Coalition)' *Lib Dem Voice* (18 November 2011), www.libdemvoice.org/the-independent-view-and-then-there-was-one-unmasked-the-only-backbench-lib-dem-mp-100-loyal-to-the-coalition-25914.html

M Crick, 'Will Lansley swap jobs with Hammond?' *BBC Newsnight Blogs* (27 April 2011), www.bbc.co.uk/blogs/newsnight/michaelcrick/2011/04

J Curtice, 'Shaping the Coalition' *Parliamentary Brief Online* (30 September 2011), www.parliamentarybrief.com/2011/09/shaping-the-coalition#all

M d'Ancona, 'The Tories couldn't deliver the goods without the Lib Dems' *Daily Telegraph* (15 January 2011), www.telegraph.co.uk/comment/columnists/matthewd_ancona/8262007/The-Tories-couldnt-deliver-the-goods-without-the-Lib-Dems.html

M D'Arcy, 'Turbulent times ahead for peers', *BBC: Mark D'Arcy's Blog* (14 December 2011), www.bbc.co.uk/news/uk-politics-16177521

I Dale, 'In conversation with . . . Patrick McLoughlin' *Total Politics* (1 November 2011), www.totalpolitics.com/articles/268817/in-conversation-with-patrick-mcloughlin.thtml

S Darrall, 'Clegg hires £500k team of seven "spies" to snoop on Tory ministers' *Daily Mail* (24 October 2011), www.dailymail.co.uk/news/article-2052440/Nick-Clegg-hires-500k-team-seven-spies-snoop-Tory-ministers.html#ixzz1ifx5tHOV

H Duffett, 'The Liberal Democrat manifesto in practice' *Liberal Democrat Voice* (28 December 2010), www.libdemvoice.org/the-liberal-democrat-manifesto-in-practice-22566.html

T Dunn and S Hawkes, 'Cameron warning on coalition course' *Sun* (27 April 2010), www.thesun.co.uk/sol/homepage/news/election2010/2949044/Cameron-warning-on-coalition-course.html

*Economist*: Bagehot's notebook, 'David Cameron: we Eurosceptics are only trying to help' (14 November 2011), www.economist.com/node/21538516

*Economist*: Bagehot's notebook, 'Britain, not leaving but falling out of the EU' (9 December 2011), www.economist.com/blogs/bagehot/2011/12/britain-and-eu-0

J Glover, 'Nick Clegg's social mobility plans should not be lost amid mockery' *Guardian* (6 April 2011), www.guardian.co.uk/commentisfree/2011/apr/06/nick-clegg-social-mobility

J Glover and N Watt, 'Coalition Government support is dramatically down, poll shows' *Guardian* (26 December 2010), www.guardian.co.uk/politics/2010/dec/26/coalition-government-support-dramatically-down

P Goodman, 'Good news about manifesto planning for the next election' *ConservativeHome* (12 January 2011), www.conservativehome.blogs.com/thetorydiary/2011/01/progess-in-forming-party-policy-for-the-next-election.html.

R Grayson, 'The Liberal Democrat journey to a Lib-Con Coalition – and where next?' (5 July 2010), www.clients.squareeye.net/uploads/compass/documents/Compass%20LD%20Journey%20WEB.pdf

T Grew, 'Lib Dems appoint backbench policy chiefs' *epolitix* (28 March 2011), www.epolitix.com/1832-blog/blog-post/newsarticle/lib-dems-appoint-backbench-policy-chiefs

A Grice, 'An age of austerity just might benefit the Tories' *Independent* (3 December 2011), www.independent.co.uk/opinion/commentators/andrew-grice/andrew-grice-an-age-of-austerity-just-might-benefit-the-tories-6271550.html

A Grice, 'Lib Dems laugh off Ed Balls' calls for a new coalition' *Independent* (22 December 2011), www.independent.co.uk/news/uk/politics/lib-dems-laugh-off-ed-balls-call-for-a-new-coalition-6280396.html?origin=internalSearch

*Guardian* Editorial, 'Coalition politics: Conflict of Tory loyalties' *Guardian* (22 February 2011), www.guardian.co.uk/commentisfree/2011/feb/22/coalition-politics-human-rights-editorial

*Guardian* Politics Blog, 'Liam Fox statement: oh no, not another victim' *Guardian* (19 October 2011), www.guardian.co.uk/politics/blog/2011/oct/19/liam-fox-statement-another- victim

P Hennessey, 'Home Secretary: scrap the Human Rights Act' *Daily Telegraph* (1 October 2011), www.telegraph.co.uk/news/politics/8801651/Home-Secretary-scrap-the-Human-Rights-Act.html

P Hennessey and L Donnelly, 'Clegg: NHS U-turn is big win for Lib Dems' *Daily Telegraph* (11 June 2011), www.telegraph.co.uk/news/politics/nick-clegg/8570422/Clegg-NHS-U-turn-is-big-win-for-Lib-Dems.html

ICM Research, *ICM Poll for the Guardian* (26 September 2011), www.icmresearch.com/wp-content/blogs.dir/1/files/2011/09/2011_sept_guardian_poll.pdf

Ipsos MORI, *Ipsos MORI Post Budget Reaction Poll Topline Results* (28 June 2011), www.ipsos-mori.com/Assets/Docs/Budget%20Reaction%20Topline.PDF

J Kirkup, 'Tory demands on EU powers are impossible for Coalition, says Nick Clegg' *Daily Telegraph* (25 October 2011), www.telegraph.co.uk/news/worldnews/europe/eu/8849273/Tory-demands-on-EU-powers-are-impossible-for-Coalition-says-Nick-Clegg.html

A Lewis, 'YouGov/Sun – CON 37, LAB 41, LDEM 10', *UK Polling Report* (13 September 2011), www.ukpollingreport.co.uk/blog/archives/4007

V Macdonald, 'Heath Bill is "biggest upheaval in NHS history"' *Channel 4 News* (6 September 2011), www.channel4.com/news/debate-on-nhs-health-and-social-care-bill

J Macintyre, 'Huhne attacks Tories "helping their friends in the City"' *Prospect* (11 September 2011), www.prospectmagazine.co.uk/2011/09/huhne-attack-osborne-50p-rate

I Martin, 'Can the Coalition survive David Cameron's veto?' *Daily Telegraph* (10 December 2011), www.telegraph.co.uk/news/worldnews/europe/eu/8948425/Can-the-Coalition-survive-David-Camerons-veto.html

T Montgomerie, 'Afraid of Being Right' *Spectator* (30 July 2011), www.spectator.co.uk/essays/7127203/afraid-of-being-right.thtml

J Murphy, 'Don't say Coalition, say Tory-led government, Labour's spin chief tells media', *Evening Standard* (18 January 2011), www.thisislondon.co.uk/standard/article-23915147-dont-say-coalition-say-tory-led-labours-spin-chief-tells-media.do

No to AV, 'Second Referendum Broadcast' (1 May 2011), *www.no2av.org/05/second-referendum-broadcast*

G Parker and E Rigby, 'Cameron's anger at claim of Osborne rift' *Financial Times* (8 November 2011), www.ft.com/cms/s/0/308fccbe-0a3b-11e1-92b5-00144feabdc0.html#axzz1jok5D0bu

*Politics Home*, 'May Day for the Queen's Speech' (3 January 2012), www.politicshome.com/uk/article/42900/may_day_for_the_queen.html

S Pope and H Cleary, 'The Coalition's balancing act' *politics.co.uk* (16 May 2011), www.politics.co.uk/comment-analysis/2011/5/16/analysis-the-coalition-s-balancing-act

A Porter, 'David Cameron sends his own spin doctors to help Lansley with NHS reforms' *Daily Telegraph* (6 May 2011), www.telegraph.co.uk/news/politics/8498648/David-Cameron-sends-his-own-spin-doctors-to-help-Lansley-with-NHS-reforms.html

Press Association, 'Nick Clegg threatens to block NHS reforms' *Guardian* (8 May 2011), www.guardian.co.uk/politics/2011/may/08/nick-clegg-veto-nhs-reforms

L Price, 'Lord Gould of Brookwood obituary' *Guardian* (7 November 2011), www.guardian.co.uk/politics/2011/nov/07/philip-gould

R Ramesh, 'NHS bill clause put on hold to stave off revolt by Liberal Democrat peers' *Guardian* (2 November 2011), www.guardian.co.uk/society/2011/nov/02/nhs-bill-clause-hold-lords

E Rigby and K Stacey, 'Cable rejects scrapping unfair firing law' *Financial Times* (26 October 2011), www.ft.com/cms/s/0/5b46e9f2-0003-11e1-ba79-00144feabdc0.html#axzz1jok5D0bu

P Routledge, 'Major hits out at Cabinet' *Observer* (25 July 1993), www.guardian.co.uk/politics/1993/jul/25/politicalnews.uk

M Savage and F Gibb, 'Tories ready for a fight on human rights "inference" from Europe' *Times* (17 February 2011), www.thetimes.co.uk/tto/news/politics/article2916641.ece

M Savage, S Coates and R Bennett, 'Clegg's big moment backfires over interns' *Times* (6 April 2011), www.thetimes.co.uk/tto/news/politics/article2974671.ece

J Slack, 'I want to scrap the Human Rights Act, but Clegg won't let me, says the PM' *Daily Mail* (3 October 2011), www.dailymail.co.uk/news/article-2044530/David-Cameron-I-want-scrap-Human-Rights-Act-Nick-Clegg-wont-let-me.html

A Sparrow, 'Tim Farron: Labour "utterly dishonest" about state of economy' *Guardian* (18 November 2011), www.guardian.co.uk/politics/2011/nov/18/tim-farron-interview-andrew-sparrow?INTCMP=SRCH

M Sowemimo, 'The next hung parliament: how Labour can prepare' (London, Compass, 2010), www.clients.squareeye.net/uploads/compass/documents/Hung_parliament_2011.pdf

A Stratton and P Wintour, 'AV dragged coalition to edge of a precipice' Guardian (5 May 2011), www.guardian.co.uk/politics/2011/may/05/av-dragged-coalition-to-edge

R Sylvester, 'From rose garden romance to secret love' *Times* (31 May 2011), www.thetimes.co.uk/tto/opinion/columnists/rachelsylvester/article3045004.ece

R Sylvester, 'Nick Clegg might not look sad much longer' *Times* (17 January 2012), www.thetimes.co.uk/tto/opinion/columnists/rachelsylvester/article3288630.ece

P Toynbee, 'Nick talks pure Cameronomics' *Guardian* (20 September 2012), www.guardian.co.uk/commentisfree/2010/sep/20/clegg-talks-pure-cameronomics

A Travis, 'David Cameron condemns supreme court ruling on sex offenders' *Guardian* (16 February 2011), www.guardian.co.uk/society/2011/feb/16/david-cameron-condemns-court-sex-offenders

H Watt and R Winnett, 'Treasury Chief David Laws, his secret lover and a £40,000 claim' *Daily Telegraph* (28 May 2010), www.telegraph.co.uk/news/newstopics/mps-expenses/7780642/MPs-Expenses-Treasury-chief-David-Laws-his-secret-lover-and-a-40000-claim.html

H Watt, R Winnett and H Blake, 'Vince Cable: "I could bring down the Government if I'm pushed"' *Daily Telegraph* (20 December 2010), www.telegraph.co.uk/news/politics/liberaldemocrats/8215462/Vince-Cable-I-could-bring-down-the-Government-if-Im-pushed.html

N Watt, 'Phone hacking: MPs "were too scared to testify in court" says MP' *Guardian* (9 September 2010), www.guardian.co.uk/media/2010/sep/09/phone-hacking-mps-scared-testify

N Watt, '"NHS reform is safe" – Andrew Lansley makes private plea for Tory support' *Guardian* (13 June 2011), www.guardian.co.uk/politics/2011/jun/13/nhs-reform-andrew-lansley

N Watt, 'NHS reforms: Cameron accepts "substantive" changes to health bill' *Guardian* (14 June 2011), www.guardian.co.uk/society/2011/jun/14/nhs-reforms-cameron-accepts-substantive-chages

N Watt, 'Nick Clegg under fire over health reform "victory"' *Guardian* (12 June 2011), www.guardian.co.uk/politics/2011/jun/12/nick-clegg-health-reform

N Watt, 'David Cameron rocked by record rebellion as Europe splits Tories again' *Guardian* (25 October 2011), www.guardian.co.uk/politics/2011/oct/24/david-cameron-tory-rebellion-europe

N Watt, 'Nick Clegg vetoes Conservative donor's idea to help firms sack workers' *Guardian* (8 November 2011), www.guardian.co.uk/politics/2011/nov/08/nick-clegg-vetoes-work-reform

M White, 'David Cameron denies Oldham byelection pact claims' *Guardian* (6 January 2011), www.guardian.co.uk/politics/2011/jan/06/david-cameron-denies-oldham-byelection-pact

G Wilson, 'Osborne raps "dodgy" Yes to AV' *Sun* (13 April 2011), www.thesun.co.uk/sol/homepage/news/3524950/Osborne-raps-dodgy-Yes-to-AV.html

R Winnett, 'Nick Clegg to boast of blocked Conservative policies' *Daily Telegraph* (11 May 2011), www.telegraph.co.uk/news/politics/nick-clegg/8505968/Nick-Clegg-to-boast-of-blocked-Conservative-policies.html

P Wintour, 'Liberal Democrats vent fury at David Cameron as party suffers election rout' Guardian (6 May 2011), www.guardian.co.uk/politics/2011/may/06/liberal-democrats-david-cameron-election

P Wintour, 'Spending cuts bind coalition partners?' *Guardian* (30 November 2011), www.guardian.co.uk/politics/2011/nov/30/spending-cuts-bind-coalition-partners

Wintour and Watt, 'Minister apologises after sailing close to the wind on byelection rules' *Guardian Blog* (13 January 2011), www.guardian.co.uk/politics/wintour-and-watt/2011/jan/13/oldham-east-and-saddleworth-liberaldemocrats

Wintour and Watt, 'Coalition's divisions over future of NHS deepen into open warfare' *Guardian Blog* (19 May 2011), www.guardian.co.uk/politics/wintour-and-watt/2011/may/18/andrewlansley-nhs?INTCMP=ILCNETTXT3487

Wintour and Watt, 'Rethink on managing coalition after Nick Clegg rejects No 10 report' *Guardian Blog* (8 November 2011), www.guardian.co.uk/politics/wintour-and-watt/2011/nov/08/liberal-conservative-coalition-nickclegg

Wintour and Watt, 'Why the Tory right no longer trusts David Cameron on Europe' *Guardian Blog* (9 December 2011), www.guardian.co.uk/politics/wintour-and-watt/2011/dec/08/davidcameron-debt-crisis?INTCMP=ILCNETTXT3487

YouGov, *YouGov/The Sun Survey Results* (13 May 2010), www.cdn.yougov.com/today_uk_import/YG-Archives-Pol-Suntopical-100513.pdf

YouGov, *The Economy* (20 December 2011), www.cdn.yougov.com/cumulus_uploads/document/7645cvwcdc/YG-Archives-Trackers-Economy-201211.pdf

YouGov, *The Party Leaders* (22 December 2011), www.cdn.yougov.com/cumulus_uploads/document/1qhe1gcvmq/YG-Archives-Trackers-Leaders-221211.pdf

## Government and Parliamentary Publications

Cabinet Office, *The Coalition: Our Programme for Government* (19 May 2010).

Cabinet Office, *List of Government Ministers as at July 2010* (7 July 2010), www.cabinetoffice.gov.uk/resource-library/government-ministers-and-responsibilities

Cabinet Office, *Cabinet Committee System* (23 September 2010), www.cabinetoffice.gov.uk/sites/default/files/resources/cabinet-committees-system.pdf

Cabinet Office, *Written Ministerial Statement on Numbers and Costs of Special Advisers* (9 December 2011), www.cabinetoffice.gov.uk/sites/default/files/resources/LIST_AND_COSTS_9_DECEMBER_0.pdf

*Coalition Agreement for Stability and Reform* (21 May 2010).

Committee on Standards in Public Life, *Political Party Finance* (November 2011), www. public-standards.gov.uk/Library/13th_Report___Political_party_finance_FINAL_ PDF_VERSION_18_11_11.pdf

Commons Library Research Paper, 'Health and Social Care Bill' (27 January 2011).

Commons Library Standard Note, 'Membership of UK Political Parties' (17 August 2009).

Commons Library Standard Note, 'Parliamentary Private Secretaries' (9 May 2011).

Commons Political and Constitutional Reform Committee, 'Fixed Term Parliaments Bill' HC (2010–11).

Department for Business, Innovation and Skills, *Securing a Sustainable Future for Higher Education: An Independent Review of Education Funding and Student Finance* (11 October 2010), www.bis.gov.uk/assets/biscore/corporate/docs/s/10-1208-securing-sustainable-higher-education-browne-report.pdf

Department of Health, *Equity and Excellence: Liberating the NHS* (2010), www.dh.gov.uk/ en/Publicationsandstatistics/Publications/PublicationsPolicyAndGuidance/DH_117353

House of Commons Library, 'General Election 2010: Preliminary Analysis', Research Paper 10/36 (18 May 2010), www.parliament.uk/documents/commons/lib/research/rp2010/ RP10-036.pdf

Intelligence and Security Commission, *Annual Report 2010–2011* (11 July 2011), isc. independent.gov.uk/files/2010-2011_ISC_AR.pdf

Joint Committee on Conventions, 'Conventions of the UK Parliament' HC (2005–06).

Joint Committee on Human Rights, 'A Bill of Rights for the UK?' HL HC (2007–08).

Lords Constitution Committee, 'Fixed Term Parliaments Bill' HL (2010–11).

Ministry of Justice, *Rights and Responsibilities: Developing our Constitutional Framework* (March 2009).

Political and Constitutional Reform Committee, 'Lessons from the process of Government formation after the 2010 General Election' HC (2010–11).

Political and Constitutional Reform Committee, 'Parliamentary Voting Systems and Constituencies Bill' HC (2010–11).

Select Committee on the Constitution, 'Parliamentary Voting Systems and Constituencies Bill: Report' HL (2010–11).

Welsh Affairs Committee, 'The Implications for Wales of the Government's proposals on constitutional reform' HC (2010–11).

**Party Publications**

Conservative Party, *Renewal: Plan for a Better NHS* (September 2008), www.conservatives. com/News/News_stories/2008/09/Our_plan_for_a_better_NHS.aspx

S Cooper, *March 2011 Federal Conference Report* (March 2011), www.nickclegg.com/site-Files/resources/PDF/2011%20March%20Sheffield%20Report.pdf

Liberal Democrat Party, *Facing the Future: Policy Development Agenda* (8 January 2011), www.libdems.org.uk/siteFiles/resources/docs/conference/100%20-%20Facing%20 the%20Future.pdf

# Index